# cooking vegetarian

healthy, delicious and easy vegetarian cuisine

## Vesanto Melina M.Sc., R.D.
## Joseph Forest

2nd Edition

Collins

*Cooking Vegetarian, 2nd Edition*
Copyright © 2011 Joseph Forest and Vesanto Melina.
All rights reserved.

Published by Collins, an imprint of HarperCollins Publishers Ltd.

Originally published by John Wiley & Sons Canada, Ltd., in both print andEPub editions: 2011

First published by Collins in this trade paperback edition and in an EPub edition: 2013

Care has been taken to trace ownership of copyright material contained in this book. The publisher will gladly receive any information that will enable them to rectify any reference or credit line in subsequent editions.

No part of this book may be used or reproduced in any manner whatsoever without the prior written permission of the publisher, except in the case of brief quotations embodied in reviews.

HarperCollins books may be purchased for educational, business, or sales promotional use through our Special Markets Department.

HarperCollins Publishers Ltd
2 Bloor Street East, 20th Floor
Toronto, Ontario, Canada
M4W 1A8

www.harpercollins.ca

Library and Archives Canada Cataloguing in Publication information is available upon request.
ISBN 978-1-44342-770-8

Printed and bound in the United States
RRD 9 8 7 6 5 4 3 2 1

*I dedicate this book to the Spirit of Love,*
*and to my mother, Louise Forest,*
*who embodies this nourishing Spirit unconditionally.*

—Joseph Forest

*I dedicate this book to the very kind and loving people throughout my life:*
*my partner Cam Doré,*
*son Chris Crawford,*
*daughter Kavyo Crawford,*
*long-time co-authors Joseph Forest*
*and Brenda Davis,*
*dear neighbours at WindSong Cohousing Community,*
*and the vegetarians I meet all over the world.*

—Vesanto Melina

# Contents

**Acknowledgements** vi
**A Word from Chef Joseph** viii
**A Word from Vesanto Melina** xi

**Part One: Making Sense of Food Choices**

Chapter 1: The Art and Science of Cooking    3
Chapter 2: Making Friends with Your Ingredients    17
Chapter 3: Nourishing Your Body    43
Chapter 4: Food Guide and Menus    53

**Part Two: Recipes**

Introduction to the Recipes    73
Breakfasts and Beverages    75
Dips, Spreads, Sandwiches, and Snacks    85
Salads    101
Dressings    117
Soups    129
Entrées    143
Side Dishes    189
Sauces and Gravies    211
Sweet Treats    223

**Appendix 1: Foods Grouped According to Six Tastes**    257
**Appendix 2: Dietary Reference Intakes (DRIs) for Minerals**    261
**Appendix 3: Dietary Reference Intakes (DRIs) for Vitamins**    262
**References and Resources**    264
**Endnotes**    265
**Index**    266

# Acknowledgements

Sincere gratitude to those who made this book possible: Alison Mclean and Lindsay Humphreys at Wiley, Judy Phillips, Pat Loi, Ian Koo and Adrian So.

We appreciate the careful recipe testing by: Misuzu Noguchi and Dan Malloy.

We greatly appreciate our taste testers: Vesanto's wonderful neighbours at WindSong Cohousing community, including Alan Carpenter, Chandra Carlson, Evan McFee, Gillian Allan, Howard Staples, Kayla Vierling, Jacob Wolfheart, Jessica Bustard, Leslie Wood, Linda Duarte, Michael Mogardo, Mina Mogardo, Miriam Evers, Oliver Bustard, Susan Collerman, Susan McFee, Trevor Erikson, Tricia Carpenter, Valerie McIntyre, and the Thursday Veggie Meal Club. Also Tobias Leenaert and Melanie Jaecques of the EVA (Ethical Vegetarian Union) in Gent, Belgium; Joseph's friends Larissa Drozenko and Siripon Pittayakornpisuth.

Special thanks to: Angelina Rogon for kitchen assistance; Cam Doré for computer assistance and inspiration; Cristina Viviani for manuscript review; Lars Warje for his baking expertise; and Maureen Butler for insightful editing help.

Love and gratitude to our families and dear ones who encouraged us throughout this project, and understood when we went into hibernation to complete the manuscript: Vesanto's partner, Cam Doré; son Chris Crawford; and daughter Kavyo Crawford; Joseph's mother, Louise; brothers Ray and Forest; sisters Donna and Nicole; teachers and friends Jeffrey Armstrong, Sandi Graham, Sarah Webster, Lee Gross, Sandra Milena Arismendy, Savey Mattu, those from Monday night class, and Sunrise Ranch, and Edenvale Retreat and Conference Centers.

**We would like to acknowledge the companies that provided us with their outstanding products:**

Asian Family Specialty Foods (www.asianfamilyfoods.com), gardein (www.gardein.com), Grainworks (www.grainworks.com), LeSaffre Human Care (lesaffre-yeast.com/red-star/vegetarian-support-formula.html), Manitoba Harvest (www.manitobaharvest.com), Nature's Path Organic, (www.naturespath.com), Omega Nutrition (www.omeganutrition.com), Sunrise Soya Foods (www.sunrise-soya.com).

# Acknowledgements

**Many thanks to the chefs and recipe innovators who generously allowed us to use or adapt their recipes for this book:**

Brenda Davis: Lemon Sesame Cookies (page 246), Cranberry Pecan Muffins (page 238), and Coconut Macaroons (page 237), the latter from *Becoming Raw* by Brenda Davis and Vesanto Melina, The Book Publishing Company, 2010

British Columbia Blueberry Board: Blueberry Mince Tart and Pie Filling (page 231)

Cherie Soria: Green Giant Juice (page 79), from *The Raw Food Revolution Diet* by Cherie Soria, Brenda Davis, and Vesanto Melina, The Book Publishing Company, 2008

David Melina: Garden of Plenty Salad (page 105)

Jennifer Cornbleet: Raw Mango Strawberry Pie (page 251), from *Raw Food Made Easy*, The Book Publishing Company, 2005

Jo Stepaniak: Gooda Cheeze (page 89) and Gee Whiz Spread (page 88), from *The Uncheese Cookbook*, The Book Publishing Company, 2003

Valerie McIntyre: Pesto-the-Best-Oh! (page 92)

# A Word from Chef Joseph

The book you hold in your hands is a work of love from two friends who greatly appreciate food and its ability to impact health and well-being. I am delighted to work with my dear colleague and mentor Vesanto Melina in bringing to you this well-researched and tested guide to adopting more plant-based foods into your daily food regime. This book contains cutting-edge scientific information on vegetarian nutrition, along with over 150 recipes that are nutritious, tasty, and easy to prepare. The full spectrum of recipes will take you through the day, from breakfast to desserts, with choices that you can revisit time and time again as you discover how truly good these recipes are. But before you make your shopping list and fill your fridge and pantry with wholesome foods, let me tell you a bit about myself.

My career as a professional chef began 27 years ago, and by today's standard, that is a long time to stay in a single occupation. The more I deepen my knowledge of food, the further I experience its ability to nourish and heal the body, mind, and spirit, and the more I appreciate my vocation. Having found my right livelihood is a blessing, and this particular path bestows gifts that go far beyond the health that I experience along the way.

As a young adult I embarked upon formal chef training that opened doors into the world of fine-dining restaurants, where the focus was serving individual plates to appreciative audiences. Later I worked in the banquet kitchens of prestigious hotels such as the Four Seasons, where I learned to transfer the high standards of quality that I had learned in smaller settings to volume cooking. These skills were eventually transferred to the world of film catering, where I worked as a team member feeding movie crews.

Highlights of my livelihood include developing a whole food catering company, working as a consultant to several natural food manufacturers, assisting in the production and revision of two corporate cookbooks, and acting as a consulting chef for the opening of two natural food restaurants. Along the way I have had the honour of feeding international rock-and-roll personalities, political leaders, dignitaries, and numerous Hollywood celebrities.

However, my favourite achievement has been co-writing the Canadian bestselling cookbook, *Cooking Vegetarian*, with Vesanto Melina, Registered Dietitian. The book was launched in 1996 and subsequently released in the United States in 1998, where it also enjoyed widespread popularity. I met Vesanto in 1991 and over the last 20 years we have collaborated on numerous projects. The nutritional knowledge I gained from working with Vesanto has been invaluable, and I consider my working relationship with her to be one of the most rewarding associations of my professional life.

The roots of my love for food go back to my youth—to when I lived in Edmonton with my parents and five siblings. Mine was a large family, and my mother spent a good amount of time making sure we were well fed. My mom and dad came from big Prairie families; they were raised on farms, so they knew the value of planting vegetable seeds in the spring to reap a harvest that would feed active, growing family members.

Soon after my mom and dad were married, they bought their first home from a gardener. That property had a large garden plot in the backyard, along with fruit trees and plenty of flowering plants. Every spring I helped plant a vegetable garden that would yield produce well into the autumn. Two crab apple trees not only offered twisting branches for good climbing but also a secret hiding place at the height of summer. Come fall, the abundant fruit from those trees was turned into jams and jellies. They took their place in the basement pantry alongside canned peaches, pears, beets, tomatoes, and Saskatoon berry jam—what seemed at the time to be countless jars of bright, multicoloured, mouth-watering food. I never went hungry.

Growing up in a large family, most kitchen duties were shared among my brothers and sisters. My preference was always to help my mom after school with the preparation of dinner, rather than with the dishwashing afterward. I didn't know it then, but the seeds of a lifelong relationship with the nourishing properties of food were being planted in my psyche.

My first formal work experience with food began at the age of 13. I worked as a baker's assistant on a part-time basis during the school year and full time during the summer months. Although, as a teenager, the thought of a career in the arena of food was not a consideration, this destiny would continue to beckon me.

Many years later, when I finally made the decision to enrol in a year-long culinary arts program, my primary intention was to work in a kitchen to pay for my university education. During the course of my chef training, I had the very good fortune of being sent on a three-week practicum to the Vancouver Four Seasons Hotel. I was awestruck at the size of the kitchen, the high standards of excellence, and the sheer number of kitchen personnel. The staff included 47 people from all over the world filling all positions of a modern-day kitchen brigade, from the executive chef all the way down the chain of command to the apprentices. That experience changed the direction of my life, and after graduation I embarked upon my career path with enthusiasm and a new vision for my self.

For the next seven years I worked in fine-dining restaurants and hotels, and to my good fortune ended up back at the Four Seasons Hotel in the banquet kitchen. After working there for a year, I met Vesanto, and was drawn to her vast knowledge of nutrition. I began collaborating with her, and over the next two years we developed a series of popular vegetarian cooking classes that received national media attention. In those classes Vesanto offered practical vegetarian nutritional theory, and I led a hands-on cooking segment. We taught hundreds of people from all walks of life, from teenagers to grandmothers, and great fun was had by all. At the end of the day, our students went home better informed and richer for the experience.

After those two years of collaboration, Vesanto embarked upon her successful writing career, which began with the publication of her international bestseller *Becoming Vegetarian*, and then continued on to our first book together, *Cooking Vegetarian*. I also did private catering with an emphasis on natural whole food ingredients, and this led to work as a caterer for film crews and movie talent. In this capacity, I took an interest in providing specialty diets to those who requested them. It was a natural fit for me, since I was equipped with a wide range of nutritional knowledge.

Over the many years of working with food, in addition to my formal training in classical French cuisine, I have studied vegetarian, vegan, macrobiotic, Ayurvedic, and diabetic diets. Through all of this, three personal perspectives have emerged. First, transition from one dietary lifestyle to another can take years. For lasting results, this important process requires time, knowledge, and patience. Feeding the body is a lifelong process that can involve adjustments from one stage of life to another for myriad reasons. Second, since each person is constitutionally different, no single diet can be considered the ideal for everybody (or every body). Although we all require carbohydrates, protein, vitamins, and minerals, the combinations and the types of foods we choose to meet those needs vary between individuals and cultural groups. Third, we are all brilliantly tailored individuals, guided by a deep source of inner intelligence. If we pay attention to the wisdom of this intelligence, we will be led into the dietary pattern that best serves who we are as individuals.

I am very pleased to collaborate with Vesanto on this book. It is our sincere wish that you expand your nutritional knowledge and increase your culinary repertoire for the purpose of sustaining your health, or of regaining your health if it is compromised. As you work with and adapt this book to suit your lifestyle, may you find inspiration to eat well to be well.

Joseph Forest, Professional Chef

# A Word from Vesanto Melina, Registered Dietitian

Welcome! This precious book is the creation of people in two food-related professions, though our perspectives have sometimes seemed worlds apart. My collaboration with Joseph Forest began in 1991 when we met at a presentation by vegan writer and inspirational speaker John Robbins. Joseph and I soon became co-hosts of a series of cooking classes that drew enthusiastic crowds and national media attention. Out of that grew our popular *Cooking Vegetarian,* the forerunner to this volume. As a dietitian, I was aware of the nutritional features of food but lacked the skills that a talented chef can bring to the table so that people lick their lips and their eyes light up. Thus, Joseph's gift of creating foods that appeal to the senses of sight, taste, smell, and touch drew me to new adventures in the world of food. I was intrigued when he shared with me experiences that he had gained during his chef training. For example, he recalled that in his apprentice cooking lab, 10 budding chefs at 10 separate work stations each followed a set of identical recipes each day. At the end of every class, all of the prepared food was brought forward for class evaluation. Invariably, the product created by each student tasted different from that of others, despite each having used the same recipe. Joseph's insights have helped to build my appreciation that although we use the same culinary map, we may each arrive at different destinations. Preparing food, including from a recipe, is truly a creative act that expresses the love and care that are part of the process. My cooking skills, along with my sensory appreciation of food, have flourished through years of association with my esteemed and capable co-author.

My diet evolved from a North American pattern that was centred on meat, dairy products, a few vegetables, and baked goods. My mother organized birthday celebrations that featured cookie-making as a party activity, and over the years these gatherings proved to be immensely popular with the neighbourhood children. She introduced me to the joy of cooking, both alone and with others. She also emphasized good nutrition as she understood it, as well as physical fitness. My mother taught early childhood education at the University of British Columbia and made life a great deal of fun. My father was a physiology professor. He did graduate work at the University of Toronto with the diabetes researchers who discovered insulin, Sir Frederick Banting and Charles Best. Later, my father's focus was on cancer research. The examples of my parents led me to value two facets of food and nutrition: the appetizing and the academic or nutritional.

Like my parents, I went on to teach in university settings; my subject was food and nutrition. After the birth of my children, Chris (Xoph) and Kavyo, I lived on an immense cattle ranch, travelled around the world several times, and lived in India and Nepal for four years. During this time I learned a great deal about the production and preparation of many cultural foods, particularly vegetarian dishes. My favourite cookbook was *The Spice Cookbook,* by A. Day and L. Stuckey (1964), and I loved learning about the origins and history of ingredients from near and far that bring such delight to the senses. My first attraction to a plant-based diet came from enjoyment of the food itself.

In 1993 while writing the "Without Dairy" chapter for my first book, *Becoming Vegetarian* (with Brenda Davis), I came face to face with my own mistaken belief that dairy products were essential to human health. From a critical review of the scientific research, I soon learned that I could survive very well without any flesh or fluids of animal origin. Over time, I learned about the profound impacts of our food choices on the environment, health, human hunger, and the lives of animals. In doing the extensive nutrition research that is a foundation of our books, I came to see that a vegan diet could provide every nutrient that we need in recommended amounts, and that such a diet makes sense for reasons that become more compelling every year. I came to appreciate how many of us are voting with our grocery dollars for good health, compassion for animals, and sustainable agriculture. My own dietary transition gave me an understanding of the challenges and solutions that people encounter as they move along a continuum from non-vegetarian through to vegan.

In recent years I have seen a great shift in attitude regarding vegetarian nutrition among those at the forefront of the dietetics profession. When I first taught university nutrition, an attitude prevailed that vegetarian diets are nutritionally risky. Vegan diets were almost unheard of. With time, scientists have recognized that centring our diet on plant foods can significantly reduce our risk of chronic disease. After the publication of *Becoming Vegetarian,* my profession awarded me the prestigious ClinTec award for leadership in dietetics. I was invited to write sections on vegetarian nutrition for diet manuals and to co-author the joint position paper by the American and Canadian dietetic associations on vegetarian diets. My vegan nutrition books are now required reading for continuing-education courses for health professionals.

I love to share with others the joy and fulfillment that comes from preparing food.

It is a pleasure to see how, right from the start, young children enjoy ingredients that are good for them. When my son, Chris, was one and a half years old, he and I demonstrated a simple recipe on television. Chris, now a tree planter and regular traveller to India, has a great appreciation for the natural, healthful, and simple foods that are easily available throughout India, far more than is the case in North America. He appreciates the long tradition of nourishing food choices that are common to so many cultures around the world.

At an early age (and before I made a similar decision), my daughter, Kavyo, decided not to eat meat. As an adult trained in geography and environmental studies, she has a productive vegetable garden and considers it very important for people to grow, prepare, and eat vegetables that they have grown. Producing one's own food can be empowering and can also create deeper respect and understanding of nature.

High in the Himalayas, I have traded tips with a Nepalese cook and porter while we made Lemon Tahini Dressing (page 122) as a sauce for our rice and spinach. It warms my heart to have my three-year-old neighbours (in our cohousing community) perched on a stool in the kitchen, with hands washed, enthusiastically putting the vegetables into a soup pot. I have enjoyed my role as a dietitian in Dr. Dean Ornish's San Francisco retreats, helping those with cardiovascular disease adopt diets that are both healing and delicious. It's deeply fulfilling to help clients and friends adopt ways of eating that are health-supportive, and it is satisfying to reassure others that we have no need to subject animals to the tortured lives and deaths they undergo when they are categorized as food animals.

Joseph and I have had such fun creating this book. It has been a pleasure to test and retest the recipes so that each one is a gem. Welcome to a recipe collection that will support your well-being, satisfy your appetite, and inspire you to enjoy cooking.

Vesanto Melina, MS, Registered Dietitian
www.nutrispeak.com

# Part One
## Making Sense of Food Choices

# Chapter 1:
# The Art and Science of Cooking
## by Chef Joseph Forest

## Cooking Is an Art

In any type of art, there are unlimited ways of assimilating, blending, and combining materials—whether musical notes, water colours, oil paints, or food ingredients—to produce an end result that satisfies in new ways. Fuse together food with creativity, motivation, and passion, throw in a bit of culinary science, mix it with an understanding of technique, and you can produce unforgettable culinary experiences.

During my apprenticeship years, I had the good fortune of working in a fine-dining restaurant in Edmonton called Walden's. At the time I worked there, it was considered one of the top restaurants in Canada. It was named after Walden Pond in Massachusetts because of its atmosphere of serenity—and the sheer number of plants and trees it housed. Walden's was a large, 180-seat garden restaurant with enormous skylights that nourished hundreds of fully grown plants, which sprawled from one end of the restaurant to the other. A fixed menu changed twice a year, and there were numerous opportunities to create daily specials to complement the main bill of fare. The emphasis on presentation was paramount and was the motivation of the kitchen team. Each plate was a little masterpiece—delicious works of art delivered to hundreds of satisfied customers every day.

The early part of my career was also completely focused on food artistry. I had the opportunity to successfully participate in provincial culinary art competitions, as well as to observe the inner workings of the most prestigious culinary art competitions at the highest international level. The culinary thinking that surrounded me in the late 1980s was that food was a medium for eye appeal and taste. Our attention centred on new ingredients, colour combinations, textures, novel ways of fusing flavour, and building artistic pyramids of food on the plate. Nutritional considerations were peripheral.

## Cooking Is a Science

Cooking is not only an art but also a science. Have you ever been curious about why a pinch of salt makes a raw apple taste sweeter, or why flour thickens a sauce? What about why it takes longer to cook potatoes in Jasper, Alberta, than in Vancouver, or why the best way to cook rice is to boil the water first, then add the grain? The answers to these questions lie in the well-documented science of cooking. Every process and technique used in the kitchen today can be understood and explained by science.

Yes, it is true that you don't need to have a PhD in order to make a pot of spicy soup or a tangy vinaigrette. However, understanding culinary technique can go a long way toward improving cooking skills and eliminating the margin of error in the kitchen.

There are usually good reasons why recipe ingredients are not all combined at once in a bowl or saucepan, stirred together, and then served. There are steps to assembling most recipes, and these procedures are based on sound culinary principles that ought to be followed before moving on to the next step. Think of cooking as a process of building layers, where one technique is followed by another. For best results, each layer ought to be developed and brought to a stage of completion before laying down the next layer.

## The Science of Nutrition

In addition to the science of cooking, there is a science of nutrition. Nutrition can be summarized as the study of nourishment, or the act of taking nutrients into the body for the purpose of building and maintaining health. Nutrition proponents have been advising humans how to eat for hundreds of years. In 400 BC, Hippocrates, the father of modern medicine, told his students, "Let your food be your medicine, and your medicine be your food." And furthermore, "A wise man should consider that health is the greatest of human blessings."

Science has expended a great deal of energy in analyzing the nature of food to discern its components: how much or how little of a particular nutrient is present in any given food, why we need specific nutrients, and the amounts of those nutrients needed to maintain physical, mental, and emotional health, or to regain it if lost. Knowing what nutrients your body needs and familiarizing yourself with their food sources can be a foundation for well-being.

This book is designed to assist vegetarians, and others who are interested in adding more plant-based foods to their diet in pursuit of optimum health. Ensuring that your dietary choice is well balanced and provides all the nutrients you need will keep you and your family in excellent health and also serve to inspire others and let them know that this is a viable choice.

## Developing a Healthy Relationship with Food

For individuals at one end of the spectrum, food is a central theme in enjoying life. Sometimes referred to as "foodies," they have a deep affinity to discovering new ingredients, eating, and cooking. There simply aren't enough meals in a day to prepare all the food they want to try. Their kitchens are full of staples and gadgets, and their fridges are overflowing with items for the next dinner party. Travel plans to exotic countries centre on culinary tourism. In visits to the marketplace, the abundance of colours, aromas, and sounds take culinary imaginations on wild-carpet rides.

For many people at the other end of the spectrum, food is just another commodity; preparing and eating it is a chore, a task that interrupts the more important things they have to do. They consider themselves inept at cooking, and their refrigerators sit empty most of the time—save for a few bottles of sauce, just in case they are forced to make a meal. For these folks, cooking is a struggle that includes a good dose of chaos and ends in frustration, disappointment, and another promise to eat prepackaged entrées for dinner starting tomorrow. Those who can afford it eat most of their meals in restaurants.

If you fall into the first camp, this book may serve you by extending your love of food into the vegetarian arena. If you struggle with the idea of preparing food and it is nothing more than a utilitarian act for you, or if you fall in between these two groups of people, what we offer in this book will help to broaden your interest in cooking, enhance your relationship with food, and establish an appreciation for preparing most of your meals at home.

## The Science of Perception: The Physical Senses

When approaching your culinary experiences, consider how your five senses might be more consciously engaged in expanding your awareness, skills, and confidence in the kitchen. Sight, smell, touch, hearing, and taste are the physical means by which you perceive and navigate through the physical world. Think of your eyes, nose, hands, ears, and tongue as extensions of your kitchen tools. They all have a role to play in your deepening relationship with food and will lead to unlocking opportunities that include a deeper appreciation of food preparation, improved cooking dexterity, expansion of kitchen wisdom, enhanced timing, greater creativity, and an improved sense of your intuitive abilities. As a result you will create wholesome food for yourself, family, and friends. Enter the kitchen without paying attention to your senses and you are more susceptible to disorganization, frustration, mistakes, and perhaps even injury.

### Awareness Starts in the Marketplace

Your senses play a significant role long before your ingredients are assembled on the kitchen counter. Think of when you shop for food. The common expression "We eat with our eyes first" reflects the strong affinity we have for artistic presentation. Look at the showcase in popular delicatessens, where a good deal of time and energy is spent arranging the food. Packaging is designed to make food visually appealing to consumers. We choose fresh ingredients according to its quality (sight) and avoid foods that are wilted, dull, or bruised.

We handle (touch) avocados, lemons, and peaches to determine how ripe they are. You may have *tasted* an olive at a Greek grocer, or been offered a sample that led to a purchase. A whiff (smell) of coffee or freshly baked bread in the market may have spurred you to buy a pound of roasted beans or a loaf of bread. Perhaps you smell melons and tomatoes to determine if they are ripe. On the other hand, a bad food odour may repulse you, in which case you steer away from it. You may buy fresh green beans or baby spring carrots because of the crisp *snap* (hearing) they make, or tap a watermelon with your knuckle in search of the right *thud* before taking it home.

## Expanding Sensory Awareness in the Kitchen

**Sight**: Learning how to look for signs before proceeding with a recipe can help reduce your reliance on the recipe's timing instructions. Often the directions will ask you to use your eyes when assembling a dish. For instance, the instructions to cook the onion "for 3 minutes or until transparent" and to cook the pancake "for 3 minutes or until the bottom is crispy brown" are visual cues. By looking for and becoming familiar with these indicators, you can relax and not be fixated on your clock, timer, or recipe instructions. This step alone will go a long way toward building your kitchen intuition.

**Smell**: Smell is a great way to connect with food. Think of garlic cooking in a skillet, freshly brewed coffee in the morning, or the scent of cinnamon and vanilla emanating from the oven when you bake a cake. As foods heat up, their volatile oils are released into the atmosphere, giving clues to what stage of cooking they're at. Kitchen aromas change as food shifts from one form to another. Some of these changes are obvious, though many are more subtle, but they can be identified if you pay attention to the fragrances in the air, which can guide and prompt you into taking the next step.

Don't be afraid to get your nose close to the cutting board and smell the food as you work with it. Smell your freshly chopped garlic and discern how it smells raw versus when it is heating up in the skillet. Slow down and smell freshly cut herbs, ground spices in your grinder, or that zest of lemon peel. Bend your head over a skillet or soup pot and take a deep whiff. Make friends with your ingredients.

**Touch**: Handling raw ingredients is an excellent way to familiarize yourself with food's consistency, texture, and other qualities, and it is a great way to connect with the process of cooking. Get your hands in there: don't be afraid to get them wet, sticky, oily, or messy.

People who love to bake their own bread often say they love it because of the kneading process. They enjoy the feel of the dough as they knead it, and the way the texture changes over a short period. Professionals often talk about "mouth feel" when describing the interaction a food has in the mouth. (Wine tasters use this term to discern the qualities of a wine.) This is a form of touch that can help you to evaluate food characteristics.

The next time you pierce a food with a sharp knife to test for doneness, feel the resistance or, alternatively, the ease in which the blade passes into the food. Bite into a green bean or spaghetti to check for al dente. These methods of using your sense of touch are ways to deepen the interaction with your nourishment and enhance your cooking skills.

**Hearing**: Here's an exercise in developing your kitchen awareness: spend time making meals without any background noise, such as the television, radio, or a CD, and see how this helps you connect with your food experience. Listen. Pay attention to the sounds around you as you cook. Listen to the sizzle of onions cooking in the skillet, the turbulent sound water makes as it comes to a boil, the popping of pumpkin seeds roasting in the oven. The sound of a lid rattling on top of a saucepan most likely means the liquid is simmering too strongly and needs a decrease in temperature for the food to cook with less vigour. Take note of the distinctive sounds liquid makes as it fills a jar or soup pot. Sounds in the kitchen are loaded with information and can indicate the need to engage with the next step of your recipe. Setting a timer is a valuable practice, but listening to your intuition is even better, as it can prompt you to check on the food before the buzzer rings.

**Taste**: As humans, we derive great pleasure and satisfaction from the taste of food and beverages. Taste is the ability to detect flavour and is perhaps the most prominent sense used in the kitchen. Taste is a component of flavour: although the terms "taste" and "flavour" are often used interchangeably, they have different meanings.

Taste is detected by approximately 9,000 elongated taste buds located on the upper surface of the tongue, throat, pharynx, and soft palate. Each taste bud has minute hairs on its surface, a barrel-shaped "bud" in the middle, and 15 to 20 taste receptors at the base, which are attached to nerve fibres that carry taste impulses to the brain. Taste buds are specialized cells in that they detect six basic tastes: salty, sweet, sour, bitter, pungent, and astringent. (Western science recognizes only the first four primary tastes listed here, whereas Eastern schools of thought recognize the other two as well.) Let's take a look at these tastes.

## Six Tastes

Have you ever had a meal that leaves you with an overwhelming sense of satisfaction? Many factors go into experiencing such a meal. The location, setting, atmosphere, occasion, company, your mood, and, last but certainly not least, the food all play important roles in the overall experience. Seasoning food to perfection always involves more than just adding salt and pepper. All six tastes play very important roles in bringing each dish into balance on its own or in relationship to the whole meal. It can be said that a dish or meal is well balanced when all six tastes are activated during the course of eating. The ideal proportions for balance vary from one individual to another and can depend on personal preference. In some cases, genetics play a role in determining inclinations toward taste.

In Appendix 1 you'll find a list of foods specific to each taste category. Examining these lists will deepen your understanding of how the tastes can interact to produce harmonious agreement when mixed together. You'll notice that some foods are found in more than one category. Foods found in more than one list typically have a predominant taste, with another taste coming through as a secondary quality.

**Salty**: There are two main sources of salt: sea water and rock salt. Sea water is evaporated to obtain the mineral, whereas rock salt is mined from enormous underground mineral deposits that were once large bodies of salt water. Salt has long been utilized as a preservative, but more commonly today it is used as a seasoning to enhance and bring out underlying flavours in food. Salt is nature's true and original flavour enhancer. It adds vigour, depth, and strength to food and stimulates the appetite by stimulating saliva and digestive juices. Used in excess, salt can blot out the other flavours. Examples of salty foods include salt (naturally), tamari, bottled sauces, and bouillon cubes and powder.

**Sweet**: Sweetness may be due to the presence of naturally occurring sugars; this is typical of fruits and root vegetables. In many prepared foods, sweetness is due to the addition of extracted sugars from beets, or from cane sugar, maple syrup, agave syrup, or barley malt, and more increasingly, high-fructose corn syrup. Such sweeteners give an immediate and strong perception of sweetness. Apart from added sugars, sweetness in food can come from the breakdown products of complex carbohydrates that start to be digested into simple sugars by salivary amylase, thus giving a sweet taste in the mouth. This occurs, for example, when you eat brown rice. Chewing a mouthful of brown rice 20 to 30 times before swallowing will begin to release the inherent sweetness of the grain, which the taste buds then discern. Knowing this, you may want to reduce your use and consumption of added sweeteners. Chewing makes you work a bit for that sweet experience.

Like salt, sweeteners enhance the flavour of food. Sweeteners have the capacity to accentuate flavour components in desserts in the way that salt does with savoury foods. Sweetness can balance the other tastes and take the edge off any harsh tones. Sweetness is soothing and relieves thirst. Sugar has another physiological effect: the simple sugar glucose raises the body's blood sugar level; the sugar that is delivered is fuel for the brain and it can satisfy the appetite. Examples of sweet foods are apricots, corn, rice, nuts, seeds, and many herbs and spices.

**Sour**: Sourness is the taste of acidic ingredients, which have the ability to sharpen the senses, stimulate the appetite, increase digestive juices, and promote digestion. They also have a cleansing effect on the palate and, indeed, the entire body. Some fine French restaurants serve lemon sorbet between courses to cleanse the palate. Sour foods added to a dish make it bright by accentuating and sharpening its inherent top notes (discussed on page 10).

Sourness enhances other flavours, adds intensity, and can decrease the need for salt. Balancing the acid content of a dish is critical to its success. Sour foods include lemons, vinegar, lemon grass, and molasses.

**Bitter**: Bitterness is detected at the very back of the tongue. Since many poisonous substances in nature are bitter, the tongue acts as a gatekeeper, providing a warning signal should a potentially toxic substance be about to be swallowed. But not all bitter taste is bad—far from it. For example, bitter-tasting foods are valued as a part of each meal in Japan, where it is recognized that this taste contributes particular health-supportive qualities. Bitter foods stimulate the digestion and have an alkalinizing effect on the blood, acting as a buffer and balancing acidity.

Many substances that we find bitter—for example in green tea, grapefruit, and vegetable greens—are actually health-promoting phytochemicals. Examples are the glucosinolates in kale, broccoli, cabbages, cauliflower, and other cruciferous vegetables with cancer-preventive properties. Our ancestors consumed a good amount of fruits and vegetables that were more bitter than their modern-day counterparts, which have been bred to increase sweetness and reduce the bitter components, at the same time reducing some of the protective phytochemicals.

Overcooking bitter vegetables can accentuate this taste, so eat them raw or lightly steamed or cooked. Add bitter vegetables to soups, stews, and stir-fries at the end of the cooking process, heating until they are just cooked and still tender to the bite. These techniques are understood in Asian cuisine, where care is taken to prepare food in ways that minimize the bitterness while still imparting their health-supportive qualities.

A bitter taste stimulates the digestion and immediately wakes up the palate, creating a desire for balance with other tastes. Think of when you had bitter medicine: there was most likely an immediate desire to balance out the taste, probably with sweetness.

Plums, Brussels sprouts, cumin, and chocolate are all bitter foods.

**Pungent**: Pungent tastes are strong, hot, spicy, acrid, and biting. Such tastes are found in mustard greens, onions, garlic, chili peppers, black pepper, cayenne, and ginger. In small amounts, pungent tastes stimulate the digestion, clear the sinuses, dispel gas from the body, and help detoxify the body. In large amounts, they will outright make you cry—think of freshly grated horseradish or wasabi. Too much pungency can cause excessive salivation, leading to a drying of the mouth and increased thirst. Pungent tastes can also burn the mouth, make the eyes water, and create excess mucus secretion. Shortly after consuming pungent foods, the body heats up and may perspire. This is a natural cooling mechanism and is the reason spicy foods are popular in hot climates. Additional examples of pungent foods are raw garlic, cilantro, cinnamon, citrus peel, and some brands of extra-virgin olive oil.

**Astringent**: Astringent tastes can make the mouth dry and puckered, causing it to feel constricted. This sensation is because of the presence of tannins. These can tighten mucous membranes, contract tissues, and decrease inflammation. They have a cleansing effect on the palate, which is why many people enjoy drinking wine with their meal. Too much astringency can cause difficulty swallowing. The drying effect of astringent taste balances out excessive salivation or perspiration of pungent taste.

Whereas foods that are sour are found to be more acidic, foods with an astringent taste tend to be more alkaline. Leafy greens, legumes (beans, peas, lentils, and soy foods), green bananas, and cranberries are astringent in their taste profile. Beans, pomegranate, potatoes, and turmeric are other astringent foods.

## Flavour

The word "flavour" is often used as a synonym for "taste." In truth, flavour includes what we perceive through our senses such as sight, and through the nerves in our mouth and nose. Our capacity to judge food with our eyes ("We eat with our eyes first") has an impact on how we filter information from the outside world, in turn impacting how we perceive flavour. Mouth feel involves the texture and temperature of food. The nose detects flavour by sensing volatile oils in the food, attaching them to receptor sites in the nasal passage, and then sending a signal to the brain, which identifies different aromas, fragrances, and odours. Other non-physical factors, such as frame of mind/mood, environment (e.g., a romantic atmosphere), and social conditioning (e.g., belief systems), play a role in how flavour is perceived by any given individual and at any given time. Flavour is subjective, the final verdict resting with each person. Taste, on the other hand, is more objective, though individuals vary physically and genetically in the extent to which their tongue perceives various tastes.

## Flavour Development

The topic of flavour development is a big one, and the world of creating artificial flavours is even bigger. Flavours are routinely synthesized in laboratories, subsequently finding their way into practically every processed food in the marketplace for the purpose of flavour enhancement and taste uniformity. In this book, however, flavour in the recipes is derived from natural, unadulterated food; it is developed by understanding the nature of taste and whether the combinations of ingredients blend well together. This is where the knowledge of the six tastes is valuable, especially for those who are inclined to move beyond the formal structure of a recipe to develop their own creations.

Although the world offers us thousands of ingredients from which to choose, and unlimited combinations, the tongue registers primarily six tastes. Good cooking may be viewed as the ability to bring these tastes into harmony with each other. The recipes in this book were created in exactly this way. If you examine the recipes and then glance at the taste lists in Appendix 1, you will see how salty, sweet, sour, bitter, pungent, and astringent foods can be assembled in order to create balanced and appealing flavour combinations.

## Food Composition

The composition of recipes has similarities to the arrangement of music within five horizontal lines known as a staff. Some musical notes are of a bass tone, or pitch, and positioned at the bottom of the staff, whereas others are found at the middle and top. Individual notes are organized into chords to produce an unlimited variation of sounds and compositions. It is the same with food ingredients. Consider the six tastes to be composed of flavours that make up a culinary musical scale. To create good food, base flavours are built upon with ingredients that have middle and top notes. A single ingredient, with its combination of tastes, is blended with another, and then another, until they all come together to create a satisfying symphony of tastes.

Just like the base line in music that carries a tune, so too in cooking. There are foods that blend well to form a base—specific chords, if you will. Take, for instance, the combination of three aromatic vegetables known as a mirepoix (pronounced "meer pwah"), which originated in 18th-century France. This classic mixture of onions, carrots, and celery is extensively used as a base for stocks, soups, stews, and sauces. This blend of food ingredients is just one example of countless food "chords" that act as a foundation in creating countless flavour combinations. Other examples of a few ingredients coming together to form a base are onion, garlic, and tomatoes in pasta sauce; ginger, curry, and coconut milk in soup; and ginger, scallions, and soy sauce in dipping sauce (and you'll find recipes with these combinations in the book).

Once the base chord in a recipe has had a chance to develop a concentrated flavour, the next step is to build the middle tier by adding another layer. This is usually the main flavour ingredient of a dish. The "main" is usually (but not necessarily) accompanied with a few more ingredients, such as vegetable stock, black beans and toasted cumin seeds that might be added to the mirepoix base in the above example

This middle note of a dish is followed by the top layer: flavours that are subtler than those in the base or middle layer. Top notes may be those ingredients that, when eaten, gives just a hint of what it is—but one can't quite identify it. That is, a well-constructed recipe will leave one guessing as to what that mysterious ingredient is. To round out the example above, a splash of freshly squeezed lime juice added at the last minute will give a bright, refreshing tone to the black bean dish.

Examples for other dishes might include lemon, freshly cut herbs or chilies, or a combination of flavours such as tamari and balsamic. This range of flavour, from the base to the top note, helps bring the dish to the peak of satisfaction.

## Adjusting the Seasoning

Now that you have some understanding of taste and flavour development, I hope you will feel more comfortable when the time comes to make that final addition to your recipes. This is an important step because natural ingredients change from one garden plot, produce market, or supermarket to the next.

For instance, carrots may all look similar, but they are not all created equal. The flavour profile can vary tremendously from one carrot to another, even within the same variety. It depends in part where and how the carrot was grown, how it was stored, how old it is, and how it is prepared. Because there is so much variation with food ingredients, the final taste of a recipe will vary from one kitchen to another, even though the instructions may have been followed exactly as written. That is why it's important to consider the final step in a recipe—"adjust the seasoning" or "season to taste."

Adjusting the seasoning is more than just adding more salt or pepper. Finer tuning may be required to tweak the final taste and bring it into balance according to your preferences. Once you have a sense of how foods are categorized into the various tastes, you will be more adept at adjusting the seasoning. Is the dish too tart? Then add some sweetness. Is the food to salty? Then add a bit of acid, and so forth.

## Recipe Development

During past centuries, recipes evolved so that skilled cooks or chefs could pass on their wisdom to those with less experience in the kitchen. In this respect, recipes have some similarities to paint-by-number kits. In both, every detail is thought through to help the user reach a consistent and favourable result. Follow the steps diligently and the image or product the creator had in mind will emerge each time. It is important to read a recipe before you start (discussed in more detail below). Reading a recipe first will help an image formulate in your mind's eye of the steps you will take, thereby making the cooking process easier and increasing the likelihood that you will reach the desired goal.

Some people follow recipes exactly, others refer to recipes for inspiration only or to consult the ratio of ingredients before rearranging a recipe as they go. Once you understand how food ingredients interact with each other, you can start to assemble them in ways that are complementary to each other, according to your creative enthusiasm, culinary ability, and dietary preferences.

## Kitchen Organization: The Key to Your Success

It's time to take these recipes to the kitchen. If this is where the system breaks down for you, the following information might help. The manner in which you approach food preparation can make or break your enjoyment of cooking. The key to success is organization.

During my chef's training, much emphasis was placed on advance preparation of ingredients before the restaurant guests arrived to maximize the efficiency of cooking hundreds of individual meals in a short period. A significant amount of time was given to this advance organization. The French term for this is *mis en place,* meaning, literally, everything in its place. We followed this system so that we could remain at our cooking station during service. In other words, once the lunch or dinner service began, it was important to have as much prep at arm's reach as possible so we didn't waste valuable time running around the kitchen once service began looking for, and cutting ingredients, or finding equipment.

Like a busy professional chef, you have deadlines, pressures, and interruptions, and you may not have as much time to spend in the kitchen as you would like. Rudimentary organizational skills can maximize your productivity and efficiency—and enjoyment—in the kitchen. Let's take a look at the four steps.

### Read Your Recipe First

Develop the habit of reading your recipe from beginning to end before you start your prep. This step cannot be overemphasized. It will give you an overview of the recipe procedures: the culinary techniques and the foods and equipment you will need. If you don't understand a particular part of the recipe, you can review the procedure before you start, rather than in the middle of cooking. If a recipe points to important information on another page in the cookbook, you can examine that material before starting your prep. Reading the recipe through will also help you visualize what you are about to do. If you can grasp the vision, you are in a good starting position.

### Gather All the Equipment

Equipment includes cutting board, knives, mixing bowls, measuring cups, spoons, food processor, pots, and so on. This step may prompt you to read the recipe again, so that you don't miss anything. Reading the recipe a second time can deepen your understanding of what you are about to achieve, especially if you have not made the recipe before. The clearer your idea of what you are about to do, the less chaos there will be in your kitchen.

## Gather All the Ingredients

Knowing up front that you have all the ingredients eliminates the frustration of discovering halfway through a recipe that you didn't replenish a needed staple on your last shopping trip. This step also saves time. It will take less time to assemble a dish if you gather all the ingredients in front of you than if you continuously interrupt your cutting or measuring to return to the refrigerator or cupboard to look for the next item called for. This step also allows you to be more present in your actions. While you are preparing ingredients for the recipe, you may preheat the oven, boil water for pasta, or warm the skillet or soup pot over low heat.

## Set Up Your Counter Space

Setting up your counter space is perhaps not so much a step as a pattern to follow each time you prepare a dish. How you arrange and organize your ingredients and equipment just before cooking determines how smoothly and quickly your recipe takes shape. As an example, here is how I would prepare the Stir-Fry 101 (page 174).

First I clear from the counter everything that I do not need for the recipe. Then I lay a damp dishcloth on the counter and set my cutting board on top to prevent it from slipping—important when using sharp knives. The kitchen utensils I need are pulled from a wicker basket that holds all my cooking spoons, spatulas, and whisks. I gather all the food ingredients to the left of the cutting board and wash those that require it. My skillet is preheating on the lowest heat setting. (Heating a pot, pan, or skillet on the lowest setting distributes the heat so that when I raise the temperature, it comes up to medium or high quickly.) As vegetables are cut they are placed in separate piles on a baking sheet or large plate to the right of the board. All the dried herbs and spices are measured into a small bowl (or bowls, if called for at different points in the recipe). Ingredient packages and containers no longer needed are returned to the cupboard or fridge, and now I proceed to the stove, where I am poised to cook.

How you set up your counter space is partly determined by how much space you have. The above method is how I operate in my own kitchen, but this might change depending whether you are right or left handed, or what side of the stove your working counter is situated. If you are short of counter space, perhaps a portable table such as a fold down TV tray could be brought into the kitchen when needed, to help in organizing your ingredients.

When all ingredients are prepped and gathered within arm's reach, the actual cooking of food—whether you are stir-frying, assembling sushi rolls, or making soup—becomes a much easier task. You won't have to worry about the onions burning while you're still cutting the carrots. Your counter space will be more tidy, and with everything you need right there for you, you can focus on cooking. Organizing yourself in this manner will go a long way toward alleviating kitchen chaos.

## Food as a Source of Nourishment and Blessing

In closing, I want to address an important consideration about food that developed early in my career, an idea that has been deeply instrumental in forming my overarching vision and approach to working with food. It is the idea that food is sacred and has the potential to act as a conduit for deep blessings unto those who partake of food that has been prepared within the context of this awareness. This is not a viewpoint that can be measured by the mechanical instruments of science, but it can be measured by the sensitive mechanism of the heart. The idea that food is sacred is not new. This concept lies at the heart of Native traditions, religious beliefs, and spiritual practices around the world, wherein food is perceived as a gift, one that in essence offers people a spiritual blessing.

Food has long been respected and revered by humans. There are many examples of food occupying a central or elevated role in a culture—for instance, it was wild rice for the First Nations of the Great Lakes region, corn for the Aztec and Mayan cultures in Mexico. Quinoa, the ancient South America grain that was revered by the Incans, was referred to as "the mother of all grains." In the spring, to show respect for what this plant provided the tribes, the Incan emperor was the first to sow quinoa seeds in the earth, using a gold-tipped shovel.

As well, major religions have sacred food traditions. The Jewish feast of Passover and Holy Communion in the Christian community are just two examples. Breaking a fresh coconut in Hindu temples dedicated to the deity Ganesha before auspicious social events and new beginnings is considered highly favourable, as is *prasad*, an offering, generally food, that is offered to a deity or saint for blessing, then distributed and consumed.

These traditions all point to food as having the capacity to offer the human body more than vitamins, minerals, and antioxidants. Central to these beliefs, customs, traditions, and rituals is the notion that at the core of human existence lies a spiritual component that can be accessed, touched, blessed, nourished, and healed with food; it is not the germ at the centre of the seed that gives and sustains life, but the living, breathing, active force of love that can manifest in daily nourishment. Imparting such a blessing is not the monopoly of Native traditions or religions; anyone with an intention of goodwill unto others or for oneself may.

When food is prepared with the awareness that it can be sacred, it can become imbued with spiritual substance. In essence, it is this substance that has the capability of transforming the server, the food, and those who partake of that sustenance. Although this subtlety cannot be measured by instruments, it can be perceived and appreciated. For instance, stories abound of apple pies baked by loving grandmothers that taste so much better than those made commercially in large volume. Is it because grandma made her pie with local, organic apples? Perhaps, but it also points to an invisible force at play: a genuine, comforting, and transforming spirit of love.

We can't eat Grandma's pie every day, but we all have the power to impart blessings on ourselves and others by the way we interact with our food. In fact, no one has more power to offer blessings upon your life than you do. The attitude and presence of mind that is brought to food preparation and its consumption is an important factor in generating health and well-being. What I want to impart here is the idea of creating sacred space regarding all aspects of food, from the way it is produced or purchased to its preparation, service to others or oneself and final intake.

One potent method of creating sacred space and imparting blessing onto your food is through gratitude. Cultivating a spirit of thankfulness for food and its ability to provide vitality, strength, and well-being is a compelling way to be mindful that food does not need to be strictly utilitarian but that instead it can be a source of blessing. The kitchen has traditionally been the heart of the home, a powerful space to generate physical, mental, emotional, and spiritual well-being, which in turn ripples out into the environment from all who share in this space. Food can be an exquisite component to everyday living. Acknowledging it as sacred rather than viewing it as just another commodity has the power to transform life, and a transformed life is a potent force in the world. May you all find comfort in body, mind, and spirit through the creation and partaking of your daily nourishment.

# Chapter 2:
# Making Friends with Your Ingredients

An acquaintance recently told me of walking into a large natural food store shortly after deciding to take greater responsibility for her health. She looked around, and then walked out without making a single purchase. When I asked her why, she told me she was simply overwhelmed by the magnitude of new ingredients all around her, on every shelf.

Deciding to take control of one's health is a significant step toward living a wholesome lifestyle. Choices that were not important yesterday are paramount today. What should I eat for breakfast? Which foods contain calcium? Is there a plant-based source of vitamin B12? What vegetable oils should I cook with? What is the truth about soy foods? Which is the optimum diet for me? Will I meet my soulmate in the produce aisle? Sifting through mountains of information to arrive at informed decisions that support one's lifestyle can be daunting, confusing, and intimidating.

The market offers thousands of food ingredients from which to choose. Picking those that are right for you, your partner, or your family boils down to what your values are and what you hold to be true about nutrition. Nutritional theory is constantly evolving. What was thought to be incorrect a decade ago all of a sudden becomes today's panacea, with headlines heralding findings from an academic study. In 10 years that remedy will begin to collect dust as new edicts from the world of nutritional science make national headlines.

The best way to navigate the market is to get clear on your personal food values. Make adjustments in your shopping as convincing information is revealed. Stay informed, keep reading labels, buy the best ingredients that your budget will allow, and remember: your values are your bedrock, despite the constantly changing market.

The aim of this chapter is to shed some light on the basic food ingredients we used in developing the recipes in this book.

## Good Fats from Whole Foods

Fat is essential to human life, and yet it has a bad reputation, likely because so much of the types and quantities that are eaten undermine human health. The nutrient-rich fat that is naturally present in fresh seeds, nuts, soybeans, avocados, olives, and other plant foods is of the highest quality. There is simply no contest between the fats found in these foods and the chemically altered fats found in margarine, shortening, and other hydrogenated vegetables oils, or the highly saturated fats found in animal products. Even vegetable oils that are thought of as being very healthful pale in comparison to the whole foods from which they were extracted. Plant foods bring with them valuable vitamins, minerals, phytochemicals, plant protein, plant sterols, essential fatty acids, and fibre. Consider what we know about the value of seeds, nuts, and the other whole foods that provide rich, creamy textures—and so much more—to our meals.

## Seeds

Seeds are the life-giving parts of plants. They are complete bundles of nutrition, designed to nourish the initial growth of seedlings. The value of seeds in human nutrition is greatly underestimated. Chia, hemp, poppy, pumpkin, sesame, and sunflower seeds are all good sources of linoleic acid, an essential omega-6 fatty acid. Even more important, chia, flax, and hemp seeds are high in the hard-to-get omega-3 fatty acid, linolenic acid. Seeds vary in their protein content, ranging from about 12 percent to more than 30 percent of calories. They are among our richest sources of vitamin E and provide an impressive selection of other vitamins, minerals (e.g., zinc), phytochemicals, and fibre.

Although some whole foods contain more fat than others, it is important to remember that a gram of fat consists of 9 calories, whether it is found in whole foods or extracted oils. Just because nuts, seeds, avocados, and olives are better eaten whole does not mean one should eat them in unlimited amounts. Typically, 1/4 cup (60 mL) of nuts or seeds provides about 1 tablespoon (15 mL) of oil.

**Flaxseeds**: Flaxseeds, also known as linseeds, are reddish-brown oval seeds, slightly bigger than sesame seeds. Flaxseeds contain lignans, which are phytochemicals with antioxidant properties that help fight cancer. These powerhouse seeds offer a significant advantage for vegetarians, as they have the greatest omega-3 content of any food, averaging about 57 percent linolenic acid. Thus, flax can go a long way toward helping correct the imbalance in essential fatty acids that exist in the modern-day diet. Flax is very high in soluble fibre, the type of fibre that lowers cholesterol, triglycerides (blood fats), and blood pressure. Flax also can improve blood sugar response in people with diabetes and may improve immune/inflammatory disorders.

Grind 1 cup (250 mL) of whole flaxseeds in the blender; store in the refrigerator or freezer. Sprinkle 2 tablespoons (30 mL) into a breakfast smoothie, into a salad dressing, over steamed vegetables or cooked rice, or use as a garnish for soup. See page 28 for how to use ground flaxseed as an egg replacer in pancakes or baked goods.

**Hemp Seeds**: Hemp is a crop that holds a lot of nutritional promise. Like other oil seeds, hemp typically contains about 31 percent fat by weight, and the ratio of omega-6s to omega-3s in hemp seeds (oil) is ideal at 3:1, which would be excellent if this were our only source of fat. But hemp seeds are far from our only source of fat. With the abundance of foods and oils high in omega-6 fatty acids in our diets, this ratio climbs as high as 10 or more parts omega-6 fatty acids to one part omega-3 fatty acids. Such high ratios reflect vegetarian as well as non-vegetarian diets. With such an imbalance, inflammatory conditions develop in the body that set the stage for common degenerative diseases.

Shelled hemp seeds are found in the Banana-Blueberry Power Drink (page 76) and Green Smoothie (page 81). They provide abundant nutrition and long-lasting energy, especially useful for athletes. Hemp seeds are very versatile and can be eaten raw; made into non-dairy milk; turned into hummus; sprinkled onto salad greens, pasta noodles, or pizza; utilized as a thickener in salad dressings; used in most baking recipes; or incorporated into a raw pie crust.

**Sesame Seeds**: Sesame seeds are primarily grown for their rich and flavourful oil content, which makes them a good candidate for choosing them as a whole food. Sesame is abundant in the minerals calcium, copper, iron, magnesium, and manganese.

Sesame seeds add a nutty taste and crunch to foods, but because the seeds are so small they can pass into the stomach without being broken open by the action of chewing, and so may not be digested. To solve this situation, grind 1 cup (250 mL) of seeds in the blender for 5 to 7 seconds to break open most of the seeds. Store the partially ground seeds in the refrigerator or freezer, ready to add to smoothies or sprinkle over salads, cooked grains, and steamed vegetables. Experiment by using the ground seeds in a pie crust. Sesame tahini is a digestible form of these seeds. This seed butter can be eaten as a spread on bread, drizzled over pancakes, or used to make a dressing or a sauce, or to thicken soups. Try it in the much-loved Heart-Healthy Hummus (page 90).

**Sunflower Seeds**: Sunflower seeds are often eaten as a mild, nutty-tasting protein snack in between meals, but they can easily be incorporated into the main meal. These seeds are a rich source of vitamin E, a powerful antioxidant that neutralizes free radicals in the body and has an anti-inflammatory effect. Sunflower seeds are also a good source of B vitamins and the minerals copper, iron, manganese, selenium, and zinc. Just 1/4 cup (60 mL) of sunflower seeds contains 6 grams of protein.

Start the day with sunflower seeds for breakfast in a smoothie (pages 76 and 81). Try the Sunflower Sesame Spread (page 96) as a snack with the Raw Vegetable Platter (page 93). Having a small bag of nutritious seeds, nuts, and raisins in the car or your purse, daypack, or office drawer will help you avoid reaching for chips or other junk food when hunger strikes.

**Pumpkin Seeds**: Pumpkin seeds are nutritional powerhouses, supplying the body with a host of nutrients, including iron, magnesium, potassium, and zinc. Most of the fatty acids in pumpkin seeds come from monounsaturated fat, and polyunsaturated fats in the form of omega-6s. One-quarter cup (60 mL) of pumpkin seeds has 184 calories from fat, and 10 grams of protein. They have slightly less fat than sunflower seeds and 30 percent more protein.

## Nuts

Nuts are loaded with good fats (mainly monounsaturated fat), are low in saturated fat, and are free of trans-fatty acids and cholesterol. Walnuts are rich in valuable omega-3 fatty acids. Almonds are particularly high in calcium, and cashews in zinc. Nuts are great sources of antioxidants, including selenium and vitamin E, and are good sources of plant protein and fibre. Important trace minerals, such as chromium, copper, magnesium, potassium, selenium, and zinc, are found in nuts.

Nuts make important additions in nutrition, flavour, and texture to meals, for instance, in the Sprouted Lentil Salad Plate (page 110) and the Brown Rice, Mushroom, and Walnut Pilaf (page 192). Nuts are also great as snacks. On their own or in combination with raisins, or dried blueberries or cranberries, nuts are valuable companions to take along on outdoor excursions such as biking, climbing, or camping trips. Trail mixes are great for long-distance trips, especially if you are flying—airport food can be a challenge, so take along your own fuel.

### Fruits: Avocados, Coconuts, and Olives

**Avocados**: Most people think "fat" when they think of avocados, and for good reason. One cup of cubed avocado contains 240 calories and 21 grams of fat. But the fat in avocados consists primarily of monounsaturated fatty acids, which have been shown to reduce total cholesterol while increasing HDL ("good") cholesterol when eaten in moderation. The fibre content of 1 cup (250 mL) of cubed avocados is impressive at 7 to 10 grams. The vitamin E for the same quantity is 2 to 3 milligrams.

**Coconut**: Coconuts have been a staple of Asian countries and the Pacific Islands for centuries. Although coconut meat is high in fat, including saturated fat, like other nuts and seeds it contains respectable amounts of the minerals copper, iron, manganese, phosphorus, selenium, and zinc, making it much more nutritious than coconut oil. Both young and mature coconuts are available in the market. The young ones contain more coconut water, and soft gel-like meat. Mature coconuts are firmer and contain less water. Coconut milk is made by blending the meat and the coconut water and additional water, if needed. (You'll find details on page 120 of how to break open a coconut to make fresh coconut milk.) Apart from its use for milk, pieces of fresh coconut can simply be eaten as a snack or blended in a smoothie. Or grate fresh coconut onto breakfast cereals or any other food where a coconut flavour is desired.

**Olives**: There are many varieties of olives, all of which are high in monounsaturated fatty acids. Most olives are cured or pickled in salty brine before being sold. This means that in addition to good fat, 1/4 cup (60 mL) of pickled olives provides 250 milligrams of sodium, or about one-sixth of your recommended daily intake. The key here, then, is moderation. With the advent of the raw food movement, raw olives that are not high in salt are now available.

## Oils: A Slippery Slope

The best way to achieve the daily recommendations for fat in our diet is by eating whole foods rich in the oils that the body requires. But what about the oils extracted from those foods, which are used in food preparation? Considering the immense variety of oils that line the grocery store shelves, choosing the right cooking oil—one that is safe and effective—can be confusing and overwhelming. Understanding how most of the oils are made can help in the selection process.

## How Oils Are Manufactured

The majority of edible oils are made using one of two extraction methods: expeller pressing or solvent extraction. Both processes generate high temperatures that strip the oil of any nutrition, particularly the omega-3 fatty acids, which are extremely sensitive to heat.

With expeller pressing, the seeds are first washed before being crushed. The crushed seed meal is then cooked for up to two hours at an average temperature of 250°F (120°C), depending on the type of seed. This step softens the cells that contain the oil, making the extraction process easier and resulting in a higher yield.

Next the seeds pass through a screw-like auger press that pushes the seed meal against the press head; the enormous pressure squeezes oil from the seed meal. At this step, heat is generated in the press head, and the hotter it gets, the more oil is extracted. Temperatures can reach 200°F (95°C). At this stage, the oil can be filtered and sold in the market as "cold pressed" or natural, unrefined oil, though the heat may have damaged essential fatty acids in the oil. In addition, the light and oxygen present during the pressing may have further deteriorated the oils.

The solvent extraction method is the predominant method used in the world today to dissolve oil from seeds, nuts, and fruit. The principal solvent used is hexane, a highly flammable by-product of the petroleum industry and a known carcinogen. Oil extracted in this manner is carefully monitored because of the highly flammable materials involved.

In the first step, the ground seed meal is mixed with hexane and constantly agitated to separate the oil from the mash. The hexane is then evaporated from the mixture, and sometimes the solvent is removed using a centrifuge. In either case, traces of hexane remain in the oil. At this point, solvent-extracted oils may be mixed with mechanically pressed oils and sold in the market as "unrefined oil."

Oils not sold as unrefined are further subjected to heat, as well as phosphoric acid, to remove naturally present gums such as lecithin. This procedure also removes chlorophyll and minerals from the oil. Caustic soda is then added to remove proteins and remaining fatty acids, which can cause an oil to go rancid.

The oil then undergoes a bleaching process to remove naturally occurring pigments, including beta-carotene, which make the oil cloudy. Deodorization is the last step, to eliminate aromatic oils and unwanted tastes. This makes the oil "pure" and tasteless, not unlike white bread. Deodorization is accomplished by steam distillation under extreme pressure and heat for up to an hour. For oils that get wide distribution through supermarkets, several synthetic antioxidants are added to replace those that were removed in the refining process. The refined oil is now inert and can last on the shelf for years.

The range of temperatures employed in the mass production of oil can range from 200°F (95°C) to 480°F (250°C), for up to an hour. Using oils produced by these methods is not recommended.

**Hydrogenation:** Large refinery-type oil manufacturing facilities take some of their refined oil and hydrogenate it. Hydrogenation is the chemical process that adds hydrogen atoms to unsaturated oil for the purpose of increasing the stability of the oil molecule. Hydrogen gas is bubbled through vegetable oil at temperatures between

250°F (120°C) and 400°F (200°C) in the presence of a catalyst such as nickel or platinum. This process can take several hours.

The result is that liquid oil is turned into solid or semi-solid fat products such as margarine, vegetable shortening, and deep-fry oil for the purpose of increasing shelf life, stability of flavour, and achieving a higher smoke point. This type of oil is severely damaged and creates a fatty-acid molecule that is harmful to human health: a trans fat. The principal health risk associated with trans fat consumption is an elevated risk of coronary heart disease. Other diseases, including cancer, diabetes, and obesity, have been linked to the consumption of trans-fatty acids.

Hydrogenated and partially hydrogenated fats are used by the truckload, in fact by the ton, in processed foods and snacks, and in the fast food industry. They keep cakes moist, cookies crisp, chips crunchy, and breads soft. The Canadian Food Inspection Agency requires food manufacturers to list the content of trans-fatty acids on food labels. Trans fat levels of less than 0.2 grams per serving can be listed as "Free of saturated fat" on the food label. Health advocates strongly believe this small amount is still too much; therefore, it best to stay away from trans fats altogether. The National Academy of Sciences has concluded there is no safe level of trans fat consumption.

**Smoke Point of Oils**: When cooking at high temperatures and deep frying, smoke point and the use of refined oil become of interest. In this book we do not feature these cooking methods. However, knowing a bit about smoke point may be helpful in choosing cooking oils. The smoke point of a particular oil is the temperature at which its molecular structure starts to break down, form a bluish smoke that may contain carcinogens, and be damaged in flavour and nutrition. Highly refined oils have higher smoke points than cold-pressed oils because vulnerable components that cause the smoke, including fatty acids, vitamins, and protective phytochemicals, have been removed.

## Cold-Pressed Oils

Buyers may have certain expectations when they purchase oils labelled "cold pressed"; however, it is important to note that this term is not subject to regulation in Canada. Process descriptions on food labels for cold-pressed products are left to the manufacturer. Consumers may believe that such oils have been extracted from seeds, nuts, or fruits (such as hemp seeds, olives, or avocados) without heat and simply by mechanical pressure against steel heads or large flat stones; this method is possible but is not typical of commercial oil production. For smaller scale operations whose emphasis is on nutritious oil, it is generally accepted that the term "cold pressed" can be used on a label when oil is produced within a tight temperature range. Oils such as flax or hemp seed oils that are valued for their content of omega-3 fatty acids are pressed between 80°F (27°C) and 92°F (33°C). Cold-pressed coconut oil and extra-virgin olive oil are pressed at or below 120°F (50°C). Oils of this nature retain important nutritional features such as vital omega-3 fatty acids and the powerful antioxidant vitamin E.

The lack of regulation leaves the responsibility with the consumer to find out which oil producers are genuine in their claims—some oils labelled "cold pressed" are actually pressed at temperatures as high as 200°F (95°C), or mixed with oils that are refined.

You can expect to pay more for cold-pressed oils because the methods used for extraction yields less oil than processes that use higher temperatures or solvents. When shopping for oil, read labels carefully. Manufacturers that produce high-quality oils will provide sufficient information indicating whether you hold a premium product in your hands. The extra cost is worth it.

Another valuable feature of cold-pressed oils is their flavour: complex aromatic fragrances and taste profiles are preserved. These components add different layers, depth, and variety to the flavour in food. Cold-pressed oils may be used in salad dressings, sprinkled over grains or steamed vegetables, tossed with noodles, or used to garnish soup. Remember, of course, that whole foods that contain oils (such as seeds, nuts, olives, and avocados) may be even better choices than liquid oil.

Unrefined cold-pressed coconut oil can have a smoke point of 350°F (180°C), whereas refined coconut oil will smoke when it is heated to 450°F (230°C). Extra-virgin olive oil will smoke at 375°F (190°C), whereas more refined virgin olive oil can be heated to 420°F (215°C) before it starts to smoke.

## Oils Used in the Recipes

The oils that are used in the recipes in this book are listed below, along with a description of their health-supportive characteristics. We use good quality oils such as those provided by Omega Nutrition. The two principal oils we use for cooking are coconut oil and olive oil. Two that are not used when heat is involved are flaxseed and hemp seed oils, both excellent sources of omega-3 fatty acids which are super sensitive to heat.

**Coconut Oil**: Coconut oil is high in saturated fat, but it's important to remember that not all saturated fats are created equal. Those found in coconut oil are medium-chain fatty acids (MCFA). These break down differently from the long-chain fatty acids that are typically found in animal products. MCFA digest more easily, are the kinds of fats found in breast milk, and are preferentially used by the liver as a source of fuel to produce energy. The predominant fatty acid present in coconut oil, lauric acid, appears to raise HDL ("good") cholesterol to an even greater extent than it raises LDL ("bad") cholesterol. Thus, the overall effect of lauric acid on the ratio of total to HDL cholesterol is consistently favourable.

Coconut oil can replace liquid oil in most baking recipes if it is heated just enough to liquefy it. If all remaining recipe ingredients are at room temperature, the warmed liquid coconut oil will remain liquid and incorporate well into the recipe.

**Olive Oil**: Ninety-five percent of olive oil on the market comes from the sunny hillsides of the Mediterranean region. The International Olive Oil Council, based in Madrid, tightly controls the classification and labelling of olive oil, and regulates that "olive oil" must not be adulterated in any way by being mixed with the oils from seeds or nuts.

There are two main categories of olive oils. *Extra-virgin, virgin, refined olive oil,* and *olive oil* are classifications of the product that is obtained directly from the fruit of the olive without the use of solvents. Oil producers are required to list which classification their oil falls in on the food label. Of these, extra-virgin is superior in terms of nutritional value and flavour, and can be used when it will not be heated above its smoke point. Other classifications of olive oil are more refined and have less and less appeal in terms of flavour as you move from extra-virgin to products simply labelled "olive oil."

*Pomace oils* are treated with solvents in an attempt to extract every last drop of oil. Ground olive pulp and pits, known as pomace, is what remains after olive oil has been extracted from the fruit. Pomace oil is cheap and nutritionally inferior.

**Flaxseed Oil**: The oil that is extracted from flaxseeds contains approximately 57 percent omega-3 fatty acids (linolenic acid). It also contains lesser amounts of the more easily obtained omega-6 fatty acids (linoleic acid). Standard North American diets typically contain at least 10 times as much omega-6 fatty acids than omega-3 fatty acids. Researchers believe this imbalance plays a significant role in the rising rate of inflammatory disorders. Omega-3 fatty acids have been shown to reduce inflammation in the body. Flaxseed oil is of value because it can help to bring the ratio back to a more desirable two or four parts omega-6 fatty acids to one part omega-3 fatty acids.

Flaxseed oil must be stored in the refrigerator or freezer. It should never be used for cooking, as heat will destroy its vital omega-3 fatty acids. Some people initially dislike the taste but later acquire a liking for its rich flavour. To get your omega-3s for the day, consume 2 teaspoons (10 mL) of flaxseed oil daily.

**Hemp Seed Oil**: Hemp seeds are approximately 44 percent oil by weight, and the oil is primarily essential fatty acids: 16 percent of the hard-to-get omega-3 fatty acid known as linolenic acid and 57 percent linoleic acid. As noted earlier, if it were our only source of dietary fat, it would provide an excellent balance of omega-6 to omega-3 fatty acids; however, the diets of most people, including vegetarians, is already heavily weighted toward omega-6 fatty acids.

Hemp seed oil is green in colour and has a pleasant nutty and grassy flavour. You can get your day's supply of omega-3 fatty acids from 1 tablespoon (15 mL) of hemp seed oil or from 1/4 cup (60 mL) of shelled hemp seeds. Like flaxseed oil, it should not be heated.

**Earth Balance Natural Spreads**: Earth Balance is a natural food company based in Boulder, Colorado, that manufactures a line of vegetarian buttery spreads and shortenings made from a combination of expeller-pressed palm fruit, canola, and olive oils. Soy oil is in some but not all of its spreads. These products are non-hydrogenated and free of genetically modified ingredients.

Culinary uses for Earth Balance are plentiful. The creamy spreads can be used wherever butter or shortening is called for in a recipe and for all regular baking, giving products a buttery taste without a trace of dairy.

**Sesame Oil**: Sesame oil is pale yellow in colour, with a light, delicate flavour. When sesame seeds are toasted and then pressed, an amber-coloured aromatic oil is produced, one that gives a delicious flavour to Asian dishes, including stir-fries, marinades, and salad dressings. As its flavour is intense, it can be used in small quantities. In this book, unrefined cold-pressed sesame seed oil and tahini, the butter made from whole sesame seeds, are used in salad dressings.

**Sunflower Oil**: Sunflower oil, made from sunflower seeds, is used for cooking, salad dressings, and baking. Sunflower oil with a high oleic (monounsaturated) acid content has a fairly high smoke point, making it stable when heated.

# Sweeteners

We all love something sweet, whether it is a ripe mango or a slice of chocolate cake with chocolate frosting. When it comes to which sweeteners we decide to stock in our cupboard and refrigerator, the choice can depend in part on our values and priorities, which may change throughout life. These same values also affect our selection of oils when, say, we opt for extra-virgin olive oil or the oil on sale that fits within a tight food budget.

In the recipes in this book, we have opted first for whole foods and dried sweeteners, and cast our vote for products that are vegetarian, organic, fair trade, and minimally refined. In recipes in this book where one of a variety of sweeteners will produce a fine product, the choice is left to the reader—you'll see, for instance, "brown sugar or other dry sweetener" or "maple syrup or other sweetener" (i.e., liquid or dry sweetener) listed in the ingredients list. You can make the choice that fits your values and priorities.

Below we discuss considerations that can influence which sweetener we selected, when we did.

## The Nutritional Value of Whole Foods

When health is our priority, whole foods such as fresh or dried fruit have the most to offer as sweeteners. Top rating goes to fresh or frozen fruit. For inspiration, see Fresh Fruit as Dessert (page 242), Watermelon Fruit Sculpture (page 255), Vegan Dasz Ice Cream (page 254). Dried fruit can give extra sweetness, as in the Raw Mango Strawberry Pie (page 251), Banana Blueberry Power Drink (page 76), and Design Your Own Muesli (page 77). Also see the list of naturally sweet foods in Appendix 1.

## Using Less Sugar

For some of us, it makes sense to accustom our palate to lower levels of sweetness. After all, who needs sugar in their peanut butter? In food preparation, this means using the minimum amount of added sweetener, if any. For instance, the Baked Stuffed Apples (page 225) contain added sugar—but only 1/2 teaspoon (2 mL) per apple. Furthermore, if we take the time to chew food well, the starch-breaking enzyme amylase in our saliva will create sugars from the complex carbohydrates in a great many plant foods.

## Ethical Aspects of Production

Some people's ingredient choices are based on the ethics surrounding the production and manufacturing of the foods. For example, the use of fair trade sugar may reflect a desire to help provide a living wage to farm labourers.

For vegetarians, compassion for animals tends to be a theme that may influence choices, including which sweetener to choose. Thus, we avoid cane sugar that has been filtered through bone char (charcoal made from animal bones). Although this practice is used less and less, some (but not all) sugar cane refineries use bone char to purify and whiten the sugar. As a result, bones from cows have been part of the production of some, but not all, white cane sugar. Beet sugar, which may be simply labelled "sugar," never undergoes this process. In the past, maple syrup was treated with a small amount of lard (fat from pigs) or other animal fat to reduce foaming during production. However, synthetic defoamers or vegetable oils are more commonly used now. Discovering which brands and products you want to use can involve some detective work. Honey is not a vegan product.

## The Environment

It sure makes sense to choose organic products, for the good of the environment as well as our health. Blackstrap molasses is rich in the minerals that are stripped from sugar cane; however, it can also be a concentrated source of pesticides and herbicides, so be sure to choose organic blackstrap molasses. The production of sugar from sugar cane involves large quantities of fossil fuels in processing and in getting the product to market.

## Flavour

Certain choices, such as maple syrup or blackstrap molasses, bring with them a wealth of flavour in addition to their inherent sweetness. Unbleached sugar, dehydrated cane juice, raw sugar, and brown or golden sugar (which are white sugar with some molasses added back in) all have added flavour, though the added nutrition is minimal.

Conversely, sometimes we want a sweetener that contributes as little flavour as possible. In this case, rice syrup is a good choice.

## Texture

Sweeteners can be dry and granular (as are various sugars), liquid (as are syrups), or somewhere in between (as are mashed dates or bananas, applesauce, and fruit juice concentrate). If you want to substitute one type for another in a recipe, you may also need to adjust the amounts of other wet or dry ingredients.

## Cost

A family or individual with a tight food budget will understandably have price as an important deciding factor in choosing sweeteners. Brown sugar is often an inexpensive choice.

# Thickeners

Thickeners are agents that when added to a liquid change its viscosity or thickness, resulting in a change in texture. Starches are the most common thickening agents. Several thickeners are of plant origin, including gums (such as xanthum gum), seaweed extracts (such as agar), ground flaxseed, and pectin. These agents often do not change the flavour of the product, though some do—for example, browned flour in a gumbo, or seed or nut butters in a soup or salad dressing. Below are brief descriptions of thickeners used in our recipes, along with examples to illustrate how they are employed.

## Agar

Agar, also known as agar-agar, is a white extract from red seaweed that can be used as a substitute for gelatine (derived from the bones of cattle and horses). This extract comes in several forms: powder, flakes, or in bars. A particularly valuable characteristic of agar is its ability to gel liquids within a wide range of pH and temperatures. Gelatine does not gel highly acidic liquids such as pineapple juice very well but agar does. Agar is readily available at larger health food stores and, generally for a much lower cost, in Asian markets.

Since agar powder, flakes, and bars differ considerably in density, care must be taken to use the specific product called for in a recipe. For instance, if you were to use an equal measure of agar powder in a recipe that calls for flakes, the end product would likely resemble a rock-hard hockey puck, since powder is much denser than flakes. If an equal measure of flakes were used in a recipe that calls for powder, the dish would not gel properly.

Agar needs to be thoroughly dissolved in a hot liquid for it to gel. Agar bars may be crumbled before measuring and then measured as flakes. Thickening power may vary from one brand of agar to another. If you find that the amount of agar called for results in too soft or too firm a product, take note and make the appropriate adjustment next time.

Gooda Cheeze (page 89) is one recipe in which we've used agar.

---

### Using Agar as a Thickening Agent

1 tablespoon (15 mL) agar flakes will thicken 1 cup (250 mL) liquid.

1/2 teaspoon (2 mL) agar powder will thicken 1 cup (250 mL) liquid.

---

## Arrowroot

Arrowroot is a perennial tropical plant that produces a large rhizome or rootlike stem from which a starch is extracted. Arrowroot powder is used to thicken sauces, gravies, custards, puddings, and the juices that result when baking fruit pies. The starch has a very delicate taste and is easily digested. Arrowroot powder can be used interchangeably with cornstarch. Arrowroot is a better choice when a transparent mixture rather than an opaque one is desired, as in a fruit sauce. Because it is gluten-free, it's often used in baking mixtures to replace wheat or other flours containing gluten. As an example, the Blueberry Orange Sauce recipe (page 212) includes arrowroot as an ingredient.

> ### Using Arrowroot as a Thickening Agent
>
> 1 tablespoon (15 mL) arrowroot powder will thicken 1 cup (250 mL) liquid.
>
> To use it, mix the desired amount of powder, based on the amount of liquid in your total recipe, in a small bowl or lidded jar and dilute with cold liquid to prevent clumping. Stir or shake until the powder is dissolved. Bring the liquid that is to be thickened to a boil and slowly pour the arrowroot mixture in a steady stream into the liquid while constantly stirring with a spoon or whisk. Do not simmer more than 10 minutes; overcooking or over-stirring can cause the thickened liquid to become thin again.

## Cornstarch

Cornstarch is extracted from the endosperm of the corn kernel. Corn is falling out of favour with a growing number of consumers as more of the North American crop becomes subjected to genetically modified organisms. Cornstarch is used just like arrowroot (see above).

## Ground Flaxseed

Ground flaxseed can be used to thicken smoothies and as an egg replacer to help bind ingredients in baked goods. Soaking ground flaxseed in a small amount of water will create a gelatinous mixture similar to egg whites, which can be used in recipes for pancakes, waffles, muffins, and in most baking recipes that call for one or two eggs. First grind the seeds by putting 1 cup (250 mL) whole flaxseeds in a blender or other grinder. Blend for 30 seconds—stopping halfway through to stir the seeds—or until the seeds are ground. Store the ground flaxseed in a lidded jar in the freezer for up to a year. The mixture of ground flaxseed and water (see below) can be used to replace one egg. Alternatively, ground flaxseed can simply be added to the wet ingredients as directed in a recipe, as in our Apple Spice Cake (page 228).

> ### Using Flaxseed as an Egg Replacer
>
> 1 tablespoon (15 mL) ground flaxseed
> 3 tablespoons (45 mL) water
>
> Place the ground flaxseed and water in a small bowl. Stir the mixture and allow it to thicken for several minutes. Use in recipes in place of 1 egg.

### Seeds, Nuts, and Their Butters

Ground seeds, nuts, and their butters make excellent thickeners for rich soups, salad dressings, and cheese-like toppings. Sesame tahini and cashews are particularly effective thickening agents, which is why we used them in our Lemon Tahini Dressing (page 122) and Cashew Cheese Lasagna (page 148). These products impart their unique flavours to the dish. Although botanically legumes rather than nuts, peanuts in the form of peanut butter are another effective thickener—which is how we used them in the African Chickpea Stew (page 145).

### Vegetables

Vegetables can thicken liquids—as when, for example, tomato paste is added to a sauce or soup. The starch in root vegetables can also thicken a liquid, as in the Ginger, Carrot, and Yam Soup (page 134). Potatoes, squash, and roasted chestnuts may be used for this purpose.

Soft, grated fresh vegetables with a high water content are a novel way of thickening liquid. This is illustrated very well in the Cucumber Dill Dressing (page 121). The grated cucumber and zucchini are blended and incorporated into the mixture to give it good consistency and body, allowing for a significant reduction in the vegetable oil that is typically found in salad dressings.

### Wheat Flour

The classic example of how wheat flour is used to thicken hot liquids is the roux, used in French cuisine since the mid-17th century. Equal parts of white flour and oil or other fat are combined and then used to thicken soup, a sauce, or a gravy. The flour makes for a very smooth end product, which is why we've used it in our Rosemary Gravy (page 217) and Light Mushroom Gravy (page 214). However, as more people become allergic, intolerant, or sensitive to wheat, other thickeners, such as those listed above, are becoming popular in dishes.

## Grains: The Staff of Life

In this section we include true grains (those in the botanical family of cereal grasses) as well as seeds from pseudograins that are used in similar ways as true grains in our diet. Pseudograins include buckwheat, the seed of a plant in the rhubarb family, and quinoa, in a botanical group that includes spinach and sugar beets. These pseudograins and others, such as wild rice, have gained popularity as many people discover that they are sensitive to wheat and other gluten-containing cereal grains. Grains and pseudograins are excellent sources of energy, protein, and B vitamins.

The use of grains in people's diets can be traced back thousands of years to when wild species of these plants first became domesticated. Many are now associated with specific regions and cultural groups: the Russians have their buckwheat, the Chinese and Japanese their rice, the Scottish and Irish have oats, and Latin Americans have corn.

On the great plains of Canada, we have wheat and rye. Grains provide 51 percent of the world's protein and are primary sources of calories in every culture.

Grains are made up of four distinct parts, with protein present in all four, though not evenly distributed. The outer layer of a grain is called the husk (also known as the chaff). This tough layer surrounds the kernel and keeps it protected from the natural elements during its growth. The husk is indigestible for humans and, once removed during processing, is discarded.

Next is the bran, a thin layer rich in protein, vitamins, minerals, and fibre that surrounds the endosperm, the biggest part of the grain. The endosperm stores most of the seed's food energy in the form of complex carbohydrate or starch.

A tiny but very important portion of the grain is the germ or embryo, abundant in vitamins, minerals, and essential fatty acids. Unfortunately, this fraction of the seed is removed during the milling and refining process, along with the bran, as its oils become rancid quickly. In the case of wheat, refining results in pure-looking white flour with a long shelf life, though it has lost much of its original wealth of vitamins (B vitamins, especially vitamin B6), protective phytochemicals, minerals (calcium, chromium, magnesium, and zinc), fibre, and essential fatty acids. Four of the B vitamins (folate, niacin, riboflavin, and thiamine) and iron are added back in the enrichment process, but this doesn't make up for what is lost. When grains are rolled, flaked, or puffed, considerable nutrient losses also occur.

## Choose Whole Grains

The best way to eat grains is the way nature grew them: completely intact. Delicious and distinctively flavoured intact or whole grains can take a central place at lunch and dinner, as they do in many parts of the world. Whole grains such as brown rice, barley, millet, Kamut, wheat or spelt berries, oat groats, and quinoa can be cooked as breakfast cereals or used for lunch and dinner in casseroles, soups, or stews, or as a pilaf.

Grains that have been "minimally processed," such as those that are cut or rolled or stone ground, with little or nothing added or removed, are also great choices, as these methods of processing do little damage to the grain. Whole grains that are slightly processed can still be good choices. The damage caused by grinding, as when making stone-ground whole-wheat flour, is only slightly higher than that from rolling or cutting.

Foods listing whole-wheat flour as a first ingredient are more nutritious than those listing refined wheat flour or unbleached wheat flour. Occasionally, refined flours may be chosen to produce a light product or appealing texture. Pancakes, muffins, and other such prepared items can be made more nutritious by adding nuts, seeds, nut butters, or dried fruit.

## Guidelines for Cooking Grains

The size of pot used for cooking cereal grains is important. For small quantities, a small, deep pot ensures that the grain is covered by water for as long as possible before all of the water is absorbed. When cooking grains, the lid should be tight-fitting, since all the water needs to be absorbed and evaporation kept to a minimum.

Generally, grains take less time to cook than legumes and do not require pre-soaking. Unless you want a sticky product, always bring water to a boil before adding the grain. (Cold water will draw some of the starch from grains into the surrounding water. When brought to a boil, the starch slightly thickens the water, resulting in a sticky final product. This is particularly true for grains that have had the bran removed, such as white basmati rice.) Once the water has come to a boil, add the grain, cover the pot, and wait for the water to return to boil before reducing the heat to simmer.

Grains are cooked when all the water has been absorbed and when the grain is soft and no longer crunchy. If the temperature is too high during cooking, and too much water has been lost through evaporation, add a small amount of hot water to the pot to complete the cooking. Do not stir the grains while they are cooking or immediately afterward, while still hot. Grains bruise very easily and stirring will make them sticky. Once the grain is cooked, allow it to rest in the pot for 5 minutes off the heat before serving. If, after the grain is fully cooked, moisture remains on the bottom of the pot, slightly open the lid and drain off the excess water.

The "Cooking Grains" chart below shows the amount of water to use, the cooking time, and the yield, based on 1 cup (250 mL) of raw grain. Generally, 1 cup (250 mL) of dry grain will yield two servings; however, the number of servings depends on how hungry the eaters are and the amounts of other foods served. Leftover grains can be easily reheated, incorporated into soups or other recipes (International Roll-Ups, on page 156, is one example), made into a salad, or served as a grain pudding for dessert.

**Cooking Grains: Water, Times, and Yields**

| 1 cup (250 mL) dry grain | Water | Cooking time (minutes) | Yield |
|---|---|---|---|
| Amaranth | 3 cups (750 mL) | 20–25 | 2 1/2 cups (625 mL) |
| Barley, pearl | 4 cups (1 L) | 50–60 | 4 cups (1 L) |
| Buckwheat or kasha | 2 cups (500 mL) | 12–15 | 4 cups (1 L) |
| Cornmeal | 4 cups (1 L) | 10 | 4 1/2 cups (1.125 L) |
| Millet | 2 1/2 cups (625 mL) | 25 | 4 cups (1 L) |
| Oats, slow-cooking | 2 1/2 cups (625 mL) | 20 | 2 1/4 cups (560 mL) |
| Quinoa | 1 1/2 cups (375 mL) | 15–20 | 3 1/2 cups (875 mL) |
| Rice, brown basmati | 2 cups (500 mL) | 40 | 3 1/4 cups (810 mL) |
| Rice, brown long-grain | 2 cups (500 mL) | 45 | 3 1/2 cups (875 mL) |
| Rice, white basmati | 2 3/4 cups (685 mL) | 18–20 | 4 cups (1 L) |
| Rice, wild | 4 cups (1 L) | 50–60 | 3 cups (750 mL) |
| Wheat, Kamut, and spelt berries | 3 1/2 cups (875 mL) | 60–70 | 3 cups (750 mL) |

## Legumes: Protein Powerhouses

Legumes are of prime importance in vegetarian diets because of their high contents of protein; iron, zinc, and other minerals; folate and other B vitamins; and fibre. Legumes are plants with seeds in pods; in North America, the term "legumes" has come to mean the seeds of these plants, though they're more commonly referred to as beans, peas, and lentils. Legumes are 20 to 30 percent protein by weight, which is double the protein content of wheat and three times that of rice. Soybeans are protein superstars, with about 36 percent of their calories from protein, making their protein content similar to that of eggs or beef (soybeans have the advantage of less fat and no cholesterol).

The protein-rich qualities of legumes are related to the fact that they, in partnership with bacteria, "fix" atmospheric nitrogen into the soil. Our atmosphere contains about 78 percent nitrogen, but in gaseous form, this essential element for building amino acids is not usable to plants. In the nodules of legumes' root systems, bacteria convert nitrogen from the air into compounds that find their way into the soil. These precious compounds are then used to form amino acids, nucleic acids such as DNA and RNA, and chlorophyll—the molecule essential for photosynthesis. This conversion process is called fixation because the nitrogen is fixed into the soil and taken up by the root hairs of plants. Science refers to this process as the nitrogen cycle, which is one of the most important transformations in nature and crucial to life on earth.

### Pre-Soaking Legumes

When beans, peas, and lentils are harvested, they have a high moisture content. Before being brought to market, they are dried to prolong their shelf life. Reconstituting the seeds by soaking them for 6 hours (or overnight) considerably reduces their cooking time as well as draws out certain carbohydrates (oligosaccharides) that can be problematic. Oligosaccharides pass into the large intestine, where they are acted upon by bacteria that inhabit our intestine. A by-product of this bacterial activity is intestinal gas, which in excessive amounts can produce discomfort in the lower bowel and be embarrassing. Because oligosaccharides are water soluble, discarding the soaking liquid and rinsing beans before they are cooked goes a long way toward reducing intestinal gas.

When legumes are soaked, their minerals become more available to us. Calcium, iron, and zinc are released from a mineral-phosphate complex known as phytate, allowing more of these and other minerals to be absorbed by the body. Thus, more nutritional value is extracted from beans that are soaked before cooking than from beans that are cooked from a dry state.

It is always a good idea to pick through legumes before soaking to remove any twigs, pieces of dirt, or small stones that may have been brought in from the field. To do this, spread them onto a baking sheet and remove the unwanted bits, including shrivelled and chipped seeds. If you travel abroad, to Nepal or India, for example, you will see women sitting together sociably doing this task between meals.

A general rule of thumb for soaking legumes is to cover them with triple their volume of water and let them sit for at least 6 hours or overnight. Legumes will expand between 2 and 3 times their dried volume, so make sure the bowl or pot you use is large enough.

> ### The Gas Crisis: Six Simple Solutions
>
> To minimize gas production:
>
> - Begin by adding small amounts of legumes to your diet, increasing amounts gradually.
> - When introducing legumes to your diet, start with well-digested smaller legumes (lentils and split peas) and with tofu.
> - Soak legumes overnight and discard the soaking water, which contains gas-producing oligosaccharides.
> - Play detective with yourself: causes vary. For example, eating sugar with certain foods may cause gas. For some people, large amounts of cabbage are problematic.
> - Don't overeat: excess undigested food can become food for bacteria.
> - Try an international solution to the gas crisis. The Japanese add kombu, a type of seaweed, to many soups. Latin Americans add an herb called epazote to certain of their dishes. Indians add asafetida, also known as hing, in small amounts to curries and lentil dishes.

## Quick-Soaking Procedure

If you forget to soak legumes or don't have time, you can still salvage your dinner plans. Rinse the legumes and place them in a pot. Add triple the amount of water, bring to a boil, cover, reduce the heat to low, and simmer for 5 minutes. Remove the pot from the heat and let rest for 1 hour. Then cook until soft, according to the directions below.

## Guidelines for Cooking Legumes

Discard the soaking liquid; rinse the legumes with fresh cold water, place in an appropriate-sized pot, and cover with 3 inches (8 cm) of fresh cold water. Bring the water to the boil, reduce heat to a simmer, and cook, covered, until the legumes are tender (see chart on page 34 for cooking times). Stir occasionally. When cooking the legumes, keeping the heat at a simmer is important; vigorous boiling can burst the skins and evaporate the cooking water before the legumes have a chance to completely cook. Some legumes produce foam in the water once it comes to a boil; skim off this foam once or twice in the first 5 to 10 minutes of cooking using a ladle or large spoon. If the water reduces before the legumes are cooked, simply add more water to cover the legumes by 1 inch (2.5 cm).

Do not add salt at the beginning of the cooking process. Salt toughens the outer skin of legumes. This makes it more difficult for water to penetrate the legume and increases the cooking time. Adding about 1/4 tsp (1 mL) salt per cup (250 mL) of dried legumes toward the end of the cooking period develops the overall flavour of legumes and decreases the need for salt when adjusting the final seasoning of the dish.

Legumes are cooked when they are no longer crunchy or grainy when bitten into. Test a few rather than just one, as some may have cooked before others. Let the legumes cool in their cooking liquid. This keeps their skins from splitting as a result of coming into contact with cooler air.

All yields in the "Cooking Legumes" chart below are based on 1 cup (250 mL) uncooked legumes and 3 cups (750 mL) cooking water and reflect a 6-hour soaking time, except for the lentils and split peas, which do not require pre-soaking, though soaking can further reduce oligosaccharides. Cooking times can vary considerably depending on the age, size, and variety of the legume. (Older beans and legumes take longer to cook.)

*A note for mountain dwellers:* At sea level, the boiling point of water is 212°F (100°C); at higher elevations, the boiling point is lower. Boiling is a function of atmospheric pressure, and since at higher elevations the pressure is lower, more time is required to cook and bake food.

**Cooking Legumes: Times and Yields**

| 1 cup (250 mL) legumes | Cooking time (minutes) | Yield* |
| --- | --- | --- |
| Adzuki beans | 35–45 | 3 cups (750 mL) |
| Ancient ancestor beans (Anasazi beans) | 50–60 | 2 2/3 cups (670 mL) |
| Appaloosa beans | 45 | 2 2/3 cups (670 mL) |
| Black beans | 45–55 | 2 1/2 cups (625 mL) |
| Black-eyed peas | 45–60 | 2 cups (500 mL) |
| Cannellini beans (white kidney beans) | 60–70 | 2 2/3 cups (670 mL) |
| Fava beans | 40–50 | 2 1/4 cups (560 mL) |
| Garbanzo beans/chickpeas | 45 | 2 3/4 cups (685 mL) |
| Great northern beans | 45 | 2 2/3 cups (670 mL) |
| Kidney beans | 35 | 2 1/2 cups (625 mL) |
| Lentils, brown | 25–35 | 2 1/4 cups (560 mL) |
| Lentils, red | 20 | 2 cups (500 mL) |
| Lima beans, small | 55–60 | 3 cups (750 mL) |
| Mung beans | 25–30 | 3 cups (750 mL) |
| Navy beans | 50–60 | 2 2/3 cups (670 mL) |
| Pinto beans | 45 | 2 2/3 cups (670 mL) |
| Split peas | 45–60 | 2 cups (500 mL) |
| Swedish brown beans | 60–70 | 2 2/3 cups (670 mL) |
| Yellow-eyed beans | 50–60 | 2 1/2 cups (625 mL) |

* Approximate yield

## Meat Analogues

Meat analogues or substitutes have textures, flavour, and appearances that resemble various types of meat, poultry, or seafood. They come in shapes and cuts that resemble sliced meats, chicken breasts, hot dogs, ground beef, and burgers. The ingredients in these veggie "meats" vary from one brand to another and include various beans, grains, and vegetables, as well as seasonings, fillers, and binders. Some are mainly composed of whole foods such as beans, grains, and corn, whereas others are highly processed, featuring ingredients such as soy protein isolate. Some contain soy, wheat, or gluten and thus are unsuitable for those with particular food sensitivities. But not to worry: a search of coolers and freezer sections of natural food stores can reveal patties and burgers that are based on rice or other gluten-free grains.

### Why Veggie Meats?

When people decide not to eat flesh foods, why do some then choose to eat products that closely resemble the meats they no longer consume? When you stop to think about it, sausages, wieners, meatballs, and patties are animal parts that are ground up and turned into consumable products that are easy to use. Since the shapes of these manufactured goods can be made from animal protein, it stands to reason that these forms could also be made from plant protein, the building blocks that animals ate to form their own bodies. Manufacturers of so-called veggie meats take ingredients from lower on the food chain—soy, pea, or grain protein, for instance—to produce an easy-to-use product that has far more health benefits than and fewer of the environmental or animal-related problems as meat products.

Furthermore, for people who eat meat but want to stop, or want to reduce their animal food intake, meat analogues are convenient transitional foods that many find useful as they build their repertoire of recipes using whole foods. Veggie meats also allow children to have sandwiches in their lunch bags that resemble those of their meat-eating peers (see Satisfying Sandwiches, Vegetarian Style, page 95), and people to share in a picnic or barbecue with ease.

### Gardein

Wholesome examples of meat analogues are found in the Gardein product line. Made from soy, wheat, and pea proteins; vegetables; and ancient grains (quinoa, amaranth, millet, and Kamut), these tasty vegan foods have meaty textures. Gardein products are easy to digest and free of cholesterol and trans and saturated fats. The majority of Gardein foods are good sources of fibre and are low in fat. (Our Veggie Chick'n Paella with Artichokes and Spinach, on page 187, calls for Gardein Chick'n Scallopini.)

## Soy Foods

In China, soybeans are known as "ta tou," the "greater bean," and with good reason. Soybeans have been highly valued in the Orient for thousands of years, due to the outstanding qualities of their protein, oil, mineral content, and versatility. Scientists have discovered the excellent amino acid profile of soybeans and recognized that highly digestible soy foods such as tofu are first rate when protein sources are compared, whether plant or animal. In addition, the isoflavones in soy function as antioxidants. Add soy to your diet and you may lower your risk of cardiovascular disease.

## Tofu: Many Textures, Many Uses

In the process of making tofu, hot soy milk is blended with a coagulant to form a curd. At this stage, to make soft tofu, the hot soy milk mixture is poured directly into its package. Soft tofu is relatively high in water and thus lower in protein and minerals when compared with firmer varieties. The coagulant was traditionally a seaweed extract called nigari, but modern processes often use magnesium or calcium salts; the latter can make the tofu an excellent source of calcium (check the Nutrition Facts box on the package).

For medium, firm, and extra-firm grades of tofu, the curd is poured into a mould, pressed to form a block, cut, and then packaged. The amount of pressure applied and water expelled determines whether the tofu will be medium, firm, or extra-firm in consistency. Since the texture varies for each type, some types work better in certain recipes than others, so be sure to note which is called for.

**Pressed Tofu:** The water content of tofu may still be too high for certain recipes. If the tofu were used without first pressing out the excess water, the liquid would weep out of the recipe and onto the serving plate or into the bread if using the Curry Sandwich Spread (page 87). To press tofu, remove it from the package and place it on a dinner plate. Place another plate or a cutting board over the tofu, and on that carefully place a 4- or 5-pound (about 2 kg) weight, for instance, several cans of food, or a bag of grain. Press the tofu in this way for 15 to 20 minutes. Once the tofu is pressed, discard the approximately 1/2 cup (125 mL) of liquid that will have pooled on the bottom plate. Transfer the tofu to a bowl and proceed with the recipe.

Both the Curry Sandwich Spread (page 87) and Scrambled Tofu (page 82) call for pressed tofu.

**Silken Tofu:** Silken tofu, of Japanese origin, is particularly silky in nature. Like other (e.g., Chinese) tofu, it is available in textures ranging from soft to extra-firm. Silken tofu is poured directly into an aseptic box and needs no refrigeration before opening. It's handy for camping trips and to keep on the shelf for when friends drop by unexpectedly—you can whip up the Lem-Un-Cheesecake with Crumb Crust (page 247) or Pumpkin Spice Pie (page 249) in a jiffy.

## Tempeh

Tempeh is a fermented soy product that originated in Indonesia, where it has long been used as a source of protein. It is made using a fermentation process that binds the soybeans into a cake or block. Unlike many other soy products, tempeh is made using the whole soybean. This gives it more fibre and a slightly higher content of protein. In Indonesia, tempeh is principally made using 100 percent soybeans, but in the West it often includes other grains, legumes, and vegetables. Look for it in the refrigerated or freezer sections of large supermarkets and natural food stores.

## Non-Dairy Milks

In choosing non-dairy milks, there are two significant points to consider: fortification and type.

### Fortification: Vitamin B12, Vitamin D, and Calcium

It is important that the non-dairy milk you select be fortified (enriched) with vitamin B12, vitamin D, and calcium. Often this is the sole source of vitamin D in a vegetarian diet. Cow's milk is fortified with vitamin D. Manufacturers are permitted to add vitamin D in just a few foods, milks, margarine, and breakfast cereals among them. The form added to some non-dairy beverages is vitamin D2 (ergocalciferol), which is vegan, whereas some non-dairy milks and other foods are fortified with vitamin D3 (cholecalciferol), which is of animal origin.

Fortified non-dairy milks can rank high as our sources of calcium. We do get calcium from greens, but non-dairy milks can make it easier to reach a daily target of 1000 to 1300 milligrams (see Appendix 2). For example, we can get 150 milligrams of calcium from either 1/2 cup (125 mL) of a fortified non-dairy beverage or from 1 2/3 cups (420 mL) of kale. Non-dairy milks labelled "natural" typically are not fortified (check the Nutrition Facts box on the package).

### Types of Non-Dairy Milk

Non-dairy milks may use almonds, hemp seeds, oat, rice, or soybeans as their primary ingredient. (For special considerations when it comes to soy milk, see below.) In many recipes, these milks may be used interchangeably, though there might be slight differences in your final products due to variations in fat, protein, or carbohydrate content between one type and another. Also, the flavours of different brands vary considerably. You'll probably find some you don't particularly like and others you really enjoy; food sensitivities may affect your choice; and your preference also may be based on the amount of added sweetener. You'll be making a good investment when you choose a non-dairy milk that is both organic and fortified.

**Soy Milk:** Soy milk is often recommended for children because its protein content is relatively high (again, check the labels). For example, the protein content of soy milk may be 7 or 8 grams per 1 cup (250 mL), whereas that of rice milk might be 0.5 grams per 1 cup (250 mL).

Soy milk is prepared commercially either from whole soybeans or from soy protein isolate. In the first instance, whole soybeans are washed, soaked, ground, and cooked. The fibrous part of the mash, called okara, is filtered out and discarded, and the remaining soy milk is packaged, with or without added flavouring and fortification.

Those soy milks with soy protein or soy protein isolate listed as ingredients are prepared by a series of steps in which fractions of the whole soybean are extracted, often using acids, alkalis, and the solvent hexane. You may prefer to use a soy beverage that is made from whole soybeans.

## Herbs and Spices

Often the secrets of a successful dish are the herbs or spices in it. These can be added in small amounts and may barely be detectable by the person eating. Adding an appropriate amount of the right seasoning requires an understanding of which ingredients fit with one another, along with a culinary knowledge—and imagination—of the possibilities. Herbs and spices are powerful agents in the development of flavour and so are invaluable allies in the kitchen.

Herbs are leafy parts of plants, prized for the flavour they impart to food. They are also often used for their medicinal qualities. In this book we focus, of course, on culinary herbs. Keep in mind that the term "culinary" does not mean that these herbs are any less medicinal in nature than those used as medicine.

Like herbs, spices are used to season food; however, they come from the roots (e.g., ginger), flowers (e.g., saffron), seeds (e.g., dill seed), berries (e.g., peppercorns), or bark (e.g., cinnamon) of the plant, rather than the leaf. Most spices are considered more exotic than herbs in that they generally originate from tropical regions such as the Caribbean, Southwest Asia, or India. In addition to providing flavour, spices can also be used to colour food, as is the case with turmeric and saffron.

The inherent strength of herbs and spices to create unforgettable eating experiences lies in their aromatic oils, which are responsible for the flavour that is imparted to a food. These oils are volatile and can easily evaporate if not stored properly.

Herbs and spices are best purchased from a store where there is a high turnover of these ingredients, to help ensure freshness. For storing these precious commodities, dark glass jars or opaque containers with tight-fitting lids are a good investment, to keep out damaging light and oxygen. Avoid storing herbs and spices near the warm environment of an oven or on a shelf just above it, as heat quickly dissipates the valuable oils, making them less effective. Instead, store them in an enclosed dark space, such as a cupboard. Store excess supplies in the freezer. Replace herbs that have lost their colour and ground spices that no longer have a vibrant, characteristic fragrance. Whole spices will last indefinitely if stored properly.

Spices are best purchased whole, as this keeps their oils locked in until they are bruised, crushed, or ground during the preparation of a recipe. Pulverizing a spice into a powder increases its surface area, and it immediately starts to lose potency. An inexpensive coffee grinder used solely for grinding spices, or a mortar and pestle, is a good kitchen investment. In this way you can grind spices and tougher herbs like rosemary as they are needed, allowing the full strength of their oils to absorb into your food.

Fresh herbs may be used instead of dried herbs in recipes, though in a different ratio: use 1 tablespoon (15 mL) of fresh herb when replacing 1 teaspoon (5 mL) of dried.

For a list of the herbs and spices used in this book, see the Shopping List on pages 39 and 40.

# Shopping List

This list of ingredients is based on the recipes in this book. Buy fresh produce as needed and in season. Dry ingredients can be purchased in appropriate amounts and stored indefinitely in sealed containers in a cool, dry place. For the best price, check out stores that sell grains and legumes in bulk.

### Vegetables

- Asparagus
- Avocados
- Beets
- Bell pepper, green, orange, red, or yellow
- Bok choy
- Broccoli
- Cabbage, Chinese (napa)
- Cabbage, red
- Carrot
- Cauliflower
- Celery
- Collard greens
- Corn on the cob or kernels
- Cucumbers
- Daikon radish
- Eggplant
- Fennel bulb
- Garlic
- Ginger
- Green beans
- Kale leaves
- Lettuce
- Mushrooms, cremini, portobello, shiitake, or white
- Onion, green
- Onion, red, yellow, or white
- Parsley
- Parsnips
- Potatoes, russet, red, or yellow
- Radishes, red, watermelon, or white
- Romaine lettuce
- Snap peas
- Snow peas
- Spinach
- Sprouts, alfalfa, lentil, mung, mustard, radish, red clover
- Sweet potatoes
- Tomatoes
- Turnips (choose young ones)
- Winter squash
- Yams
- Zucchini

### Fruits, fresh

- Apples
- Bananas
- Blueberries
- Lemons
- Limes
- Oranges
- Pineapple
- Raspberries
- Strawberries
- Watermelon

### Fruits, dried

- Blueberries
- Coconut, unsweetened shredded
- Cranberries
- Currants
- Dates
- Raisins, sultana
- Tamarind pulp

### Nuts, Seeds, and Butters

- Almonds, whole
- Almond butter
- Cashews, raw, unsalted
- Peanut butter
- Pumpkin seeds
- Sesame seeds
- Sesame tahini
- Sunflower seeds
- Walnuts

### Grains

- Amaranth
- Barley
- Buckwheat
- Flour, whole wheat or whole-wheat pastry or all-purpose
- Kamut berries
- Millet
- Oat flakes, slow-cooking
- Oat groats
- Quinoa
- Rice, brown or white basmati
- Rice, short-grain brown
- Rice, sticky (sushi)
- Rice, wild
- Spelt or wheat berries

### Legumes

- Adzuki beans
- Black beans
- Cannellini beans
- Chickpeas
- Great northern beans
- Green split peas
- Lentils, French or Puy
- Lentils, green
- Lentils, red
- Lima beans
- Mung beans
- Pinto beans
- White beans

### Soy foods

| | | | |
|---|---|---|---|
| Miso, dark or light | Tempeh | Tofu, medium-firm | Tofu, soft |
| Soy milk, fortified | Tofu, extra-firm | Tofu, silken, extra-firm | Veggie meats |
| Tamari or soy sauce | Tofu, firm | Tofu, silken, firm | |

### Beverages

| | | | |
|---|---|---|---|
| Almond milk | Apple juice concentrate | Hemp seed milk, unsweetened | Orange juice concentrate |
| Apple juice, unsweetened | Fortified rice milk | | Pineapple juice |

### Groceries

| | | | |
|---|---|---|---|
| Agar flakes or powder | Earth Balance spread | Pesto | Tomatoes, canned |
| Almond extract | Hemp seeds, shelled | Pimento, jarred | Tortilla shells |
| Arrowroot powder | Lasagna noodles | Prepared yellow mustard | Vanilla extract, pure |
| Artichoke hearts, canned | Macaroni noodles | Refried beans | Vegetable stock, powder, or cubes |
| Baking powder | Mayonnaise, eggless | Sake | |
| Bread crumbs | Nori seaweed | Salsa | Vinegar, apple cider |
| Capers | Nutritional yeast, Red Star | Sun-dried tomatoes | Vinegar, balsamic |
| Coconut milk | | Thai curry paste | Vinegar, rice |
| Dijon mustard | Olives, black, green or Kalamata | Tomato paste | Wasabi |
| Dry active yeast | | Tomato sauce | White flour, unbleached |
| | Patak's mild curry paste | | Whole-wheat patty buns |

### Culinary Oils

| | | | |
|---|---|---|---|
| Coconut oil | Hemp seed oil | Sunflower seed oil | Toasted sesame seed oil |
| Extra-virgin olive oil | | | |

### Herbs and Spices

| | | | |
|---|---|---|---|
| Allspice, ground | Chipotle pepper | Dill | Paprika |
| Basil | Cilantro | Fennel seeds | Pepper, black |
| Bay leaves | Cinnamon, ground | Garam masala | Pepper, white |
| Cardamom, ground | Cloves, ground | Garlic powder | Peppercorns |
| Cayenne pepper | Cloves, whole | Lemon grass | Rosemary |
| Celery seeds | Coriander seed, ground | Marjoram | Salt |
| Chili flakes, dried | Coriander seeds, whole | Mint | Spike seasoning |
| Chili paste | Cumin seeds | Mustard seeds | Thyme, dried |
| Chili pepper, red fresh | Cumin, ground | Onion powder | Turmeric powder |
| Chili powder | Curry powder | Oregano | Yellow mustard powder |

### Sweeteners

| | | | |
|---|---|---|---|
| Blackstrap molasses | Maple syrup | Sugar, brown | Sugar, white |
| | Molasses | | |

### Secondary Items *(for recipe variations)*

| | | | |
|---|---|---|---|
| Almond extract | Pickled ginger | Rice pasta | Veggie wieners |
| Barley flakes | Pickles | Rye flakes | Water chestnuts |
| Celeriac | Pita bread | Veggie protein slices | Whole-wheat flakes |
| Corn pasta | Rice flakes | | |

# Kitchen Equipment List

Whether you work with computers, musical instruments, or electric tools, you probably know the difference between working with bad equipment and working with functional equipment that always performs well. Working with good equipment makes you feel capable and increases your willingness to perform the task at hand. It's the same with kitchen equipment.

Consider your kitchen equipment as an investment in your health. Budget what you can afford to get some foundational tools and build on them over time. Having the necessary tools will boost your confidence and can help pave the way to wanting to spend more time in the kitchen, cooking nourishing and appealing food. The number of people you will be feeding will determine the size of stock pot, skillet, and so on, that you need. Go with the largest your budget will allow or whatever you have space for in your kitchen.

The following equipment list is a basic inventory of what is needed to prepare the recipes in this book. If your budget is limited, check out the thrift stores, where you can find many of the items listed here. Visit a store that specializes in kitchen knives to acquire basic knowledge on how to purchase and utilize them, and maintain a good edge. More serious cooks will want to purchase both a sharpening stone and steel for best results in maintaining their knives.

| Knives and Accessories | |
|---|---|
| Chef knife, 10-inch (25 cm) | Sharpening steel |
| Serrated bread knife | Sharpening stone |
| Paring knife | |

| Cooking Utensils | |
|---|---|
| Pots with lids, small, medium, and large | Pie plates (2), 8-inch (20 cm) |
| Stock pot with lid, 12-quart (12 L) | Cookie sheets (2) |
| Skillets, small and large | Muffin tins (2) |
| Steamer basket | Pizza pan, 12-inch (30 cm) |
| Wok | Baking dish, 9 × 13-inch (23 × 33 cm) |

| Electric Appliances | |
|---|---|
| Blender | Coffee grinder for grinding spices |
| Food processor | |

| Hand-Held Tools ||
|---|---|
| Can opener | Pancake flipper |
| Citrus juicer | Rolling pin |
| Colander | Rubber spatulas, small, medium, and large |
| Cutting boards, large and small | Scissors |
| Food grater | Slotted spoon |
| Funnels, small and medium | Soup ladle |
| Kitchen timer | Spring-loaded tongs |
| Measuring cup set (1/4 cup – 1 cup size) | Strainers, small and medium |
| Measuring cups, medium and large (2 cup and 8 cup) | Vegetable peeler |
| | Vegetable scrub brush |
| Measuring spoon set | Whisks, small and medium |
| Mortar and pestle (as an alternative to a coffee grinder for grinding spices) | Wooden spoons (2) |
| | Zester or food rasp |
| Mixing bowls, small, medium, and large | |

| Storage Containers and Wraps ||
|---|---|
| Canisters for grains, legumes, etc. | Plastic wrap |
| Foil | Storage containers with lids, in many sizes |
| Freezer containers | |

# Chapter 3: Nourishing Your Body

Imagine...

*The scrumptious aroma of potatoes baking in the oven on a cold winter afternoon.*

*Black bean soup simmering on the stove, with onion, oregano, and cumin wafting upward from the pot.*

*The youthful green of lightly steamed broccoli, the glistening red of sweet bell peppers, the sunshine yellow of crunchy corn.*

*Your first mouthful of a toasted sandwich, heaped with slices of fresh tomato and avocado.*

*The explosion of flavour awakening your senses when you bite into a warm cranberry-pecan muffin.*

*The delectable taste and feel of a mouthful of mango-strawberry pie.*

*The comforting warmth of rice pudding with raisins.*

Food gives us so much pleasure. Those mentioned above delight our senses, yet they do much more. Every one of them is vegetarian. The choice to build menus around such foods expresses compassion for animals and a love for the environment, and it is an act that supports excellent health. If you have ever had the notion that nutritious foods don't taste good, prepare to be very pleasantly surprised.

In the creative collaboration for *Cooking Vegetarian*, we choose *healthful*, *delicious*, and *easy* as central themes in assembling this all-star cast of recipes. Our vision is to enable people with full and busy lives to assemble appetizing and nourishing meals. The dishes made from recipes in this book consist of plant-based ingredients that are simple to obtain and nourishing.

Typically, people have 10 well-loved recipes that they make over and over. In this book, you can discover the 10—or many more—that will become lifetime favourites for you, your family, and your friends. The nutritional analysis for each recipe is a special feature of this book. In this chapter you'll find an overview of nutrition guidelines for good health.

Recipes and menus in this book are suitable for those people—

- With an interest in fitness and whose food choices must deliver energy and build a body with power and endurance
- Who are vegetarian or are moving in that direction
- Who want to include more plant-based meals in their diet
- Who want their families and friends to enjoy comforting, tasty, familiar foods
- Who wish to experience excellent health
- Who want to know how many calories and how much protein, fat, iron, sodium, or other nutrients are in the delicious meals they consume
- Who love simplicity and want readily available ingredients and easy recipes
- Who have diabetes and need to know the carbohydrate content of their food choices
- On weight-loss diets, with an interest in the calories, fat, and fibre contents of foods
- At risk for chronic diseases in which good nutrition can play a healing role
- Who want foods in which the six tastes are superbly balanced, giving an ideal blend

This book will appeal to the full spectrum of cooks, from beginners whose priority is simplicity to gourmet chefs seeking depths and nuances of flavour that will delight the palate.

## Protein-Rich Plant Foods

Vegetarians are sometimes asked, Where do you get your protein? The simple truth is that plant foods deliver abundant protein, as illustrated by large herbivores such as elephants, bulls, and many elite vegetarian athletes (see sidebar, page 46). We can get all the protein we need, and then some, from a wide variety of plant foods.

At the same time, integrating protein-rich foods, such as legumes (beans, peas, and lentils), into the day's menus proves to be the single most common challenge for vegetarians. (These foods also tend to be high in the minerals iron and zinc. Fortified soy milks and tofu are rich sources of the mineral calcium as well.) The typical questions asked by vegetarians reflect potential stumbling blocks on the path to a protein-rich diet. For example, What do I do with these foods to make them taste good? How do I fit these into menus? How do I create protein-rich meals that my family or housemates will like too? Which foods deliver significant amounts of protein, iron, zinc, and calcium, and how much do they provide, compared with how much I need?

The recipes in this book come complete with nutritional analyses that list amounts in each cup (250 mL) or serving for protein and for carbohydrates, fats, fibre, vitamins, and minerals. The nutrients provided can be compared with the recommended intakes that are summarized in this chapter and, for minerals and vitamins, in Appendices 2 and 3 respectively. For those recipes made with nutritional yeast, the analysis was done using Red Star Vegetarian Support Formula nutritional yeast, a source of vitamin B12.

Recommended intakes for protein may be stated in one of two ways: either in grams of dietary protein per kilogram of body weight or in calories from protein as a percentage of the total calories in the diet. The nutritional analyses for the recipes in this book state both: the grams of protein per serving and also the percentage of calories in the recipe that are derived from protein.

## Recommended Protein Intake in Grams

The Recommended Dietary Allowance (RDA) for both men and women is 0.8 grams of good-quality protein per kilogram of body weight per day. (For more on protein quality, see page 47.) This recommendation includes a safety margin to cover individual variation in protein requirements. **The recommended protein intake for vegetarians aged 15 and older is 1 gram of protein per kilogram body weight.** This figure includes an extra margin of safety to cover the lower digestibility of some plant foods.

To determine your recommended protein intake, first calculate your weight in kilograms (divide your weight in pounds by 2.2). A few examples of recommended protein intakes at different weights are shown in the table below. During pregnancy and lactation, recommended intakes for protein are further increased by 25 grams per day.

**Recommended Daily Protein Intakes\***

| Weight (pounds) | Weight (kilograms) | Recommended protein intake (grams) |
| --- | --- | --- |
| 110 | 50 | 50 |
| 132 | 60 | 60 |
| 154 | 70 | 70 |
| 176 | 80 | 80 |

\* Age 18 years and over

## Recommended Protein as a Percentage of Total Calories

Protein is one of the macronutrients that provide us with calories; the others are fat, carbohydrate, and, where this is part of the diet, alcohol. (In contrast, vitamins and minerals are nutrients that do not provide calories.) Both the Institute of Medicine (IOM) and the World Health Organization (WHO) give guidelines as to what percentage of calories in our diets should come from protein, fat, and carbohydrate. There is no recommendation for alcohol, as people can manage fine without any. The recommendations from the two groups overlap but differ slightly from each other. Those from the IOM are known as "Acceptable Macronutrient Distribution Ranges" (AMDR) and those from the WHO are ranges of population nutrient intake goals. Figures in the table below reflect a simple blending of the two organizations' recommendations.

**Distribution of Calories from Protein, Fat, and Carbohydrate[1]**

| Macronutrient | Recommended intake as a percentage of calories |
| --- | --- |
| Protein | 10–20 |
| Fat | 15–35 |
| Carbohydrate | 45–75 |

Worldwide, protein contributes an average of about 11 percent of total calories to human diets. Surveys show that in vegetarian diets, protein typically contributes 10 to 14 percent of calories. When people adopt weight-loss diets that are low in total calories, the percentage derived from protein must be greater. Each recipe's nutritional analysis lists the percentage of calories derived from protein, carbohydrate, fat.

## Protein for Vegetarian Athletes

For those who make the excellent choice to keep fit with regular exercise, 1 gram of protein per kilogram body weight is plenty. Endurance and strength athletes need somewhat more; the recommendation by the Canadian and American dietetic associations is 1.3 to 1.8 grams of protein per kilogram of body weight for vegetarian athletes. This intake is relatively easy to achieve, since people who are doing a great deal of exercise tend to have high caloric intakes. Diets that include legumes, soy foods, and nuts and seeds or their butters, and perhaps plenty of whole grains, will supply sufficient protein for vegetarian athletes. It isn't difficult to meet the requirements of competitive athletes who start the day with Banana Blueberry Power Drink (page 76), a Green Smoothie (page 81), or hearty portions of Scrambled Tofu (page 82) and then lunch and dine on protein-rich spreads, soups, or entrées based on recipes in this book—many provide at least 15 to 20 grams of protein per serving. (Again, you'll find this information in the nutritional analysis following each recipe.) Hungry athletes easily can consume double or even triple portions.

### Vegetarian Athletes

Many vegetarian (in fact, vegan) athletes inspire us with their achievements. Here are a few examples:

- Holder of ten Olympic medals in two sports, Carl Lewis
- NBA (National Basketball Association) champion John Salley
- Marathon winners Scott Jurek, Fiona Oakes, and Pat Reeves
- Ironman triathletes Brendan Brazier and Ruth Heidrich
- Professional ice hockey player Georges Laraque
- Bodybuilders Robert Cheeke, Jane Black, Mike Mahler, and Kenneth Williams
- World-record high jumper Weia Reinboud
- Stuntwoman Spice Williams-Crosby
- Cyclocross racing cyclists Molly Cameron and Adam Myerson
- Professional skateboarder Ed Templeton
- Wrestlers Bryan Danielson (aka Daniel Bryan or the American Dragon) and Taryn Terrell
- Major League baseball pitcher Patrick J. Neshek
- Mixed martial arts professional Mac Danzig
- Personal trainer Bob Harper (of *The Biggest Loser*)

Body builders can require as much as 2.0 to 2.3 grams of protein per kilogram of body weight when they are adding to their muscle mass. Even such high requirements can be met simply using plant-based diets, for instance, by adding protein powders based on soy, peas, or rice to smoothies.

A common challenge for athletes is to find simple and practical ways to prepare protein-rich vegetarian foods. It can take ingenuity to include these at sports events and while travelling—but with a little preparation and planning, it can be accomplished. Just over half of the world's protein comes from grains (in which 10 to 15 percent of the calories come from protein), so cereals, breads, and pasta should not be discounted. Vegetables, seeds, and nuts can also add significantly to daily protein intake. For suggested menus providing several levels of caloric intake, see pages 59 to 70.

### Protein for Children

Children require more protein per kilogram of body weight than do adults. The values in the table below give examples of suggested protein intakes for children at a variety of ages and body weights. These protein intakes are approximate and include a significant safety margin.

Although grains and vegetables are significant protein providers, beans, peas, lentils, and soy foods tend to be the most concentrated sources. Protein is present in most plant foods, with the notable exceptions of sugar, fats, and oils. There is not a lot of room for candy, chips, and sweet beverages in any diet that meets recommended intakes for protein, minerals, and vitamins. Note that fortified soy milk typically provides about 7 grams of protein per 1 cup (250 mL), whereas rice beverages contain only about 0.5 grams of protein; other non-dairy beverages can be similarly low in protein.

**Suggested Daily Protein Intake for Vegetarian Children**

| Age (years) | Suggested protein (grams per kilogram of body weight) | Typical body weight (kilograms) | Daily protein intake (grams,* at typical body weight) |
|---|---|---|---|
| 1–2 | 1.6–1.7 | 11 | 18–19 |
| 2–4 | 1.4–1.6 | 13 | 18–21 |
| 4–6 | 1.3–1.4 | 20 | 26–28 |
| 7–10 | 1.1–1.2 | 28 | 31–34 |
| 11–14 | 1.1–1.2 | 46 | 51–55 |

* Figures are rounded

### Protein Quality

Protein quality depends on digestibility and on the similarity of the amino acid content to the pattern of amino acids required by humans. Soy foods such as tofu and tempeh rival animal products in protein quality because soy foods contain excellent proportions of indispensible (essential) amino acids and digestibility has been improved by heat and by the removal of tough plant cell walls.

The idea that originated forty years ago that complementary proteins must be eaten at the same meal to receive the full range of amino acids is no longer credited. Good protein quality in a vegetarian menu can be easily achieved by including an appealing assortment of plant foods over the course of a day. The recommended intake of 1 gram of protein per kilogram of body weight takes into account the slightly lower digestibility of whole plant foods, when plant foods are compared with animal products or certain refined foods. Every one of the indispensible amino acids originates from plant foods, and from these, our bodies can build any other amino acids we need. The amino acids in all animal products can be traced back to their plant origins.

> Getting enough protein is easily accomplished with a diet centred on plant foods. At the same time, this aspect of menu planning may present challenges until people learn simple and tasty ways to prepare beans, peas, lentils, and soy foods. These high-protein ingredients also deliver plenty of other nutrients. For that reason, this book emphasizes the use of such legumes in dips, spreads, soups, entrées, and other recipes so that these can be included in the diet on a daily basis.

## Meeting Your Needs for Minerals

Recommended daily intakes for minerals at various ages are listed in Appendix 2. The nutritional analysis accompanying each recipe lists amounts of the minerals discussed below.

### Iron and Zinc

Among non-vegetarians and vegetarians alike, iron deficiency is the most widely recognized nutritional deficiency in North America, particularly in women and children. Just like those on any other diet, vegetarians should know good iron sources. Foods that are good protein sources also tend to be high in iron and zinc. For example, 1 cup (250 mL) of cooked beans, peas, or lentils or 1/2 cup (125 mL) of tofu provides 4 to 8 milligrams (mg) of iron and 2 to 4 mg of zinc. This can be compared with a recommended intake of 8 mg of iron for a man or for a woman over the age of 50 (see Appendix 2.) Premenopausal women have higher iron requirements, at 18 mg.

One cup (250 mL) of cooked whole grains provides 1 to 4 mg of iron and 1 to 2 mg of zinc. Seeds, nuts, dried fruit (raisins, currants, and prunes), green veggies (broccoli, green beans, and kale), mushrooms, and potatoes also are significant sources of iron and zinc. Seeds and cashews are especially good sources of zinc. A good source of vitamin C, eaten at the same time, can greatly increase iron absorption (you'll find a list of vitamin C–rich fruits on page 243). Cast-iron cookware contributes iron to foods cooked in it, especially acidic foods such as tomato sauce. Sprouting foods increases mineral availability, so does fermentation (which is part of the production of tempeh and miso).

## Magnesium

Magnesium is the central atom in the chlorophyll molecule, making greens good sources; this mineral is also present in other vegetables, nuts, seeds, legumes, fruit, and chocolate.

## Phosphorus

Phosphorus is present in seeds, nuts, whole grains, and legumes.

## Potassium

Although bananas have somehow become known as potassium-rich foods, a great many fruits and vegetables are packed with potassium. In fact, mushrooms, tomatoes, potatoes, green beans, and strawberries have even more potassium per calorie than bananas.

## Sodium

Although sodium is essential for life, most North Americans get too much, rather than too little, of it. Adults are advised to limit sodium intake to between 1500 and 2300 milligrams (mg) per day. From age 50, we should reduce the lower end of this range to 1300 mg, and further reduce it to 1200 mg at age 71. Those who are most sensitive to the blood-pressure effects of sodium should take care to limit their sodium intakes.

## Calcium

From advertising, we may have the impression that achieving good bone health is entirely reliant on the mineral calcium—or perhaps even on dairy products. Yet, rather than one mineral or a single animal product being necessary for strong bones, these complex structures rely on the teamwork of a number of nutrients, all of which can be found in a vegetarian diet. We need protein; the minerals calcium, magnesium, boron, copper, zinc, manganese, and fluoride; and the vitamins D, K, C, B12, B6, and folic acid. In addition, physical activity plays a vital role in lifelong bone health.

Vegetarian diets provide many good plant sources of calcium, including:

- Greens, especially broccoli, collards, kale, mustard or turnip greens, napa cabbage, and okra
- Calcium-fortified beverages (fortified soy milk, orange juice, and other non-dairy beverages)
- Calcium-set tofu (see the calcium contribution on the label)
- White beans and black beans
- Almonds, sesame seeds, almond butter, and tahini
- Blackstrap molasses (contains minerals that are stripped from sugar cane during refining)
- Figs

You'll notice that certain greens (spinach, Swiss chard, and beet greens) are not listed above as calcium sources. This is because the calcium present is tightly bound by plant acids called oxalates and is unavailable to our bodies for absorption.

## Meeting Your Needs for Vitamins

Recommended daily intakes for vitamins at various ages are listed in Appendix 3. For the most part, a vegetarian diet is an *excellent* choice when it comes to vitamins, and meeting recommended intakes is easily achieved. Two vitamins require special attention: vitamins D and B12.

### Vitamin D

Vitamin D is essential for our absorption and utilization of calcium, and it has numerous other roles in supporting our health. We can derive vitamin D from sunlight, dietary sources, or supplements. Sensible sun exposure can provide an adequate amount of vitamin D production in the body. For people with light skin colour, average daily exposure of the face and forearms to warm sunlight for 10 to 15 minutes (depending on time of day, latitude, age, and skin pigmentation) several times a week is often adequate. People with dark skin may need considerably more time, up to two hours. Winter sun can be ineffective in supporting vitamin D production. For example, at latitudes above 35 degrees north there is little or no vitamin D production between November and March; at 49 degrees north, this "vitamin D winter" extends from October to April. It can be difficult to achieve the balance between insufficient and too much sun exposure, and at many latitudes and seasons, the body's production of vitamin D can be insufficient. Vitamin D–fortified beverages or supplements, therefore, are helpful in supplementing our body's production of vitamin D from sunlight. For recommended intakes, see page 57.

In vegetarian diets, fortified non-dairy beverages such as soy milk are good sources; to determine amounts, check labels. Grown in certain conditions, mushrooms contain a little vitamin D, but amounts are insufficient to meet our needs. Supplements provide either vitamin D3, which is typically of animal origin, or vitamin D2, which is vegan. Despite earlier suggestions to the contrary, it has been established that vitamin D2 is equally as effective as vitamin D3 in maintaining adequate blood levels of vitamin D.

### Vitamin B12

We require a tiny amount of vitamin B12, an essential nutrient that is produced by bacteria. Plant foods, including tempeh, seaweeds, and organic produce, are not reliable sources. We can get our recommended intake from two to three servings of vitamin B12–fortified foods (such as non-dairy milks, veggie meats, or breakfast cereals that are fortified with a total of 4 micrograms—mcg—of vitamin B12 or 100 percent of the Dietary Value of vitamin B12). Another option is 2 tablespoons (30 mL or 8 grams) of Red Star Vegetarian Support Formula nutritional yeast. Supplements are very reliable sources of this vitamin; choose either a daily supplement that provides 25 mcg of vitamin B12 or a supplement that provides 1000 mcg of vitamin B12, the latter to be taken twice a week.

## Meeting Your Needs for Carbohydrates and Fibre

### Carbohydrates

Carbohydrates are the most efficient source of energy for the body; protein and fat are less efficient as energy sources. Carbohydrates are the preferred energy source for the brain, nervous system, and red blood cells. The Recommended Dietary Allowance (RDA) or minimum intake of carbohydrate for the day is 130 grams. Carbohydrates should provide between 45 and 75 percent of the calories in our diet. (The IOM suggests that 45 to 65 percent of our calories come from carbohydrate; the WHO recommends 55 to 75 percent of calories from carbohydrate.) Both groups of experts agree our best sources are the starches in whole grains, legumes, and vegetables and the simple sugars in fruits, in addition to the relatively small amounts available from nuts and seeds. They do not recommend pop, sweets, and the refined and processed food that currently provide most of the carbohydrates in North American diets.

### Fibre

Fibre is a structural component in the cell walls of plants and thus is present in all whole plant foods (though not in animal products). Fibre plays a major role in keeping waste products and toxins moving along through the intestine so they can be eliminated. High-fibre foods allow carbohydrates to be released slowly into the bloodstream, thereby helping us to maintain normal blood glucose levels and as a result stave off hunger.

Recommendations for fibre intake vary with caloric intake. The average daily fibre intake suggested for women is a minimum of 25 grams to age 50 and 21 grams above age 50; for men it is 38 grams to age 50 and 30 grams above age 50. The average fibre intake in North America falls far short of this at 15 grams per day. In contrast, fibre intakes of those on vegetarian diets consistently meet and exceed the suggested levels. Fibre is one of many important components present in whole grains but are lost when grains are refined. (Other losses are B vitamins, minerals, and protective phytochemicals.)

Legumes include a fibre component that can give rise to gas (flatulence); however, this potential problem can be averted—see the sidebar "The Gas Crisis: Six Simple Solutions," on page 33.

## Meeting Your Needs for Fats

Fat is a part of all plant cells and of every plant food. For example, in lettuce, 10 percent of the calories are derived from fat. So, even if you don't spread your toast with margarine or cook with oil, your diet will contain some fats. From a health perspective, our best sources of these essential fats are whole foods such as avocado, olives, seeds, and nuts, rather than extracted oils that have lost fibre, fat-soluble vitamins, essential fats, and other nutrients.

The IOM recommends that our diets contain between 20 and 35 percent calories from fat, and the WHO suggests 15 to 30 percent calories from fat. Many health experts advise us to aim for intakes at the lower end of this range (15 to 20 percent calories from fat) in order to reduce risk of disease.

## Essential Fats: Omega-3 and Omega-6 Fatty Acids

Two fat components are essential to life:

- The omega-6 fatty acid known as linoleic acid, which is present in seeds (hemp, sesame, pumpkin, sunflower), nuts (butternuts, pine nuts, walnuts), grains (corn, wheat germ), and soybeans and in small amounts in many other plant foods
- The omega-3 fatty acid known as linolenic acid, which is present in seeds (chia, flax, hemp), nuts (butternuts, pine nuts, walnuts), and in small amounts in green leafy vegetables and sea vegetables

These fatty acids serve as raw material for building our cell membranes, brain, and nervous systems and certain hormone-like substances. It is recommended that we get at least 5 to 8 percent of our calories from omega-6 fatty acids and 1 to 2 percent of our calories from omega-3 fatty acids. In a vegetarian menu providing 2000 calories, this means that we should aim for at least:

- 9 grams of linoleic acid, the omega-6 fatty acid, plus
- 2.2 to 4.4 grams of linolenic acid, the omega-3 fatty acid

These amounts give ratios of omega-6 to omega-3 fatty acids that support our good health. This amount of linoleic acid (9 grams) is easily obtained by eating a variety of plant foods. You can obtain 2.2 grams of linolenic acid with 1 teaspoon (5 mL) of flaxseed oil or other choices discussed in Chapter 2.

You may choose to increase your intake of omega-3 fatty acids by adding DHA (docosahexaenoic acid), which is another omega-3 fatty acid. Our bodies can make DHA from linolenic acid, yet it is possible that supplemental DHA may be helpful for women during pregnancy or for those people with diabetes, as their DHA production may be inefficient. Further research is needed to clarify whether supplemental DHA can be beneficial on a wider basis. The vegetarian source of DHA is microalgae; a suitable choice might be a supplement that provides about 200 to 300 milligrams of DHA. (Fish contain DHA, and they derive this substance from microalgae.)

### For More Information

If you wish to delve more deeply into vegetarian nutrition, *Becoming Vegetarian* by Vesanto Melina and Brenda Davis, and *Becoming Raw* by Brenda Davis and Vesanto Melina, are good starting points. In these books you'll also find charts outlining the nutrient contents of individual foods and ingredients.

# Chapter 4:
# Food Guide and Menus

In this chapter you'll find a vegetarian food guide, followed by menus that meet your nutrient needs and can take you through the day. The menus incorporate recipes in this book, along with other plant foods. None of this is intended to be followed rigidly every day, but rather to be an enjoyable travel guide to keep you on course—and in excellent health.

## Putting It All Together

Our vegetarian food guide is based on foods that together meet recommended intakes for all of the nutrients you need. The guide encompasses food groups, plus suggestions for getting your omega-3 fatty acids and vitamins B12 and D. It is not essential to meet the minimum intake from every food group every single day, though this could be a goal for your average intakes over time. Eating patterns can vary greatly and still meet recommended intakes. This guide works for family meal planning, for individuals or couples, for those who want well-designed menus for weight loss, for people whose energy requirements have decreased with age, for those on a raw food diet, and for athletes with high energy requirements.

### Vegetables

Vegetables are the most nutrient-dense food group of any. These plant foods contain more vitamins (especially vitamins A, C, and folate), protective phytochemicals, protein, and minerals per calorie than the other food groups.

### Legumes

This food group includes beans, peas, lentils, and soy foods. Legumes and especially soyfoods are the protein powerhouses of the plant kingdom and also are rich in iron and zinc. Whole legumes are the most concentrated natural sources of fibre in the diet, whereas highly processed products that are made from legumes, such as veggie meats, are low in fibre and tend to be relatively higher in sodium. If intake from this group is very low (such as with raw vegan diets), the intake of some higher protein seeds and nuts should be increased.

## Nuts and Seeds

Nuts and seeds are less concentrated sources of protein than legumes, though many contribute significant amounts. For example 1/4 cup (60 mL) of pumpkin, sesame, or sunflower seeds, or pine nuts provides 8.5 grams protein; of almonds or black walnuts provides 7.5 grams protein; of chia seeds, cashews, pistachios, or poppy seeds provides 6 to 6.5 grams protein. Nuts and seeds (and butters made from these) are good sources of trace minerals such as copper, magnesium, and selenium, and important sources of vitamin E. Seeds and cashews are especially rich in zinc. Flax, hemp, and chia seeds and walnuts provide omega-3 fatty acids. Sesame seeds and almonds are good sources of calcium. Peanuts are actually legumes and as such are high in protein, iron, and zinc; however, they are typically grouped with nuts, as we've done here, because of their content of fat and other nutrients, as well as the way they're used in recipes.

## Fruits

Fruits are rich in phytochemicals, the antioxidant vitamins, and potassium and are nature's healers and protectors. Fruits are lower in protein than vegetables. Much of the sugar shown in the nutritional analyses accompanying each menu in this chapter is from fruit.

## Grains

The grains food group includes cereals, breads, and pasta. These energy foods (especially whole grains and whole-grain products) are excellent sources of carbohydrate, fibre, protein, and most of the B vitamins, apart from vitamin B12. Those whose caloric requirements are relatively low, wish to lose weight, or are on a raw food diet may opt for intakes at the low end of this range (for example, three servings). Athletes or others with high energy needs can choose much higher intakes, for example, 12 servings, or even more.

Some people prefer rice, millet, corn, and the gluten-free pseudograins—those foods that are botanically not grains but classified as such for culinary purposes, for instance, amaranth, buckwheat, quinoa, and wild rice. Starchy vegetables provide similar amounts of energy to grains, so those people who avoid grains could consume starchy vegetables such as parsnips, potatoes, squash, sweet potatoes, turnips, and yams. Placing starchy vegetables in this food group is a reasonable option, though they tend to be higher in potassium and vitamin A, whereas the grains are higher in B vitamins.

## Calcium-Rich Foods

The food guide on page 56 emphasizes the calcium-rich foods in each food group discussed above. By following the guidelines listed, you'll ensure an adequate calcium intake. Each serving of the calcium-rich foods listed in the third column of the guide provides about 100 to 150 milligrams of calcium. As you make your choices from the five food groups (listed in the first column), take care to include foods from the calcium-rich foods. These foods do double duty. For example, if you consume 1/2 cup (125 mL) of fortified soy milk or calcium-set tofu, either of these counts as a serving from the legumes group and also as a serving toward your calcium-rich foods quota. If you prefer not to use calcium-fortified beverages or tofu, taking a calcium supplement is a very good choice. Note that beyond the items listed in the calcium-rich foods column, we get small amounts of calcium from many, many plant foods. For more on calcium-rich foods, see Chapters 2 and 3.

## Non-Dairy Milks

Choose non-dairy milks that are fortified with calcium and vitamin D. Fortified almond, rice, and hemp milk are excellent sources of calcium and vitamin D, yet their protein content is significantly lower than that of soy milk. It is fine to include these other milks in your diet, and they boost intakes of calcium and vitamin D. Just take into account that dietary protein must come from other sources—an important consideration in designing children's diets.

# Number of Servings

The guide may seem to recommend a lot of servings. Is it possible to fit all these servings into one day? Yes. People usually eat more than one serving from a particular food group at a meal. For example, someone may eat 3 ounces (90 grams) of a veggie meat (three servings), 1 cup (250 mL) of fortified soy milk or oatmeal (each two servings), or 2, 3, or more cups (500, 750, or more mL) of salad (two, three, or more servings). Also, servings of calcium-rich foods do double duty in also counting as one or even two servings of the food groups.

Following this guide means that most of our calories come from wholesome, nutritious foods. Although extra foods that are high in sugar or fat but lack other nutrients might be included occasionally, there is not a lot of room for such items in any diet that meets recommended intakes.

**Vegetarian Food Guide[2]**

| Food group, servings per day | Foods | Calcium-rich foods,* 6 to 8 servings | Notes |
|---|---|---|---|
| **Vegetables**, 5 or more servings | 1/2 cup (125 mL) raw or cooked vegetables<br>1 cup (250 mL) raw leafy vegetables<br>1/2 cup (125 mL) vegetable juice | 1 cup (250 mL) cooked bok choy, broccoli, collard greens, Chinese (napa) cabbage, kale, mustard greens, or okra<br>2 cups (500 mL) raw bok choy, broccoli, collard greens, Chinese (napa) cabbage, or kale<br>1/2 cup (125 mL) calcium-fortified tomato or vegetable juice | Aim for at least 2 servings per day of the calcium-rich greens. Enjoy the full rainbow of colourful vegetables: red, orange, yellow, green, blue, purple, and white. |
| **Legumes**, 4 or more servings | 1/2 cup (125 mL) cooked beans or lentils<br>1/4–1/2 (60–125 mL) cup tofu<br>1/4 cup (60 mL) tempeh or peanuts<br>1 cup raw or sprouted lentils or peas<br>1 cup (250 mL) soymilk<br>1 ounce (28 g) veggie "meat"<br>2 tablespoons (30 mL) peanut butter | 1/2 cup (125 mL) fortified soy milk or soy yogurt<br>1/2 cup (125 mL) calcium-set tofu (look for calcium on the label), cooked soybeans, or soy nuts<br>1 cup (250 mL) black or white beans | These are powerful providers of iron, zinc, and protein, with about 8 grams protein per serving. Include a choice from this group at most meals. |
| **Nuts and Seeds**, 1 or more servings | 1/4 cup (60 mL) seeds or nuts<br>2 tablespoons (30 mL) nut or seed butter | 1/4 cup (60 mL) almonds<br>2 tablespoons (30 mL) almond butter or tahini | Seeds and nuts contribute copper, selenium, vitamin E, and fat; some are rich in omega-3s. |
| **Fruits**, 4 or more servings | 1/2 cup (125 mL) fruit or fruit juice<br>1/4 cup (60 mL) dried fruit<br>1 medium fruit | 1/2 cup (125 mL) calcium-fortified fruit juice<br>1/4 cup (60 mL) chopped dried figs<br>2 oranges | Make these your sweet treats. They are important potassium sources. Enjoy the full spectrum of colourful fruits. |
| **Grains**, 3 or more servings | 1/2 cup (125 mL) cooked cereal, rice, pasta, quinoa, or other grain<br>1 ounce (28 g) ready-to-eat cereal<br>1 slice bread<br>1/2 cup (125 mL) raw corn or sprouted quinoa, buckwheat, or other grain | 1 ounce (28 g) calcium-fortified cereal or bread<br>1 calcium-fortified tortilla | Select whole grains as often as possible. Adjust the number of grain servings to your energy needs. Some fortified cereals and tortillas are particularly high in calcium; check labels. |

*Each serving provides about 100 to 150 milligrams of calcium

# Essential Extras[2]

## Omega-3 Sources

Although greens and soy foods provide some omega-3 fatty acids, to get your recommended intake for the day, include at least *one* of the following:

- 2 tablespoons (30 mL) ground flaxseed or chia seeds
- 1/4 cup (60 mL) hemp seeds or walnuts
- 1 teaspoon (5 mL) flaxseed oil
- 1 tablespoon (15 mL) hemp seed oil
- 2 tablespoons (30 mL) canola oil

A vegan DHA or DHA with EPA supplement is optional and may be beneficial for some individuals (such as those who are pregnant or have diabetes).

## Vitamin B12

Be sure to include *one* of the following:

- Two to three servings per day of vitamin B12–fortified foods (for example, non-dairy milks, veggie meats, or breakfast cereals that are fortified with at least 4 micrograms of vitamin B12 or 100 percent of the Dietary Value; check the label)
- 2 tablespoons (30 mL or 8 grams) Red Star Vegetarian Support Formula nutritional yeast
- A daily supplement that provides at least 25 micrograms of vitamin B12
- Twice a week, a supplement that provides at least 1000 micrograms of vitamin B12

## Vitamin D

Get your vitamin D from sunlight, fortified foods, a supplement, or a combination of these:

- *Sunlight.* Exposure of the face and forearms to warm sunlight (from 10 a.m. to 2 p.m.) without sunscreen, on a day that is not cloudy and not in winter can provide your day's supply of vitamin D. The amount of time required is 15 minutes daily for light-skinned people; 20 minutes for dark-skinned people; and 30 minutes for the elderly.
- *Fortified foods or supplements.* Use vitamin D supplements or fortified foods if your sun exposure is insufficient. The recommended vitamin D intake for adults is 15 micrograms (600 IUs or International Units) to age 70 and 20 micrograms (800 IUs) above the age of 70 years. Amounts of vitamin D as high as 1000 IU of vitamin D and 2000 IU above the age of 70 years also are considered suitable and safe. Note that 5 micrograms of vitamin D is equivalent to 200 IU of vitamin D.

## Iodine

We can get our day's recommended intake of 150 micrograms of iodine from a multivitamin mineral supplement or from about 1/3 teaspoon (2 mL) of iodized salt. (A teaspoon of iodized salt provides 400 micrograms of iodine.) Sea salt is generally not iodized. Sea vegetables such as kelp also contain iodine, though amounts vary greatly. A reliable source of iodine is an iodine supplement or a multivitamin mineral supplement that includes iodine. Without sources such as these, iodine intake from a vegetarian diet can be insufficient or vary considerably, as it will depend on the amounts of iodine in the soil where the plant foods were grown.

# Twelve Tempting Menus
## Menus That Meet Recommended Intakes

On pages 59 to 70 you will find menus that fit the vegetarian food guide and meet recommended intake for protein, fats, carbohydrates, vitamins, and minerals. The menus are offered at three caloric levels: the standard 2000 calories; 1600 calories (for a small person or for weight loss); and 2500 calories (for a larger or more active person). Caloric intakes can be further increased (for example, for an athlete) with larger servings of the foods listed. While all menus are suitable for families with children, the first menu was designed with this in mind. The second provides healthful versions of typical North American favourites. The third is designed for someone with few cooking skills or who is too busy to do much food preparation; and the fourth menu is entirely raw. We then move through a variety of ethnic menus: Asian, East Indian, French, Italian, Japanese (and gluten-free), Mexican, and Middle Eastern. We end with a menu that includes a few more complex dishes, from which you can select menus for celebration or holiday meals.

Foods may be shifted from one meal to another within the same menu. Also, you may replace a recipe with simple plant foods that involve little or no preparation and that are similar nutritionally. Although it takes a little time to adapt to any new dietary pattern, creating a balanced and nutritionally adequate vegetarian diet is easier than it may appear at first glance.

> All menus require reliable sources of vitamin D and vitamin B12!

## Children's and Family Favourites Menu

A great way to entice children and teenagers to eat vegetables is to set out a raw veggie platter and a nutritious dip when the starving hordes return from school or play. The colourful array is likely to be preferred over steamed broccoli at suppertime. The high intakes of B vitamins come from nutritional yeast in the Gee Whiz Spread. For alternative sandwich ideas, see page 95. Young, small children can get 1000 calories and double their protein needs with half portions of the foods listed here.

## Breakfast

Good Morning Granola (page 78), or cooked or ready-to-eat cereal, 1 cup (250 mL)
Fortified soy milk, 1 cup (250 mL)
Blueberries, 1/2 cup (125 mL)

## Lunch

Sandwich: 2 slices bread, 2 tablespoons (30 mL) almond butter
Carrot sticks, 1/2 cup (125 mL)
Grapes, 1 cup (250 mL)
Fortified soy milk, 1/2 cup (125 mL)

## Supper

Timesaving Tacos (page 183), 1 (taco shell, refried beans, avocado, tomato, lettuce)
Fortified soy milk, 1 cup (250 mL)

## Snacks and Desserts

Gee Whiz Spread (page 88), 1/2 cup (125 mL), with 1 teaspoon (5 mL) flaxseed oil stirred in
Raw Vegetable Platter (page 93), 2 cups (500 mL)
Vegan Dasz Ice Cream (page 254), 1 cup (250 mL)
Blueberry Cornmeal Muffins (page 230), 1

**Nutritional analysis of menu:** calories: 1949, protein: 66 g, fat: 65 g, carbohydrate: 300 g (113 g from sugar), dietary fibre: 39 g, calcium: 1368 mg, iron: 18 mg, magnesium: 479 mg, phosphorus: 1940 mg, potassium: 4447 mg, sodium: 1620 mg, zinc: 12 mg, thiamine: 7.5 mg, riboflavin: 8 mg, niacin: 58 mg, vitamin $B_6$: 8 mg, folate: 585 mcg, pantothenic acid: 6 mg, vitamin $B_{12}$: 7.6 mcg, vitamin A: 847 mcg, vitamin C: 179 mg, vitamin E: 17 mg, omega-6 fatty acids: 17 g, omega-3 fatty acids: 3 g

Percentage of calories from protein 13%, fat 28%, carbohydrate 59%

**1600 calories (59 grams protein) variation**
Have 3/4 cup (185 mL) of the granola and eliminate the muffin.

**2500 calorie (80 grams protein) variation**
For a hungry athlete or teenage boy, provide 1 1/2 cups (375 mL) of the granola, 2 tacos, and 2 muffins (or increase menu options as desired).

## North American Menu

This menu is packed with nutritious versions of North American favourites. The high levels of B vitamins shown in the nutritional analysis, including vitamin B12, are thanks to the nutritional yeast in the scrambled tofu. Adding condiments such as mayo, mustard, and ketchup will significantly increase the sodium in a menu.

## Breakfast

Scrambled Tofu (page 80) using calcium-set tofu, 1/2 cup (125 mL)
Toast, 1 slice with jam or marmalade
Calcium-fortified juice, 1 cup (250 mL)

## Lunch

Multi-Coloured Bean and Vegetable Salad (page 106), 1 cup (250 mL)
Salad Bar (page 168): broccoli, napa cabbage, romaine lettuce, other veggies, 3 cups (750 mL)
Flaxseed or hemp seed oil, 2 teaspoons (10 mL) in dressing
Sunflower seeds, 2 tablespoons (30 mL)

## Supper

Portobello Mushroom Burgers with Chickpea Topping (page 164), 1
Whole-wheat hamburger bun, 1
Mustard or vegan mayo (optional)
Leaf lettuce and slices of tomato, cucumber, and red onion, as desired
Seasoned Potato Wedges (page 202), 6

## Snacks and Desserts

Raw Lime Pie (page 248), 1 slice
2 oranges or other pieces of fruit

**Nutritional analysis of menu:** calories: 1996, protein: 70 g, fat: 72 g, carbohydrate: 296 g (119 g from sugar), dietary fibre: 55 g, calcium: 1219 mg, iron: 19 mg, magnesium: 571 mg, phosphorus: 1460 mg, potassium: 5919 mg, sodium: 2190 mg, zinc: 13.6 mg, thiamine: 9 mg, riboflavin: 9 mg, niacin: 72 mg, vitamin $B_6$: 9 mg, folate: 1037 mcg, pantothenic acid: 8.5 mg, vitamin $B_{12}$: 6 mcg, vitamin A: 760 mcg, vitamin C: 532 mg, vitamin E: 19 mg, omega-6 fatty acids: 17 g, omega-3 fatty acids: 6 g

Percentage of calories from protein 13%, fat 31%, carbohydrate 56%

**1600 calorie (65 grams protein) variation**
Omit the pie.

**2500 calorie (79 grams protein) variation**
Have 2 mushroom burgers with buns or 2 pieces of pie.

## Super Simple Menu

This is a nutritionally adequate menu for a busy day or if your food preparation skills are minimal. There is just one meal to prepare—a stir-fry with rice. Stir-fries allow for infinite variation. Apart from that, you can rely on your toaster, can opener, and a bag of trail mix. For variety, the canned soup may be replaced with another bean or lentil soup or Stovetop "Baked" Beans (page 176). The stir-fry may be replaced with Coconut Mango Black Beans (page 147).

## Breakfast

Whole-grain toast, 2 slices
Almond butter, 2 tablespoons (30 mL)
Calcium-fortified juice, 1 cup (250 mL)

## Lunch

Black bean soup, 2 cups (500 mL)
Banana or other fruit, 1

## Supper

Stir-Fry 101 (page 174): broccoli, carrots, chickpeas, napa cabbage, onion, red bell pepper, snow peas, 2 cups (500 mL)
Brown rice, 1 1/2 cups (375 mL)

## Snacks

Trail mix: 1/4 cup (60 mL) walnuts, 1/4 cup (60 mL) almonds or cashews, 1/2 cup (125 mL) figs or other dried fruit
Fresh or canned peach, 1

**Nutritional analysis of menu:** calories: 2009, protein: 61 g, fat: 71 g, carbohydrate: 307 g (94 g from sugar), dietary fibre: 44 g, calcium: 981 mg, iron: 20 mg, magnesium: 676 mg, phosphorus: 1343 mg, potassium: 4639 mg, sodium 1012 mg,* zinc: 11 mg, thiamine: 1.4 mg, riboflavin: 1.3 mg, niacin: 27 mg, vitamin $B_6$: 2.3 mg, folate: 503 mcg, pantothenic acid: 4.7 mcg, vitamin $B_{12}$: 0 mcg, vitamin A: 746 mcg, vitamin C: 362 mg, vitamin E: 23 mg, omega-6 fatty acids: 221 g, omega-3 fatty acids: 3 g

*The sodium content of this menu depends mainly on choice of soup; check the label and add this amount to 1012 mg sodium.

Percentage of calories from protein 12%, fat 30%, carbohydrate 58%

**1600 calories (52 grams protein) variation**
Have 1 slice of toast and almond butter rather than 2 slices, and 1/2 cup (125 mL) rice at supper instead of 1 1/2 cups (375 mL).

**2500 calorie (70 grams protein) variation**
Add 2 ounces (55 g) crackers at lunch; 1/2 cup (125 mL) rice at supper, and 2 small oatmeal cookies.

## Raw Vegan Menu

For a raw food diet to meet recommended calcium intakes it is necessary to include greens throughout the day (or to include a calcium supplement, preferably one with vitamin D). Here greens are ingredients in the smoothie, salad, vegetable platter (broccoli), and juice. Oranges (in the smoothie) and tahini contribute additional calcium. Greens and tahini are sources of protein and of other minerals too. This is a powerfully protective menu.

## Breakfast

Green Smoothie (page 81), 1

## Lunch

Garden of Plenty Salad (page 105), 6 cups (1.5 L)
Lemon Tahini Dressing (page 122), 1/4 cup (60 mL)
Raw corn on the cob, 2 ears

## Supper

Sprouted Lentils (page 112), 1 cup (250 mL)
Cucumber Dill Dressing (page 121), 2 tablespoons (30 mL)
Raw green peas, 1 cup (250 mL)
Raw Vegetable Platter (page 93), 2 cups (500 mL)
Pesto-the-Best-Oh! (page 92) *or* Limey Avocado Dip (page 91), 1/4 cup (60 mL)

## Snacks and Desserts

Green Giant Juice (page 79), 1 1/2 cups (375 mL)
Raw Mango Strawberry Pie (page 251), 1 slice

**Nutritional analysis of menu:** calories 1962, protein: 73 g, fat: 81 g, carbohydrate: 286 g (112 g from sugar), dietary fibre: 52 g, calcium: 967 mg, iron: 22 mg, magnesium: 741 mg, phosphorus: 1752 mg, potassium: 6764 mg, sodium: 1602 mg, zinc: 12 mg, thiamine: 3.6 mg, riboflavin: 1.8 mg, niacin: 32 mg, vitamin $B_6$: 3.3 mg, folate: 917 mcg, pantothenic acid: 9 mg, vitamin $B_{12}$: 0.1 mcg, vitamin A: 2276 mcg, vitamin C: 876 mg, vitamin E: 27 mg, omega-6 fatty acids: 33 g, omega-3 fatty acids: 4 g

Percentage of calories from protein 13%, fat 34%, carbohydrate 54%

**1600 calorie (65 grams protein) variation**
Eliminate either the pie or the pesto, and have just a half portion of the other.

**2500 calorie (80 grams protein) variation**
Double the pesto or the pie. Add 1 1/2 cups (375 mL) fruit or vegetables of your choice.

## Asian Fusion Menu

Throughout Asia, people may start the day with rice, miso soup, tofu, soy milk, fruit, or pancakes. In this menu we include pancakes, though, for an instant version of this breakfast, you might try frozen vegan waffles with fruit or fruit syrup. The lunch and supper bring us exotic flavours from Vietnam, Thailand, China, and other parts of Asia. Thai Pasta Salad with Spicy Peanut Dressing (page 113) would be another tasty lunch option. The calcium content of tofu varies from brand to brand, so choose one that is a good source of calcium.

### Breakfast

**Whole-Wheat Pancakes (page 83), 3**
**Blueberry Orange Sauce (page 212), 1/2 cup (125 mL)**
**Ground flaxseed, 1 tablespoon (15 mL)**

### Lunch

**Ginger, Carrot, and Yam Soup (page 134), 2 cups (500 mL)**
**Vietnamese Salad Roll (page 114), 1**

### Supper

**Sweet and Sour Tofu (page 177), 1 cup (250 mL),** *or* **Marinated Tofu (page 160), 1/2 cup (125 mL)**
**Brown rice or millet, 2 cups (500 mL)**
**Bok choy or Chinese greens, steamed, 1 cup (250 mL)**

### Snacks and Desserts

**Lemon Sesame Cookies (page 246), 1**
**Green Smoothie (page 81), 1 cup (250 mL)**

**Nutritional analysis of menu:** calories: 2037, protein: 52 g, fat: 64 g, carbohydrate: 333 g (86 g from sugar), dietary fibre: 42 g, calcium: 1190 mg, iron: 16 mg, magnesium: 567 mg, phosphorus: 1192 mg, potassium: 4996 mg, sodium: 2084 mg, zinc: 8.2 mg, thiamine: 3.2 mg, riboflavin: 1.2 mg, niacin: 27 mg, vitamin $B_6$: 2.9 mg, folate: 491 mcg, pantothenic acid: 6.2 mg, vitamin $B_{12}$: 0 mcg, vitamin A: 1982 mcg, vitamin C: 507 mg, vitamin E: 13 mg, omega-6 fatty acids: 15 g, omega-3 fatty acids: 3 g

Percentage of calories from protein 10%, fat 27%, carbohydrate 63%

**1600 calories (44 grams protein) variation**
Decrease the Blueberry Orange Sauce to 1/4 cup (60 mL) and the rice to 1 cup (250 mL).

**2500 calorie (66 grams protein) variation**
Have 2 salad rolls with lunch and double the smoothie to a full recipe. The cookie is optional.

## Indian Menu

In India, menus throughout the day contain legumes, including varieties that are not well known in North America. It is not unusual to include a lentil dish at breakfast. Another Indian breakfast delight, as in many parts of the world, is freshly squeezed orange juice. Here we use fortified juice to increase the calcium intake—but you might prefer yours freshly squeezed. Vitamin B12 is in nutritional yeast (in sandwich spread) and fortified soy milk. Check product labels.

## Breakfast

Hearty Whole-Grain Cereal (page 80), 1 cup (250 mL)
Fortified non-dairy milk, 1 cup (250 mL)
Calcium-fortified orange juice, 1 cup (250 mL)

## Lunch

Curried Kabocha Squash and Chickpea Soup (page 132), 1 cup (250 mL)
Curry Sandwich Spread (page 87), 1/2 cup (125 mL)
Chapatti or naan bread or crackers, 1 1/2 ounces (45 g)
Tomato, 1

## Supper

Dhal-icious (page 151), 1 cup (250 mL)
Coconut Saffron Rice with Cardamom and Lime (page 191), 1/2 cup (125 mL)
Aloo Gobi (page 190), 1 1/2 cups (375 mL)
Apple Plum Chutney (page 211) (optional)

## Snacks and Desserts

Almond-Butter Balls (page 224), 2
Walnuts, 1/4 cup (60 mL)
Mango, cubes or slices, 1 1/2 cups (375 mL)

**Nutritional analysis of menu:** calories: 2000, protein: 63 g, fat: 74 g, carbohydrate: 296 g (109 g from sugar), dietary fibre: 36 g, calcium: 1195 mg, iron: 22 mg, magnesium: 512 mg, phosphorus: 1312 mg, potassium: 4326 mg, sodium: 1813 mg, zinc: 8.6 mg, thiamine: 1.8 mg, riboflavin: 1.2 mg, niacin: 22 mg, vitamin $B_6$: 2.4 mg, folate: 599 mcg, pantothenic acid: 4.6 mg, vitamin $B_{12}$: 3.2 mcg, vitamin A: 953 mcg, vitamin C: 285 mg, vitamin E: 18 mg, omega-6 fatty acids: 18 g, omega-3 fatty acids: 3 g

Percentage of calories from protein 12%, fat 31%, carbohydrate 57%

**1600 calories (54 grams protein) variation**
Decrease the chapatti to 1 ounce (28 g), the mango to 1 cup (250 mL), and omit the Almond-Butter Balls.

**2500 calorie (76 grams protein) variation**
Have 2 chapattis at lunch. At supper, increase the amounts of Dhal-icious and Coconut Saffron Rice each to 1 1/2 cups (375 mL).

## French Menu

Enjoy this elegant menu on a special day. Although not as rich in calcium as leafy greens (such as kale), pea soup, carrots, parsnips, oranges, and figs are all sources. For dessert you might choose instead Lem-Un-Cheesecake with Crumb Crust (page 247), or Fresh Fruit as Dessert (page 242). The B vitamins in this menu, including vitamin B12, are primarily from the nutritional yeast in the Gooda Cheeze.

## Breakfast

Design Your Own Muesli (page 77), made with calcium-fortified juice, 1 serving
Orange, 1, *or* figs, 2

## Lunch

Classic Split Pea Soup (page 131), 2 cups (500 mL)
Gooda Cheeze (page 89), 1/2 cup (125 mL)
Whole-grain Melba toast, 5 pieces

## Supper

Watercress, Avocado, and Grapefruit Salad (page 115), 1 serving
French Lentils with Fennel and Lemon (page 153), 1 cup (250 mL)
Mashed Parsnips and Apple with Toasted Walnuts (page 195), 1/2 cup (125 mL)
Carrots with Dijon Mustard and Tarragon (page 189), 1 cup (250 mL)
Seasoned Greens (page 203), 1 cup (250 mL)

## Snacks and Desserts

Baked Stuffed Apples (page 225), 1
Cashew Cream Topping (page 234), 1 tablespoon (15 mL)

**Nutritional analysis of menu**: calories: 1980, protein: 74 g, fat: 74 g, carbohydrate: 291 g (88 g from sugar), dietary fibre: 68 g, calcium: 998 mg, iron: 25 mg, magnesium: 614 mg, phosphorus: 1566 mg, potassium: 6020 mg, sodium: 2294 mg, zinc: 13 mg, thiamine: 5.2 mg, riboflavin: 4 mg, niacin: 44 mg, vitamin $B_6$: 5 mg, folate: 921 mcg, pantothenic acid: 7.2 mg, vitamin $B_{12}$: 2 mcg, vitamin A: 3840 mcg, vitamin C: 520 mg, vitamin E: 12 mg, omega-6 fatty acids: 21 g, omega-3 fatty acids: 3 g

Percentage of calories from protein 14%, fat 31%, carbohydrate 55%

**1600 calories (59 grams protein) variation**
Serve 1 cup (250 mL) Classic Split Pea Soup and 1/4 cup (60 mL) Gooda Cheeze at lunch, and eliminate the parsnips at supper. For omega-3s, include 2 tablespoons (30 mL) ground flaxseed somewhere in the menu.

**2500 calorie (87 grams protein) variation**
Have 8 pieces Melba toast at lunch; 1 cup (250 mL) parsnips at supper; and enjoy 1/4 cup (60 mL) Cashew Cream Topping with the baked apple. Add 1 piece of fruit.

*Italian Menu*

Imagine yourself by the blue Mediterranean or in the rolling hills of Tuscany while you enjoy this menu. The vitamin B12 is from the nutritional yeast in the pesto. Many foods in this menu provide calcium: the muffin, figs, soup, pesto, and bread, plus the tofu in the lasagna and cheesecake.

## Breakfast

Good-quality Italian coffee
Blueberry Cornmeal Muffins (page 230), 1
Fresh or dried figs, 2, and grapes, 2 cups (500 mL)

## Lunch

Tuscan Minestrone Soup (page 141), 1 cup (250 mL)
Pesto-the-Best-Oh! (page 92) *or* Walnut, Olive, and Sun-Dried Tomato Tapenade (page 97), 1/4 cup (60 mL)
Whole-wheat bread or focaccia, 2 ounces (55 g)

## Supper

Cashew Cheese Lasagna (page 148), 1 serving
Garden of Plenty Salad (page 105), 3 cups (750 mL)
Tomato Herb Dressing (page 127), 3 tablespoons (45 mL)

## Snacks and Desserts

Lem-Un-Cheesecake with Crumb Crust (page 247), 1 slice, with Blueberry Orange Sauce (page 212), 1/2 cup (125 mL)
Calcium-fortified fruit juice, 1 cup (250 mL)

**Nutritional analysis of menu:** calories: 1999, protein: 60 g, fat: 71 g, carbohydrate: 310 g (136 g from sugar), dietary fibre: 41 g, calcium: 1076 mg, iron: 19 mg, magnesium: 564 mg, phosphorus: 1190 mg, potassium: 5391 mg, sodium: 2396 mg, zinc: 9.4 mg, thiamine: 4 mg, riboflavin: 3.6 mg, niacin: 42 mg, vitamin $B_6$: 4.1 mg, folate: 648 mcg, pantothenic acid: 5 mg, vitamin $B_{12}$: 1.8 mcg, vitamin A: 1660 mcg, vitamin C: 583 mg, vitamin E: 14 mg, omega-6 fatty acids: 16 g, omega-3 fatty acids: 4 g

Percentage of calories from protein 12%, fat 30%, carbohydrate 58%

**1600 calories (50 grams protein) variation**
Decrease the grapes to 1 1/2 cups (375 mL), pesto to 2 tablespoons (30 mL), bread at lunch to 1 slice, and the pie and topping to a half serving.

**2500 calorie (70 grams protein) variation**
Add another muffin to your day's menu and increase the amount of pesto to 1/2 cup (125 mL).

## Japanese Menu (Gluten-Free)

This menu has a Japanese flair. Many recipes in this book are wheat- and gluten-free; here is an example of a day's menu that can be used by those who are sensitive to wheat and gluten. For this purpose, choose wheat- and gluten-free varieties of rice syrup, tamari, miso, and other ingredients. This menu can be enjoyed by anyone, not only those with food sensitivities.

## Breakfast

**Banana Blueberry Power Drink (page 76), 2 1/2 cups (625 mL)**

## Lunch

**Ginger Lemon Adzuki Beans (page 144), 1/2 cup (125 mL)**

**Rice, 1/2 cup (125 mL)**

**Calcium-Rich Greens (page 101), 2 cups (500 mL)**

**Cherry tomatoes, 8**

**Oriental Dressing (page 125)** *or* **extra-virgin olive oil and lemon juice dressing, 3 tablespoons (45 mL)**

## Supper

**Maki-Sushi Rolls (page 178), 1 roll**

**Teriyaki Tofu with Japanese Vegetables (page 182), 1/2 cup (125 mL)**

**Shiitake Mushrooms, Kale, and Sesame (page 205), 1 cup (250 mL)**

## Snack

**Calcium-fortified orange juice, 1 cup (250 mL)**

**Nutritional analysis of menu:** calories: 1991, protein: 58 g, fat: 58 g, carbohydrate: 327 g (112 g from sugar), dietary fibre: 53 g, calcium: 991 mg, iron: 18 mg, magnesium: 494 mg, phosphorus: 1053 mg, potassium: 4822 mg, sodium: 1650 mg, zinc: 9 mg, thiamine: 1.9 mg, riboflavin: 1 mg, niacin: 23 mg, vitamin $B_6$: 2.6 mg, folate: 521 mcg, pantothenic acid: 6.3 mg, vitamin $B_{12}$: 0 mcg, vitamin A: 2727 mcg, vitamin C: 677 mg, vitamin E: 19 mg, omega-6 fatty acids: 22 g, omega-3 fatty acids: 3 g

Percentage of calories from protein 12%, fat 25%, carbohydrate 63%

**1600 calorie (49 grams protein) variation**
Serve a half recipe of the Blueberry Banana Power Drink and reduce the rice at lunch to 1/2 cup (125 mL).

**2500 calorie (71 grams protein) variation**
Increase the rice at lunch to 1 cup (250 mL). Add 1/4 cup (60 mL) seeds or nuts. Add a serving of Apple Pear Crumble (page 226). (For a gluten-free menu, use oats that are processed in a gluten-free facility.) Alternatively, have a second maki-sushi roll instead of the crumble.

## Mexican Menu

The flavourful lunch and supper in this menu have a Mexican theme. The foods highest in calcium include fortified soy milk, oranges, black beans, almonds, and figs. For another simple lunch, you might choose a commercial bean soup, crackers, and a carrot, plus a handful of walnuts for your omega-3s.

## Breakfast

Hearty Whole-Grain Cereal (page 80), 1 cup (250 mL)
Fortified soy milk, 1 cup (250 mL)
Oranges, 2

## Lunch

Savoury Black Bean Soup (page 138), 2 cups (500 mL)
Fiesta Quinoa Salad with Lime Dressing (page 103) made with flaxseed oil, 1 cup (250 mL)
Carrot, 1

## Supper

Lima Beans, Corn, and Chipotle Pepper (page 158), 1 cup (250 mL)
Spanish Rice (page 207), 1 cup (250 mL)

## Snacks and Dessert

Almonds, 1/4 cup (60 mL)
Figgy Pudding (page 241), 3/4 cup (185 mL)
Papaya, cubes or slices, 1 cup (250 mL), *or* Coconut Macaroons (page 237), 1

**Nutritional analysis of menu:** calories: 1993, protein: 73 g, fat: 54 g, carbohydrate: 328 g (96 g from sugar), dietary fibre: 63 g, calcium: 991 mg, iron: 22 mg, magnesium: 740 mg, phosphorus: 1597 mg, potassium: 5048 mg, sodium: 1492 mg, zinc: 11 mg, thiamine: 2 mg, riboflavin: 1.8 mg, niacin: 29 mg, vitamin $B_6$: 2 mg, folate: 792 mcg, pantothenic acid: 6.8 mg, vitamin $B_{12}$: 3.1 mcg, vitamin A: 1131 mcg, vitamin C: 341 mg, vitamin E: 18 mg, omega-6 fatty acids: 11 g, omega-3 fatty acids: 4 g

Percentage of calories from protein 14%, fat 23%, carbohydrate 63%

**1600 calorie (60 grams protein) variation**
Decrease grains servings (cereal, quinoa salad, rice) at each meal from 1 cup (250 mL) to 1/2 cup (125 mL). Use unsweetened soy milk. Have just 2 tablespoons (30 mL) almonds.

**2500 calorie (84 grams protein) variation**
Increase grains servings (cereal, quinoa salad, rice) at each meal from 1 cup (250 mL) to 1 1/2 cups (375 mL) each. Add 3 more macaroons or other cookies, or increase portions as desired.

## Middle Eastern Menu

Enjoy some exotic flavours and ingredients. Middle Eastern restaurants and takeout counters at food courts often provide a tasty lunch or supper in the form of a falafel or pita bread with hummus and veggies.

### Breakfast

**Calcium-fortified soy yogurt, 1 cup (250 mL)**
**Bread or toast, 2 slices**
**Tahini, 2 tablespoons (30 mL)**

### Lunch

**Pita bread pocket with 1/2 cup (125 mL) each Heart-Healthy Hummus (page 90), lettuce, onion, and tomato**
**Lemon Tahini Dressing (page 122), 2 tablespoons (30 mL)**

### Supper

**Mediterranean Lentil Soup (page 135)** *or* **Spicy Eggplant Soup with Chickpeas and Olives (page 140), 1 cup (250 mL)**
**Kamut, Tomato, and Avocado Salad (page 107)** *or* **Brown Rice, Mushroom, and Walnut Pilaf (page 192), 1 1/2 cups (375 mL)**

### Snacks and Dessert

**Walnuts, 1/4 cup (60 mL)**
**Fresh Fruit as Dessert (page 242), 2 cups (500 mL)**
**Fortified almond milk or other non-dairy beverage, 1 cup (250 mL)**

**Nutritional analysis of menu:** calories: 2059, protein: 66 g, fat: 84 g, carbohydrate: 283 g (61 g from sugar), dietary fibre: 46 g, calcium: 982 mg, iron: 18 mg, magnesium: 379 mg, phosphorus: 1643 mg, potassium: 3648 mg, sodium: 2114 mg, zinc: 9 mg, thiamine: 2 mg, riboflavin: 1 mg, niacin: 19 mg, vitamin $B_6$: 1.8 mg, folate: 534 mcg, pantothenic acid: 3.8 mg, vitamin $B_{12}$: 0 mcg, vitamin A: 366 mcg, vitamin C: 98 mg, vitamin E: 17 mg, omega-6 fatty acids: 27 g, omega-3 fatty acids: 3 g

Percentage of calories from protein 12%, fat 35%, carbohydrate 53%

**1600 calorie (52 grams protein) variation**
Have 1 slice of toast and tahini, 1/2 cup (125 mL) Kamut, Tomato, and Avocado Salad with 1 tablespoon (15 mL) ground flaxseed sprinkled on top of it, and 1 tablespoon (15 mL) walnuts.

**2500 calorie (83 grams protein) variation**
At lunch, double the pita bread and fillings. At some point during the day, add one-third of an avocado or a cookie.

## Holiday Menu

For a lovely celebration lunch or dinner, select courses from this list.

**Gooda Cheeze (page 89) with crackers**
**Ginger, Carrot, and Yam Soup (page 134)**
**Wild Rice, Walnut, and Cranberry Salad (page 116)** or **Holiday Stuffed Winter Squash (page 154)**
**Kale and Red Pepper Holly Ring (page 106)**
**Rosemary Gravy (page 217)** or **Light Mushroom Gravy (page 214)**
**Cranberry Ginger Relish (page 213)**
**Blueberry Mince Tarts or Pies (page 232)**
**Pumpkin Spice Pie (page 249) with Cashew Cream Topping (page 234)** or **Holiday Pie Topping (page 244)**

# Part Two
Recipes

# Introduction to the Recipes

Welcome to recipes that were developed for their outstanding taste and ease of preparation. Each was guided by sound nutritional information. The majority of ingredients called for are easy to obtain in the marketplace; there are just a few less common items, which can be found in health food stores, specialty markets, ethnic stores, or over the Internet. A comprehensive shopping list that includes all the food items used in the recipes can be found on pages 39 and 40.

If you do not already have a good knife, we recommend that it be your first investment. Visit a store that specializes in knives to get free instruction on what to look for and how to use a good quality knife. Also essential is a cutting board that is large enough to easily hold the food you are working on. From there, continue to invest in your health by adding to your equipment, one purchase at a time, so that you are happy to spend time working with real food in your kitchen. For a list of equipment used to make all of the recipes in this book, see pages 41 and 42.

## How to Approach the Recipes

- Read each recipe fully before you start. This will help ensure that you understand the task at hand and have a successful outcome.
- If possible, make the recipe exactly as it is written the first time you try it. After that, use your creativity to explore new taste possibilities.
- Look at the variations and ingredient options for the recipe, as you may find a version you prefer.
- At the beginning of each recipe you will find the yield, usually in cups (1 = 250 mL) or occasionally in servings. We generally use a volume measure for the yield as we recognize that appetites vary immensely, and what could be considered several servings in one group might be a single serving for one hungry, high-energy person.
- To increase your understanding of cooking and learn how to balance flavour, read Chapter 1 ("The Art and Science of Cooking").

## How to interpret the Nutritional Analyses

A special feature of these recipes is the nutritional analysis that accompanies each one. Following is some information on how the analyses should be interpreted.

- The nutritional analysis provided for each recipe does not include optional ingredients.
- Where two or more choices are given for an ingredient, the analysis is based on the first choice.
- Where there is a range in the amount of an ingredient, the smaller amount is used for the analysis.
- Metric measures were used for the analyses.
- Certain nutrients—such as choline, chromium, iodine, manganese, molybdenum, and selenium—are not included due to insufficient data. The databases used are those of the US Department of Agriculture (www.nal.usda.gov/fnic/foodcomp/search) and the professional nutritional analysis program ESHA/The Food Processor (www.esha.com).
- Although we list a specific amount of each nutrient per serving of a recipe, the actual amount can vary due to differences in plant varieties, growing conditions, and farming practices.
- Most of the values for sugar in the nutritional analyses reflect naturally occurring sugars in fruits and vegetables. Added sugars, such as those from maple syrup, also are included in this figure.
- For recipes calling for nutritional yeast, the analysis was done using Red Star Vegetarian Support Formula nutritional yeast, a source of vitamin B12.

## Percentage of Calories from Protein, Fat, and Carbohydrate

The amounts of protein, carbohydrate, and fat are listed in grams in the nutritional analyses. Foods and beverages also can be described in terms of the percentage of calories that are derived from these 3 energy-giving nutrients. The bottom line of the analysis shows the percentage of calories that come from protein, fat, and carbohydrate. Note that 35 percent *calories from fat* is very different from 35 percent or less of the food's *weight* coming from fat.

By weight, 2% milk contains 2 grams of fat per 100 grams of milk (and 89 percent water). When our bodies convert fat, protein, and carbohydrate to calories, we derive 9 calories from each gram of fat and 4 calories from each gram of protein or carbohydrate, but no calories from water. Thus in 2% milk, 27 percent of the calories is derived from protein, 35 percent from fat, and 38 percent from carbohydrate (lactose sugar). (So from another perspective it might be called 35% milk rather than 2% milk.) The Dahl-icious recipe (page 151) provides 23 percent calories from protein, 27 percent calories from fat, and 50 percent from carbohydrate.

It is recommended that in our overall diet we get 10-20 percent of our calories from protein, 15-35 percent of our calories from fat, and 45-75 percent of our calories from carbohydrate. In a few recipes, such as African Chickpea Stew (page 145) and Coconut Mango Black Beans (page 147), the amounts of protein, fat, and carbohydrates will fit neatly into these ranges. In other recipes, the amounts will be quite different. For example, the tasty Marinated Tofu (page 160) and Dahl-icious (page 151) recipes are relatively high in protein. These can be balanced at a meal and also over the course of the day by foods that are higher in carbohydrate and fat. Salad dressings tend to be relatively high in fat; this can be offset by choosing more fruits, vegetables, grains, and legumes.

# Breakfasts and Beverages

## Apple Cinnamon Topping

Makes 2 cups (500 mL)

Apples are one of the most widely cultivated tree fruits, with over 7,500 varieties grown worldwide. Cooking apples are less sweet than eating apples; therefore, only add the maple syrup if the apples you are using are tart. The classic combination of apples and cinnamon is fabulous in this warm topping. Serve with Whole-Wheat Pancakes (page 83), hot cereal recipes (see pages 80 and 81), Lem-Un-Cheescake with Crumb Crust (page 247), or Vegan Dasz Ice Cream (page 254).

**3 apples**
**3 tablespoons (45 mL) chopped toasted almonds (optional)**
**1 tablespoon (15 mL) freshly squeezed lemon juice**
**1 tablespoon (15 mL) maple syrup (optional)**
**1/4 teaspoon (1 mL) grated lemon peel**
**Pinch of cinnamon**

Quarter the apples, remove and discard the core, and cut into 1/4-inch (5 mm) thick slices. Put the apples, almonds, lemon juice, syrup, lemon peel, and cinnamon in a medium skillet over medium heat. Cover and cook, stirring occasionally, for 5 minutes or until the apples are soft and moist.

Per 1/2 cup (125 mL): calories: 72, protein: 0.3 g, fat: 0.2 g, carbohydrate: 19 g (15 g from sugar), dietary fibre: 3 g, calcium: 11 mg, iron: 0.2 mg, magnesium: 7 mg, phosphorus: 13 mg, potassium: 135 mg, sodium: 2 mg, zinc: 0.3 mg, thiamin: 0 mg, riboflavin: 0 mg, niacin: 0.1 mg, vitamin $B_6$: 1 mg, folate: 4 mcg, pantothenic acid: 0.1 mg, vitamin $B_{12}$: 0 mcg, vitamin A: 3 mcg, vitamin C: 7 mg, vitamin E: 0.2 mg, omega-6 fatty acids: 0 g, omega-3 fatty acids: 0 g

Percentage of calories from protein 2%, fat 2%, carbohydrate 96%

# Banana Blueberry Power Drink

Makes 2 1/2 cups (625 mL), enough for 1 to 2 servings

The fruit, sunflower seeds, and hemp seeds in this smoothie provide abundant protein, minerals, vitamin E, and omega-3 fatty acids. As a single serving, this is a power-packed breakfast that will stave off hunger all morning. Although soaking the seeds and dates will increase their mineral availability and improve the smoothness of the final product, you can skip this step if you prefer.

**1/4 cup (60 mL) raw sunflower seeds**
**3 pitted dates**
**1 1/4 cups (310 mL) water**
**1 banana**
**1 cup (250 mL) fresh or frozen blueberries**
**1/4 cup (60 mL) hemp seeds**

Put the sunflower seeds and dates in a small bowl. Add water to cover and let soak at room temperature for 6 to 10 hours. Transfer the sunflower seeds, dates, and their soaking liquid to a blender. Add banana, blueberries, and hemp seeds and process on high speed until smooth. For a thinner consistency, add a little more water.

Per 2 1/2 cups (625 mL): calories: 584, protein: 18 g, fat: 28 g, carbohydrate: 74 g (44 g from sugar), dietary fibre: 21 g, calcium: 85 mg, iron: 5 mg, magnesium: 146 mg, phosphorus: 339 mg, potassium: 852 mg, sodium: 10 mg, zinc: 2 mg, thiamin: 1 mg, riboflavin: 0.1 mg, niacin: 4.3 mg, vitamin $B_6$: 0.4 mg, folate: 92 mcg, pantothenic acid: 2.7 mg, vitamin $B_{12}$: 0 mcg, vitamin A: 63 mcg, vitamin C: 17 mg, vitamin E: 13 mg, omega-6 fatty acids: 17 g, omega-3 fatty acids: 6 g

Percentage of calories from protein 11%, fat 41%, carbohydrate 48%

---

### Frozen Bananas

Use frozen bananas in Banana Blueberry Power Drink (above), Green Smoothie (page 81), and Vegan Dasz Ice Cream (page 254). Select ripe bananas, as they are much sweeter and have a less-starchy aftertaste. Peel the bananas and leave them whole or break them into chunks. A squeeze of lemon juice sprinkled over the fruit will keep it from turning brown. Place the bananas in zipper-lock freezer bags or airtight containers and freeze them. Frozen bananas will keep for several weeks before turning brown, depending on their ripeness and the temperature of your freezer.

# Design Your Own Muesli

Makes about 3 cups (700 mL), enough for 2 servings

The original muesli recipe consisting of soaked raw oats, fruit, and ground nuts was developed by Dr. Maximilian Bircher-Benner (1867–1939), a Swiss physician and pioneer in nutritional research, at his renowned healing clinic in Zurich as an easily digested, nourishing meal. This version takes less than three minutes to prepare. Refrigerate any leftovers and enjoy them for breakfast another day or as a snack. Be sure to check out the many variations that follow the main recipe; you can adjust the ingredients to best suit your dietary needs and preferences.

**1 cup (250 mL) rolled oats**
**1/4 cup (60 mL) raw sunflower seeds**
**1/4 cup (60 mL) raisins**
**Pinch of cinnamon**
**1 1/4 cups (310 mL) unsweetened apple juice**
**1 chopped banana or fruit of your choice**

Put the oats, seeds, raisins, and cinnamon in a bowl. Stir in the juice, cover, and refrigerate for 6 to 10 hours. Top with the banana just before serving. For a thinner consistency, add a little more juice.

Per 1 1/2 cups (375 mL): calories: 455, protein: 12 g, fat: 12 g, carbohydrate: 80 g (21 g from sugar), dietary fibre: 9 g, calcium: 67 mg, iron: 4 mg, magnesium: 158 mg, phosphorus: 374 mg, potassium: 839 mg, sodium: 16 mg, zinc: 2 mg, thiamin: 0.7 mg, riboflavin: 0.2 mg, niacin: 5 mg, vitamin $B_6$: 0.5 mg, folate: 62 mcg, pantothenic acid: 2 mg, vitamin $B_{12}$: 0 mcg, vitamin A: 4 mcg, vitamin C: 8 mg, vitamin E: 7 mg, omega-6 fatty acids: 7 g, omega-3 fatty acids: 0.1 g

Percentage of calories from protein 10%, fat 23%, carbohydrate 67%

### Barley, Rye, or Wheat Muesli
Replace the oats with 1 cup (250 mL) rolled barley, rye, or wheat.

### Gluten-free Muesli
Use rolled oats that were processed in a certified gluten-free facility; alternatively, use 1 cup (250 mL) rice flakes and decrease the soaking time to 30 minutes.

### Almond, Pumpkin Seed, or Walnut Muesli
Replace the sunflower seeds with 1/4 cup (60 mL) chopped raw almonds, raw pumpkin seeds, or chopped walnuts.

### Blueberry, Cranberry, or Date Muesli
Replace the raisins with 1/4 cup (60 mL) dried blueberries, cranberries, or dates.

### Cardamom or Fennel Muesli
Replace the cinnamon with a pinch of ground cardamom or fennel.

### Muesli with Non-Dairy Milk
Replace the apple juice with 1 1/4 cups (310 mL) almond milk, hemp milk, rice milk, or soy milk.

### Apple or Berry Muesli
Replace the banana with 1 cup (250 mL) chopped apple, blueberries, raspberries, or sliced strawberries.

### Muesli with Topping
To serve, add a dollop of Cashew Cream Topping (page 234) or Holiday Pie Topping (page 244).

# Good Morning Granola

Makes 12 cups (3 L)

This recipe makes a large quantity—enough to give your days a quick, wholesome, delicious start for a week or two.

**1/2 cup (125 mL) frozen apple juice concentrate, thawed**
**1/2 cup (125 mL) almond butter or tahini**
**1/2 cup (125 mL) maple syrup**
**1 teaspoon (5 mL) cinnamon**
**1 teaspoon (5 mL) vanilla or almond extract**
**8 cups (2 L) rolled oats**
**1 cup (250 mL) raw sunflower seeds or chopped almonds (optional)**
**1 cup (250 mL) currants, raisins, and/or chopped dates**

Preheat the oven to 350°F (180°C).

Put the apple juice concentrate, almond butter, syrup, cinnamon, and vanilla in a bowl and stir until well combined. Alternatively, process them in a blender until smooth.

Combine the oats and seeds in a roasting pan or large bowl. Pour the almond butter mixture over the oats and toss well to distribute it evenly.

Spread the oat mixture evenly in the roasting pan, or on two baking sheets, or along the sides of a large metal bowl. Bake for 10 minutes, then stir to prevent burning. Bake for 10 minutes longer or until golden brown.

Cool thoroughly and then stir in the currants. Transfer to glass jars or heavy-duty zipper-lock storage bags. Keeps for up to 6 months in the refrigerator or freezer.

Per cup (250 mL): calories: 381, protein: 11 g, fat: 10 g, carbohydrate: 64 g (10 g from sugar), dietary fibre: 7 g, calcium: 84 mg, iron: 4 mg, magnesium: 126 mg, phosphorus: 344 mg, potassium: 480 mg, sodium: 57 mg, zinc: 3 mg, thiamin: 0.4 mg, riboflavin: 0.2 mg, niacin: 4 mg, vitamin $B_6$: 0.1 mg, folate: 17 mcg, pantothenic acid: 0.6 mg, vitamin $B_{12}$: 0 mcg, vitamin A: 67 mcg, vitamin C: 1 mg, vitamin E: 3 mg, omega-6 fatty acids: 2.6 g, omega-3 fatty acids: 0.1 g

Percentage of calories from protein 11%, fat 23%, carbohydrate 66%

**Apple Granola**
Replace the maple syrup with an additional 1/2 cup (125 mL) apple juice concentrate.

**Coconut Granola**
Stir in 1 1/2 cups (375 mL) unsweetened shredded dried coconut 5 minutes before the granola is finished baking.

# Green Giant Juice

Makes 3 cups (750 mL), enough for 2 servings

A serving of this juice delivers 150 milligrams of calcium and 5 grams of protein, plus iron, magnesium, manganese, potassium, zinc, and beta carotene (converted in the body to vitamin A), vitamins B6 and K, and folate, and less than half a gram of fat. As a bonus, the calcium in kale is about twice as available to the body as the calcium from cow's milk.

**8 ounces (220 g) kale, including stems**
**1/2 head romaine lettuce**
**1 cucumber, quartered lengthwise**
**1 apple**
**4 stalks celery**
**1 lemon, peeled**
**1-inch (3 cm) piece of fresh ginger or to taste (optional)**

Juice the kale, lettuce, cucumber, apple, celery, lemon, and ginger. Serve immediately.

Per 1 1/2 cups (375 mL): calories: 57, protein: 5 g, fat: 0.4 g, carbohydrate: 8 g, dietary fibre: 3 g, calcium: 155 mg, iron: 1.4 mg, magnesium: 48 mg, potassium: 835 mg, sodium: 110 mg, zinc: 0.6 mg, vitamin $B_{12}$: 0 mcg, vitamin C: 15 mg, vitamin E: 1.5 mg, omega-6 fatty acids: 0.1 g, omega-3 fatty acids: 0.2 g

Percentage of calories from protein 35%, fat 7%, carbohydrate 58%

---

### Juicing Kale with Different Juicers

*Champion juicer*: If you use a Champion juicer, roll the kale leaves tightly and feed them through the chute in small quantities. To maximize your yield, you may want to put the pulp through the juicer a second time.

*Green Power juicer*: If you use a Green Power or Green Star juicer, feed the stem end of the leaves in first and allow the twin gears to pull the leaves through the gears. You do not need to chop or roll the leaves.

*Centrifugal juicer*: Centrifugal juicers are not efficient at juicing greens.

## Hearty Whole-Grain Cereal

Makes 4 cups (1 L)

A hearty cereal is a great way to add whole grains to your diet. Leftovers can be refrigerated and served as a cold pudding over several days or reheated as needed and served as a warm cereal. If you haven't made this recipe before, try it first with three whole grains; later you can experiment by creating your own mixes with as many grains as you like. Serve the cereal with your choice of fresh or dried fruit, nuts, seeds, and non-dairy milk.

**1 cup (250 mL) uncooked grain (such as amaranth, barley, brown rice, buckwheat, Kamut berries, millet, oat groats, quinoa, spelt berries, wheat berries, or wild rice)**
**4 cups (1 L) water**

### Stovetop Method

Put the grains and water in a heavy pot and bring to a boil over high heat. Reduce heat to low, cover, and simmer for 2 to 3 hours, until the grains are tender and the water is absorbed. Add more water as needed so the grains don't dry out during cooking.

### Double-Boiler Method

Put the grains and water in the top portion of a double boiler, above plenty of simmering water in the lower pot. Cover and cook the grains for 2 to 3 hours. Check periodically to make sure there is sufficient water in the lower pot.

### Slow-Cooker Method

Put the grains and water in a slow cooker and cook on low heat for 8 to 10 hours, until the water has been absorbed. Letting the cereal cook overnight is a great way to have a hot breakfast ready to go in the morning.

Per cup (250 mL): calories: 167, protein: 5 g, fat: 2 g, carbohydrate: 34 g (0 g from sugar), dietary fibre: 3 g, calcium: 7 mg, iron: 1 mg, magnesium: 71 mg, phosphorus: 142 mg, potassium: 111 mg, sodium: 3 mg, zinc: 1 mg, thiamin: 0.2 mg, riboflavin: 0.1 mg, niacin: 3 mg, vitamin $B_6$: 0.2 mg, folate: 23 mcg, pantothenic acid: 0.5 mg, vitamin $B_{12}$: 0 mcg, vitamin A: 0 mcg, vitamin C: 0 mg, vitamin E: 0.3 mg, omega-6 fatty acids: 0.6 g, omega-3 fatty acids: 0 g

Percentage of calories from protein 11%, fat 8%, carbohydrate 81%

**Note:** Analysis was done using brown rice, millet, and oat groats.

## Tasty and Nutritious Grain Combinations

- 1/3 cup (85 mL) each of barley, Kamut berries, and oat groats
- 1/3 cup (85 mL) each of barley, brown rice, and wheat or spelt berries
- 1/3 cup (85 mL) each of brown rice, millet, and oat groats (this combination is gluten-free)

## Green Smoothie

Makes about 2 1/2 cups (625 mL), enough for 1 or 2 servings

This smoothie provides a satisfying breakfast for one or two people. It is rich in protein, calcium, iron, potassium, zinc, and folate and is a powerhouse of antioxidants, including vitamins A, C, and E, and selenium. Soaking the seeds will increase their mineral availability, although this smoothie tastes just as good without that step. If you use hemp seeds, the protein and mineral content will be a little lower; however, this choice will provide twice your daily supply of omega-3 fatty acids.

**1/4 cup (60 mL) raw sunflower or hemp seeds**
**1 cup (250 mL) orange juice or a blend of orange and apple juice**
**2 cups (500 mL) chopped kale leaves**
**1 orange, peeled and quartered**
**1 banana**

Soak the sunflower seeds in the juice for 15 minutes at room temperature or for 6 to 10 hours in the refrigerator. (Skip this step if using hemp seeds.)

Transfer the seeds and juice to a blender. Add the kale, orange, and banana and process on high speed for 1 minute or until smooth.

Per 2 1/2 cups (625 mL): calories: 552, protein: 17 g, fat: 20 g, carbohydrate: 88 g (49 g from sugar), dietary fibre: 13 g, calcium: 310 mg, iron: 6 mg, magnesium: 246 mg, phosphorus: 420 mg, potassium: 2006 mg, sodium: 62 mg, zinc: 3 mg, thiamin: 1.4 mg, riboflavin: 0.5 mg, niacin: 8 mg, vitamin $B_6$: 1.2 mg, folate: 262 mcg, pantothenic acid: 4 mg, vitamin $B_{12}$: 0 mcg, vitamin A: 1088 mcg, vitamin C: 371 mg, vitamin E: 14 mg, omega-6 fatty acids: 12 g, omega-3 fatty acids: 0.3 g

Percentage of calories from protein 11%, fat 30%, carbohydrate 59%

## Scrambled Tofu

Makes 2 1/2 cups (625 mL), enough for 2 to 3 servings

Turmeric adds an appealing yellow colour to this tasty, high-protein dish. It resembles scrambled eggs but is cholesterol-free. For breakfast, serve it with whole-grain toast and juice or a hot beverage. Later in the day, it makes an easy-to-assemble lunch or dinner packed with vitamins and minerals. Add your favourite salsa for extra colour and flavour.

1 pound (454 g) medium-firm tofu
2 teaspoons (10 mL) coconut or olive oil
1 cup (250 mL) sliced mushrooms
1 cup (250 mL) sliced napa cabbage
1/2 cup (125 mL) diced red bell pepper
1 clove garlic, minced
1 teaspoon (5 mL) tamari or soy sauce
1/4 teaspoon (1 mL) ground cumin
Pinch of turmeric
2 tablespoons (30 mL) chopped green onion
1 tablespoon (15 mL) nutritional yeast (optional)
1 tablespoon (15 mL) chopped fresh cilantro or parsley
1/4 teaspoon (1 mL) salt (optional)

Press the tofu for 20 minutes (see page 36). Discard the liquid. Place tofu in a bowl and mash with a fork. Heat the oil in a large skillet over medium heat. Add the mushrooms, cabbage, bell pepper, and garlic and cook, stirring, for 5 minutes or until the moisture has evaporated. Stir in the tofu, tamari, cumin, and turmeric and cook for 5 minutes, stirring occasionally. Stir in the green onion, yeast, cilantro, and salt. Serve immediately.

Per 1 1/4 cups (310 mL): calories: 243, protein: 23 g, fat: 14 g, carbohydrate: 12 g (5 g from sugar), dietary fibre: 4 g, calcium: 514 mg, iron: 5 mg, magnesium: 102 mg, phosphorus: 396 mg, potassium: 695 mg, sodium: 877 mg, zinc: 3 mg, thiamin: 0.2 mg, riboflavin: 0.4 mg, niacin: 9 mg, vitamin $B_6$: 0.4 mg, folate: 66 mcg, pantothenic acid: 1.1 mg, vitamin $B_{12}$: 0 mcg, vitamin A: 100 mcg, vitamin C: 92 mg, vitamin E: 1 mg, omega-6 fatty acids: 4 g, omega-3 fatty acids: 0.5 g

Percentage of calories from protein 34%, fat 48%, carbohydrate 18%

**Note**: Analysis was done using calcium-set tofu. Adding the optional nutritional yeast will significantly increase the B vitamins.

# Whole-Wheat Pancakes

Makes eight or nine 4-inch (10 cm) pancakes

These light pancakes are free of eggs, dairy, and (if you wish) soy. Serve them with your choice of toppings, such as Apple Cinnamon Topping (page 75), fresh fruit, or maple syrup.

**1 cup (250 mL) whole-wheat pastry flour**
**2 tablespoons (30 mL) baking powder**
**1/2 teaspoon (2 mL) cinnamon**
**Pinch of salt**
**1 cup (250 mL) non-dairy milk**
**2 1/2 tablespoons (37 mL) coconut or olive oil**
**1 tablespoon (15 mL) sweetener (optional)**
**Additional oil for frying**

Combine the flour, baking powder, cinnamon, and salt in a medium bowl. Combine the milk, oil, and sweetener in a small bowl or measuring cup. Put a skillet over medium-high heat. When it is hot, add about 1 tablespoon of oil to coat the surface.

To make the batter, pour the milk mixture into the flour mixture and lightly whisk until just combined. (Overmixing will make the pancakes flatter and less fluffy.) For each pancake, pour about 3 tablespoons (45 mL) of the batter into the hot pan. Cook for about 3 minutes or until bubbles form on the surface and the bottom of the pancake is lightly browned. Turn the pancake over and cook until the other side is browned, about 2 minutes. Serve hot.

Per pancake: calories: 98, protein: 3 g, fat: 5 g, carbohydrate: 11 g (0 g from sugar), dietary fibre: 1 g, calcium: 137 mg, iron: 0.5 mg, magnesium: 1 mg, phosphorus: 37 mg, potassium: 80 mg, sodium: 244 mg, zinc: 0.1 mg, thiamin: 0.4 mg, riboflavin: 0.1 mg, niacin: 0.3 mg, vitamin $B_6$: 0 mg, folate: 3 mcg, pantothenic acid: 0 mg, vitamin $B_{12}$: 0.4 mcg, vitamin A: 13 mcg, vitamin C: 0 mg, vitamin E: 0 mg, omega-6 fatty acids: 0.1 g, omega-3 fatty acids: 0 g

Percentage of calories from protein 10%, fat 45%, carbohydrate 45%

**Note**: Analysis was done using fortified soy milk.

# Dips, Spreads, Sandwiches, and Snacks

## Black Bean Chipotle Dip

Makes 2 cups (500 mL)

Black beans have a slightly earthy taste that is reminiscent of mushrooms. These beans often are combined with assertive flavours, like the chipotle pepper in this recipe. Keep this dip or spread in your refrigerator ready to serve as a quick snack with carrot sticks, crackers, or bread. It's a great source of protein, trace minerals, and folate.

2 cups (500 mL) cooked or canned black beans, drained and rinsed
1/4 cup (60 mL) tahini
1/4 cup (60 mL) lime juice
1/4 cup (60 mL) water
1 teaspoon (5 mL) minced chipotle pepper
1 clove garlic, chopped
1/2 teaspoon (2 mL) ground toasted cumin seeds (see page 133)
1/2 teaspoon (2 mL) oregano
1/4 teaspoon (1 mL) salt
2 tablespoons (30 mL) chopped fresh cilantro or parsley
1 tablespoon (15 mL) extra-virgin olive oil

Combine the beans, tahini, lime juice, water, chipotle, garlic, cumin, oregano, and salt in the bowl of a food processor and purée until smooth. Add cilantro and olive oil and blend for 5 seconds. Adjust the seasoning to taste.

Per 1/2 cup (125 mL): calories: 247, protein: 11 g, fat: 12 g, carbohydrate: 27 g (0 g from sugar), dietary fibre: 9 g, calcium: 55 mg, iron: 3 mg, magnesium: 81 mg, phosphorus: 253 mg, potassium: 423 mg, sodium: 125 mg, zinc: 2 mg, thiamin: 0.5 mg, riboflavin: 0.1 mg, niacin: 3 mg, vitamin $B_6$: 0.1 mg, folate: 153 mcg, pantothenic acid: 0.2 mg, vitamin $B_{12}$: 0 mcg, vitamin A: 5 mcg, vitamin C: 7 mg, vitamin E: 1 mg, omega-6 fatty acids: 4 g, omega-3 fatty acids: 0.2 g

Percentage of calories from protein 17%, fat 42%, carbohydrate 41%

# Black Bean, Corn, and Avocado Salsa

Makes 3 1/2 cups (875 mL)

Black beans are pivotal to the cuisines of Central and South America, Mexico, the Caribbean, and Cuba, where these delicious beans are practically a daily staple. This hearty salsa has a Mexican influence, from a part of the world where salsas are served as a condiment or side dish at virtually every meal. It is rich in protein, dietary fibre, iron, potassium, zinc, and folate.

2 cups (500 mL) cooked or canned black beans, drained and rinsed
1 cup (250 mL) diced tomato
1 cup (250 mL) corn kernels, fresh, frozen, or canned
1/4 cup (60 mL) chopped green onion
2 tablespoons (30 mL) lime juice
2 tablespoons (30 mL) chopped fresh cilantro or parsley
1 teaspoon (5 mL) ground cumin
1/4 teaspoon (1 mL) salt
1/2 fresh green chili, finely minced, or hot sauce to taste
1 clove garlic, minced
1 ripe avocado, diced

Combine the black beans, tomato, corn, green onion, lime juice, cilantro, cumin, salt, green chili, and garlic in a medium bowl. Mix well. Gently fold in the avocado and transfer the salsa to a serving bowl.

Per cup (250 mL): calories: 142, protein: 6 g, fat: 5 g, carbohydrate: 21 g (2 g from sugar), dietary fibre: 7 g, calcium: 27 mg, iron: 2 mg, magnesium: 61 mg, phosphorus: 116 mg, potassium: 501 mg, sodium: 77 mg, zinc: 1 mg, thiamin: 0.2 mg, riboflavin: 0.1 mg, niacin: 1.4 mg, vitamin $B_6$: 0.2 mg, folate: 112 mcg, pantothenic acid: 0.6 mg, vitamin $B_{12}$: 0 mcg, vitamin A: 18 mcg, vitamin C: 17 mg, vitamin E: 0.3 mg, omega-6 fatty acids: 0.7 g, omega-3 fatty acids: 0.1 g

Percentage of calories from protein 17%, fat 29%, carbohydrate 54%

# Curry Sandwich Spread

Makes 2 cups (500 mL)

This mild curry sandwich filling has the look and texture of egg salad, along with a little more protein and no cholesterol. The recipe makes enough filling for four sandwiches. It can also be served as an appetizer with raw vegetables, crackers, or bread.

1 pound (454 g) medium-firm tofu
1/4 cup (60 mL) eggless mayonnaise
1 tablespoon (15 mL) chopped green onion
1 tablespoon (15 mL) chopped fresh parsley
2 teaspoons (10 mL) tamari or soy sauce
1 clove garlic, minced
1/2 teaspoon (2 mL) curry powder
1/2 teaspoon (2 mL) chili powder
1/2 teaspoon (2 mL) nutritional yeast
Salt

Press the tofu for 20 minutes (see page 36). Discard the liquid. Mash the tofu in a small bowl with a fork. Stir in the mayonnaise, green onion, parsley, tamari, garlic, curry powder, chili powder, yeast, and salt to taste.

Per 1/2 cup (125 mL): calories: 119, protein: 10 g, fat: 8 g, carbohydrate: 4 g (1 g from sugar), dietary fibre: 1 g, calcium: 234 mg, iron: 2 mg, magnesium: 45 mg, phosphorus: 145 mg, potassium: 219 mg, sodium: 281 mg, zinc: 1 mg, thiamin: 0.2 mg, riboflavin: 0.2 mg, niacin: 4 mg, vitamin $B_6$: 0.3 mg, folate: 29 mcg, pantothenic acid: 0.2 mg, vitamin $B_{12}$: 0.1 mcg, vitamin A: 5 mcg, vitamin C: 2 mg, vitamin E: 0.1 mg, omega-6 fatty acids: 2 g, omega-3 fatty acids: 0.2 g

Percentage of calories from protein 33%, fat 55%, carbohydrate 12%

# Gee Whiz Spread

Makes 2 cups (500 mL)

Here's a tasty, easy-to-make spread, without the saturated fat and cholesterol of cheese. It's rich in protein, minerals, and B vitamins, and low in fat. It's great on crackers, in sandwiches, and in combination with veggie burgers to make "cheeseburgers." Try it as the dairy-free cheese replacement in Mac Un-Cheese (page 159). If you prefer, replace great northern beans with navy or white kidney beans.

1 1/2 cups (375 mL) cooked or canned great northern beans, drained and rinsed
1/2 cup (125 mL) chopped pimento
6 to 8 tablespoons (90 to 125 mL) nutritional yeast
3 tablespoons (45 mL) lemon juice
2 to 3 tablespoons (30 to 45 mL) tahini
1/2 teaspoon (2 mL) onion powder
1/2 teaspoon (2 mL) prepared yellow mustard
1/2 teaspoon (2 mL) salt

Combine the beans, pimento, yeast, lemon juice, tahini, onion powder, mustard, and salt in the bowl of a food processor and process until smooth. Chill thoroughly before serving.

Per 1/2 cup (125 mL): calories: 173, protein: 12 g, fat: 5 g, carbohydrate: 23 g (1 g from sugar), dietary fibre: 6 g, calcium: 69 mg, iron: 3 mg, magnesium: 57 mg, phosphorus: 282 mg, potassium: 549 mg, sodium: 252 mg, zinc: 3 mg, thiamin: 6 mg, riboflavin: 6 mg, niacin: 36 mg, vitamin $B_6$: 6 mg, folate: 219 mcg, pantothenic acid: 0.8 mg, vitamin $B_{12}$: 4.6 mcg, vitamin A: 34 mcg, vitamin C: 28 mg, vitamin E: 0.6 mg, omega-6 fatty acids: 2 g, omega-3 fatty acids: 0.1 g

Percentage of calories from protein 26%, fat 24%, carbohydrate 50%

# Gooda Cheeze

Makes 3 cups (750 mL)

This creamy, dome-shaped cheese can be sliced or cut into wedges, making it appealing for sandwiches and as an appetizer. The agar dissolves after simmering in water for a few minutes. When removed from the heat, the liquid mixture begins to firm up quickly, so complete the procedure without interruption. (To learn more about the characteristics of agar, see page 27.) Nutritional yeast makes this dish an excellent source of B vitamins, and along with the turmeric and paprika, gives it a golden colour.

1 3/4 cups (435 mL) water
1/2 cup (125 mL) chopped carrots
1/3 cup (85 mL) agar flakes or 2 teaspoons (10 mL) agar powder
1/2 cup (125 mL) unsalted raw cashew pieces
1/4 cup (60 mL) nutritional yeast
3 tablespoons (45 mL) tahini
3 tablespoons (45 mL) lemon juice
1 tablespoon (15 mL) Dijon mustard
2 teaspoons (10 mL) onion powder
1 teaspoon (5 mL) salt
1/2 teaspoon (2 mL) garlic powder
1/2 teaspoon (2 mL) dry mustard
1/4 teaspoon (1 mL) turmeric
1/4 teaspoon (1 mL) paprika
1/4 teaspoon (1 mL) ground cumin

Bring the water, carrots, and agar to a boil in a covered saucepan. Lower the heat and cook for 10 minutes. Pour the carrot mixture into a blender and add the cashews, yeast, tahini, lemon juice, Dijon mustard, onion powder, salt, garlic powder, mustard, turmeric, paprika, and cumin and process until very smooth. Pour immediately into a lightly oiled 3-cup (750 mL) bowl or mould with a rounded bottom. Cover and chill for at least 2 hours. To serve, turn out of mould and slice into thin wedges.

Per 1/2 cup (125 mL): calories: 147, protein: 6 g, fat: 10 g, carbohydrate: 11 g (1 g from sugar), dietary fibre: 1 g, calcium: 38 mg, iron: 2 mg, magnesium: 55 mg, phosphorus: 178 mg, potassium: 259 mg, sodium: 471 mg, zinc: 2 mg, thiamin: 2.7 mg, riboflavin: 2.6 mg, niacin: 16 mg, vitamin $B_6$: 2.5 mg, folate: 86 mcg, pantothenic acid: 0.5 mg, vitamin $B_{12}$: 2 mcg, vitamin A: 185 mcg, vitamin C: 4.8 mg, vitamin E: 0.4 mg, omega-6 fatty acids: 2.7 g, omega-3 fatty acids: 0.1 g

Percentage of calories from protein 16%, fat 58%, carbohydrate 28%

## Heart-Healthy Hummus

Makes 2 1/2 cups (625 mL)

Originating in the Middle East, hummus is popular worldwide thanks to its nutritional profile and excellent taste. This soothing version can be a staple and perhaps even rival your jar of peanut butter. It is a thoroughly nourishing spread to keep near the front of the refrigerator for hungry children and teens.

2 cups (500 mL) cooked or canned chickpeas, drained and rinsed
1/3 cup (85 mL) tahini
1/4 cup (60 mL) water
1/4 cup (60 mL) lemon juice
1 to 2 tablespoons (15 to 30 mL) extra-virgin olive oil (optional)
1 1/2 teaspoons (7 mL) ground cumin
1 clove garlic, chopped
1/2 teaspoon (2 mL) salt
1/4 cup (60 mL) chopped fresh parsley

Combine the chickpeas, tahini, water, lemon juice, oil, cumin, garlic, and salt in the bowl of a food processor. Purée until smooth, occasionally scraping down the sides of the bowl. Add parsley and blend for 5 seconds. Adjust the seasoning and serve.

Per 1/2 cup (125 mL): calories: 223, protein: 9 g, fat: 11 g, carbohydrate: 24 g (4 g from sugar), dietary fibre: 4 g, calcium: 70 mg, iron: 3 mg, magnesium: 54 mg, phosphorus: 259 mg, potassium: 326 mg, sodium: 203 mg, zinc: 2 mg, thiamin: 0.4 mg, riboflavin: 0.1 mg, niacin: 2.4 mg, vitamin $B_6$: 0.1 mg, folate: 142 mcg, pantothenic acid: 0.2 mg, vitamin $B_{12}$: 0 mcg, vitamin A: 30 mcg, vitamin C: 12 mg, vitamin E: 0.7 mg, omega-6 fatty acids: 4.7 g, omega-3 fatty acids: 0.1 g

Percentage of calories from protein 16%, fat 42%, carbohydrate 42%

# Limey Avocado Dip

Makes 1 cup (250 mL)

Many Mexican foods are low in fat—black beans, chili beans, corn, tomato products, and tortilla shells, for instance. Avocados are the exception. They add a creamy, soothing, and colourful touch to a meal or festive occasion. Nutritional yeast packs extra B vitamins into this dip that can be served with crackers or rice cakes, or spread on bread.

2 ripe avocados
1 clove garlic, minced
1 tablespoon (15 mL) lime juice
1 teaspoon (5 mL) nutritional yeast
1/2 teaspoon (2 mL) tamari or soy sauce
1/4 teaspoon (1 mL) chili powder
2 teaspoons (10 mL) chopped green onion
2 teaspoons (10 mL) chopped fresh cilantro or parsley

Scoop the avocado flesh into a small bowl and mash with a fork until smooth. Blend in the garlic, lime juice, yeast, tamari, and chili powder. Stir in the green onion and cilantro. Adjust the seasoning and serve.

Per 1/4 cup (60 mL): calories: 167, protein: 2 g, fat: 15 g, carbohydrate: 8 g (0 g from sugar), dietary fibre: 5 g, calcium: 15 mg, iron: 1 mg, magnesium: 41 mg, phosphorus: 50 mg, potassium: 626 mg, sodium: 46 mg, zinc: 0.5 mg, thiamin: 0.4 mg, riboflavin: 0.4 mg, niacin: 4 mg, vitamin $B_6$: 0.6 mg, folate: 71 mcg, pantothenic acid: 1 mg, vitamin $B_{12}$: 0.2 mcg, vitamin A: 67 mcg, vitamin C: 10 mg, vitamin E: 1 mg, omega-6 fatty acids: 2 g, omega-3 fatty acids: 0.1 g

Percentage of calories from protein 6%, fat 76%, carbohydrate 18%

# Pesto-the-Best-Oh!

Makes 1 1/4 cups (310 mL)

This spread delivers the rich flavours of basil and garlic, along with plenty of valuable omega-3 fatty acids. Enjoy it as a gourmet appetizer on fresh bread, as a pizza sauce (page 164), or on pasta (see the variation to this recipe). Be sure to use fresh walnuts; rancid nuts will overpower the other ingredients. When basil and garlic are in season, make plenty of this pesto and freeze it in small containers for use all winter.

**1 cup (250 mL) walnuts**
**4 cups (1 L) fresh basil leaves and tender stems**
**1/4 cup (60 mL) extra-virgin olive or hemp seed oil**
**2 tablespoons (30 mL) lemon juice**
**2 tablespoons (30 mL) tamari or soy sauce**
**3 to 6 cloves garlic**
**Pinch of black pepper**

Put the walnuts in a food processor and process until fine. Add the basil, oil, lemon juice, tamari, garlic, and pepper and process until smooth.

Per 1/4 cup (60 mL): calories: 253, protein: 5 g, fat: 25 g, carbohydrate: 6 g (1 g from sugar), dietary fibre: 3 g, calcium: 81 mg, iron: 2 mg, magnesium: 66 mg, phosphorus: 111 mg, potassium: 290 mg, sodium: 410 mg, zinc: 1 mg, thiamin: 0.1 mg, riboflavin: 0.1 mg, niacin: 2 mg, vitamin $B_6$: 0.2 mg, folate: 46 mcg, pantothenic acid: 0.2 mg, vitamin $B_{12}$: 0 mcg, vitamin A: 95 mcg, vitamin C: 10 mg, vitamin E: 2 mg, omega-6 fatty acids: 9 g, omega-3 fatty acids: 2 g

Percentage of calories from protein 7%, fat 84%, carbohydrate 9%

**Pesto Pasta**
To use as a pasta sauce, combine 1/2 cup (125 mL) pesto with 1/3 cup (85 mL) hot water or vegetable stock and stir to make a sauce. Add tamari to taste. Stir into 4 cups (1 L) cooked pasta.

## Raw Vegetable Platter

Vegetables deliver more vitamins and protective phytochemicals per calorie than any other food group. A colourful platter of these will balance the high fat content of many dips and thick salad dressings. Cut the veggies in similar shapes or create a variety, such as diagonal slices, cubes, discs, strips, julienne, and spirals.

| Asparagus tips | Cauliflower | Green onions | Snow peas | Turnips (choose young ones) |
|---|---|---|---|---|
| Bok choy | Celery | Jicama | Sweet bell peppers | |
| Broccoli | Cucumbers | Parsnips | | Yams |
| Carrots | Daikon | Radishes | Tomatoes | Zucchini |

Per cup (250 mL) assorted veggies: calories: 38, protein: 1.5 g, fat: 0.3 g, carbohydrate: 8 g (3 from sugar), dietary fibre: 2 g, calcium: 31 mg, iron: 0.6 mg, magnesium: 16 mg, phosphorus: 38 mg, potassium: 292 mg, sodium: 25 mg, zinc: 0.3 mg, thiamin: 0.1 mg, riboflavin: 0.1 mg, niacin: 1 mg, vitamin $B_6$: 0.1 mg, folate: 39 mcg, pantothenic acid: 0.3 mg, vitamin $B_{12}$: 0 mcg, vitamin A: 181 mcg, vitamin C: 41 mg, vitamin E: 0.6 mg, omega-6 fatty acids: 0.1 g, omega-3 fatty acids: 0 g

Percentage of calories from protein 15%, fat 6%, carbohydrate 79%

## Tasty Ways to Stuff Your Pockets

Spread your pita with one or more fillings or spreads, then add veggies and perhaps a sauce and your pita is ready to go. Examples of combinations are hummus, lettuce or sprouts, and Lemon Tahini Dressing (page 122); and warmed refried beans, grated non-dairy cheese, avocado, sprouts, tomato, and salsa.

| Filling or Spread | | |
|---|---|---|
| Black Bean Chipotle Dip (page 85) | Gooda Cheeze (page 89) | Marinated Tofu (page 160) |
| Non-dairy cheese | Hummus (page 90 or commercial) | Walnut, Olive, and Sun-Dried Tomato Tapenade (page 97) |
| Crispy Tofu Slices (page 143) | Lemon Ginger Tempeh (page 155) | Refried beans |
| Curry Sandwich Spread (page 87) | Limey Avocado Dip (page 91) | Sunflower Sesame Spread (page 96) |
| Gee Whiz Spread (page 88) | | |
| **Veggie** | | |
| Avocado, sliced | Jicama, grated | Peppers (red, orange, yellow, green), chopped |
| Beet, grated | Lettuce, chopped | |
| Carrot, shredded | Olives, pitted or sliced | Sprouts (alfalfa, broccoli, lentil, sunflower) |
| Cucumber, sliced | Onion (green, red, sweet, yellow, white), sliced | Tomato, chopped |
| **Sauce** | | |
| Eggless mayonnaise | Salsa | Tabasco |
| Lemon Tahini Dressing (page 122) | Spicy Peanut Sauce (page 218) | |

# Roasted Sunflower or Pumpkin Seeds

Makes 2 cups (500 mL)

These seeds make a savoury alternative to deep-fried potato chips or corn chips. They are great for snacking and to take on hikes or picnics. Or use them as a garnish for salads, baked potatoes, and cooked grains. Easy to make, they provide protein, B vitamins, vitamin E, iron, and zinc.

**2 cups (500 mL) raw sunflower or pumpkin seeds**
**1 tablespoon (15 mL) tamari**
**2 tablespoons (30 mL) nutritional yeast**

Preheat the oven to 300°F (150°C).

Spread seeds evenly on a baking sheet and bake for 7 to 9 minutes. Do not overcook, as they easily can burn (the seeds heat up faster on dark baking pans than on light or glass pans). Transfer seeds to a bowl, stir in the tamari and yeast, and toss to coat evenly. Return the seeds to the baking sheet, then the oven for 1 minute to dry. Let cool before transferring to a jar with a lid for storage. Seeds keep for up to 2 or 3 weeks refrigerated or for up to 6 months in the freezer.

Per 2 tablespoons (30 mL): calories: 112, protein: 5 g, fat: 9 g, carbohydrate: 4 g (0.5 g from sugar), dietary fibre: 2 g, calcium: 23 mg, iron: 1 mg, magnesium: 69 mg, phosphorus: 144 mg, potassium: 149 mg, sodium: 65 mg, zinc: 1 mg, thiamin: 1 mg, riboflavin: 0.5 mg, niacin: 4 mg, vitamin $B_6$: 0.6 mg, folate: 55 mcg, pantothenic acid: 1 mg, vitamin $B_{12}$: 0.4 mcg, vitamin A: 1 mcg, vitamin C: 0 mg, vitamin E: 7 mg, omega-6 fatty acids: 6 g, omega-3 fatty acids: 0 g

Percentage of calories from protein 16%, fat 71%, carbohydrate 13%

**Spicy Toasted Seeds**
For additional flavour, toss the roasted nuts or seeds with 2 teaspoons (10 mL) hot sauce and 1/2 teaspoon (2 mL) garlic powder when adding the tamari, reducing the tamari to 2 teaspoons (10 mL).

## Satisfying Sandwiches, Vegetarian-Style

Let this handy chart inspire you to discover tasty sandwich combinations that include a grain product, filling, and veggies. Add spreads of your choice, such as soy mayonnaise, Dijon mustard, relish, pesto, or salsa. If you like, mix and match any of the grain, filling, and veggie suggestions, or add your own creative touches.

| Grain product | Filling | Veggies |
| --- | --- | --- |
| Baguette or roll | Sunflower Sesame Spread (page 96) | Cucumber slices, thinly sliced red onion, sprouts |
| Crusty roll | Veggie pizza pepperoni (small) slices<br>Walnut, Olive, and Sun-Dried Tomato Tapenade (page 97) | Shredded lettuce, tomatoes, onions, sliced green or red bell pepper |
| Multigrain bread | Curry Sandwich Spread (page 87) | Lettuce, sprouts, tomato slices |
| Pita bread | Heart-Healthy Hummus (page 90) or store-bought, or Black Bean Chipotle Dip (page 85) | Diced tomato, chopped onion, sprouts, olives, romaine lettuce |
| Rice or corn cakes | Gee Whiz Spread (page 88) or Gooda Cheeze (page 89) | Sliced olives, cucumber slices |
| Rice paper wrap | Marinated Tofu (page 160) or Crispy Tofu Slices (page 143) | Shredded carrot, cucumber strips, lettuce, sprouts, sunflower seeds, chopped peanuts |
| Rye bread or roll | Veggie salami or deli slices | Pickles or sauerkraut, onions, lettuce |
| Sourdough or whole-grain roll | Veggie burger | Lettuce, tomato, onion |
| Toasted whole-wheat bread | Canadian veggie bacon, non-dairy cheese slices | Tomato slices, red onion slices |
| Tortilla (plain, tomato, or spinach) | Refried beans, Limey Avocado Dip (page 91), or avocado slices | Sunflower sprouts, shredded carrot, green onions |
| Whole-wheat submarine roll | Veggie ham or turkey and soy cheese slices | Onions, shredded lettuce, cucumber, tomatoes, sprouts |

This is just a beginning. Try International Roll-Ups (page 156), Portabello Mushroom Burgers with Chickpea Topping (page 166), and Vietnamese Salad Roll (page 114). Explore the selection of marinated or smoked tofu, seasoned tempeh or seitan, and flavourful veggie meats at supermarkets. Combine slices and veggies to create a hero sandwich. Japan's contribution to the world of sandwiches is the maki-sushi roll: rice and fillings rolled up and held together by a sheet of nori seaweed. Vegetarian maki-sushi rolls make an excellent lunch-on-the-go that is available at supermarkets, Japanese restaurants, and Japanese food outlets at airports and food courts. To make your own Maki-Sushi Rolls, see page 178.

## Sunflower Sesame Spread

Makes 2 1/4 cups (560 mL)

Commercial sunflower seed butter can be expensive. Here is a way to make your own spread that combines two seeds that are rich in protein, iron, zinc, and vitamin E: sunflower and sesame seeds (in the tahini). This spread can be used in a sandwich, as a filling in the channel of a celery stick, as a stuffing for Baked Stuffed Apples (page 225), or as a dip.

1 cup (250 mL) **sunflower seeds**
1 cup (250 mL) **water**
1/2 cup (125 mL) **tahini**
1/4 cup (60 mL) **lemon juice**
4 teaspoons (20 mL) **tamari**
1 **small clove garlic**
1/2 teaspoon (2 mL) **dried dill**

Soak the sunflower seeds in the water overnight. Drain and reserve the soaking liquid. Place the seeds, 1/2 cup (125 mL) of the soaking liquid, tahini, lemon juice, tamari, garlic, and dill in the bowl of a food processor. Process until smooth.

Per 1/4 cup (60 mL): calories: 184, protein: 7 g, fat: 16 g, carbohydrate: 7 g (1 g from sugar), dietary fibre: 2 g, calcium: 42 mg, iron: 2 mg, magnesium: 75 mg, phosphorus: 235 mg, potassium: 198 mg, sodium: 157 mg, zinc: 2 mg, thiamin: 0.6 mg, riboflavin: 0.1 mg, niacin: 3 mg, vitamin $B_6$: 0.2 mg, folate: 53 mcg, pantothenic acid: 1 mg, vitamin $B_{12}$: 0 mcg, vitamin A: 2 mcg, vitamin C: 4 mg, vitamin E: 6 mg, omega-6 fatty acids: 9 g, omega-3 fatty acids: 0.1 g

Percentage of calories from protein 14%, fat 14%, carbohydrate 72%

## Walnut, Olive, and Sun-Dried Tomato Tapenade

Makes 1 1/4 cups (310 mL)

Tapenade is a spread that originates in the French region of Provence and is traditionally made with olives and capers. In this recipe, the substitution of walnuts for most of the olives reduces the sodium and provides a significant amount of omega-3 fatty acids. This recipe tastes best with fresh basil but can also work with the dried herb.

1 cup (250 mL) walnuts
1/2 cup (125 mL) pitted black kalamata olives
1/2 cup (125 mL) sun-dried tomatoes, soaked in water for 4 hours, then drained
2 tablespoons (30 mL) capers
2 tablespoons (30 mL) lemon juice
1 small clove garlic, chopped
1 tablespoon (15 mL) chopped fresh parsley
1 1/2 teaspoons (7 mL) chopped fresh basil or 1/2 teaspoon (2 mL) dried

Place the walnuts in the bowl of a food processor and process for 15 seconds or until the walnuts are a mealy crumb texture. Add the olives, sun-dried tomatoes, capers, lemon juice, and garlic and process until the mixture turns into a paste, stopping two or three times to scrape down the sides of the bowl. Add the parsley and process for 10 seconds. Transfer to a serving bowl.

Per 1/4 cup (60 mL): calories: 74, protein: 2 g, fat: 6 g, carbohydrate: 6 g (2 g from sugar), dietary fibre: 2 g, calcium: 31 mg, iron: 1 mg, magnesium: 24 mg, phosphorus: 44 mg, potassium: 242 mg, sodium: 348 mg, zinc: 0.4 mg, thiamin: 0.1 mg, riboflavin: 0 mg, niacin: 1 mg, vitamin $B_6$: 0.1 mg, folate: 13 mcg, pantothenic acid: 0.2 mg, vitamin $B_{12}$: 0 mcg, vitamin A: 19 mcg, vitamin C: 7 mg, vitamin E: 0.3 mg, omega-6 fatty acids: 2.4 g, omega-3 fatty acids: 0.6 g

Percentage of calories from protein 10%, fat 61%, carbohydrate 29%

## What Will I Spread On My Bread or Toast?

Which is the lesser of two evils, butter or margarine? If you've become tired of this debate, opt for spreads that offer nutritional pluses found in neither. For example, almond butter is a tasty source of calcium. Cashew butter provides zinc. The combination of tahini and blackstrap molasses is sweet and rich in calcium, iron, and other minerals. Gee Whiz Spread (page 88) is high in nutritional value yet low in calories. All of the suggestions below offer wonderfully satisfying flavour.

### Commercial Spreads

- Nut butters (such as almond or cashew butter)
- Fruit-sweetened jams
- Miso (thinly spread)
- Seed butters (such as sunflower butter or tahini)
- Tahini, along with a thin layer of blackstrap molasses
- Pestos
- Tapenades
- Bean dips

### Recipes

- Black Bean Chipotle Dip (page 85)
- Curry Sandwich Spread (page 87)
- Gee Whiz Spread (page 88)
- Gooda Cheeze (page 89)
- Heart-Healthy Hummus (page 90)
- Limey Avocado Dip (page 91)
- Sunflower Sesame Spread (page 96)
- Walnut, Olive, and Sun-Dried Tomato Tapenade (page 97)
- White Bean, Olive, and Thyme Spread (page 99)

# White Bean, Olive, and Thyme Spread

Makes 2 1/4 cups (560 mL)

Common white beans include navy, great northern, and cannellini (white kidney) beans. These often are used in soups, casseroles, and baked with tomato sauce. Try any of these white beans in this spread and serve with vegetable sticks, crackers, or any of the grain products listed in the Satisfying Sandwiches chart (page 95). The flavour of this mineral-rich spread will deepen if it is allowed to sit for a couple of hours before serving.

2 1/2 cups (625 mL) cooked or canned white beans, drained and rinsed
1 clove garlic, chopped
1/4 cup (60 mL) lemon juice
1 tablespoon (15 mL) extra-virgin olive oil
1 teaspoon (5 mL) dried thyme
1/2 teaspoon (2 mL) salt
1/4 teaspoon (1 mL) black pepper
1/4 cup (60 mL) pitted and chopped green or black olives, about 8 medium olives
2 tablespoons (30 mL) chopped fresh parsley

Place beans, garlic, lemon juice, oil, thyme, salt, and pepper in the bowl of a food processor and purée until smooth. Add the olives and parsley and pulse mixture for about 5 seconds to incorporate. Season to taste. Transfer the spread into a bowl or covered container and refrigerate to marry and deepen the flavours.

Per 1/2 cup (125 mL): calories: 272, protein: 10 g, fat: 14 g, carbohydrate: 29 g (0 g from sugar), dietary fibre: 11 g, calcium: 95 mg, iron: 4 mg, magnesium: 75 mg, phosphorus: 182 mg, potassium: 520 mg, sodium: 281 mg, zinc: 1 mg, thiamin: 0.3 mg, riboflavin: 0.1 mg, niacin: 2 mg, vitamin $B_6$: 0.2 mg, folate: 149 mcg, pantothenic acid: 0.3 mg, vitamin $B_{12}$: 0 mcg, vitamin A: 19 mcg, vitamin C: 9 mg, vitamin E: 2 mg, omega-6 fatty acids: 1 g, omega-3 fatty acids: 0.2 g

Percentage of calories from protein 14%, fat 44%, carbohydrate 42%

# Salads

## Calcium-Rich Greens

Makes 7 1/2 cups (1.875 L)

Kale can be eaten raw, as in this dish, or steamed. When raw, it is best sliced very fine, since it's fibrous. Here kale is combined with napa cabbage (also known as Chinese cabbage or sui choy) and broccoli, two other greens chosen for their high calcium availability. Greens are potent providers of protein, beta carotene (converted in the body to vitamin A), folate, and beneficial plant oils. Serve with Oriental Dressing (page 127) or Lemon Tahini Dressing (page 124).

To cut the kale, remove the leaves from the stems and slice matchstick thin. Cut the cabbage leaves in half lengthwise and then slice.

**2 cups (500 mL) very thinly sliced kale leaves (stems removed)**
**2 cups (500 mL) 1/4-inch (5 mm) thick strips napa cabbage**
**2 1/2 cups (625 mL) broccoli florets and peeled, sliced stem**
**1 cup (250 mL) diced red bell pepper**

Toss the kale, napa cabbage, broccoli, and red pepper together in a bowl or serve on a platter.

Per 2 cups (500 mL): calories: 52, protein: 4 g, fat: 0.6 g, carbohydrate: 11 g (2 g from sugar), dietary fibre: 4 g, calcium: 112 mg, iron: 1 mg, magnesium: 43 mg, phosphorus: 85 mg, potassium: 484 mg, sodium: 36 mg, zinc: 0.6 mg, thiamin: 0.1 mg, riboflavin: 0.1 mg, niacin: 2 mg, vitamin $B_6$: 0.4 mg, folate: 64 mcg, pantothenic acid: 0.4 mg, vitamin $B_{12}$: 0 mcg, vitamin A: 460 mcg, vitamin C: 185 mg, vitamin E: 1 mg, omega-6 fatty acids: 0.1 g, omega-3 fatty acids: 0.2 g

Percentage of calories from protein 24%, fat 8%, carbohydrate 68%

# Curry Basmati Rice Salad with Currants

Makes 4 1/2 cups (1.125 L)

Basmati is long-grain rice that has been grown in the foothills of the Himalayas since ancient times; either white or the slower-cooking brown basmati can be used (see variation). Its name means "the fragrant one" in Sanskrit, and in this recipe its mild, nutty aroma and flavour combine well with the sweetness of the currants. Both turmeric and coriander contain potent antioxidants. Turmeric has cancer-protective qualities, and coriander seed has long been used as an aid to digestion.

1/4 cup (60 mL) currants, soaked in 1/4 cup (60 mL) water
1 3/4 cups (435 mL) water
1 cup (250 mL) white basmati rice
1/2 teaspoon (2 mL) salt
Pinch of turmeric
1 tablespoon (15 mL) Indian curry paste
2 tablespoons (30 mL) lime juice
1 cup (250 mL) finely diced red bell pepper
2 tablespoons (30 mL) chopped fresh cilantro or parsley
1 teaspoon (5 mL) coriander seed, crushed (optional)

Soak currants in their soaking water for 20 minutes. In the meantime, bring 1 3/4 cups (435 mL) water to a boil. Stir in the rice, salt, and turmeric. Reduce heat to low, cover, and simmer for 20 minutes, then remove from heat and allow the rice to cool.

Put the curry paste in a small bowl. Strain the soaking water from the currants and gradually add this water to the curry paste, stirring to form a smooth mixture. Stir in lime juice. Add the curry mixture to the rice, along with the red pepper, cilantro, coriander seed, and currants. Stir until the ingredients are evenly distributed.

Per cup (250 mL): calories: 220, protein: 3 g, fat: 2 g, carbohydrate: 52 g (7 g from sugar), dietary fibre: 3 g, calcium: 22 mg, iron: 2 mg, magnesium: 13 mg, phosphorus: 26 mg, potassium: 181 mg, sodium: 215 mg, zinc: 0.2 mg, thiamin: 0.2 mg, riboflavin: 0.1 mg, niacin: 2 mg, vitamin $B_6$: 0.1 mg, folate: 12 mcg, pantothenic acid: 0.1 mg, vitamin $B_{12}$: 0 mcg, vitamin A: 63 mcg, vitamin C: 71 mg, vitamin E: 1 mg, omega-6 fatty acids: 0.2 g, omega-3 fatty acids: 0 g

Percentage of calories from protein 6%, fat 6%, carbohydrate 88%

**Variation:**
Replace the white rice with brown basmati rice, increasing the cooking water to 2 cups (500 mL) and cooking for 45 minutes.

# Fiesta Quinoa Salad with Lime Dressing

Makes 4 1/2 cups (1.125 L)

Quinoa (pronounced "keen-wa") is an ancient grain native to the high Andes regions of South America. It was introduced to North America in the 1980s. It is often called a supergrain because of its excellent protein content and nutritional profile. In nature, quinoa is coated with a slightly bitter resin, a natural repellent that is unpopular with birds and insects. Most commercial quinoa has been pre-rinsed; however, before cooking, it's best to wash the grain in a fine sieve until the rinse water is no longer foamy.

## Quinoa

1 1/2 cups (375 mL) water
1 cup (250 mL) quinoa, rinsed and thoroughly drained
1/2 teaspoon (2 mL) salt

## Lime Dressing

1/4 cup (60 mL) lime juice
2 tablespoons (30 mL) extra-virgin olive or flaxseed oil
1 teaspoon (5 mL) toasted sesame oil
Pinch of black pepper

## Salad

1/2 cup (125 mL) diced cucumber
1/2 cup (125 mL) corn kernels, fresh or frozen
1/4 cup (60 mL) diced red bell pepper
2 tablespoons (30 mL) finely chopped green onion
4 teaspoons (20 mL) finely chopped fresh cilantro

To make quinoa, bring water to a boil over high heat, stir in quinoa and salt, reduce heat, then cover and simmer for 15 minutes or until all the water is absorbed. Set aside to cool.

To make dressing, combine lime juice, olive oil, sesame oil, and pepper in a small bowl. Pour over cooled quinoa and toss gently with a fork. Adjust seasoning.

To assemble the salad, add the cucumber, corn, red pepper, green onion, and cilantro to the dressed quinoa. Stir well to incorporate all ingredients, adjust the seasoning, and serve.

Per cup (250 mL): calories: 249, protein: 7 g, fat: 10 g, carbohydrate: 35 g (3 g from sugar), dietary fibre: 4 g, calcium: 32 mg, iron: 4 mg, magnesium: 89 mg, phosphorus: 171 mg, potassium: 437 mg, sodium: 221 mg, zinc: 1 mg, thiamin: 0.1 mg, riboflavin: 0.2 mg, niacin: 2 mg, vitamin $B_6$: 0.1 mg, folate: 26 mcg, pantothenic acid: 0.5 mg, vitamin $B_{12}$: 0 mcg, vitamin A: 36 mcg, vitamin C: 23 mg, vitamin E: 1 mg, omega-6 fatty acids: 2 g, omega-3 fatty acids: 0.1 g

Percentage of calories from protein 11%, fat 35%, carbohydrate 54%

# French Potato Salad

Makes 10 cups (2.5 L)

This delicious marinated potato salad is ideal for a large family gathering, potluck dinner, or picnic. The best potatoes to use are the waxy or boiling potatoes, rather than the baking varieties such as the russet. Pick red or yellow potatoes, as they hold their shape well when boiled. This salad will keep for several days stored in the refrigerator in a sealed container. Fresh peppers add crispiness and contrast well with the soft texture of the cooked potatoes.

3 1/2 pounds (1.6 kg) red potatoes, scrubbed and cut into 1-inch (2.5 cm) dice, about 11 cups (2.75 L)
1/3 cup (85 mL) red wine vinegar
1/4 cup (60 mL) extra-virgin olive oil
2 tablespoons (30 mL) Dijon mustard
1 teaspoon (5 mL) caraway seeds
1 teaspoon (5 mL) paprika
1 teaspoon (5 mL) salt
1/2 teaspoon (2 mL) black pepper
1/2 cup (125 mL) sliced black or green olives
1/2 cup (125 mL) chopped red bell peppers, cut into 1/4-inch (5 mm) dice
1/2 cup (125 mL) chopped yellow, orange, or green bell peppers, cut into 1/4-inch (5 mm) dice
1/4 cup (60 mL) diced green onion
1/4 cup (60 mL) chopped fresh parsley

Place potatoes in a large pot, pour in enough water to cover, and cook over medium-low heat for 8 to 10 minutes or until soft when pierced with a knife. Do not overcook. Drain and place in a large bowl.

Combine vinegar, oil, mustard, caraway, paprika, salt, and pepper in a small bowl and mix thoroughly. While the potatoes are still warm, pour the oil-and-vinegar mixture over the potatoes. Refrigerate for 1 hour to allow potatoes to absorb the flavour. Add the olives, red and yellow peppers, green onion, and parsley. Toss gently to mix.

Per cup (250 mL): calories: 194, protein: 4 g, fat: 9 g, carbohydrate: 31 g (3 g from sugar), dietary fibre: 3 g, calcium: 29 mg, iron: 2 mg, magnesium: 38 mg, phosphorus: 88 mg, potassium: 933 mg, sodium: 383 mg, zinc: 1 mg, thiamin: 0.2 mg, riboflavin: 0.2 mg, niacin: 4 mg, vitamin $B_6$: 0.5 mg, folate: 28 mcg, pantothenic acid: 1 mg, vitamin $B_{12}$: 0 mcg, vitamin A: 28 mcg, vitamin C: 64 mg, vitamin E: 1.2 mg, omega-6 fatty acids: 0.6 g, omega-3 fatty acids: 0.1 g

Percentage of calories from protein 8%, fat 30%, carbohydrate 62%

# Garden of Plenty Salad

Makes 7 1/2 quarts (7.5 L)

Spend half an hour assembling this recipe and you will have abundant salad for a big gathering or fresh salad, at a moment's notice, for up to 5 days. Store it in one or two large containers with a good seal. To keep salad for more than 2 days, it works well to add the romaine lettuce and red pepper fresh every 2 days. Serve it with Liquid Gold Dressing (page 123), Lemon Tahini Dressing (page 122), Oriental Dressing (page 125), or another favourite dressing.

5 large kale leaves
5 large romaine leaves
5 napa cabbage leaves
1/4 medium head of red cabbage, about 7 ounces (200 g)
1 stalk broccoli, about 10 ounces (284 g)
1/2 small head cauliflower, about 10 ounces (284 g)
3 to 4 carrots, about 10 ounces (284 g)
1 red bell pepper, about 7 ounces (200 g)

Remove the stems from the kale and cut the leaves into matchsticks. Tear the lettuce into bite-size pieces. Cut the napa cabbage leaves in half lengthwise, and slice into 1/4-inch (5 mm) long strips. Slice the red cabbage into thin slices. Cut the broccoli and cauliflower into bite-size florets. The broccoli stem can be peeled and diced. Slice the carrots and red pepper into 1/4-inch (5 mm) strips. Combine and toss all in a large bowl.

Per 3 cups (750 mL): calories: 56, protein: 3 g, fat: 0.5 g, carbohydrate: 12 g (5 g from sugar), dietary fibre: 4 g, calcium: 90 mg, iron: 1 mg, magnesium: 29 mg, phosphorus: 75 mg, potassium: 523 mg, sodium: 56 mg, zinc: 0.5 mg, thiamin: 0.1 mg, riboflavin: 0.2 mg, niacin: 2 mg, vitamin $B_6$: 0.3 mg, folate: 84 mcg, pantothenic acid: 0.6 mg, vitamin $B_{12}$: 0 mcg, vitamin A: 461 mcg, vitamin C: 128 mg, vitamin E: 1 mg, omega-6 fatty acids: 0.1 g, omega-3 fatty acids: 0.1 g

Percentage of calories from protein 21%, fat 7%, carbohydrate 72%

# Kale and Red Pepper Holly Ring

Makes about 5 1/2 cups (1.375 L)

The deep green kale tossed with bright red bell peppers resembles a small holly wreath when presented in a circle on a platter. This simple yet elegant dish is perfect for the holiday season and adds colour and a festive touch to a dinner any time of the year. For smaller gatherings, you may want to divide the recipe in half, or for larger gatherings, double it. This dish is a rich source of calcium; iron; potassium; the antioxidant vitamins A, C, and E; and omega-3 fatty acids.

12 cups (3 L) packed thinly sliced kale leaves, stems removed
3 tablespoons (45 mL) flaxseed or extra-virgin olive oil
4 teaspoons (20 mL) balsamic vinegar
4 teaspoons (20 mL) tamari or soy sauce
1/2 cup (125 mL) diced red bell pepper

Place kale in a steamer. Cover and steam over medium-high heat until kale is soft to the bite. Drain in a colander and squeeze out any excess water. Combine the oil, vinegar, and tamari in a large bowl. Add kale, toss to coat the leaves with dressing, and arrange on a warm platter. Create a round wreath shape by pushing the kale toward the edges of the platter, leaving an open space in the centre. Sprinkle with the red pepper and serve.

Per cup (250 mL): calories: 153, protein: 6 g, fat: 9 g, carbohydrate: 17 g (1 g from sugar), dietary fibre: 3 g, calcium: 210 mg, iron: 3 mg, magnesium: 56 mg, phosphorus: 96 mg, potassium: 730 mg, sodium: 315 mg, zinc: 1 mg, thiamin: 0.2 mg, riboflavin: 0.2 mg, niacin: 3 mg, vitamin $B_6$: 0.5 mg, folate: 48 mcg, pantothenic acid: 0.2 mg, vitamin $B_{12}$: 0 mcg, vitamin A: 1210 mcg, vitamin C: 212 mg, vitamin E: 3 mg, omega-6 fatty acids: 1.2 g, omega-3 fatty acids: 4.3 g

Percentage of calories from protein 14%, fat 46%, carbohydrate 40%

# Kamut, Tomato, and Avocado Salad

Makes 4 1/2 cups (1.125 L)

Kamut is a trademark name for an ancient grain that is a close relative to durum wheat—the wheat used for making pasta. Some people with sensitivities to wheat find that they can tolerate Kamut or spelt (see the variation of this recipe). Kamut has a sweet taste, soft chewy texture, and blends well with the other flavours in this simple, nutritious, and refreshing salad.

3 cups (750 mL) water
1 cup (250 mL) Kamut berries, rinsed
1/2 teaspoon (2 mL) salt
2 medium tomatoes, diced
1 ripe avocado, diced
1/2 cup (125 mL) diced cucumber
3 tablespoons (45 mL) lemon juice
2 tablespoons (30 mL) extra-virgin olive or hemp seed oil
1/2 teaspoon (2 mL) ground toasted cumin seeds (see page 133)
1/4 cup (60 mL) chopped fresh parsley

Bring the water to a boil over high heat, then stir in the Kamut berries and salt. Reduce heat to low, cover, and simmer for 45 minutes or until berries are soft to the bite. Drain the excess water and set the grain aside to cool. In the meantime, combine the tomatoes, avocado, cucumber, lemon juice, oil, cumin, and parsley in a medium bowl. Add the cooled Kamut, adjust the seasoning, and serve.

Per cup (250 mL): calories: 304, protein: 7 g, fat: 14 g, carbohydrate: 40 g (3 g from sugar), dietary fibre: 12 g, calcium: 29 mg, iron: 2 mg, magnesium: 86 mg, phosphorus: 167 mg, potassium: 614 mg, sodium: 224 mg, zinc: 2 mg, thiamin: 0.2 mg, riboflavin: 0.1 mg, niacin: 2 mg, vitamin $B_6$: 0.2 mg, folate: 44 mcg, pantothenic acid: 0.5 mg, vitamin $B_{12}$: 0 mcg, vitamin A: 105 mcg, vitamin C: 20 mg, vitamin E: 2 mg, omega-6 fatty acids: 2 g, omega-3 fatty acids: 0.1 g

Percentage of calories from protein 9%, fat 40%, carbohydrate 51%

**Variation:**
Replace Kamut with whole spelt berries.

# Multi-Coloured Bean and Vegetable Salad

Makes 6 cups (1.5 L)

Enjoy different-coloured beans in this salad, perhaps trying others beyond those listed below. When chlorophyll-containing green vegetables are immersed in acids such as lemon juice or vinegar, their lovely colour becomes dull. To retain a bright green colour, it is best to put green peppers, broccoli, and other greens in the marinade, which contains vinegar, immediately before serving.

## Marinade

1/4 cup (60 mL) lemon juice or apple cider vinegar
2 tablespoons (30 mL) extra-virgin olive oil
1 teaspoon (5 mL) garlic powder
1 teaspoon (5 mL) dried dill
1 teaspoon (5 mL) Dijon mustard
1/2 teaspoon (2 mL) salt
1/2 teaspoon (2 mL) black pepper

## Beans

3 cups (750 mL) cooked or canned beans, such as black, pinto, red, white, or garbanzo

## Vegetables

1 cup (250 mL) diced yellow bell pepper
1 cup (250 mL) cherry tomatoes, sliced in half
1 cup (250 mL) chopped celery

To make the marinade, put lemon juice, oil, garlic powder, dill, mustard, salt, and pepper in a jar and shake, or in a bowl and whisk, until blended.

To prepare the beans, rinse the beans to remove the cooking or canning liquid. Drain well. Place the beans and marinade in a large bowl and gently toss to coat the beans. Refrigerate for 6 hours so the marinade flavours penetrate the beans. Stir occasionally.

Stir in the bell pepper, cherry tomatoes, and celery just before serving.

Per cup (250 mL): calories: 197, protein: 9 g, fat: 6 g, carbohydrate: 29 g (3 g from sugar), dietary fibre: 10 g, calcium: 50 mg, iron: 2 mg, magnesium: 66 mg, phosphorus: 171 mg, potassium: 470 mg, sodium: 426 mg, zinc: 1 mg, thiamin: 0.2 mg, riboflavin: 0.1 mg, niacin: 3 mg, vitamin $B_6$: 0.2 mg, folate: 147 mcg, pantothenic acid: 0.4 mg, vitamin $B_{12}$: 0 mcg, vitamin A: 18 mcg, vitamin C: 58 mg, vitamin E: 1 mg, omega-6 fatty acids: 0.2 g, omega-3 fatty acids: 0.1 g

Percentage of calories from protein 19%, fat 24%, carbohydrate 57%

**Variation:**
Replace the 3 cups (750 mL) of vegetables with any combination of the following: yellow cherry tomatoes; olives; trimmed snow peas; chopped asparagus; chopped red, orange, or green bell peppers; chopped napa cabbage; chopped green beans sliced zucchini; broccoli florets; or cauliflower florets.

# Spicy Marinated Tofu Salad

Makes 7 cups (1.75 L)

Just one-quarter of this colourful salad provides 17 grams of protein and 11 milligrams of iron. After straining the tofu from the marinade, reserve the flavour-rich liquid—it will keep for up to 3 or 4 days in the refrigerator or for up to 6 months in the freezer. Thicken the drained marinade with arrowroot powder to make a sauce for Stir-Fry 101 (page 174) or reuse it to make another batch of Marinated Tofu (page 160).

1 recipe Marinated Tofu (page 160), cut into 1/2-inch (1 cm) cubes
1 tablespoon (15 mL) extra-virgin olive oil
1 teaspoon (5 mL) toasted sesame oil
1 teaspoon (5 mL) chili paste
1 teaspoon (5 mL) tamari or soy sauce
1 teaspoon (5 mL) rice vinegar
1 cup (250 mL) thinly sliced carrots
1 cup (250 mL) thinly sliced celery
1 cup (250 mL) snow peas, quartered diagonally
1 cup (250 mL) sliced cucumber
1 cup (250 mL) diced red bell pepper
1/4 cup (60 mL) sliced green onion
1/4 cup (60 mL) chopped fresh cilantro or parsley
1 tablespoon (15 mL) toasted sesame seeds (optional; see page 133)

Strain the tofu and reserve the liquid. Combine the olive oil, sesame oil, chili paste, tamari, and vinegar in a small bowl. Put the carrots, celery, snow peas, cucumber, red pepper, green onion, and cilantro in large bowl and toss with the dressing. Mix in the tofu, sprinkle the sesame seeds on top, and serve.

Per cup (250 mL): calories: 132, protein: 10 g, fat: 8 g, carbohydrate: 9 g (3 g from sugar), dietary fibre: 3 g, calcium: 371 mg, iron: 6 mg, magnesium: 45 mg, phosphorus: 133 mg, potassium: 362 mg, sodium: 246 mg, zinc: 1 mg, thiamin: 0.2 mg, riboflavin: 0.1 mg, niacin: 0.2 mg, vitamin B$_6$: 0.2 mg, folate: 42 mcg, pantothenic acid: 0.4 mg, vitamin B$_{12}$: 0 mcg, vitamin A: 204 mcg, vitamin C: 60 mg, vitamin E: 1 mg, omega-6 fatty acids: 3 g, omega-3 fatty acids: 0.3 g

Percentage of calories from protein 27%, fat 49%, carbohydrate 24%

# Sprouted Lentil Salad Plate

Makes 1 serving

Salads are an excellent way of incorporating the recommended nine or more servings of fruit and vegetables a day. Lentils, which can be sprouted in as short a time as 2 days (see page 112), occupy the centre of this plate; along with the tomatoes, walnuts, and olives, they make for an attractive, nourishing, and protein-rich meal. See the Salad Bar recipe (page 172) for ideas of other vegetable choices that you might enjoy. If you like, add Cucumber Dill Dressing (page 121), Coconut Almond Dressing (page 119), or another favourite dressing.

**1 cup (250 mL) Sprouted Lentils (page 112)**
**5 tomato wedges**
**5 whole, unpitted kalamata olives**
**5 walnut halves**
**1/2 avocado**

Place the sprouts in the centre of the plate. Arrange the tomato wedges above the sprouts. Flank the tomatoes with the olives on one side and the walnuts on the other. Remove the avocado pit. Insert the edge of a soup spoon between the avocado pulp and its skin. Carefully scoop out the pulp in one piece and place it on a cutting board. Make thin strips lengthwise starting 1/2-inch (1 cm) from narrow end of the avocado through to the bottom. With light pressure from your hand and at a 45-degree angle, push the avocado so that it fans out. Place the narrow end of the avocado near the edge of the plate and the fanned part spread out against the bed of sprouts.

Per serving: calories: 448, protein: 13 g, fat: 34 g, carbohydrate: 34 g (4 g from sugar), dietary fibre: 11 g, calcium: 61 mg, iron: 5 mg, magnesium: 109 mg, phosphorus: 270 mg, potassium: 1123 mg, sodium: 332 mg, zinc: 2 mg, thiamin: 0.4 mg, riboflavin: 0.3 mg, niacin: 5 mg, vitamin $B_6$: 0.6 mg, folate: 175 mcg, pantothenic acid: 2 mg, vitamin $B_{12}$: 0 mcg, vitamin A: 114 mcg, vitamin C: 36 mg, vitamin E: 2 mg, omega-6 fatty acids: 10 g, omega-3 fatty acids: 2 g

Percentage of calories from protein 11%, fat 62%, carbohydrate 27%

# Sprouted Mung Beans and Lentils

Mung beans and lentils are seeds with the potential and life force to grow into large, strong plants. As such, these little embryos contain a rich store of vitamins, minerals, proteins, fats, and carbohydrates, waiting and ready for the right conditions of heat, moisture, and oxygen to be present in order to grow. As soon as seeds germinate, chemical changes occur, including some that provide us with health benefits. For example—

- When mung beans and lentils are sprouted, protein is created; protein quality improves (with increased amounts of essential amino acids) and the digestibility of the protein present increases.
- Trypsin inhibitors (anti-nutrients that reduce protein digestibility) are destroyed during germination.
- Starch is converted to the more easily assimilated simple sugars; glucose and fructose increase tenfold when mung beans are sprouted.
- Sprouting significantly increases the content of enzymes, including those that break down or begin the digestion of protein and starch.
- The carbohydrates that can produce gas (flatulence) largely disappear when mung beans are sprouted.
- Sprouting stimulates the production of quantities of antioxidants that protect us against disease.
- The vitamin C content of the original legume increases 17 times in the case of sprouted lentils and eight times in the case of mung beans.
- The riboflavin content of mung bean triples and that of lentils increases by 50 percent during germination. The content of other B vitamins also increases.
- Phytate-mineral complexes are broken down during sprouting, greatly increasing mineral availability.
- The small amounts of hemagglutinins that are present in raw lentils and mung beans are destroyed by germination, making these raw sprouts safe to eat. (Most legumes contain too much of these illness-producing proteins to be eaten in a raw form, though hemagglutinins are completely destroyed by cooking. Thus, though sprouted mung beans and lentils are safe, other legumes should be eaten in the cooked form only.)

Take mung beans, lentils, and other sproutable seeds along on a sailing trip away from ports or when camping in remote areas, when access to produce markets is limited—fresh sprout salads can provide wholesome nutrition. During winter months when garden produce is not available, sprouts can provide fresh food and an excellent source of vitamin C.

The equipment needed to grow sprouts is simple and economical. A wide mouth 1-quart (1 L) canning (Mason) jar is sufficient for kitchen sprouting. A sprouting lid or mesh screen is needed for the top, to allow rinse water to flow out without the sprouts falling out of the jar. Plastic sprouting lids can be purchased at natural foods stores for this purpose, or you can use a piece of mesh screen or cotton cheesecloth across the mouth of the jar and hold in place with a rubber band. A dish rack is helpful, though not essential, to hold the jar at an angle to completely drain the water after rinsing.

## Sprouted Mung Beans and Lentils

Makes 3 to 4 cups (750 mL to 1 L) sprouts

**1/4 cup (60 mL) dried mung beans or 1/2 cup (125 mL) dried lentils, picked over and rinsed**
**2 cups (500 mL) water**

Put the mung beans or lentils in a 1-quart (1 L) sprouting jar and add the water. Put a mesh screen or sprouting lid on the jar and let sit at room temperature for 12 to 24 hours. Drain the beans or lentils, then rinse them thoroughly with cool water, and drain again. Repeat this two or three times.

Place the jar, with its screen in place, upside down at a 45-degree angle over a saucer (so that water may run off) or in a dish rack. Cover the jar with a tea towel or place it away from sunlight so the sprouts can grow in the dark.

Rinse and drain the beans two or three times a day for 3 to 5 days, until a 1/4-inch (5 mm) tail is visible on the lentils and a 1-inch (2.5 cm) tail is visible on the mung beans. Store the sprouts in a sealed container in the refrigerator for up to 1 week. Rinse every 3 days.

**Note:** Homegrown mung bean sprouts will have much shorter tails than commercially grown sprouts. The tails become longer if mung beans are grown under a weight that exerts pressure on them.

---

### Roasting Nuts and Seeds (Oven Method)

Preheat the oven to 300°F (150°C).

Lightly dry-roasting nuts such as almonds, cashews, hazelnuts, pecans, and walnuts, and seeds such as pumpkin, sesame, and sunflower seeds, accentuates their flavour. Spread the nuts or seeds in a single layer on a cookie sheet—this is so that they heat evenly and don't burn. Pick through them and remove any foreign matter, such as pieces of the husk, dirt, and pebbles. Place the sheet on the middle rack of the oven. For nuts, remove the cookie sheet every 5 minutes to check doneness during a cooking time of up to 15 minutes. For seeds, check every 3 to 4 minutes; they will be roasted after 7 or 8 minutes. Allow the nuts and seeds to cool before storing them in air-tight, sealed jars or containers in a cool, dry place. Refrigerating or freezing the nuts and seeds will prolong their shelf life and flavour.

# Thai Pasta Salad with Spicy Peanut Dressing

Makes 8 cups (2 L)

The appetizing dressing for this pasta salad is inspired by the rich flavours of Thai cuisine. The majority of Thai noodles are made from rice, a staple cereal grain that grows throughout Southeast Asia. If you have wheat or gluten sensitivity, replace the wheat pasta in this recipe with rice pasta or noodles. Other fresh vegetables that work well in this salad include thinly sliced carrots, broccoli, Chinese cabbage, celery, mung sprouts, shelled peas, snap peas, yellow beans, and zucchini.

**2 quarts (2 L) water**
**1/2 teaspoon (2 mL) salt**
**2 1/2 cups (625 mL) uncooked whole-wheat pasta spirals**
**3/4 cup (185 mL) Spicy Peanut Sauce (page 218)**
**1 cup (250 mL) diced cucumber**
**1 cup (250 mL) diced tomatoes**
**1 cup (250 mL) sliced green beans**
**1 cup (250 mL) trimmed and sliced snow peas**
**1/2 cup (125 mL) roasted peanuts (optional)**
**1/4 cup (60 mL) chopped green onion**
**2 tablespoons (30 mL) lime juice**
**2 tablespoons (30 mL) chopped fresh cilantro or parsley**

Pour the water into a large pot, add the salt, and bring to a boil. Stir in the pasta and cook according to the package directions. When the pasta is cooked, plunge it into cold water, drain well, and transfer to a mixing bowl. Add the peanut sauce, cucumber, tomatoes, green beans, snow peas, peanuts, green onion, lime juice, and cilantro. Mix well and serve.

Per cup (250 mL): calories: 196, protein: 7 g, fat: 6 g, carbohydrate: 30 g (5 g from sugar), dietary fibre: 3 g, calcium: 39 mg, iron: 2.4 mg, magnesium: 44 mg, phosphorus: 95 mg, potassium: 332 mg, sodium: 355 mg, zinc: 1 mg, thiamin: 0.4 mg, riboflavin: 0.2 mg, niacin: 4 mg, vitamin $B_6$: 0.2 mg, folate: 94 mcg, pantothenic acid: 0.6 mg, vitamin $B_{12}$: 0 mcg, vitamin A: 17 mcg, vitamin C: 21 mg, vitamin E: 1 mg, omega-6 fatty acids: 1.4 g, omega-3 fatty acids: 0 g

Percentage of calories from protein 14%, fat 27%, carbohydrate 59%

# Vietnamese Salad Roll

Makes 1 roll

After the ingredients for this salad roll are laid out before you, the rolls can be assembled with ease. For inside the roll and for dipping, Spicy Peanut Sauce (page 218), Lemon Tahini Dressing (page 122), Teriyaki Sauce (page 220), or a plum sauce create a deliciously wide range of flavour possibilities. Experiment with filling ingredients too, for example by replacing avocado with Crispy Tofu Slices (page 143).

8 cups (2 L) warm water
8 1/2-inch (21 cm) sheet of rice paper
1/3 cup (85 mL) cooked brown rice
1 teaspoon (5 mL) Spicy Peanut Sauce (page 218)
2 tablespoons (30 mL) grated carrot
3 slices avocado
6-inch (15 cm) strip green onion
1/2 teaspoon (2 mL) chopped fresh cilantro or parsley
1/2 teaspoon (2 mL) julienne pickled ginger (optional)

Pour the warm water into a large bowl. Dip the sheet of rice paper into the warm water for 5 seconds, then lay it on a cutting board. Pat with a dry cloth to absorb excess water. Spread the rice onto the paper in a square, leaving a 1-inch (2.5 cm) border on all sides. Layer the sauce, carrot, avocado, green onion, cilantro, and ginger along the bottom portion of the rice. Fold right and left margins toward the centre, followed by the bottom margin. Moisten top margin of paper. Using both hands, tightly roll the paper toward the top. Apply a bit of pressure with your hands to seal the roll.

Per roll: calories: 259, protein: 7 g, fat: 13 g, carbohydrate: 31 g (4 g from sugar), dietary fibre: 5 g, calcium: 33 mg, iron: 2 mg, magnesium: 73 mg, phosphorus: 129 mg, potassium: 522 mg, sodium: 596 mg, zinc: 1 mg, thiamin: 0.2 mg, riboflavin: 0.1 mg, niacin: 5 mg, vitamin $B_6$: 0.3 mg, folate: 57 mcg, pantothenic acid: 1 mg, vitamin $B_{12}$: 0 mcg, vitamin A: 118 mcg, vitamin C: 6 mg, vitamin E: 1 mg, omega-6 fatty acids: 3 g, omega-3 fatty acids: 0.1 g

Percentage of calories from protein 10%, fat 44%, carbohydrate 46%

# Watercress, Avocado, and Grapefruit Salad

Makes 4 servings

This artistic salad is designed to be served as a side salad. Add more watercress if you want to serve it as a main dish. The dressing for this elegant salad uses mirin, a Japanese rice wine that is subtle, delicious, and clean on the palate. The grapefruit juice for the dressing can be squeezed from the remaining pulp after the segments are removed from the fruit.

## Salad

16 stems watercress greens (1/2 bunch)
2 ripe avocados
1 to 2 large grapefruits
1 teaspoon (5 mL) toasted sesame seeds (see page 133)

## Dressing

2 tablespoons (30 mL) grapefruit juice
2 tablespoons (30 mL) mirin
2 teaspoons (10 mL) rice vinegar
1/2 teaspoon (2 mL) tamari or soy sauce

To prepare the salad, wash the watercress and spin or pat dry. Arrange 4 stems each on the top third of four plates. Set aside. Cut avocados in half lengthwise and remove pits. Insert the edge of a soup spoon between the avocado pulp and the skin. Carefully scoop out the pulp in one piece and put it on a cutting board. Make thin strips lengthwise, starting 1/2-inch (1 cm) down from the narrow end of the avocado through to the bottom. With light pressure from your hand and at a 45-degree angle, push avocado so that it fans out. Arrange half of each avocado fan on each bed of watercress so that the fanned area is near the bottom of the plate.

Put the grapefruit on a cutting board. Slice off the top and bottom of the grapefruit. Using a sharp knife, cut away the skin and the white part of the peel. Cut along both sides of each segment toward the centre to loosen and remove all of the segments. Reserve the pulp for its juice. Garnish each plate with 4 grapefruit segments to form two Xs, one on either side of the avocado.

To prepare the dressing, squeeze into a small bowl the juice from the reserved pulp of the grapefruit after the segments are removed. Add the mirin, vinegar, and tamari and stir to combine. Spoon about 1 tablespoon (15 mL) of dressing over each individual salad. Sprinkle each salad with a pinch of sesame seeds.

Per serving: calories: 216, protein: 3 g, fat: 16 g, carbohydrate: 16 g (2 g from sugar), dietary fibre: 6 g, calcium: 39 mg, iron: 1 mg, magnesium: 49 mg, phosphorus: 59 mg, potassium: 729 mg, sodium: 48 mg, zinc: 1 mg, thiamin: 0.2 mg, riboflavin: 0.2 mg, niacin: 3 mg, vitamin $B_6$: 0.3 mg, folate: 71 mcg, pantothenic acid: 1 mg, vitamin $B_{12}$: 0 mcg, vitamin A: 1164 mcg, vitamin C: 34 mg, vitamin E: 2 mg, omega-6 fatty acids: 2 g, omega-3 fatty acids: 0.1 g

Percentage of calories from protein 5%, fat 63%, carbohydrate 28%, alcohol 4%

# Wild Rice, Walnut, and Cranberry Salad

Makes 6 cups (1.25 L)

Wild rice is not true rice but an annual species of grass that grows in shallow freshwater streams and lakes. Once harvested only in the wild, today this rice is available worldwide, thanks to large commercial operations. Wild rice has a nutty flavour that goes very well with fruits such as oranges and cranberries. The walnuts in this recipe enhance the taste and provide a good measure of omega-3 fatty acids. If making this salad in the summer, consider adding a cup (250 mL) of fresh blueberries for their protective antioxidant content.

4 cups (1 L) water
1 cup (250 mL) wild rice
1/2 teaspoon (2 mL) salt
1/4 cup (60 mL) thawed orange juice concentrate
1 tablespoon (15 mL) extra-virgin olive oil
1 teaspoon (5 mL) minced ginger
1/4 teaspoon (1 mL) salt
Pinch of black pepper
1 cup (250 mL) walnuts, chopped
1/2 cup (125 mL) dried cranberries
1/2 cup (125 mL) diced red bell pepper

Bring the water to a boil over high heat. Add the rice and salt, cover, reduce heat, and simmer for 45 minutes or until the kernels of rice have fully puffed open. Drain the water and set the rice aside to cool. Whisk together the orange juice concentrate, oil, ginger, salt, and black pepper. Stir into the rice. Add the walnuts, cranberries, and red pepper to the rice and mix thoroughly. Adjust the seasoning and serve.

Per cup (250 mL): calories: 310, protein: 8 g, fat: 16 g, carbohydrate: 37 g (9 g from sugar), dietary fibre: 4 g, calcium: 34 mg, iron: 1 mg, magnesium: 90 mg, phosphorus: 204 mg, potassium: 321 mg, sodium: 321 mg, zinc: 2 mg, thiamin: 0.1 mg, riboflavin: 0.1 mg, niacin: 4 mg, vitamin $B_6$: 0.3 mg, folate: 68 mcg, pantothenic acid: 0.5 mg, vitamin $B_{12}$: 0 mcg, vitamin A: 21 mcg, vitamin C: 44 mg, vitamin E: 1 mg, omega-6 fatty acids: 8 g, omega-3 fatty acids: 2 g

Percentage of calories from protein 9%, fat 45%, carbohydrate 46%

# Dressings

## Adding Oil and Lemon to Salad Greens

The classic French vinaigrette is a simple dressing to enrich salad greens. The basic ingredients are oil, vinegar, mustard, garlic, salt, and pepper, with a ratio of three parts oil to one part vinegar. Making this type of dressing at home is simple. Vinegar, mustard, minced garlic, salt, and pepper are mixed in a bowl with a fork or whisk, then a thin steady stream of oil is whisked in until it is incorporated and the mixture has emulsified; it's then seasoned to taste. People who prefer less vinegar may adjust the ratio to 4:1, whereas others may like more vinegar.

Even more basic than making a vinaigrette from scratch is dressing your greens with oil right out of the bottle, followed by fresh juice squeezed directly from the lemon (remove any visible seeds after cutting the lemon in half), and a dash of Bragg Liquid Aminos or tamari. Use one of three premium oils: extra-virgin olive, flaxseed, or hemp seed oil. You might like to have all three oils on hand for variety, as each is distinctive in flavour and nutritional benefits. A suggested ratio for 3 cups (750 mL) of greens is approximately 1 to 2 teaspoons (5 to 10 mL) oil, 1/2 teaspoon (2 mL) lemon juice, and a light sprinkling of Bragg Liquid Aminos. If you prefer, replace the lemon juice with lime juice, unpasteurized apple cider vinegar, balsamic vinegar, or another vinegar of your choice, and the Bragg or tamari with soy sauce.

# Avocado, Grapefruit, and Chipotle Dressing

Makes 1 3/4 cups (435 mL)

Avocados were known to the Aztecs as the fertility fruit. They contain both soluble and insoluble fibre, and more potassium than bananas. Although naturally high in fat, the fat is mainly monounsaturated. Add more grapefruit or lime juice to the dressing if it's too thick. The acidity in these juices prevents the avocado from turning brown.

1 medium avocado
2 tablespoons (30 mL) green onion, including white part
1 small clove garlic, chopped
3/4 cup (185 mL) freshly squeezed grapefruit juice
1/4 cup (60 mL) freshly squeezed lime juice
2 tablespoons (30 mL) maple syrup
1/2 teaspoon (2 mL) chopped chipotle pepper
1/4 teaspoon (1 mL) salt

Put the avocado flesh, green onion, garlic, grapefruit juice, lime juice, maple syrup, chipotle, and salt in a blender and blend for 30 seconds or until smooth. Dressing will keep in the refrigerator for 3 to 4 days.

Per 1/4 cup (60 mL): calories: 106, protein: 1 g, fat: 6 g, carbohydrate: 13 g (5 g from sugar), dietary fibre: 2 g, calcium: 18 mg, iron: 1 mg, magnesium: 23 mg, phosphorus: 26 mg, potassium: 346 mg, sodium: 100 mg, zinc: 1 mg, thiamin: 0.1 mg, riboflavin: 0.1 mg, niacin: 1 mg, vitamin B6: 0.1 mg, folate: 32 mcg, pantothenic acid: 0.5 mg, vitamin B12: 0 mcg, vitamin A: 23 mcg, vitamin C: 22 mg, vitamin E: 1 mg, omega-6 fatty acids: 0.8 g, omega-3 fatty acids: 0.1 g

Percentage of calories from protein 4%, fat 49%, carbohydrate 47%

# Coconut Almond Dressing

Makes 1 1/2 cups (375 mL)

The exotic flavours in this salad dressing are borrowed from Thai cuisine. Allow this dressing to slightly thicken in the refrigerator for 1 hour before using over a crisp, leafy green salad or as a marinade in Tofu: An Easy Entrée (page 184). It also is good on cooked brown rice or steamed broccoli or cauliflower. Two tablespoons (30 mL) provide a tenth of your day's supply of the antioxidant vitamin E.

**1/2 cup (125 mL) coconut milk**
**1/2 cup (125 mL) water**
**1/4 cup (60 mL) almond butter**
**2 tablespoons (30 mL) minced ginger**
**2 tablespoons (30 mL) lime juice**
**1 tablespoon (15 mL) maple syrup or other sweetener**
**1 teaspoon (5 mL) curry powder**
**1 small clove garlic, chopped**
**Pinch of salt**

Put the coconut milk, water, almond butter, ginger, lime juice, maple syrup, curry powder, garlic, and salt in a blender and process for 30 seconds or until smooth. Dressing will keep for 3 to 4 days if using freshly made coconut milk, or 1 to 2 weeks if using canned milk.

Per 2 tablespoons (30 mL): calories: 60, protein: 1 g, fat: 5 g, carbohydrate: 3 g (1 g from sugar), dietary fibre: 0.4 g, calcium: 19 mg, iron: 1 mg, magnesium: 22 mg, phosphorus: 40 mg, potassium: 76 mg, sodium: 31 mg, zinc: 0.3 mg, thiamin: 0 mg, riboflavin: 0 mg, niacin: 0.5 mg, vitamin B6: 0 mg, folate: 5 mcg, pantothenic acid: 0 mg, vitamin B12: 0 mcg, vitamin A: 0 mcg, vitamin C: 1 mg, vitamin E: 1.5 mg, omega-6 fatty acids: 1 g, omega-3 fatty acids: 0 g

Percentage of calories from protein 7%, fat 74%, carbohydrate 19%

## Making Your Own Coconut Milk

Making fresh coconut milk is easy, and the reward is worth the effort. You will need a hammer to crack open the hard shell of the coconut seed, a dull knife to pry the meat away from the shell, a blender, 1 cup (250 mL) water for every coconut, a fine-mesh strainer, and a spoon to push the pulp through the strainer. One average-sized coconut will make 2 to 3 cups (500 to 750 mL) of coconut milk.

Hold the coconut shell over the sink and strike it with the hammer to crack it open. The thin coconut water inside can be used in the milk or drunk on its own. Split the shell into three or four pieces. Remove the tender white meat using a knife—make sure it's dull, like a dinner knife, so that you don't injure yourself. Before digging the flesh out, score it in a number of places by pressing the knife all the way through the meat to the shell; this will help when prying the meat away from the shell. Removal of the brown skin on the outside of the meat is not necessary.

Wash the chunks of coconut and cut into 1- to 2-inch (2.5 to 5 cm) pieces. Put 1 cup (250 mL) water into a blender. Take out the removable portion of the blender lid, and secure the lid in place. With the blender on low speed, drop a piece or two of coconut at a time into the blender. Add enough water to keep the milk moving. You don't want too thick or thin a liquid; about the consistency of light puréed soup is just right. Increase the blender speed to high and blend until the milk is smooth, about 1 minute.

Pour the milk through the strainer into a bowl. Press down on the contents of the strainer to extract as much liquid as possible. Discard the pulp or use it in a soup, raw fruit pie crust, or in other imaginative ways, and store the coconut milk in a sealed container in the refrigerator, where it will keep for up to 2 or 3 days. It's best not to freeze the milk, as it may curdle when thawed, so use it while it's fresh.

# Cucumber Dill Dressing

Makes 1 1/2 cups (375 mL)

This simple-to-make salad dressing is refreshing and cool; making it an ideal accompaniment to salads in the summer, but don't let the seasons stop you from making it all year round. If you prefer, you may replace the dried dill with 1 tablespoon (15 mL) fresh dill. Made with hemp seed oil, this dressing is an excellent source of omega-3 fatty acids and has an ideal balance between omega-6 and omega-3 fatty acids.

1 cup (250 mL) chopped or grated, peeled cucumber
1 cup (250 mL) chopped or grated zucchini
1/4 cup (60 mL) hemp seed or extra-virgin olive oil
1/4 cup (60 mL) lemon juice
2 teaspoons (10 mL) Dijon mustard
1 teaspoon (5 mL) nutritional yeast
1 teaspoon (5 mL) dried dill
1 teaspoon (5 mL) maple syrup or agave sweetener
1/2 teaspoon (2 mL) salt
1/2 teaspoon (2 mL) hot sauce
1 clove garlic, chopped

Put the cucumber, zucchini, oil, lemon juice, mustard, yeast, dill, maple syrup, salt, hot sauce, and garlic in a blender and blend for 20 seconds. Scrape down the sides of the blender, then blend another 10 seconds or until all ingredients are well incorporated. Dressing will keep in the refrigerator for 3 to 4 days.

Per 2 tablespoons (30 mL): calories: 41, protein: 0.5 g, fat: 5 g, carbohydrate: 2 g (1 g from sugar), dietary fibre: 0.4 g, calcium: 6 mg, iron: 0.1 mg, magnesium: 5 mg, phosphorus: 9 mg, potassium: 61 mg, sodium: 104 mg, zinc: 0.1 mg, thiamin: 0.1 mg, riboflavin: 0.1 mg, niacin: 1 mg, vitamin B6: 0.1 mg, folate: 8 mcg, pantothenic acid: 0.1 mg, vitamin B12: 0.1 mcg, vitamin A: 1 mcg, vitamin C: 4 mg, vitamin E: 0 mg, omega-6 fatty acids: 3 g, omega-3 fatty acids: 1 g

Percentage of calories from protein 4%, fat 82%, carbohydrate 14%

# Lemon Tahini Dressing

Makes 1 1/2 cups (375 mL)

Tahini is a delicious sesame seed butter that became well known in the West with the rise in popularity of Middle Eastern cuisine. Use tahini to flavour sauces and soups, or to give a creamy texture to a dressing, as with this one. Since tahini is not hydrogenated, oil may rise to the surface during storage, so you may need to stir the dressing before using. Try this one on salads, steamed broccoli, and baked potatoes.

**1/2 cup (125 mL) tahini**
**1/2 cup (125 mL) water**
**1/4 cup (60 mL) lemon juice**
**1/4 cup (60 mL) tamari or soy sauce**
**2 cloves garlic, chopped**
**1 teaspoon (5 mL) ground cumin**
**1/2 teaspoon (2 mL) toasted sesame oil**
**Pinch of cayenne pepper**

Put the tahini, water, lemon juice, tamari, garlic, cumin, sesame oil, and cayenne in a blender and process for 30 seconds or until smooth. This dressing will keep, in a covered container and refrigerated, for up to 3 weeks.

Per 2 tablespoons (30 mL): calories: 70, protein: 3 g, fat: 6 g, carbohydrate: 3 g (0 g from sugar), dietary fibre: 1 g, calcium: 19 mg, iron: 1 mg, magnesium: 14 mg, phosphorus: 93 mg, potassium: 73 mg, sodium: 344 mg, zinc: 0.5 mg, thiamin: 0.2 mg, riboflavin: 0 mg, niacin: 1 mg, vitamin B6: 0 mg, folate: 12 mcg, pantothenic acid: 0 mg, vitamin B12: 0 mcg, vitamin A: 1 mcg, vitamin C: 3 mg, vitamin E: 0.3 mg, omega-6 fatty acids: 2 g, omega-3 fatty acids: 0 g

Percentage of calories from protein 14%, fat 69%, carbohydrate 17%

## Liquid Gold Dressing

Makes 1 3/4 cups (435 mL)

The name "Liquid Gold" suits this dressing made with Omega Nutrition Flaxseed Oil for reasons beyond the colour. Just 2 tablespoons (30 mL) provides half of your day's supply of omega-3 fatty acids—along with 40 percent of your vitamin B12 for the day when made with Red Star Vegetarian Support Formula nutritional yeast. This creamy dressing is packed with riboflavin and other B vitamins. The ground flaxseed not only provides omega-3s, it also allows the dressing to thicken on standing, making it smooth to the taste.

1/2 cup (125 mL) **flaxseed oil**
1/2 cup (125 mL) **water**
1/3 cup (85 mL) **lemon juice**
1/4 cup (60 mL) **tamari, soy sauce, or Bragg Liquid Aminos**
1/4 cup (60 mL) **nutritional yeast**
2 tablespoons (30 mL) **cider or balsamic vinegar**
2 tablespoons (30 mL) **ground flaxseed**
2 teaspoons (10 mL) **Dijon mustard**
1 teaspoon (5 mL) **ground cumin**

Put the flaxseed oil, water, lemon juice, tamari, nutritional yeast, vinegar, flaxseed, mustard, and cumin in a blender and blend until smooth. Dressing will keep in a jar with a lid, refrigerated, for up to 2 weeks.

Per 2 tablespoons (30 mL): calories: 99, protein: 2 g, fat: 9 g, carbohydrate: 2 g (0 g from sugar), dietary fibre: 1 g, calcium: 11 mg, iron: 0.5 mg, magnesium: 15 mg, phosphorus: 45 mg, potassium: 80 mg, sodium: 311 mg, zinc: 0.5 mg, thiamin: 1.2 mg, riboflavin: 1.2 mg, niacin: 7 mg, vitamin B6: 1 mg, folate: 31 mcg, pantothenic acid: 0.2 mg, vitamin B12: 1 mcg, vitamin A: 0 mcg, vitamin C: 3 mg, vitamin E: 1.5 mg, omega-6 fatty acids: 5 g, omega-3 fatty acids: 1.2 g

Percentage of calories from protein 8%, fat 82%, carbohydrate 10%

# Orange Ginger Dressing

Makes 1 3/4 cups (435 mL)

With its combination of orange and lemon juices, miso, tamari, and the bite of fresh ginger, this recipe combines four flavours that are fundamental to our enjoyment of food. These are sweet, sour, salty, and pungent. When used as a dressing for greens that contribute a slight bitterness, such as raw or cooked kale, we end up with a superb blend of five flavours.

**4 pitted dates**
**1 cup (250 mL) freshly squeezed orange juice**
**2 tablespoons (30 mL) almond butter**
**2 tablespoons (30 mL) grated ginger**
**2 tablespoons (30 mL) miso**
**2 tablespoons (30 mL) lemon juice**
**2 tablespoons (30 mL) tamari**
**Pinch of cayenne pepper**

Soak the dates in the orange juice for 6 to 10 hours. Put the dates and orange juice in a blender along with the almond butter, ginger, miso, lemon juice, tamari, and cayenne, and process for 30 seconds or until smooth. Dressing will keep in the refrigerator for 1 week.

Per 1/4 cup (60 mL): calories: 73, protein: 2 g, fat: 3 g, carbohydrate: 10 g (6 g from sugar), dietary fibre: 1 g, calcium: 22 mg, iron: 0.5 mg, magnesium: 25 mg, phosphorus: 48 mg, potassium: 170 mg, sodium: 498 mg, zinc: 0.3 mg, thiamin: 0.1 mg, riboflavin: 0.1 mg, niacin: 1 mg, vitamin B6: 0.1 mg, folate: 18 mcg, pantothenic acid: 0.2 mg, vitamin B12: 0 mcg, vitamin A: 4 mcg, vitamin C: 21 mg, vitamin E: 1 mg, omega-6 fatty acids: 0.7 g, omega-3 fatty acids: 0.1 g

Percentage of calories from protein 11%, fat 36%, carbohydrate 53%

# Oriental Dressing

Makes 1 1/4 cups (310 mL)

Rice vinegar has a delicate flavour and about half the acidity of other vinegars. The intriguing blend of flavours in this low-fat dressing in part comes from the Chinese five-spice powder, composed of cinnamon, fennel, star anise, and pepper. Allow the dressing to sit for 1 hour to develop the flavours. Agave syrup can be substituted for the rice syrup. Serve it with Calcium-Rich Greens (page 101) or Sprouted Lentil Salad Plate (page 110), or use it as a marinade for Tofu: An Easy Entrée (page 184).

1/2 cup (125 mL) rice vinegar
1/2 cup (125 mL) rice syrup
2 tablespoons (30 mL) water
2 tablespoons (30 mL) unrefined sesame oil
1 clove garlic, minced
2 teaspoons (10 mL) minced ginger
1/2 teaspoon (2 mL) toasted sesame oil
1/4 teaspoon (1 mL) five-spice powder

Put the rice vinegar, rice syrup, water, unrefined sesame oil, garlic, ginger, toasted sesame oil, and five-spice powder in a blender and process for 15 seconds. Alternatively, put all ingredients in a jar, cover with a lid, and shake for 15 seconds or until the rice syrup is dissolved. (It dissolves more easily at room temperature.) Dressing will keep in the refrigerator for up to 3 weeks.

Per 2 tablespoons (30 mL): calories: 88, protein: 0.2 g, fat: 3 g, carbohydrate: 15 g (9 g from sugar), dietary fibre: 0.1 g, calcium: 6 mg, iron: 0 mg, magnesium: 0 mg, phosphorus: 1 mg, potassium: 46 mg, sodium: 30 mg, zinc: 0 mg, thiamin: 0 mg, riboflavin: 0 mg, niacin: 0 mg, vitamin B6: 0 mg, folate: 0 mcg, pantothenic acid: 0 mg, vitamin B12: 0 mcg, vitamin A: 0 mcg, vitamin C: 0 mg, vitamin E: 0 mg, omega-6 fatty acids: 1 g, omega-3 fatty acids: 0 g

Percentage of calories from protein 1%, fat 30%, carbohydrate 69%

# Serrano Chili and Cilantro Dressing

Makes 3/4 cup (185 mL)

This versatile recipe can be used as a salad dressing, or served with Vietnamese Salad Roll (page 114), International Roll-Ups (page 156), Timesaving Tacos (page 183), or Baked Potato and Fixin's Bar (page 146). It also makes an excellent sauce for Tofu: An Easy Entrée (page 184).

2 serrano chilies, chopped
1 large bunch cilantro leaves, about 2 cups (500 mL) loosely packed leaves
1/3 cup (85 mL) lemon or lime juice
2 tablespoons (30 mL) hemp seed or extra-virgin olive oil
1 tablespoon (15 mL) tamari or soy sauce
1 clove garlic, chopped

Put the chilies, cilantro, lemon juice, oil, tamari, and garlic in a blender and blend for 20 seconds. Scrape down the sides of the blender, then blend for another 10 seconds or until smooth. Dressing will keep in the refrigerator for 1 week.

Per 2 tablespoons (30 mL): calories: 40, protein: 0.5 g, fat: 5 g, carbohydrate: 2 g (0.4 g from sugar), dietary fibre: 0.2 g, calcium: 3 mg, iron: 0.1 mg, magnesium: 3 mg, phosphorus: 7 mg, potassium: 36 mg, sodium: 171 mg, zinc: 0 mg, thiamin: 0 mg, riboflavin: 0 mg, niacin: 0.3 mg, vitamin B6: 0 mg, folate: 3 mcg, pantothenic acid: 0 mg, vitamin B12: 0 mcg, vitamin A: 2 mcg, vitamin C: 8 mg, vitamin E: 0 mg, omega-6 fatty acids: 3 g, omega-3 fatty acids: 1 g

Percentage of calories from protein 4%, fat 82%, carbohydrate 14%

# Tomato Herb Dressing

Makes 1 1/4 cups (310 mL)

This healthful, low-oil dressing can be varied according to your preferred herbs—for example, dill, oregano, or marjoram on their own or in combination. If you use dried herbs, use one-third the amount of the fresh herbs called for. The tomato juice provides body and considerably reduces the amount of oil required.

1 cup (250 mL) tomato juice
2 tablespoons (30 mL) lemon juice
2 tablespoons (30 mL) apple cider vinegar
2 tablespoons (30 mL) extra-virgin olive oil
1 1/2 teaspoons (7 mL) chopped fresh basil
1 teaspoon (5 mL) Dijon mustard
1/2 teaspoon (2 mL) dried tarragon, crushed
Pinch of black pepper

Put the tomato juice, lemon juice, vinegar, oil, basil, mustard, tarragon, and pepper in a jar with a lid and shake for 30 seconds. This dressing will keep, refrigerated, for up to 2 weeks.

Per 2 tablespoons (30 mL): calories: 30, protein: 0.3 g, fat: 3 g, carbohydrate: 1 g (1 g from sugar), dietary fibre: 0.2 g, calcium: 4 mg, iron: 0.2 mg, magnesium: 3 mg, phosphorus: 7 mg, potassium: 64 mg, sodium: 106 mg, zinc: 0 mg, thiamin: 0 mg, riboflavin: 0 mg, niacin: 0 mg, vitamin B6: 0 mg, folate: 6 mcg, pantothenic acid: 0.1 mg, vitamin B12: 0 mcg, vitamin A: 15 mcg, vitamin C: 4 mg, vitamin E: 0.2 mg, omega-6 fatty acids: 0 g, omega-3 fatty acids: 0 g

Percentage of calories from protein 3%, fat 79 %, carbohydrate 18%

# Soups

## Vegetable Stock

Makes 6 cups (1.5 L)

This simple stock can be kept on hand in the refrigerator for up to 4 or 5 days or made in larger quantities and frozen. When making stock from scratch, try substituting different vegetables, such as tomatoes, fennel, leeks, and mushrooms, or herbs, such as basil, rosemary, and coriander. Avoid cabbage-family vegetables in your stock, as their taste and odour will be overpowering. If using commercial stock cubes or powders, choose one that does not contain MSG, hydrogenated fats, or hydrolyzed protein.

6 cups (1.5 L) water
2 carrots, chopped
2 stalks celery, sliced
2 large cloves garlic, chopped
1 large onion, chopped
1/2 fennel bulb and stalks, chopped (optional)
1/4 cup (60 mL) whole fresh parsley leaves and stems
1/2 teaspoon (2 mL) dried thyme
10 peppercorns, crushed
3 bay leaves
3 whole cloves

Put the water, carrots, celery, garlic, onion, fennel, parsley, thyme, peppercorns, bay leaves, and cloves in a large pot; bring to a boil, then reduce heat, cover, and simmer for 30 minutes. Strain the liquid through a sieve or colander, discard vegetables, and let stock cool before refrigerating or freezing.

# Carrot, Lemon Grass, and Basil Soup

Makes 8 cups (2 L)

Native to India and Sri Lanka, lemon grass is a tropical grass that has a citrus flavour without the sourness associated with lemons. The leafy, long-stemmed, aromatic stalks are popular in Thai cuisine and are often combined with coconut milk, ginger, and vegetables as the basis for a wide variety of dishes. Here, these ingredients form a creamy, delicious soup with a bright yellow-orange colour, indicative of its plentiful amounts of the antioxidant beta carotene.

1 tablespoon (15 mL) coconut or olive oil
1/2 medium onion, diced
3 cloves garlic, minced
2 tablespoons (30 mL) minced ginger
2 tablespoons (30 mL) thinly sliced lemon grass bulb
4 cups (1 L) sliced carrots
3 1/2 cups (875 mL) water
1 3/4 cups (435 mL) coconut milk or 1 can (12 ounces/355 mL)
3 tablespoons (45 mL) fresh basil or 1 tablespoon (15 mL) dried
1/2 teaspoon (2 mL) salt
1 tablespoon (15 mL) lime juice

Heat the oil in a pot over medium heat; add the onion and cook for 3 to 5 minutes or until translucent. Add the garlic, ginger, and lemon grass and cook for another 2 minutes. Add the carrots, water, coconut milk, basil, and salt; bring to a boil, then reduce heat, cover, and simmer for 15 minutes or until the carrots are soft. Transfer soup to a blender and blend until smooth. Pour the soup back into the pot and reheat it, then add the lime juice, adjust the seasoning, and serve.

Per cup (250 mL): calories: 159, protein: 2 g, fat: 14 g, carbohydrate: 10 g (3 g from sugar), dietary fibre: 2 g, calcium: 50 mg, iron: 2 mg, magnesium: 39 mg, phosphorus: 84 mg, potassium: 386 mg, sodium: 175 mg, zinc: 1 mg, thiamin: 0.1 mg, riboflavin: 0.1 mg, niacin: 2 mg, vitamin B6: 0.2 mg, folate: 24 mcg, pantothenic acid: 0.3 mg, vitamin B12: 0 mcg, vitamin A: 571 mcg, vitamin C: 6 mg, vitamin E: 0.5 mg, omega-6 fatty acids: 0.2 g, omega-3 fatty acids: 0 g

Percentage of calories from protein 5%, fat 71%, carbohydrate 24%

# Classic Split Pea Soup

Makes 9 cups (2.25 L)

Served with a wholesome bread and salad, this protein-rich soup satisfies the heartiest appetites. A 2-cup (500 mL) portion provides 24 grams of protein, along with iron, other minerals, and folate. Freeze leftovers in individual portions for quick lunches and suppers.

1 tablespoon (15 mL) coconut or olive oil
1/2 onion, diced
1 cup (250 mL) diced carrots
1 cup (250 mL) diced celery
2 cloves garlic, minced
8 cups (2 L) water
2 cups (500 mL) dried green split peas, picked over and rinsed
3 bay leaves
5 whole cloves
1/2 teaspoon (2 mL) salt or to taste
Pinch of black pepper
1 tablespoon (15 mL) chopped fresh parsley

Put the oil in a pot over medium heat; add the onion and cook for 3 to 5 minutes or until translucent. Add the carrots, celery, and garlic and cook for 3 minutes. Add the water, split peas, bay leaves, and cloves; bring to a boil, reduce heat, cover, and simmer for 1 hour or until the peas are soft. Add more water if soup gets too thick. Add the salt and pepper. Garnish each serving with parsley.

Per cup (250 mL): calories: 189, protein: 12 g, fat: 2 g, carbohydrate: 32 g (5 g from sugar), dietary fibre: 13 g, calcium: 56 mg, iron: 2.5 mg, magnesium: 63 mg, phosphorus: 183 mg, potassium: 575 mg, sodium: 146 mg, zinc: 1.5 mg, thiamin: 0.4 mg, riboflavin: 0.1 mg, niacin: 4 mg, vitamin B6: 0.2 mg, folate: 136 mcg, pantothenic acid: 1 mg, vitamin B12: 0 mcg, vitamin A: 169 mcg, vitamin C: 5 mg, vitamin E: 1 mg, omega-6 fatty acids: 0.4 g, omega-3 fatty acids: 0.1 g

Percentage of calories from protein 24%, fat 11%, carbohydrate 65%

# Curried Kabocha Squash and Chickpea Soup

Makes 9 1/2 cups (2.375 mL)

Kabocha squash is a Japanese variety of winter squash with a hard shell and deep orange-yellow flesh. Although the skin is hard, it need not be peeled, as it's edible and will soften as it cooks. This creamy, sweet squash is exceptional roasted or cooked in a soup. Measure all the ground spices into a small bowl and add them all at once. Butternut squash is a perfect substitute for kabocha, though it will need to be peeled.

2 tablespoons (30 mL) coconut or olive oil
1 onion, diced
1 tablespoon (15 mL) minced ginger
4 cloves garlic, minced
2 tablespoons (30 mL) ground coriander
1 1/2 tablespoons (22 mL) ground toasted cumin seeds (see page 133)
1/2 teaspoon (2 mL) salt
1/2 teaspoon (2 mL) turmeric
1/2 teaspoon (2 mL) cayenne pepper
1/4 teaspoon (1 mL) ground cardamom
1/4 teaspoon (1 mL) cinnamon
4 cups (1 L) water
4 cups (1 L) diced, unpeeled Kabocha squash
2 cups (500 mL) chopped tomatoes
2 cups (500 mL) cooked or canned chickpeas, drained and rinsed

Heat the oil in a large pot over medium heat and cook the onion, ginger, and garlic for 5 minutes or until the onion is translucent. Stir in the coriander, cumin, salt, turmeric, cayenne, cardamom, and cinnamon and cook for 2 minutes, stirring frequently to avoid scorching. Add 1/2 cup (125 mL) of the water and stir to loosen any spices that may have stuck to the bottom to the pot. Add remaining water along with the squash, tomatoes and chickpeas. Bring the soup to a boil, reduce heat to medium-low, cover and cook for 20 minutes or until the squash is soft.

Per cup (250 mL): calories: 135, protein: 5 g, fat: 5 g, carbohydrate: 22 g (5 g from sugar), dietary fibre: 4 g, calcium: 77 mg, iron: 3 mg, magnesium: 54 mg, phosphorus: 107 mg, potassium: 482 mg, sodium: 260 mg, zinc: 1 mg, thiamin: 0.1 mg, riboflavin: 0.1 mg, niacin: 2 mg, vitamin B6: 0.2 mg, folate: 88 mcg, pantothenic acid: 0.4 mg, vitamin B12: 0 mcg, vitamin A: 350 mcg, vitamin C: 20 mg, vitamin E: 1 mg, omega-6 fatty acids: 0.6 g, omega-3 fatty acids: 0.1 g

Percentage of calories from protein 13%, fat 27%, carbohydrate 60%

## Roasting Spices and Sesame Seeds (Stovetop Method)

Dry-roasting Indian spices such as cumin, coriander, fenugreek, and mustard seed releases non-volatile oils known as oleoresins, which will enhance and deepen the flavours of the dish in which they are used. Sesame seeds also can be roasted by this method. Put the seeds in a heavy-bottomed skillet over medium heat. When the seeds start to warm up, stir them continuously for several minutes with a wooden spoon. The amount of time needed to roast seeds depends on the volume of the seed, the skillet, and the type of spice. As a general rule, from the time the skillet is fully warmed, 1/4 cup (60 mL) of seeds will roast within 3 to 5 minutes. After the seeds are roasted, transfer them to a bowl so they do not continue to cook. Allow the seeds to cool then store them in air-tight, sealed jars or containers in a cool, dry place. They can be refrigerated or frozen for months to retain their flavour.

# Ginger, Carrot, and Yam Soup

Makes 9 cups (2.25 L)

Vitamins and phytochemicals in vegetables provide the splendid array of colours you see when you walk down the produce aisle. Three of these vitamins are bright yellow: riboflavin, folate, and vitamin A (converted in the body from the antioxidant beta carotene). This warming, golden soup is packed with all three.

1 tablespoon (15 mL) coconut or olive oil
1/2 small onion, sliced
1/4 cup (60 mL) chopped ginger
4 cups (1 L) water
4 cups (1 L) chopped carrots
2 cups (500 mL) peeled, chopped yams
1 medium orange, peeled, seeded, and chopped
2 teaspoons (10 mL) whole coriander seed or 1 teaspoon (5 mL) ground coriander
1/2 teaspoon (2 mL) salt
1/4 teaspoon (1 mL) allspice
1/4 teaspoon (1 mL) nutmeg
1/2 cup (125 mL) apple juice

Heat the oil in a large pot over medium heat and cook the onion and ginger for 3 to 5 minutes or until translucent. Add the water, carrots, yams, orange, coriander, salt, allspice, and nutmeg and bring to a boil. Reduce heat, cover, and simmer for 15 to 20 minutes or until the carrots and yams are soft. Transfer the soup to a blender and blend until smooth. Return the soup to the pot, add the apple juice, and reheat.

Per cup (250 mL): calories: 98, protein: 1 g, fat: 2 g, carbohydrate: 20 g (6 g from sugar), dietary fibre: 4 g, calcium: 38 mg, iron: 0.5 mg, magnesium: 20 mg, phosphorus: 46 mg, potassium: 543 mg, sodium: 153 mg, zinc: 0.3 mg, thiamin: 0.1 mg, riboflavin: 0.1 mg, niacin: 1 mg, vitamin B6: 0.2 mg, folate: 25 mcg, pantothenic acid: 0.3 mg, vitamin B12: 0 mcg, vitamin A: 508 mcg, vitamin C: 18 mg, vitamin E: 1 mg, omega-6 fatty acids: 0.1 g, omega-3 fatty acids: 0 g

Percentage of calories from protein 6%, fat 16%, carbohydrate 78%

# Mediterranean Lentil Soup

Makes 6 cups (1.5 L)

Lentils have been feeding populations in various parts of the world since antiquity. There is a good reason for this choice—these little gems contain 26 percent protein by weight. Thus, a hearty 2-cup (500 mL) portion provides about one-third to one-half of the recommended protein intake for the day. (For details about recommended protein intakes, see pages 45 and 47.) In addition, this tasty soup is rich in minerals. This lentil soup simmers quietly for 1 hour while you do other things. It has a deep, rich flavour thanks to the addition of the molasses, which also gives the soup a robust appearance.

1 tablespoon (15 mL) coconut or olive oil
1/2 onion, chopped
2 large cloves garlic, minced
5 cups (1.25 L) water
2 cups (500 mL) chopped fresh or canned tomatoes
1 cup (250 mL) dried lentils, picked over and rinsed
2 teaspoons (10 mL) dried basil or 2 tablespoons (30 mL) fresh
1 teaspoon (5 mL) dried oregano or 1 tablespoon (15 mL) fresh
2 bay leaves
1 tablespoon (15 mL) blackstrap molasses or brown sugar
1 tablespoon (15 mL) balsamic vinegar
1 teaspoon (5 mL) salt
**Pinch of black pepper**

Put the oil in a pot over medium heat; add the onion and cook for 3 to 5 minutes or until translucent. Add the garlic and cook for another 2 minutes. Stir in the water, tomatoes, lentils, basil, oregano, and bay leaves and bring to a boil, then reduce heat, cover, and simmer for 1 hour. Add molasses, vinegar, salt, and pepper. Adjust the seasoning and serve.

Per cup (250 mL): calories: 164, protein: 10 g, fat: 3 g, carbohydrate: 26 g (6 g from sugar), dietary fibre: 5 g, calcium: 78 mg, iron: 4 mg, magnesium: 56 mg, phosphorus: 175 mg, potassium: 589 mg, sodium: 407 mg, zinc: 1.5 mg, thiamin: 0.2 mg, riboflavin: 0.1 mg, niacin: 3 mg, vitamin B6: 0.3 mg, folate: 158 mcg, pantothenic acid: 0.7 mg, vitamin B12: 0 mcg, vitamin A: 61 mcg, vitamin C: 12 mg, vitamin E: 1 mg, omega-6 fatty acids: 0.4 g, omega-3 fatty acids: 0.1 g

Percentage of calories from protein 24%, fat 15%, carbohydrate 61%

# Mulligatawny Soup

Makes 4 cups (1 L)

In one of the languages of southern India, "mulligatawny" means, literally, "pepper water." The spiciness in this light soup varies according to how much pepper and ginger you add. If you like it hot, adjust the amounts; this version is mildly spicy. The sweetness of apple and celery balances the spice, and the crunch of uncooked apple as a garnish adds an appealing texture.

**1 tablespoon (15 mL) coconut or olive oil**
**1/2 onion, diced**
**2 cloves garlic, minced**
**1 tablespoon (15 mL) minced ginger**
**1 cup (250 mL) sliced celery**
**1 tablespoon (15 mL) tomato paste**
**1 1/2 teaspoons (7 mL) curry powder**
**1/4 teaspoon (1 mL) celery seeds**
**1/4 teaspoon (1 mL) salt**
**1/4 teaspoon (1 mL) black pepper**
**4 cups (1 L) water**
**1/4 cup (60 mL) white basmati rice**
**1 apple, diced**

Put the oil in a pot over medium heat; add onion, garlic, ginger, and celery and sauté for 5 minutes or until the onion is translucent. Stir in the tomato paste, curry powder, celery seeds, salt, and pepper. Cook for 3 minutes, stirring frequently to prevent sticking and scorching. Add the water and basmati rice, bring to a boil, cover, reduce heat, and simmer for 30 minutes. Adjust seasoning, garnish with apple, and serve.

Per cup (250 mL): calories: 118, protein: 2 g, fat: 4 g, carbohydrate: 22 g (6 g from sugar), dietary fibre: 3 g, calcium: 34 mg, iron: 1 mg, magnesium: 14 mg, phosphorus: 21 mg, potassium: 221 mg, sodium: 152 mg, zinc: 0.2 mg, thiamin: 0.1 mg, riboflavin: 0 mg, niacin: 1 mg, vitamin B6: 0.1 mg, folate: 13 mcg, pantothenic acid: 0.1 mg, vitamin B12: 0 mcg, vitamin A: 29 mcg, vitamin C: 7 mg, vitamin E: 1 mg, omega-6 fatty acids: 0.4 g, omega-3 fatty acids: 0 g

Percentage of calories from protein 6%, fat 26%, carbohydrate 68%

**Mulligatawny Soup with Brown Rice**
Replace the white rice with brown basmati rice and simmer for 45 minutes.

# Red Lentil Miso Soup

Makes 6 1/2 cups (1.625 L)

Miso is a Japanese fermented paste made from soybeans, salt, a grain—most commonly rice or barley—and a living culture that is used to initiate the fermentation process. The nutrient-rich soybeans are made more digestible by fermentation. Miso can be used to flavour many different dishes such as gravies, dressings, dips, and soups.

1 tablespoon (15 mL) coconut or olive oil
1/2 onion, diced
2 cloves garlic, minced
2 cups (500 mL) diced carrots
5 cups (1.25 L) water
1 cup (250 mL) red lentils, picked over and rinsed
1/2 teaspoon (2 mL) ground cumin
2 tablespoons (30 mL) dark miso
1/2 teaspoon (2 mL) salt

Heat the oil in a pot over medium heat and cook the onion for 3 to 5 minutes or until translucent. Add the garlic and carrots and cook for 3 minutes. Add the water, lentils, and cumin, bring to a boil, reduce heat, cover, and simmer for 20 to 25 minutes or until lentils have disintegrated. Mix miso and salt in small bowl, adding a small amount of soup liquid; stir paste until smooth. Stir miso into soup and serve.

Per cup (250 mL): calories: 160, protein: 9 g, fat: 3 g, carbohydrate: 25 g (3 g from sugar), dietary fibre: 5 g, calcium: 39 mg, iron: 3 mg, magnesium: 32 mg, phosphorus: 116 mg, potassium: 343 mg, sodium: 379 mg, zinc: 1.5 mg, thiamin: 0.2 mg, riboflavin: 0.1 mg, niacin: 2 mg, vitamin B6: 0.2 mg, folate: 72 mcg, pantothenic acid: 0.2 mg, vitamin B12: 0 mcg, vitamin A: 334 mcg, vitamin C: 4 mg, vitamin E: 0.5 mg, omega-6 fatty acids: 0.2 g, omega-3 fatty acids: 0 g

Percentage of calories from protein 22%, fat 18%, carbohydrate 60%

## Savoury Black Bean Soup

Makes 6 cups (1.5 L)

Black beans are a staple legume in Latin American and Caribbean countries, and their popularity has spread across North America. Here is a tasty recipe that combines flavours from Europe, Mexico, and the Caribbean. This soup has an outstanding balance of protein, fat, and carbohydrate and is rich in fibre, iron, and potassium. Adding lime juice just before serving adds a bright accent that would be lost if it were added while the soup is still cooking.

1 tablespoon (15 mL) coconut or olive oil
1/2 onion, diced
1 clove garlic, minced
1 cup (250 mL) diced carrots
1 cup (250 mL) diced celery
4 cups (1 L) water
3 cups (750 mL) cooked or canned black beans, drained and rinsed
1/4 cup (60 mL) tomato paste
1 1/2 teaspoons (7 mL) ground cumin
1 teaspoon (5 mL) dried oregano
1 teaspoon (5 mL) dried thyme
1/2 teaspoon (2 mL) salt
2 teaspoons (10 mL) lime juice

Put the oil in a pot over medium heat; add the onion and cook for 3 to 5 minutes or until translucent. Add the garlic, carrots, and celery and cook for 3 minutes. Add the water, black beans, tomato paste, cumin, oregano, and thyme, bring to a boil, reduce heat, cover, and simmer for 30 minutes. Add the salt and, just before serving, stir in the lime juice and adjust the seasoning.

Per cup (250 mL): calories: 172, protein: 9 g, fat: 3 g, carbohydrate: 29 g (2 g from sugar), dietary fibre: 10 g, calcium: 65 mg, iron: 3 mg, magnesium: 82 mg, phosphorus: 158 mg, potassium: 618 mg, sodium: 205 mg, zinc: 1 mg, thiamin: 0.3 mg, riboflavin: 0.1 mg, niacin: 3 mg, vitamin B6: 0.2 mg, folate: 153 mcg, pantothenic acid: 0.5 mg, vitamin B12: 0 mcg, vitamin A: 187 mcg, vitamin C: 10 mg, vitamin E: 1 mg, omega-6 fatty acids: 0.4 g, omega-3 fatty acids: 0.2 g

Percentage of calories from protein 21%, fat 15%, carbohydrate 64%

# Shiitake Mushroom Miso Soup

Makes 7 1/2 cups (1.875 L)

Most people believe that miso originated in Japan, but it can be traced back to China, to as early as the fourth century. Miso is a dark, rich, fermented paste made from beans (usually soybeans) and grain. It contains active friendly bacteria that can aid digestion. Each miso brand has its own distinct aroma, colour, and flavour that determine how it should best be used. Light miso is sweeter and more subtle; it is suitable for dishes that call for a delicate flavour. Dark miso is more robust and salty; it is appropriate for recipes that need more assertive seasoning.

5 ounces (150 g) shiitake mushrooms
2 tablespoons (30 mL) coconut or olive oil
1/2 onion, diced
4 cloves garlic, chopped
1 cup (250 mL) diced carrots
6 cups (1.5 L) water or vegetable stock
1/2 cup (125 mL) brown rice
2 teaspoons (10 mL) dried marjoram
2 teaspoons (10 mL) dried thyme
1/4 cup (60 mL) dark miso
1/4 cup (60 mL) chopped fresh parsley

Wash the mushrooms and remove and discard the tough stems. Thinly slice the caps.

Put the oil in a large soup pot over medium heat. When the oil is hot, add the onion and mushrooms and cook for 3 to 5 minutes or until the moisture from the mushrooms has evaporated. Add the garlic and carrots and cook for about 3 minutes. Reduce heat to low and add the water, rice, marjoram, and thyme. Increase heat to medium-high and bring to a boil. Reduce heat to low, cover, and simmer for 45 minutes or until the rice is tender.

Put the miso in a small bowl and stir in about 1/2 cup (125 mL) of the soup broth to make a thin paste. Remove the soup from the heat and stir in the miso mixture and parsley. Serve at once.

Per cup (250 mL): calories: 121, protein: 3 g, fat: 5 g, carbohydrate: 17 g (2 g from sugar), dietary fibre: 2 g, calcium: 37 mg, iron: 2 mg, magnesium: 31 mg, phosphorus: 63 mg, potassium: 144 mg, sodium: 369 mg, zinc: 1 mg, thiamin: 0.1 mg, riboflavin: 0.1 mg, niacin: 1 mg, vitamin B6: 0.2 mg, folate: 14 mcg, pantothenic acid: 0.3 mg, vitamin B12: 0 mcg, vitamin A: 155 mcg, vitamin C: 6 mg, vitamin E: 0.3 mg, omega-6 fatty acids: 0.5 g, omega-3 fatty acids: 0.1 g

Percentage of calories from protein 10%, fat 34%, carbohydrate 56%

# Spicy Eggplant Soup with Chickpeas and Olives

Makes 9 cups (2.25 L)

Since there are references to eggplant in the ancient language of Sanskrit, it is thought that this fruit is native to the Indian subcontinent. Historians believe that eggplant was introduced to the Middle East, Africa, and Europe along the Silk Road as early as the sixth century. This soup has an excellent balance of protein, fat, and carbohydrate and provides iron and other minerals.

1 tablespoon (15 mL) coconut or olive oil
1/2 onion, diced
3 cups (750 mL) diced eggplants
1 cup (250 mL) diced carrots
1 cup (250 mL) diced red bell pepper
2 cloves garlic, minced
5 cups (1.25 L) water or vegetable stock
2 cups (500 mL) cooked or canned chickpeas, rinsed and drained
1 cup (250 mL) chopped fresh or canned tomatoes
1/2 cup (125 mL) pitted kalamata olives, chopped
2 teaspoons (10 mL) ground cumin
1/4 teaspoon (1 mL) cayenne pepper
1 teaspoon (5 mL) salt (less if using salted vegetable stock)
1/4 cup (60 mL) chopped fresh parsley

Heat the oil in a large pot over medium heat. Cook the onion for 3 to 5 minutes or until translucent. Add the eggplant, carrots, bell pepper, and garlic and cook for 5 minutes. Add the water, chickpeas, tomatoes, olives, cumin, cayenne, and salt. Bring to a boil, reduce heat, cover, and cook on low heat for 20 minutes. Adjust the seasoning, stir in the parsley, and serve.

Per cup (250 mL): calories: 112, protein: 4 g, fat: 4 g, carbohydrate: 17 g (5 g from sugar), dietary fibre: 4 g, calcium: 47 mg, iron: 2 mg, magnesium: 33 mg, phosphorus: 92 mg, potassium: 338 mg, sodium: 350 mg, zinc: 1 mg, thiamin: 0.1 mg, riboflavin: 0.1 mg, niacin: 2 mg, vitamin B6: 0.2 mg, folate: 85 mcg, pantothenic acid: 0.3 mg, vitamin B12: 0 mcg, vitamin A: 167 mcg, vitamin C: 41 mg, vitamin E: 1 mg, omega-6 fatty acids: 0.6 g, omega-3 fatty acids: 0 g

Percentage of calories from protein 15%, fat 28%, carbohydrate 57%

# Tuscan Minestrone Soup

Makes 8 cups (2 L)

Tuscany, a region in central Italy, is a charmed land blessed with copious amounts of sunshine. The cuisine from this famed tourist destination incorporates plenty of olives, garlic, tomatoes, cannellini beans (white kidney beans), and herbs that readily grow throughout the region. Although minestrone soups vary from one Italian kitchen to another, the ingredients in this recipe are typical. So that the vegetables cook evenly, it is best to cut pieces of uniform size, such as a 1/3-inch (8 mm) dice. Other varieties of white beans such as navy or great northern beans can be substituted for the cannellini beans in this recipe.

- 2 tablespoons (30 mL) olive oil
- 1/2 onion, diced
- 2 cloves garlic, minced
- 1 cup (250 mL) diced carrots
- 1 cup (250 mL) diced celery
- 1 cup (250 mL) diced potato
- 1/2 cup (125 mL) chopped green beans
- 2 tablespoons (30 mL) chopped fresh basil or 2 teaspoons (10 mL) dried
- 1 tablespoon (15 mL) minced fresh rosemary or 1 teaspoon (5 mL) dried
- 4 cups (1 L) water
- 1 cup (250 mL) tomato sauce
- 1 cup (250 mL) cooked or canned white beans, drained and rinsed
- 1 teaspoon (5 mL) salt
- 1 cup (250 mL) diced zucchini

Heat the oil in a pot over medium heat. Cook the onion for 3 to 5 minutes or until translucent. Add the garlic, carrots, celery, potato, and green beans and cook for 3 minutes. Add the basil, rosemary, water, tomato sauce, white beans, and salt, bring to a boil, then reduce heat, cover, and simmer for 15 minutes or until potatoes are al dente. Add the zucchini. Simmer for about 5 minutes or until vegetables are tender-crisp. Adjust the seasoning and serve.

Per cup (250 mL): calories: 107, protein: 4 g, fat: 4 g, carbohydrate: 16 g (3 g from sugar), dietary fibre: 4 g, calcium: 50 mg, iron: 2 mg, magnesium: 35 mg, phosphorus: 66 mg, potassium: 512 mg, sodium: 494 mg, zinc: 1 mg, thiamin: 0.1 mg, riboflavin: 0.1 mg, niacin: 2 mg, vitamin B6: 0.2 mg, folate: 42 mcg, pantothenic acid: 0.4 mg, vitamin B12: 0 mcg, vitamin A: 157 mcg, vitamin C: 12 mg, vitamin E: 2 mg, omega-6 fatty acids: 0.4 g, omega-3 fatty acids: 0.1 g

Percentage of calories from protein 14%, fat 30%, carbohydrate 56%

# Zucchini, Corn, and Amaranth Soup

Makes 8 cups (2 L)

Summertime is a good time to make this soup, when fresh local produce and herbs are at their peak. To remove corn kernels from the ear, slice off the stem and place the ear of corn, stem end down, on a damp cloth to avoid slipping. Hold a knife at the top of the ear and slice from top to bottom. Slightly rotate the ear and repeat until all of the corn is removed. If fresh herbs are not available, use dried herbs but only one-third the amount.

1 tablespoon (15 mL) coconut or olive oil
1/2 onion, diced
2 cloves garlic, minced
2 cups (500 mL) diced tomatoes
3 tablespoons (45 mL) chopped fresh basil
1 tablespoon (15 mL) fresh thyme leaves
1 fresh red chili pepper or 1/2 teaspoon (2 mL) dried chili flakes
4 cups (1 L) vegetable stock
1/3 cup (85 mL) amaranth
2 cups (500 mL) corn kernels
2 cups (500 mL) diced zucchini

Heat the oil in a pot over medium heat and cook the onion for 3 minutes or until translucent. Add the garlic, tomatoes, basil, thyme, and chili pepper and cook for 3 minutes. Add the stock and amaranth, bring to a boil, then reduce heat to simmer, cover, and cook for 20 minutes. Add the corn and zucchini, bring back to a simmer, and cook another 5 minutes or until the zucchini is cooked but still crisp. Adjust seasoning and serve.

Per cup (250 mL): calories: 109, protein: 4 g, fat: 3 g, carbohydrate: 19 g (4 g from sugar), dietary fibre: 3 g, calcium: 34 mg, iron: 1 mg, magnesium: 53 mg, phosphorus: 108 mg, potassium: 394 mg, sodium: 159 mg, zinc: 1 mg, thiamin: 0.1 mg, riboflavin: 0.1 mg, niacin: 2 mg, vitamin B6: 0.2 mg, folate: 43 mcg, pantothenic acid: 0.5 mg, vitamin B12: 0 mcg, vitamin A: 101 mcg, vitamin C: 24 mg, vitamin E: 0.5 mg, omega-6 fatty acids: 0.6 g, omega-3 fatty acids: 0 g

Percentage of calories from protein 13%, fat 25%, carbohydrate 62%

**Note:** Analysis was done without added salt.

# Entrées

## Crispy Tofu Slices

Makes 3 servings (each about 6 slices)

If you want to introduce tofu to family or friends, this is a form they'll likely enjoy. You'll find Spike at supermarkets. Red Star Vegetarian Support Formula nutritional yeast is found at natural foods stores and is a source of vitamin B12. When cooked, the tofu takes on a crispy Southern-fried taste. Some people like tofu moist, others like it dry, so experiment with the cooking time. Crispy Tofu Slices can be used as the high-protein part of a meal, as an appetizer, pizza topping, tossed into a salad, or in sandwiches.

1 package (12.3 ounces/349 g) extra-firm or firm tofu
2 tablespoons (30 mL) low-sodium or regular tamari or soy sauce
1/3 cup (85 mL) nutritional yeast
1 teaspoon (5 mL) salt-free or regular Spike
1 tablespoon (15 mL) coconut or olive oil

Cut the tofu into 1/4-inch (5 mm) thick slices. Pour the tamari onto a small plate. Combine the yeast and Spike on another plate or in a wide, shallow bowl. Dip each tofu slice into the tamari, coating both sides, then into the yeast mixture to again coat both sides. Pan-fry the coated tofu in oil over medium heat for 3 to 4 minutes or until crispy brown. Turn the tofu and repeat on the other side.

Per serving (about 6 slices): calories: 238, protein: 27 g, fat: 11 g, carbohydrate: 13 g (0 g from sugar), dietary fibre: 7 g, calcium: 789 mg, iron: 13 mg, magnesium: 93 mg, phosphorus: 417 mg, potassium: 634 mg, sodium: 859 mg, zinc: 5 mg, thiamin: 11 mg, riboflavin: 11 mg, niacin: 67 mg, vitamin $B_6$: 10 mg, folate: 286 mcg, pantothenic acid: 1.3 mg, vitamin $B_{12}$: 8.3 mcg, vitamin A: 19 mcg, vitamin C: 0 mg, vitamin E: 0 mg, omega-6 fatty acids: 5 g, omega-3 fatty acids: 1 g

Percentage of calories from protein 43%, fat 37%, carbohydrate 20%

**Spicy Tofu Slices**
Replace Spike with powdered ginger, cumin, or another seasoning, such as Mrs. Dash.

# Ginger Lemon Adzuki Beans

Makes 5 cups (1.25 L)

Genetic evidence suggests that adzuki beans originated in the Himalayas. These reddish beans have been used for thousands of years in Chinese, Korean, and Japanese cuisine as a low-fat source of protein, iron, zinc, potassium, many B vitamins, and fibre. Nutty and sweet, the cooked beans are ground into a paste that is used as a filling in confections such as buns and cakes. Here, adzuki beans are seasoned and served as a hot savoury dish. Try this recipe in combination with Coconut Saffron Rice with Cardamom and Lime (page 193).

1 tablespoon (15 mL) coconut or olive oil
2 teaspoons (10 mL) toasted sesame oil
1/2 onion, diced
3 large cloves garlic, minced
2 tablespoons (30 mL) minced ginger
6 cups (1.5 L) cooked adzuki beans
2 cups (500 mL) water
2 tablespoons (30 mL) tamari or soy sauce
1/2 teaspoon (2 mL) salt
2 tablespoons (30 mL) lemon juice

Heat the coconut and sesame oils in a large pot over medium heat; add the onion and cook for 3 to 5 minutes or until translucent. Add garlic and ginger and cook for 1 minute. Add adzuki beans, water, tamari, and salt, reduce heat to low, and cook for 10 minutes. Stir in the lemon juice and serve.

Per cup (250 mL): calories: 439, protein: 23 g, fat: 6 g, carbohydrate: 75 g (1 g from sugar), dietary fibre: 22 g, calcium: 92 mg, iron: 6 mg, magnesium: 159 mg, phosphorus: 506 mg, potassium: 1608 mg, sodium: 623 mg, zinc: 5 mg, thiamin: 0.4 mg, riboflavin: 0.2 mg, niacin: 6 mg, vitamin $B_6$: 0.3 mg, folate: 357 mcg, pantothenic acid: 1.3 mg, vitamin $B_{12}$: 0 mcg, vitamin A: 1 mcg, vitamin C: 4 mg, vitamin E: 0 mg, omega-6 fatty acids: 1 g, omega-3 fatty acids: 0 g

Percentage of calories from protein 20%, fat 12%, carbohydrate 68%

# African Chickpea Stew

Makes 6 cups (1.5 L), enough for 4 servings

Peanut butter makes a wonderful creamy sauce for this nutrition-packed stew that is likely to become a family favourite. It is well loved by children and adults alike and has a good balance of protein, fat, and carbohydrate. Lemon juice, added at the end of cooking, adds a lively note to the flavour. If you like, add a dash of hot pepper sauce, fiery chipotle sauce, or Vietnamese chili sauce.

1 tablespoon (15 mL) coconut or olive oil
1 onion, diced
2 cloves garlic, minced
4 cups (1 L) vegetable stock or water
2 cups (500 mL) peeled, diced sweet potatoes or yams
1 cup (250 mL) cooked or canned chickpeas, drained and rinsed
1/2 cup (125 mL) uncooked brown rice
1/4 teaspoon (1 mL) salt
1/4 cup (60 mL) peanut butter
2 cups (500 mL) thinly sliced kale or collard leaves
2 tablespoons (30 mL) freshly squeezed lemon juice
1/2 teaspoon (2 mL) black pepper
Tamari
Hot chili pepper sauce

Heat the oil in a pot over medium heat. Add onion and cook for 3 to 5 minutes or until translucent. Add garlic and cook for 3 more minutes. Add stock, sweet potatoes, chickpeas, rice, and salt; bring to a boil, reduce heat, cover, and simmer for 45 minutes or until the rice is cooked. In a small bowl, blend peanut butter with enough liquid from the stew to make a smooth paste. Stir this paste into the stew along with kale, lemon juice, pepper, and tamari and chili pepper sauce to taste and cook for another 5 minutes. Adjust the seasoning.

Per cup (250 mL): calories: 383, protein: 12 g, fat: 14 g, carbohydrate: 55 g (8 g from sugar), dietary fibre: 7 g, calcium: 102 mg, iron: 3 mg, magnesium: 106 mg, phosphorus: 247 mg, potassium: 661 mg, sodium: 530 mg, zinc: 2 mg, thiamin: 0.3 mg, riboflavin: 0.1 mg, niacin: 7.6 mg, vitamin $B_6$: 0.6 mg, folate: 142 mcg, pantothenic acid: 1.7 mg, vitamin $B_{12}$: 0 mcg, vitamin A: 498 mcg, vitamin C: 15 mg, vitamin E: 3 mg, omega-6 fatty acids: 3.2 g, omega-3 fatty acids: 0.1 g

Percentage of calories from protein 13%, fat 32%, carbohydrate 55%

# Baked Potato and Fixin's Bar

Makes 1 potato with assorted toppings

There are many options for topping a baked potato apart from butter and sour cream; two excellent choices are Lemon Tahini Dressing (page 122) and Liquid Gold Dressing (page 123). Build a meal around baked potatoes and assorted toppings by adding soup, salad, or Crispy Tofu Slices (page 143). Potatoes bake very well without oil, though coating with a minimal amount will soften the skin, which some people prefer.

**1 russet potato or other baking potato, washed**
**Olive oil, to coat potatoes (optional)**

Preheat the oven to 375°F (190°C). Pierce the potato 3 or 4 times with knife or fork. Put the olive oil into the palm of your hand and rub on to the potato. Bake the potato for about 45 minutes or until soft when a skewer is inserted into the potato.

## Low-Calorie Toppings

- Diced red bell pepper, tomato, cucumber
- Dulse or kelp powder or flakes
- Fresh chopped herbs such as parsley or basil
- Gomasio (a Japanese condiment made of sesame seeds and salt)
- Miso, thinned with a little water
- Nutritional yeast
- Salsa or hot sauce such as Tabasco
- Sliced green or diced red onion
- Your favourite low-fat salad dressing
- Salt and freshly cracked pepper
- Veggie (soy) bacon bits

## Creamy Toppings

- Earth Balance spread (see page 26)
- Grated non-dairy cheese
- Lemon Tahini Dressing (page 122)
- Light Mushroom Gravy (page 214)
- Limey Avocado Dip (page 91)
- Liquid Gold Dressing (page 123)
- Pesto-the-Best-Oh! (page 92)
- Rosemary Gravy (page 217)
- Walnut, Olive, and Sun-Dried Tomato Tapenade (page 97)

## Other

- Roasted Sunflower or Pumpkin Seeds (page 94)

# Coconut Mango Black Beans

Makes about 2 cups (500 mL)

By having a few staples on hand, such as canned black beans and frozen mango pieces, this simple entrée can be made in a matter of minutes. Experiment with different seasonings by replacing the chili powder with any, or a combination, of the following flavours to suit your preference: allspice, fresh chili peppers such as ancho, chipotle, or jalapeño, cilantro, ground coriander, ground cumin (regular or toasted), curry powder, garlic, minced ginger, or minced lemon grass. Serve with rice and salsa.

1 3/4 cups (435 mL) cooked or canned black beans, drained and rinsed
1/4 cup (60 mL) coconut milk
1 tablespoon (15 mL) freshly squeezed lime juice
1 teaspoon (5 mL) chili powder
1/4 teaspoon (1 mL) salt
2 cups (500 mL) fresh or frozen mango pieces

Put the black beans, coconut milk, lime juice, chili powder, and salt in a medium saucepan and heat until the coconut milk comes to a boil. Reduce heat to medium-low, cover, and cook for 10 minutes. Add the mango, cover, and cook for 3 minutes or until heated through, stirring occasionally.

Per cup (250 mL): calories: 396, protein: 16 g, fat: 8 g, carbohydrate: 71 g (26 g from sugar), dietary fibre: 16 g, calcium: 78 mg, iron: 5 mg, magnesium: 148 mg, phosphorus: 283 mg, potassium: 985 mg, sodium: 285 mg, zinc: 2 mg, thiamin: 1 mg, riboflavin: 0.2 mg, niacin: 5 mg, vitamin $B_6$: 0.5 mg, folate: 269 mcg, pantothenic acid: 1 mg, vitamin $B_{12}$: 0 mcg, vitamin A: 125 mcg, vitamin C: 53 mg, vitamin E: 3 mg, omega-6 fatty acids: 0.6 g, omega-3 fatty acids: 0.3 g

Percentage of calories from protein 15%, fat 18%, carbohydrate 67%

**Coconut Black Beans with Papaya**
Replace the mango with 1 small papaya, peeled, seeded, and cut into 1/2-inch (1 cm) cubes

**Coconut Black Beans with Avocado**
Replace the mango with 1 avocado, sliced or cubed, added to the plate or bowl after the beans are cooked.

# Cashew Cheese Lasagna

Makes 12 servings, each about 4 × 2 inches (10 × 5 cm)

Cashews provide a wonderful cheesy-tasting topping for this delicious lasagna. Each serving is rich in protein, iron, zinc, other minerals, and B vitamins. Salt is typically added to canned tomato products, so to lower your sodium intake, try one of the low-sodium tomato sauces that are available. For best flavour in the topping, use freshly squeezed lemon juice; however, good-quality bottled lemon juice also will work.

## Lasagna

- 12 ounces (340 g) lasagna noodles (12 noodles)
- 3 packages (each 12.3 ounces/349 g) extra-firm silken tofu
- 2 tablespoons (30 mL) coconut or olive oil
- 1 onion, diced
- 3 cups (750 mL) chopped mushrooms
- 2 cups (500 mL) diced celery
- 1 teaspoon (5 mL) dried basil
- 1 teaspoon (5 mL) dried oregano
- 1/2 teaspoon (2 mL) salt (optional)
- 1/4 teaspoon (1 mL) black pepper
- 3 cups (750 mL) tomato sauce
- 1 large tomato, sliced

## Cashew Cheese Topping

Makes 3 cups (750 mL)

- 1 1/2 cups (375 mL) unsalted raw cashew pieces
- 1 1/2 cups (375 mL) water
- 1/3 cup (85 mL) nutritional yeast
- 1/3 cup (85 mL) lemon juice
- 4 teaspoons (20 mL) tamari or soy sauce
- 2 teaspoons (10 mL) onion powder
- 1 teaspoon (5 mL) celery seed
- 1/2 teaspoon (2 mL) garlic powder

To prepare the lasagna, cook the noodles according to the package directions. Drain in a colander, then immediately plunge into cold water to stop the cooking. Drain the noodles again and then lay them side by side on cookie sheets or trays to prevent them from sticking together. If stacking, place clear film between the layers of noodles.

Place the tofu in a large bowl and mash it well with a masher or fork. Heat the oil in a skillet over medium heat and cook the onion for 5 minutes or until translucent. Add mushrooms, celery, basil, oregano, salt, and pepper and cook for 5 minutes or until the water from the mushrooms has evaporated. Add the vegetable mixture to the mashed tofu and mix well.

To make the topping, combine the cashews, water, yeast, lemon juice, tamari, onion powder, celery seed, and garlic powder in a blender. Process at high speed for 1 minute or until mixture is smooth.

Preheat the oven to 350°F (180°C).

To assemble the lasagna, spread 1 cup of the tomato sauce on the bottom of a 9 × 13-inch (23 × 33 cm) baking dish to prevent noodles from sticking to the dish. Arrange 3 noodles over the sauce, followed by one-third of the tofu mixture. Spread on another cup of the tomato sauce, followed by 3 noodles and another one-third of the tofu mixture. Repeat this sequence one more time using the remaining ingredients and ending with noodles. Pour the cashew topping evenly over the top layer of noodles. Arrange the tomato slices on top and bake for 30 to 40 minutes or until the topping has set and the lasagna bubbles along the sides of the dish.

Per serving: calories: 316, protein: 17 g, fat: 13 g, carbohydrate: 37 g (5 g from sugar), dietary fibre: 4 g, calcium: 72 mg, iron: 4 mg, magnesium: 117 mg, phosphorus: 319 mg, potassium: 774 mg, sodium: 582 mg, zinc: 3 mg, thiamin: 2.3 mg, riboflavin: 2.2 mg, niacin: 17 mg, vitamin $B_6$: 2 mg, folate: 129 mcg, pantothenic acid: 0.9 mg, vitamin $B_{12}$: 1.5 mcg, vitamin A: 12 mcg, vitamin C: 11 mg, vitamin E: 1.4 mg, omega-6 fatty acids: 1.6 g, omega-3 fatty acids: 0 g

Percentage of calories from protein 20%, fat 35%, carbohydrate 45%

**Lasagna with Firm Tofu**
Replace the silken tofu with 3 packages (each 12.3 ounces/349 g) firm tofu

## Curried Vegetables with Tofu

Makes 6 cups (1.5 L)

This dish provides a delightful blend of colours, textures and flavours, and it's rich in minerals and vitamins. It is best served with basmati rice, though it also goes well with other types of rice, millet, or quinoa. For a change, make this curry without tofu and serve it with Indian Chickpeas (page 152).

- 1/4 cup (60 mL) boiling water
- 1/4 cup (60 mL) raisins
- 2 tablespoons (30 mL) coconut or olive oil
- 1 large onion, diced
- 2 cloves garlic, minced
- 1 tablespoon (15 mL) minced ginger
- 1 teaspoon (5 mL) curry powder
- 1 teaspoon (5 mL) ground cumin
- 1/2 teaspoon (2 mL) ground coriander
- 1/2 teaspoon (2 mL) salt
- 7 ounces (210 mL) coconut milk
- 1 cup (250 mL) diced carrots
- 1 cup (250 mL) diced red bell pepper
- 1 cup (250 mL) broccoli florets
- 1 cup (250 mL) cauliflower florets
- 1 package (12.3 ounces/349 g) firm tofu, diced
- 1 tablespoon (15 mL) lime juice
- 2 tablespoons (30 mL) chopped fresh cilantro or parsley

Pour the boiling water over the raisins and let soak for 15 minutes. Heat the oil in a pan over medium heat and cook the onion for 3 to 5 minutes until translucent. Add the garlic and ginger and cook for 1 minute. Stir in the curry, cumin, coriander, and salt; cook for 1 minute, stirring frequently to avoid scorching. Add the raisins and soaking liquid to the pan and then the coconut milk, carrots, red pepper, broccoli, cauliflower, and tofu. Simmer, covered, until vegetables are tender-crisp. Stir in lime juice. Adjust the seasoning, garnish with cilantro, and serve.

Per cup (250 mL): calories: 266, protein: 12 g, fat: 18 g, carbohydrate: 21 g (9 g from sugar), dietary fibre: 5 g, calcium: 437 mg, iron: 8 mg, magnesium: 72 mg, phosphorus: 200 mg, potassium: 592 mg, sodium: 198 mg, zinc: 1.5 mg, thiamin: 0.2 mg, riboflavin: 0.2 mg, niacin: 4 mg, vitamin $B_6$: 0.3 mg, folate: 61 mcg, pantothenic acid: 0.5 mg, vitamin $B_{12}$: 0 mcg, vitamin A: 250 mcg, vitamin C: 76 mg, vitamin E: 1 mg, omega-6 fatty acids: 3 g, omega-3 fatty acids: 0.4 g

Percentage of calories from protein 16%, fat 55%, carbohydrate 29%

# Dhal-icious

Makes 3 cups (750 mL)

*Dhal* is the Indian word for beans, peas, and lentils and the dishes made from them. In this recipe, the popped mustard seeds and the other Indian spices when cooked release their fragrant oils and acids to create a rich and appetizing dish. Although the dhal is ready to eat when the lentils or mung beans are soft—after about 60 minutes of cooking—the best flavour is achieved by simmering on very low heat for 2 hours, adding water if necessary.

2 tablespoons (30 mL) coconut or olive oil
1 teaspoon (5 mL) mustard seeds
1/2 onion, diced
1 clove garlic, minced
1 tablespoon (15 mL) minced ginger
1 teaspoon (5 mL) curry powder
1 teaspoon (5 mL) garam masala
1 cup (250 mL) dried lentils or mung beans, picked over and rinsed
3 cups (750 mL) water
1/2 teaspoon (2 mL) salt
1/4 teaspoon (1 mL) black pepper
1 tablespoon (15 mL) lemon juice

Heat the oil in a large pot over medium heat. Add mustard seeds, cover, and cook for 1 to 2 minutes or until seeds start to pop. Add onion, garlic, and ginger and cook until the onion is translucent. Stir in curry powder and garam masala and cook for 1 to 2 minutes, stirring frequently to avoid scorching. Add lentils and water; bring to a boil, reduce heat, cover, and simmer for 60 minutes. Add salt, pepper, and lemon juice and adjust seasoning.

Per cup (250 mL): calories: 341, protein: 20 g, fat: 11 g, carbohydrate: 45 g (5 g from sugar), dietary fibre: 9 g, calcium: 73 mg, iron: 8 mg, magnesium: 92 mg, phosphorus: 340 mg, potassium: 732 mg, sodium: 330 mg, zinc: 3 mg, thiamin: 0.4 mg, riboflavin: 0.2 mg, niacin: 5 mg, vitamin $B_6$: 0.5 mg, folate: 304 mcg, pantothenic acid: 1.3 mg, vitamin $B_{12}$: 0 mcg, vitamin A: 2 mcg, vitamin C: 9 mg, vitamin E: 2 mg, omega-6 fatty acids: 1 g, omega-3 fatty acids: 0.2 g

Percentage of calories from protein 23%, fat 27%, carbohydrate 50%

# Indian Chickpeas

Makes 4 cups (1 L)

Once you've discovered curry pastes, you'll enjoy the ease with which you can put together a vegetable, lentil, or bean curry. Even the mild pastes are hot enough for many people. The Patak's brand is our favourite. Use a little or a lot, depending on your preference. Chickpeas are rich in protein, minerals, and the B vitamin folate.

1/2 onion, diced
1 tablespoon (15 mL) coconut or olive oil
2 cloves garlic, minced
2 cups (500 mL) chopped fresh or canned tomatoes
1 tablespoon (15 mL) mild Indian curry paste
3 cups (750 mL) cooked or canned chickpeas, drained and rinsed
1 tablespoon (15 mL) lemon juice
1 teaspoon (5 mL) tamari or soy sauce
1/4 teaspoon (1 mL) salt (optional)

Cook the onion in the oil in a pan over medium heat for 3 to 5 minutes or until translucent. Add the garlic, tomatoes, and curry paste and cook for 3 minutes. Add chickpeas, lemon juice, tamari, and salt; cook for 15 minutes. Adjust the seasoning.

Per cup (250 mL): calories: 288, protein: 13 g, fat: 9 g, carbohydrate: 42 g (9 g from sugar), dietary fibre: 8 g, calcium: 83 mg, iron: 4 mg, magnesium: 77 mg, phosphorus: 252 mg, potassium: 649 mg, sodium: 100 mg, zinc: 2 mg, thiamin: 0.2 mg, riboflavin: 0.1 mg, niacin: 3 mg, vitamin $B_6$: 0.3 mg, folate: 242 mcg, pantothenic acid: 0.5 mg, vitamin $B_{12}$: 0 mcg, vitamin A: 40 mcg, vitamin C: 17 mg, vitamin E: 2 mg, omega-6 fatty acids: 2 g, omega-3 fatty acids: 0.1 g

Percentage of calories from protein 17%, fat 27%, carbohydrate 56%

# French Lentils with Fennel and Lemon

Makes 6 cups (1.5 L)

Lentils have a mild earthy flavour and contain good amounts of protein, iron, and many of the B vitamins, while being very low in fat. The best lentils for this recipe are the small, delicate French green lentils, considered to be the Rolls-Royce of the lentil world. Puy lentils are grown near Puy-en-Velay in Auvergne, a rugged mountainous region with volcanic soil in the south of France. The Puy lentil is controlled by a French governing agency that allows the name to be given to only those lentils grown in the region.

1 tablespoon (15 mL) coconut or olive oil
1/2 onion, chopped
2 cloves garlic, minced
1 bulb fennel, chopped, about 2 cups (500 mL)
5 cups (1.25 L) water
1 cup (250 mL) Puy or other French lentils
2 cups (500 mL) diced tomatoes
1 teaspoon (5 mL) dried thyme
1 teaspoon (5 mL) dried basil
1/2 teaspoon (2 mL) minced lemon peel
1 teaspoon (5 mL) salt
1/4 teaspoon (1 mL) black pepper

Heat the oil in a pan over medium heat. Add the onion, garlic, and fennel and cook for 5 minutes or until the onion is translucent. Add the water, lentils, tomatoes, thyme, basil, and lemon peel. Bring to a boil, reduce heat to low, cover, and cook for 45 to 60 minutes or until the lentils are soft to the bite. Add the salt and pepper and serve.

Per cup (250 mL): calories: 157, protein: 10 g, fat: 3 g, carbohydrate: 24 g (4 g from sugar), dietary fibre: 5 g, calcium: 45 mg, iron: 4 mg, magnesium: 49 mg, phosphorus: 181 mg, potassium: 539 mg, sodium: 407 mg, zinc: 1 mg, thiamin: 0.2 mg, riboflavin: 0.1 mg, niacin: 3 mg, vitamin $B_6$: 0.3 mg, folate: 162 mcg, pantothenic acid: 0.7 mg, vitamin $B_{12}$: 0 mcg, vitamin A: 29 mcg, vitamin C: 13 mg, vitamin E: 0.5 mg, omega-6 fatty acids: 0.1 g, omega-3 fatty acids: 0 g

Percentage of calories from protein 26%, fat 15%, carbohydrate 59%

# Holiday Stuffed Winter Squash

Makes 1 stuffed squash, about 8 servings

For many, getting together to cook is one of the best parts of a celebration. Assembling this stuffed, baked squash can be the central activity for a wonderful day spent with the people you love. Serve it with Light Mushroom Gravy (page 214), Miso Gravy (page 216) or Rosemary Gravy (page 217), plus other items from the Holiday Menu (page 72). Choose a soft-skinned squash such as kabocha, butternut or acorn. Several smaller squashes work too, if you can't find a single large one, as called for in this recipe.

**1 winter squash, about 5 pounds (2.27 kg)**
**1 recipe Quinoa Stuffing for Vegetables (page 168)**

Preheat the oven to 350°F (180°C).

Pierce the top of the squash with a sharp knife at a 45-degree angle, 2 inches (5 cm) from the centre of the top. Pushing the knife blade away from your body, cut around the top of the squash, and remove the cone-shaped top piece. Remove any fibrous material from the top and then set it aside. Using a spoon, remove the seeds and pulp from the cavity of the squash. Put the top back on the squash, place on a baking sheet, and pre-bake for 30 minutes. Remove from the oven and set aside to cool for 15 minutes.

Spoon the stuffing into the squash cavity. Leave 1 inch (2.5 cm) of room to allow the stuffing to expand while baking. Set squash lid in place, return squash to the baking sheet, and bake for 45 to 60 minutes or until a toothpick can be easily inserted into the side of the squash. Leftover stuffing can be placed in a loaf pan, sprinkled with 2 to 3 tablespoons (30 to 45 mL) water, covered, and heated in the oven for the last 20 minutes of the cooking time for the squash. Remove the squash from the oven and place on a warm serving platter. Slice into wedges and serve. Any leftover stuffing can be served on the platter or in a bowl.

Per serving: calories: 293, protein: 12 g, fat: 9 g, carbohydrate: 48 g (2 g from sugar), dietary fibre: 10 g, calcium: 82 mg, iron: 4 mg, magnesium: 148 mg, phosphorus: 247 mg, potassium: 1264 mg, sodium: 156 mg, zinc: 2 mg, thiamin: 0.5 mg, riboflavin: 0.3 mg, niacin: 6 mg, vitamin $B_6$: 0.6 mg, folate: 96 mcg, pantothenic acid: 2 mg, vitamin $B_{12}$: 0 mcg, vitamin A: 781 mcg, vitamin C: 53 mg, vitamin E: 4 mg, omega-6 fatty acids: 4 g, omega-3 fatty acids: 0.4 g

Percentage of calories from protein 15%, fat 26%, carbohydrate 59%

**Variations:**
Replace the quinoa in the stuffing with rice, buckwheat, millet, or lentils, or a mixture of these, and cook as directed in the recipe. Replace the sunflower seeds with cashews, walnuts or almonds.

# Lemon Ginger Tempeh

Makes two 4-ounce (113 g) servings

Tempeh is a traditional Indonesian food that is made with cooked, dehulled soybeans and a live culture; the combination is fermented for a day or two. Tempeh is easy to digest and has excellent protein quality, abundant minerals (including calcium, iron, magnesium, and zinc), and B vitamins. Tempeh is stored in the refrigerator and freezer sections of natural foods stores in order to keep the fermentation process in check. There, you may discover tempeh that includes cereal grains, vegetables, and various seasonings.

8 ounces (220 g) tempeh
3 tablespoons (45 mL) freshly squeezed lemon juice
4 teaspoons (20 mL) tamari or soy sauce
2 teaspoons (10 mL) minced ginger
1 teaspoon (5 mL) minced garlic
1/2 teaspoon (2 mL) onion powder

Tempeh packages often provide 2 slices of tempeh, each about 1/2 inch (1 cm) thick; if not, make 2 such slices. Quarter each slice so that you have 8 quarters each about $2 \times 2 \times 1/2$ inches ($5 \times 5 \times 1$ cm). Put the tempeh on a pie plate or pan. In a small bowl combine the lemon juice, tamari, ginger, garlic, and onion powder. Pour the lemon juice mixture over the tempeh and refrigerate for a minimum of 2 hours, turning occasionally to ensure both sides marinate evenly.

Once the tempeh has marinated, preheat the oven for 5 minutes on the broiler setting. Put the tempeh under the broiler for 2 minutes, turn, and heat for another 2 minutes. Alternatively, bake at 350°F (180°C) for 10 minutes.

Per serving: calories: 238, protein: 23 g, fat: 12 g, carbohydrate: 15 g (1 g from sugar), dietary fibre: 7 g, calcium: 135 mg, iron: 3 mg, magnesium: 100 mg, phosphorus: 324 mg, potassium: 541 mg, sodium: 691 mg, zinc: 1 mg, thiamin: 0.1 mg, riboflavin: 0.4 mg, niacin: 9 mg, vitamin B$_6$: 0.3 mg, folate: 33 mcg, pantothenic acid: 0.4 mg, vitamin B$_{12}$: 0 mcg, vitamin A: 0 mcg, vitamin C: 11 mg, vitamin E: 0 mg, omega-6 fatty acids: 4 g, omega-3 fatty acids: 0.2 g

Percentage of calories from protein 35%, fat 22%, carbohydrate 43%

**Fried Lemon Ginger Tempeh**
Marinate the tempeh as described above. Heat 2 teaspoons (10 mL) coconut or olive oil in a skillet over medium heat. Add the tempeh and cook for 3 minutes on each side or until brown.

**Tempeh with Tofu Marinade**
Marinate tempeh with Tofu Marinade (page 221) for 2 hours or more and broil or fry as described in recipe and variation above.

# International Roll-Ups

Each version makes one 9-inch (23 cm) tortilla roll

Here we've provided recipes for six possible fillings, based on various cuisines.

## African Style

1/3 cup (85 mL) cooked brown rice
1/3 cup (85 mL) cooked mashed yam
1/3 cup (85 mL) sliced kale, lightly steamed
1/4 cup (60 mL) alfalfa sprouts
2 tablespoons (30 mL) Spicy Peanut Sauce (page 218)
Dash of hot pepper sauce

## Indonesian Style

1/2 cup (125 mL) cooked brown rice
2 ounces (55 g) Lemon Ginger Tempeh (page 155)
1/4 cup (60 mL) sliced napa cabbage
2 tablespoons (30 mL) sliced water chestnuts
1 teaspoon (5 mL) sliced pickled ginger
2 tablespoons (30 mL) Tamarind Date Sauce (page 219)

## Italian Style

1/2 cup (125 mL) cooked brown rice
1/2 cup (125 mL) chopped spinach
2 fresh or canned artichoke hearts, sliced
1 teaspoon (5 mL) chopped fresh basil
1 lettuce leaf, cut into strips
2 tablespoons (30 mL) tomato sauce

## Japanese Style

1/2 cup (125 mL) cooked brown rice
1/4 cup (60 mL) grated carrot
1/4 cup (60 mL) grated daikon radish
2 teaspoons (10 mL) eggless mayonnaise
2 teaspoons (10 mL) sliced pickled ginger
1/2 teaspoon (2 mL) toasted sesame seeds (see page 133)
1 tablespoon (15 mL) thinly sliced green onion
2 tablespoons (30 mL) Teriyaki Sauce (page 220)

## Mexican Style

- 1/2 cup (125 mL) cooked brown rice
- 1/4 cup (60 mL) grated carrot
- 1/4 cup (60 mL) shredded non-dairy cheese
- 1 teaspoon (5 mL) chopped fresh cilantro
- 2 teaspoons (10 mL) eggless mayonnaise
- 1 lettuce leaf, cut into strips
- 2 tablespoons (30 mL) salsa

## Middle Eastern Style

- 1/2 cup (125 mL) Heart-Healthy Hummus (page 90)
- 1/4 cup (60 mL) chopped fresh tomato
- 1/4 cup (60 mL) grated carrot
- 1 tablespoon (15 mL) chopped fresh parsley
- 1 lettuce leaf, cut into strips
- 2 tablespoons (30 mL) Lemon Tahini Dressing (page 122)

Decide how many rolls you would like to make, prepare the appropriate amount of ingredients, and have them ready on the counter. To assemble each roll, spread the rice or hummus, depending on which version you're making, across the bottom third of the tortilla, leaving a 2-inch (5 cm) margin that is free of ingredients on the side nearest you and along the right edge. Place the remaining ingredients on top of the rice or hummus. Lift the right edge of the tortilla and fold it toward the centre. Take the edge nearest you and proceed to snugly roll the tortilla toward the centre and continue rolling until you have reached the top of the tortilla and have a roll in your hands.

Per one African-Style International Roll-Up: calories: 247, protein: 8 g, fat: 7 g, carbohydrate: 41 g (9 g from sugar), dietary fibre: 6 g, calcium: 77 mg, iron: 2 mg, magnesium: 80 mg, phosphorus: 152 mg, potassium: 499 mg, sodium: 709 mg, zinc: 1 mg, thiamin: 0.2 mg, riboflavin: 0.1 mg, niacin: 5 mg, vitamin $B_6$: 0.4 mg, folate: 29 mcg, pantothenic acid: 1 mg, vitamin $B_{12}$: 0 mcg, vitamin A: 2 mcg, vitamin C: 33 mg, vitamin E: 2 mg, omega-6 fatty acids: 2 g, omega-3 fatty acids: 0.1 g

Percentage of calories from protein 12%, fat 24%, carbohydrate 64%

# Lima Beans, Corn, and Chipotle Pepper

Makes 4 cups (1 L)

Lima beans originate in South America; indeed, they are named after the capital of Peru. They have a flat, oblong shape, a creamy, starchy texture, and a sweet flavour. This recipe is a variation of the classic southern American dish, succotash, but it has a Mexican twist through the addition of chipotle pepper, lime juice, and cilantro.

1 tablespoon (15 mL) coconut or olive oil
1/2 onion, diced
2 cloves garlic, minced
2 1/2 cups (625 mL) cooked baby lima beans
1 cup (250 mL) corn kernels
1/2 cup (125 mL) diced red bell pepper
1/2 cup (125 mL) water
1/4 cup (60 mL) lime juice
1 to 2 teaspoons (5 to 10 mL) minced chipotle pepper
1/2 teaspoon (2 mL) salt
1/4 cup (60 mL) chopped fresh cilantro or parsley

Heat the oil in a skillet over medium heat and cook the onion for 3 to 5 minutes or until translucent. Add the garlic and cook for 2 minutes. Stir in the lima beans, corn, bell pepper, water, lime juice, chipotle, and salt. Cook for 10 minutes, stirring occasionally and adding more water if the mixture gets too dry. Stir in cilantro, adjust seasoning, and serve.

Per cup (250 mL): calories: 233, protein: 11 g, fat: 4 g, carbohydrate: 40 g (3 g from sugar), dietary fibre: 11 g, calcium: 46 mg, iron: 3 mg, magnesium: 85 mg, phosphorus: 203 mg, potassium: 680 mg, sodium: 248 mg, zinc: 2 mg, thiamin: 0.3 mg, riboflavin: 0.1 mg, niacin: 4 mg, vitamin $B_6$: 0.2 mg, folate: 207 mcg, pantothenic acid: 1 mg, vitamin $B_{12}$: 0 mcg, vitamin A: 36 mcg, vitamin C: 48 mg, vitamin E: 1 mg, omega-6 fatty acids: 0.4 g, omega-3 fatty acids: 0.1 g

Percentage of calories from protein 19%, fat 16%, carbohydrate 65%

# Mac Un-Cheese

Makes 4 1/2 cups (1.125 L)

This is a vegan version of a creamy, cheesy, childhood favourite. A cup (250 mL) provides most of your B vitamins for the day, including vitamin B12 when made with Red Star Vegetarian Support Formula nutritional yeast. One cup (250 mL) of Mac Un-Cheese also provides 12 grams of protein (and more in the variation with wieners). Some children prefer this dish without the onion or tomatoes, as in the very simple variation listed below.

1 1/2 cups (375 mL) uncooked macaroni, about 12 ounces (340 g)
1 tablespoon (15 mL) coconut or olive oil
1/2 onion, finely chopped
1 3/4 cups (435 mL) canned, diced tomatoes (14-ounce/398 g can)
1 tablespoon (15 mL) nutritional yeast
1 cup (250 mL) Gee Whiz Spread (page 88) or grated non-dairy cheese

Cook pasta in simmering water according to package directions or until al dente. Drain well and return to the cooking pot.

Heat the oil in a saucepan over medium heat. Add the onion and cook until translucent. Stir in the tomatoes and yeast. Add the Gee Whiz Spread, mix well, and heat through. Stir into the hot pasta, thoroughly coating with the sauce. Season to taste.

Per cup (250 mL): calories: 267, protein: 12 g, fat: 6 g, carbohydrate: 43g (4 g from sugar), dietary fibre: 5 g, calcium: 68 mg, iron: 3 mg, magnesium: 58 mg, phosphorus: 216 mg, potassium: 517 mg, sodium: 229 mg, zinc: 2 mg, thiamin: 3.9 mg, riboflavin: 3.7 mg, niacin: 26 mg, vitamin $B_6$: 3.5 mg, folate: 216 mcg, pantothenic acid: 0.8 mg, vitamin $B_{12}$: 2.7 mcg, vitamin A: 21 mcg, vitamin C: 21 mg, vitamin E: 1 mg, omega-6 fatty acids: 1 g, omega-3 fatty acids: 0.1 g

Percentage of calories from protein 17%, fat 20%, carbohydrate 63%

**Gluten-Free Mac Un-Cheese**
Replace wheat macaroni with rice pasta or corn pasta.

**Mac Un-Cheese and Wieners**
Add 3 or 4 chopped veggie wieners at the same time as the tomatoes and heat through.

**Simple Mac Un-Cheese**
Omit the oil, onion, tomatoes, and pepper. Stir the non-dairy cheese into the hot pasta, with optional nutritional yeast and salt.

**Mac Un-Cheese with Zip**
Add 1 teaspoon (5 mL) minced garlic plus hot sauce or cayenne pepper to taste, along with the onion.

**Note:** As this dish cools or if leftovers are refrigerated, the macaroni will continue to absorb moisture from the sauce. When the dish is reheated, add a little tomato juice, water, non-dairy milk, or chopped, fresh tomatoes for moisture.

# Marinated Tofu

Makes 2 cups (500 mL)

Tofu is made from soy milk, to which a coagulant is added. The mixture is then poured into a mould, and pressed in order to make it firm. Sold in a variety of styles, textures, and flavours, its firmness depends on the amount of pressure that is applied after the soy milk is poured into the mould. The firmness, or sponginess, of the final product determines how readily it absorbs the flavours it comes in contact with (see below).

**1 package (12.3 ounces/349 g) medium-firm, firm, or extra-firm tofu, cut into cubes**
**1 cup (250 mL) Tofu Marinade (page 221)**

Place tofu cubes in a container with a lid. Pour marinade over tofu so that it covers the tofu. Cover the container and refrigerate for 6 hours. Drain excess marinade from tofu.

Per 1/2 cup (125 mL): calories: 139, protein: 14 g, fat: 9 g, carbohydrate: 4 g (0 g from sugar), dietary fibre: 2 g, calcium: 599 mg, iron: 9 mg, magnesium: 53 mg, phosphorus: 174 mg, potassium: 228 mg, sodium: 296 mg, zinc: 1 mg, thiamin: 0.1 mg, riboflavin: 0.1 mg, niacin: 4 mg, vitamin $B_6$: 0.1 mg, folate: 27 mcg, pantothenic acid: 0.1 mg, vitamin $B_{12}$: 0 mcg, vitamin A: 18 mcg, vitamin C: 1 mg, vitamin E: 0 mg, omega-6 fatty acids: 4 g, omega-3 fatty acids: 1 g

Percentage of calories from protein 38%, fat 51%, carbohydrate 11%

**Note**: Analysis was done on the basis of 1/4 cup (60 mL) marinade being absorbed and retained by the 12.3 ounces (349 g) tofu. Calcium content depends on the brand of tofu used; check the labels.

---

### Marinating Tofu

Tofu has a sponge-like texture, which allows it to absorb flavour well when marinated. Tofu can be cut into cubes of different sizes depending on how it is to be used in the recipe. For example, for the Spicy Marinated Tofu Salad (page 109), the cube will be smaller than for the Vegetable Kebabs (page 186). Smaller cubes will absorb more marinade than larger cubes, thereby increasing the sodium intake for the meal. Though you'll need enough marinade to cover the tofu cubes, only part of the liquid will be absorbed. Leftover marinade can be heated and served over brown rice or thickened with arrowroot powder or cornstarch and used as a sauce for Stir-Fry 101 (page 174). The marinating time depends on the type of tofu and the marinade. Medium-firm tofu is more sponge-like and soaks up the marinade faster than other types, followed by firm, then extra-firm tofu. If you are marinating the tofu for less than 1 hour, it can be done at room temperature. For longer periods, marinating should be done in a refrigerator to prevent bacterial growth and spoilage.

# Moroccan Black Beans with Yams and Currants

Makes about 4 cups (1 L)

This recipe complements the Fiesta Quinoa Salad with Lime Dressing (page 103) for a hearty, tasty meal. It is low in fat yet rich in protein, minerals (calcium, iron, magnesium, phosphorus, potassium, and zinc), folate, and other B vitamins. To toast cumin, see the sidebar on page 133. If you prefer a milder dish, decrease the amount of chilies.

1 tablespoon (15 mL) coconut or olive oil
1/2 onion, diced
2 cloves garlic, minced
2 red chilies, minced
3 cups (750 mL) cooked or canned black beans, drained and rinsed
2 cups (500 mL) peeled, chopped yams, cut into 1/2-inch (1 cm) dice
2 1/2 cups (625 mL) water
1/2 cup (125 mL) currants
1 tablespoon (15 mL) toasted ground cumin
1 tablespoon (15 mL) ground coriander
1/2 teaspoon (2 mL) cinnamon
1/2 teaspoon (2 mL) salt
1/4 cup (60 mL) chopped fresh cilantro or parsley (optional)
1 tablespoon (15 mL) lemon juice

Heat the oil in a pot over medium heat; add the onion and cook for 3 to 5 minutes or until translucent. Add the garlic and chilies and cook for 1 minute. Stir in the black beans, yams, water, currants, cumin, coriander, cinnamon, and salt and bring to a boil. Cover, reduce heat to low, and simmer for 20 to 30 minutes or until the yams are soft. Just before serving, stir in the cilantro and lemon juice.

Per cup (250 mL): calories: 382, protein: 15 g, fat: 5 g, carbohydrate: 74 g (15 g from sugar), dietary fibre: 17 g, calcium: 97 mg, iron: 5 mg, magnesium: 135 mg, phosphorus: 282 mg, potassium: 1433 mg, sodium: 255 mg, zinc: 2 mg, thiamin: 0.5 mg, riboflavin: 0.2 mg, niacin: 5 mg, vitamin $B_6$: 0.5 mg, folate: 232 mcg, pantothenic acid: 0.7 mg, vitamin $B_{12}$: 0 mcg, vitamin A: 19 mcg, vitamin C: 50 mcg, vitamin E: 1 mg, omega-6 fatty acids: 0.4 g, omega-3 fatty acids: 0.2 g

Percentage of calories from protein 15%, fat 11%, carbohydrate 74%

## Mushroom Lentil Patties

Makes 5 patties

These veggie burgers, made with lentils and rice, are full of flavour, protein, B vitamins, and the minerals iron and zinc. Be creative and vary the seasoning with celery seed, cumin, or Cajun spice; serve with Light Mushroom Gravy (page 214) or your favourite tomato sauce. When you don't have time to make them from scratch, check the refrigerator and freezer sections of local supermarkets, as new brands and flavours of veggie burgers arrive every few months.

2 cups (500 mL) water
1/2 cup (125 mL) brown rice
1/2 cup (125 mL) dried green lentils, picked over and rinsed
1 tablespoon (15 mL) coconut or olive oil
1/2 onion, diced
2 cups (500 mL) sliced mushrooms
1/4 cup (60 mL) bread crumbs
3 tablespoons (45 mL) chopped fresh parsley
2 tablespoons (30 mL) nutritional yeast
1/2 teaspoon (2 mL) salt
1/4 teaspoon (1 mL) dried thyme
1/4 teaspoon (1 mL) dried basil
1/4 teaspoon (1 mL) paprika
Pinch of black pepper
1 tablespoon (15 mL) oil, for frying

Bring the water to a boil; add the rice and lentils, reduce heat to low, and cook for 50 minutes or until all the water is absorbed. Transfer rice and lentils to a bowl and mash with the back of a large spoon until they bind together.

While the rice and lentils are cooling, heat the coconut oil in a skillet over medium-high heat and cook the onion and mushrooms for 5 minutes or until the moisture from the mushrooms has evaporated. Stir in the bread crumbs, parsley, yeast, salt, thyme, basil, paprika, and pepper. Mix well. Form the mixture into five 4-inch (10 cm) patties. (An easy way to do this is to line a 4-inch/10 cm wide jar lid with clear wrap, tightly fill the lid with the patty mixture, then turn the patty out onto a plate.)

Heat the oil for frying in a skillet over medium heat. Cook the patties for 2 to 3 minutes on each side or until golden brown and crispy.

Per patty: calories: 222, protein: 11 g, fat: 5 g, carbohydrate: 35 g (3 g from sugar), dietary fibre: 4 g, calcium: 41 mg, iron: 3 mg, magnesium: 64 mg, phosphorus: 222 mg, potassium: 466 mg, sodium: 239 mg, zinc: 2 mg, thiamin: 2 mg, riboflavin: 2 mg, niacin: 14 mg, vitamin $B_6$: 2 mg, folate: 149 mcg, pantothenic acid: 2 mg, vitamin $B_{12}$: 1.3 mcg, vitamin A: 16 mcg, vitamin C: 7 mg, vitamin E: 0.3 mg, omega-6 fatty acids: 0.5 g, omega-3 fatty acids: 0 g

Percentage of calories from protein 18%, fat 21%, carbohydrate 61%

## Pesto Pizza

Makes two 12-inch (30 cm) pizzas

Pizza is so ingrained in North American culture that we may encounter the familiar aroma on every city block. For vegetarians with a hankering for pizza, this recipe will tingle your taste buds and warm your soul. If you like, garnish the top with chopped fresh basil after baking.

**1 recipe Pizza Dough (page 165)**
**2 cups (500 mL) Pesto-the-Best-Oh! (page 92)**
**8 tomatoes, cut into 1/4-inch (5 mm) thick slices**
**Extra-virgin olive oil, for drizzling (optional)**

Preheat the oven to 375°F (190°C).

Roll out the pizza dough, cut in half, and spread it to fit two 12-inch (30 cm) round baking trays. Spread 1 cup (250 mL) of the pesto sauce evenly over each of the crusts. Spread the tomato slices evenly over the pizzas. If you like, drizzle a thin line of extra-virgin olive oil along the edge of the unbaked pizza. Bake for 10 to 12 minutes or until the edge and crust bottoms are golden brown.

Per 1/3 pizza: calories: 616, protein: 15 g, fat: 37 g, carbohydrate: 62 g (7 g from sugar), dietary fibre: 8 g, calcium: 143 mg, iron: 6 mg, magnesium: 122 mg, phosphorus: 277 mg, potassium: 878 mg, sodium: 954 mg, zinc: 2 mg, thiamin: 0.7 mg, riboflavin: 0.5 mg, niacin: 9 mg, vitamin $B_6$: 0.5 mg, folate: 214 mcg, pantothenic acid: 1 mg, vitamin $B_{12}$: 0 mcg, vitamin A: 195 mcg, vitamin C: 34 mg, vitamin E: 3 mg, omega-6 fatty acids: 12 g, omega-3 fatty acids: 3 g

Percentage of calories from protein 9%, fat 52%, carbohydrate 39%

**Pita Pizza**
To make an individual pita bread pizza, spread 2 1/2 tablespoons (37 mL) Pesto-the-Best-Oh! (page 92) across one 6-inch (15 cm) piece of pita bread. Top with 1/4-inch (5 mm) thick slices from 1 tomato. Bake at 375°F (190°C) for 6 minutes or until the bottom starts to brown.

# Pizza Dough

Makes 2 thin 12-inch (30 cm) crusts

This dough can be used in Pesto Pizza (page 164), Tapenade Pizza (page 180), and Veggie Pepperoni Pizza (page 188). If you do not have a cooking thermometer, it's helpful to know that water that is 100°F (38°C) is just slightly warm to the touch. We suggest using a glass or ceramic bowl for this recipe because these materials retain warmth better than stainless steel. Soy milk or hemp seed milk are not essential but result in increased growth of the yeast.

2 tablespoons (30 mL) soy milk or hemp seed milk (optional)
1 tablespoon (15 mL) olive oil
1 teaspoon (5 mL) brown sugar or other sweetener
1 cup (250 mL) warm water (100°F/ 38°C)
1 package (1 tablespoon/15 mL) dry active yeast
2 3/4 cups (685 mL) unbleached all-purpose flour
1 teaspoon (5 mL) salt
Additional flour, for kneading
Additional olive oil

Heat a large glass or ceramic bowl under running hot water for 2 minutes. Place the soy milk, oil, sugar, and then the warm water in the bowl and mix thoroughly. Sprinkle yeast on top of the mixture. Fill a sink one-quarter full with slightly warm water that is about 100°F (38°C). Place the bowl in the water and leave it for 10 minutes or until the yeast appears to have doubled in size.

Slowly stir 1 cup (250 mL) of the flour into the yeast mixture to make it a porridge consistency and then add the salt. Gradually add the remaining flour and form a ball of dough. Knead the dough on a lightly floured countertop for 5 to 10 minutes. Form a round ball, lightly oil the bottom of the bowl and surface of the dough ball to prevent the dough from sticking, and return it to the bowl. Cover the top with a cloth to retain the heat. Replace the water in the sink with fresh warm water and place the bowl in the sink for 30 minutes for the dough to rise. Proceed to make your pizza of choice.

Per 1/6 recipe: calories: 247, protein: 7 g, fat: 3 g, carbohydrate: 47 g (2 g from sugar), dietary fibre: 2 g, calcium: 12 mg, iron: 3 mg, magnesium: 15 mg, phosphorus: 85 mg, potassium: 97 mg, sodium: 396 mg, zinc: 0.5 mg, thiamin: 0.5 mg, riboflavin: 0.4 mg, niacin: 6 mg, vitamin $B_6$: 0.1 mg, folate: 128 mcg, pantothenic acid: 0.5 mg, vitamin $B_{12}$: 0 mcg, vitamin A: 0 mcg, vitamin C: 0 mg, vitamin E: 0 mg, omega-6 fatty acids: 0.2 g, omega-3 fatty acids: 0 g

Percentage of calories from protein 11%, fat 11%, carbohydrate 78%

**Whole-Wheat Pizza Crust**
Replace the all-purpose flour with whole-wheat flour and add an extra 3 tablespoons (45 mL) water.

# Portobello Mushroom Burgers with Chickpea Topping

Makes 4 burgers, with 3 cups (750 mL) topping

Portobello mushrooms are large, mature cremini mushrooms with what might be called a meaty texture, making them ideal as burgers. These mushroom burgers are delicious and can be eaten with or without a bun. They are excellent sources of protein, iron, zinc, and B vitamins. If you like, add 2 to 4 tablespoons (30 to 60 mL) walnuts (to further increase the omega-3 fatty acids) or pine nuts to the topping.

## Mushroom Burgers

Four 4-inch (10 cm) portobello mushrooms

## Mushroom Marinade

1 tablespoon (15 mL) extra-virgin olive oil
1 teaspoon (5 mL) balsamic vinegar
1 teaspoon (5 mL) tamari or soy sauce

## Chickpea Topping

2 cups (500 mL) cooked or canned chickpeas, drained and rinsed
1 cup (250 mL) diced zucchini
1/4 cup (60 mL) dry-packed sun-dried tomatoes, soaked in water for 15 minutes, then chopped
2 cloves garlic, minced
2 teaspoons (10 mL) freshly squeezed lemon juice
1/2 teaspoon (2 mL) dried basil
1/2 teaspoon (2 mL) salt

## Optional Garnishes

- 4 whole-wheat buns
- Mayonnaise
- Dijon, grainy, or regular prepared mustard
- Thinly sliced red onion
- Sliced tomato
- Sliced cucumber
- Sliced pickle
- Lettuce leaf

Preheat the oven to 375°F (190°C).

Gently remove and chop the stems of the mushrooms. Put the stems in a medium bowl. Put the portobello mushrooms on a baking tray with the gills facing up.

To make the mushroom marinade, combine the oil, vinegar, and tamari in a small bowl. Drizzle the marinade over the gills of each mushroom.

To make the chickpea topping, put the chickpeas in the bowl of a food processor and pulse until the chickpeas are pulverized but not puréed. Transfer to the bowl with the chopped mushroom stems and add the zucchini, sun-dried tomatoes, garlic, lemon juice, basil, and salt. Stir to mix. Spoon one-quarter of the filling on top of each mushroom and pack down the mixture. Bake the mushrooms, uncovered, in the oven for 15 minutes or until the mushrooms and filling are heated through. Serve on a whole-wheat bun with your choice of garnishes.

Per burger: calories: 333, protein: 15 g, fat: 8 g, carbohydrate: 54 g (11 g from sugar), dietary fibre: 9 g, calcium: 110 mg, iron: 5 mg, magnesium: 92 mg, phosphorus: 272 mg, potassium: 1001 mg, sodium: 614 mg, zinc: 3 mg, thiamin: 0.3 mg, riboflavin: 0.6 mg, niacin: 8 mg, vitamin $B_6$: 0.4 mg, folate: 194 mcg, pantothenic acid: 2 mg, vitamin $B_{12}$: 0 mcg, vitamin A: 5 mcg, vitamin C: 11 mg, vitamin E: 1 mg, omega-6 fatty acids: 2 g, omega-3 fatty acids: 0.1 g

Percentage of calories from protein 17%, fat 21%, carbohydrate 62%

**Note:** Analysis includes marinade, topping, mushrooms, and buns but does not include optional garnishes.

# Quinoa Stuffing for Vegetables

Makes 6 cups (1.5 L)

Quinoa is not a true cereal grain but a seed in the goosefoot family. Other members of this plant family include spinach, beets, and lamb's quarters. In its natural state, quinoa has a bitter, resinous coating that foams up like soap when the seeds are rinsed with water. Most of this resin is removed after harvest, but the seeds should be rinsed to ensure the complete removal of this natural compound before cooking. This nutrition-packed stuffing can be used for a variety of vegetables, such as bell peppers (see variation on page 169), tomatoes, and zucchini.

1 1/2 cups (375 mL) water
1 cup (250 mL) quinoa, rinsed
1/2 teaspoon (2 mL) salt
1 tablespoon (15 mL) coconut or olive oil
1/2 onion, diced
2 cloves garlic, minced
2 stalks celery, diced
1 cup (250 mL) corn kernels
1/2 cup (125 mL) diced red bell pepper
1/2 cup (125 mL) sunflower seeds
1 tablespoon (15 mL) lime juice
1 1/2 teaspoons (7 mL) dried basil
1 1/2 teaspoons (7 mL) dried dill
1/2 teaspoon (2 mL) dried thyme
Pinch of black pepper

Bring the water to a boil over high heat in a small saucepan. Stir in quinoa and salt, reduce heat to low (just below boiling), cover, and cook for 20 minutes or until the liquid is absorbed. Transfer the quinoa to a large bowl and set aside to cool.

Heat the oil in a skillet over medium heat and cook onion for 3 to 5 minutes or until translucent. Add the garlic and celery and cook for 3 minutes. Stir into the cooled quinoa along with the corn, red pepper, sunflower seeds, lime juice, basil, dill, thyme, and pepper. Stir to mix and adjust the seasoning.

Per cup (250 mL): calories: 240, protein: 8 g, fat: 11 g, carbohydrate: 31 g (2 g from sugar), dietary fibre: 5 g, calcium: 57 mg, iron: 4 mg, magnesium: 125 mg, phosphorus: 250 mg, potassium: 485 mg, sodium: 181 mg, zinc: 2 mg, thiamin: 0.4 mg, riboflavin: 0.2 mg, niacin: 4 mg, vitamin $B_6$: 0.3 mg, folate: 66 mcg, pantothenic acid: 1 mg, vitamin $B_{12}$: 0 mcg, vitamin A: 29 mcg, vitamin C: 29 mg, vitamin E: 5 mg, omega-6 fatty acids: 5 g, omega-3 fatty acids: 0.1 g

Percentage of calories from protein 13%, fat 38%, carbohydrate 49%

**Stuffed Bell Peppers**
Preheat the oven to 350°F (180°C). Slice the tops from 6 medium-sized red, yellow, orange, or green peppers and remove the seeds and membranes to create a cavity that can be filled with quinoa stuffing. Stuff the peppers; each will require about 1 cup (250 mL) of stuffing. Put the peppers into a baking dish with a lid, cover, and bake for 30 minutes or until a knife easily pierces the skin of the peppers. Remove the lid and bake for another 10 minutes or until the tops are crispy but not too dry.

# Salad Bar

To create an appealing meal for your family or for a crowd, place bowls of colourful salad components on the table and let diners select their favourites. Your salad buffet can be simple or gourmet and can serve people with various food sensitivities or preferences. You might select one or two items from a few or many of the sections below. You could prepare the ingredients using a single technique, such as julienne, or get creative and give some ingredients a unique treatment or shape. Alternatively, make a few choices from those listed here and toss them together in a big salad bowl. Include one or more prepared salads from the salad recipes in this book for additional variety and nutrition.

## Dressings

Adding Oil and Lemon to Salad Greens (page 117)
Avocado, Grapefruit, and Chipotle Dressing (page 118)
Coconut Almond Dressing (page 119)
Cucumber Dill Dressing (page 121)
Lemon Tahini Dressing (page 122)
Liquid Gold Dressing (page 123)
Orange Ginger Dressing (page 124)
Oriental Dressing (page 125)
Serrano Chili and Cilantro Dressing (page 126)
Tomato Herb Dressing (page 127)

## Pods, Peas, and Beans

Black, garbanzo, lima, white, or other cooked beans
Green peas, raw or steamed
Snow peas, raw
Sugar snap peas, raw

## Flowering and Cruciferous Vegetables

Broccoflower florets
Broccoli florets
Broccolini florets
Cauliflower florets
Collard greens or kale, thinly sliced
Napa cabbage, sliced
Red or green cabbage, chopped

## Fruit-Vegetables

Avocado slices
Bell pepper slices (green, red, orange, or yellow)
Cherry tomatoes
Corn, young raw kernels
Olives
Tomato wedges
Zucchini slices

## Leafy Greens

Arugula, endive, radicchio, or watercress
Butterhead, leaf, or romaine lettuce, chopped
Spinach
Spring mix

# Entrées

## Nuts and Seeds

Almonds
Cashews
Roasted Sunflower or Pumpkin Seeds (page 94)
Sunflower or pumpkin seeds, raw

## Bulbs

Fennel, chopped
Green onions, chopped
Red or sweet white onion, thinly sliced

## Roots and Tubers

Beets, chopped or grated
Carrots, sliced or grated
Celeriac, chopped or grated
Daikon radish, chopped or grated
Jerusalem artichokes, sliced
Jicama, grated
Red radishes, whole, sliced, or grated
Rutabaga, chopped
Turnip, chopped or grated

## Sprouts

Alfalfa, broccoli, radish, sunflower, mustard, red clover
Lentil
Mung bean

## Stalk Vegetables

Asparagus tips
Celery, sliced

## Chopped Fresh Herbs

Basil, chives, cilantro, dill, fennel leaves, mint, oregano, parsley, sage, tarragon, thyme

# Shepherd's Pie

Makes 8 hearty servings, each about 3 × 4 inches (8 × 10 cm)

This classic comfort food may stir up fond memories from childhood, with its dark, rich, meaty-flavoured bottom layer, a mid-layer of bright yellow corn, and a smooth topping of mashed potato, baked until golden brown. The nutritional profile is superb, with a serving providing about half of your protein for the day plus most of the recommended intake for iron, zinc, potassium, and B vitamins. (It provides much of your day's supply of sodium too.) This is a fine entrée to serve non-vegetarians (including parents) when they come to dinner, along with a colourful salad.

## Potato Topping

5 large russet potatoes, peeled, about 4 pounds (1.8 kg)
3 tablespoons (45 mL) olive oil
1/2 cup (125 mL) soy or other non-dairy milk
1/2 teaspoon (2 mL) salt
1/4 teaspoon (1 mL) black pepper

## Pie Mixture

1 tablespoon (15 mL) coconut or olive oil
2 cups (500 mL) diced onion
2 cups (500 mL) chopped celery
6 cloves garlic, minced
2 packages (each 340 g) Yves Meatless Ground Round Original
2 tablespoons (30 mL) vegetarian Worcestershire sauce
2 tablespoons (30 mL) tamari or soy sauce
2 teaspoons (10 mL) dried tarragon, crushed
1/2 teaspoon (2 mL) black pepper
1/2 teaspoon (2 mL) salt (optional)
1 1/2 cups (375 mL) fresh, canned or frozen corn kernels
1/4 teaspoon (1 mL) paprika

Preheat the oven to 350°F (180°C).

To make the potato topping, cut each potato into thirds and cook in boiling water until tender.

Meanwhile, to make the pie mixture, heat the oil in a skillet over medium heat and cook the onion, celery, and garlic for 3 minutes or until the onion is translucent. Turn off heat, add crumbled veggie ground round, Worcestershire sauce, tamari, tarragon, pepper, and salt and stir to mix thoroughly. Transfer the mixture to a lightly oiled 9 × 13-inch (23 × 33 cm) casserole dish. Spread the mixture and pack evenly. Sprinkle the corn kernels over top.

Drain the potatoes, add the olive oil, soy milk, salt, and pepper and mash until fluffy. Spread the mashed potato over the corn and sprinkle with the paprika. Bake the pie for 20 minutes or until it is heated through.

Per serving: calories: 399, protein: 26 g, fat: 8 g, carbohydrate: 60 g (5 g from sugar), dietary fibre: 5 g, calcium: 89 mg, iron: 9 mg, magnesium: 78 mg, phosphorus: 198 mg, potassium: 1588 mg, sodium: 855 mg, zinc: 10 mg, thiamin: 0.7 mg, riboflavin: 0.4 mg, niacin: 5 mg, vitamin $B_6$: 1.3 mg, folate: 67 mcg, pantothenic acid: 2 mg, vitamin $B_{12}$: 6 mcg, vitamin A: 9 mcg, vitamin C: 52 mg, vitamin E: 1 mg, omega-6 fatty acids: 1 g, omega-3 fatty acids: 0.1 g

Percentage of calories from protein 25%, fat 17%, carbohydrate 58%

**Note:** Analysis was done using Yves Meatless Ground Round Original and fortified soy milk, both sources of vitamin B12.

### Caramelizing Onions

Caramelizing white, yellow, or red onions breaks down the naturally present starches, transforming the starches to sugars and creating an aromatic flavour sensation. Caramelize onions to deepen the flavour of soups or stews, as a topping for pizza, or simply serve them as a sweet, nutty side dish. Sweet onions such as the Vidalia, Maui, and Walla Walla varieties will caramelize more quickly than other varieties due to their higher sugar content.

Cut the onions in half and then into crescent-shaped slices. Heat a small amount of coconut or olive oil in a skillet over medium heat. Add the onions and a pinch of salt, then cook, stirring occasionally, until the onions turn brown. If the onions stick to the skillet, add 1 to 2 tablespoons (15 to 30 mL) water to deglaze the skillet and continue cooking until the desired colour has been achieved. Add 1/2 teaspoon (2 mL) dried basil, rosemary, or thyme per medium onion for added flavour, and a touch of balsamic vinegar at the end of cooking for an even deeper sweet taste.

# Stir-Fry 101

Makes 4 1/2 cups (1.125 L)

If you only learn one recipe from this book, make it this one. The process is fun, you can create your masterpiece alone or with company, and the combinations are unlimited. (See ideas for variations below.) A stir-fry is typically cooked over high heat in a round-bottomed cooking vessel known as a wok. This recipe can be made in a wok or large skillet and uses very little oil. Serve with cooked rice or noodles.

**1 tablespoon (15 mL) coconut or olive oil**
**1/2 onion, cut into large dice**
**1 cup (250 mL) sliced carrots, cut diagonally**
**1 cup (250 mL) broccoli florets**
**1 cup (250 mL) cooked or canned chickpeas, drained and rinsed**
**1 cup (250 mL) sliced red bell peppers**
**1 cup (250 mL) trimmed snow peas**
**1 cup (250 mL) sliced bok choy**
**1/4 cup (60 mL) commercial stir-fry sauce, or to taste**

Heat the oil in a wok or large skillet over medium-high heat. If using an electric wok or skillet, heat to 375°F (190°C). Add the onion and cook for 3 to 5 minutes or until translucent. Add the carrots, broccoli, and chickpeas and cook until the carrots and broccoli are half cooked or almost tender-crisp. Add the peppers, snow peas, bok choy, and sauce and cook for 1 minute or until the vegetables are warm and wilted.

Per cup (250 mL): calories: 168, protein: 7 g, fat: 4 g, carbohydrate: 27 g (7 g from sugar), dietary fibre: 5 g, calcium: 80 mg, iron: 3 mg, magnesium: 51 mg, phosphorus: 138 mg, potassium: 591 mg, sodium: 269 mg, zinc: 1 mg, thiamin: 0.2 mg, riboflavin: 0.2 mg, niacin: 3 mg, vitamin $B_6$: 0.4 mg, folate: 143 mcg, pantothenic acid: 1 mg, vitamin $B_{12}$: 0 mcg, vitamin A: 333 mcg, vitamin C: 137 mg, vitamin E: 2 mg, omega-6 fatty acids: 0.8 g, omega-3 fatty acids: 0.1 g

Percentage of calories from protein 15%, fat 23%, carbohydrate 62%

**Note**: Analysis was done using 2 tablespoons (30 mL) minced or grated ginger, 2 tablespoons (30 mL) tamari, and 1/4 cup (60 mL) orange juice concentrate for the sauce.

**Stir-Fry Variations:**
- Replace 1 teaspoon (5 mL) coconut or olive oil with toasted sesame oil.
- Add 2 cloves garlic, minced.
- Add 1 tablespoon (15 mL) minced ginger
- Replace any of the vegetables with others such as sliced celery, green or yellow beans, green onions, green or yellow bell peppers, mushrooms, napa cabbage, okra, mung bean sprouts, or sugar snap peas.
- Replace the chickpeas with cubed firm tofu, marinated tofu, veggie chicken, sliced seitan, or tempeh.
- Omit the stir-fry sauce. Instead add 2 tablespoons (30 mL) minced or grated ginger along with the onion, and add 1 tablespoon (15 mL) tamari or soy sauce plus 1/4 cup (60 mL) orange juice concentrate along with the peppers, snow peas, and bok choy.
- Replace the stir-fry sauce with Teriyaki Sauce (page 220) or Tofu Marinade (page 221).
- Top your stir-fry with 1/2 cup (125 mL) cashew nuts.

## Stir-Frying

A stir-fry is an Asian dish that is prepared in a large bowl-shaped cooking pan called a wok. Food is cooked at high heat and constantly stirred or lifted away from the heat, not giving the food any chance to sit idle. If a wok is not available, use a large skillet. There are three keys for making a good stir-fry:

- Cut each vegetable in uniform pieces so they cook at the same rate.
- Add the vegetables in batches, starting with the onion, followed by dense vegetables that take the longest to cook, and finishing with light vegetables that are more tender.
- Do not overcrowd the wok or skillet. Putting too much food in the wok will lower the cooking temperature and the vegetables will steam rather than remain crisp.

### Preparation

Prepare all the vegetables first by washing them and assembling them on the counter near your cutting board. As you cut each vegetable, group them in piles or rows on a cookie sheet, platter, or flat serving dish in the order that you will add them to the wok. It can be a pleasure to see the colourful chopped veggies lined up in preparation for a stir-fry!

### Cooking

First heat the oil until it is hot—but not so hot that it begins to smoke (see page 22). When the oil is hot, add the onion and cook it until it is translucent. This develops an underlying sweetness to the dish. You can add whole slightly crushed garlic with the onion, if you like. If the garlic is chopped or minced, wait until the onions are soft; it might burn if added at the beginning with the onions. Ginger may be added at the same time as the garlic.

The sequence of adding the vegetables to the wok is important. After the onions, garlic, and ginger are cooked, add the vegetables that are most dense and cook them for a few minutes. This group will include carrots, cauliflower, and broccoli. Cook these until they are half cooked. Progressively add softer vegetables such as bell peppers, daikon radish, or zucchini and cook these until they are tender to the bite. Kale leaves and chard stems could be added at this stage as well since they are fibrous. Next add the leafy greens such as boy choy, Chinese cabbage, mung sprouts, and spinach.

A final addition is a liquid such as stir-fry sauce, tamari, or lemon juice. Because water can only be heated to 212°F (100°C) before it evaporates, unlike oil which can be heated much higher, the addition of watery liquids changes the nature of the food. If liquids are added to a stir-fry too early, they will change the texture of vegetables from tender-crisp to soggy, from having been steamed.

# Stovetop "Baked" Beans

Makes 5 cups (1.25 L)

Pinto beans have a mottled appearance similar to the pinto or "painted" horse from which they derive their name. They are a member of the common bean family and are related to kidney and black beans. This flavourful combination can be baked in the oven (see the variation) or made more quickly on the stovetop, as in this recipe. A serving of these "baked" beans is an excellent source of protein, dietary fibre, calcium, iron, potassium, zinc, and B vitamins, while being very low in fat.

**1 tablespoon (15 mL) coconut or olive oil**
**1 medium onion, diced**
**5 cups (1.25 L) cooked pinto beans**
**1 1/2 cups (375 mL) water**
**1/4 cup (60 mL) apple cider vinegar**
**1/4 cup (60 mL) maple syrup or brown sugar**
**2 teaspoons (10 mL) dried dill**
**2 teaspoons (10 mL) Dijon mustard**
**1 teaspoon (5 mL) salt**
**1/2 teaspoon (2 mL) black pepper**
**1/4 teaspoon (1 mL) ground cloves**

Heat the oil in a skillet over medium heat and cook the onion for 5 minutes or until translucent. Add the beans, water, vinegar, maple syrup, dill, mustard, salt, pepper, and cloves and stir to mix well. Bring the beans to a boil, reduce heat, cover, and cook, stirring occasionally, for 45 to 60 minutes or until the liquid has turned into a well-bodied sauce.

Per cup (250 mL): calories: 367, protein: 20 g, fat: 6 g, carbohydrate: 60 g (11 g from sugar), dietary fibre: 17 g, calcium: 112 mg, iron: 5 mg, magnesium: 101 mg, phosphorus: 306 mg, potassium: 913 mg, sodium: 537 mg, zinc: 3 mg, thiamin: 0.4 mg, riboflavin: 0.1 mg, niacin: 5 mg, vitamin $B_6$: 0.5 mg, folate: 314 mcg, pantothenic acid: 0.5 mg, vitamin $B_{12}$: 0.4 mcg, vitamin A: 1 mcg, vitamin C: 2 mg, vitamin E: 2 mg, omega-6 fatty acids: 0.3 g, omega-3 fatty acids: 0.2 g

Percentage of calories from protein 22%, fat 14%, carbohydrate 64%

**Oven-Baked Beans**
To bake, preheat the oven to 350°F (180°C). After beans and liquid are brought to a boil in the skillet, pour them into a casserole dish, cover, and bake for 45 minutes.

**Beans with Molasses**
To increase the calcium content to 253 milligrams per cup, which is one-quarter of the recommended intake for the day, replace the maple syrup with organic blackstrap molasses.

# Sweet and Sour Tofu

Makes 4 cups (1 L)

Vinegar is less acidic when made from rice than from fruit such as apples; the rice vinegar in this stir-fry creates a dish that is more smooth than sharp. This allows a smaller amount of sweetener to be added and the inherent sweetness of the vegetables to come through. Serve this dish on a bed of rice for two hungry adults, or for four if other items are included in the meal.

1 cup (250 mL) diced onion
1 tablespoon (15 mL) coconut or olive oil
1 cup (250 mL) diagonally sliced carrots
2 cloves garlic, minced
1 tablespoon (15 mL) minced ginger
3/4 cup (185 mL) pineapple juice
1/2 cup (125 mL) diced pineapple
1/4 cup (60 mL) brown sugar or other dry sweetener
1/4 cup (60 mL) rice vinegar
2 tablespoons (30 mL) tamari or soy sauce
1 tablespoon (15 mL) arrowroot powder or cornstarch
1 cup (250 mL) diced red or yellow bell pepper
1 cup (250 mL) diced green bell pepper
1 cup (250 mL) diced firm tofu
1 tablespoon (15 mL) chopped fresh parsley (optional)

In a pot over medium heat, cook the onion in the oil for 3 to 5 minutes or until translucent. Add the carrots, garlic, and ginger and cook for 3 minutes. In a bowl or jar, mix together the pineapple juice, diced pineapple, sugar, vinegar, and tamari. Add the arrowroot powder and stir until it is dissolved, then add to the skillet along with the red and green peppers and tofu. Stir constantly until thickened, then cover and simmer for 3 minutes. Garnish with parsley.

Per cup (250 mL): calories: 305, protein: 16 g, fat: 11 g, carbohydrate: 40 g (16 g from sugar), dietary fibre: 5 g, calcium: 632 mg, iron: 10 mg, magnesium: 83 mg, phosphorus: 225 mg, potassium: 678 mg, sodium: 545 mg, zinc: 2 mg, thiamin: 0.3 mg, riboflavin: 0.2 mg, niacin: 2 mg, vitamin $B_6$: 0.5 mg, folate: 68 mcg, pantothenic acid: 0.6 mg, vitamin $B_{12}$: 0 mcg, vitamin A: 319 mcg, vitamin C: 156 mg, vitamin E: 2 mg, omega-6 fatty acids: 4 g, omega-3 fatty acids: 1 g

Percentage of calories from protein 20%, fat 31%, carbohydrate 49%

**Note:** Analysis was done using calcium-set tofu.

**Mixed Vegetable Sweet and Sour Tofu**
Replace the carrot with cauliflower, and some of the peppers with snow peas or bok choy. If using the peas and bok choy, stir in 1 minute before the end of cooking so as not to overcook them.

## Maki-Sushi Rolls

Makes 3 rolls, 8 pieces per roll

Sushi is a small bundle-shaped parcel of rice with a protein topping of some kind such as fish, egg, etc. Sushi that is served rolled in a sheet of nori seaweed is called maki-sushi. These rolls are made using a bamboo sushi mat, which can be purchased at any Asian market. Sticky (glutinous) Japanese rice works well in these rolls, though brown rice can also be used (see variation on page 179). Use the ingredients listed below, or get creative.

1 1/2 cups (375 mL) water
1/4 teaspoon (1 mL) salt
1 cup (250 mL) white sushi rice
2 tablespoons (30 mL) rice vinegar
1 tablespoon (15 mL) sugar or other dry sweetener
3 sheets nori seaweed
3 tablespoons (45 mL) eggless mayonnaise
1 1/2 cups (375 mL) grated carrot
1/2 avocado, cut into 6 slices
6 cucumber sticks, each 1/4 × 2 inches (5 mm × 5 cm)
2 lettuce leaves, cut into 1/2-inch (1 cm) wide strips
1 tablespoon (15 mL) thinly sliced pickled ginger

## Garnishes

1 teaspoon (5 mL) wasabi powder mixed with 1/2 teaspoon (2 mL) water
2 tablespoons (30 mL) thinly sliced pickled ginger
2 tablespoons (30 mL) tamari or soy sauce

Bring the water and salt to a boil. Add the rice, reduce heat to low, cover, and cook for 20 minutes or until the water is absorbed.

Stir the rice vinegar and sugar in a small bowl until the sugar is dissolved. Drizzle vinegar mixture over the hot cooked rice and fluff with a fork. Set aside to cool completely before assembling the rolls.

Place all the filling ingredients on the counter. Place the sushi mat on the counter so that the bamboo strips are lying horizontal to you. Lay a sheet of nori on the mat. Spoon 3/4 cup (185 mL) of the rice onto the nori and push the rice out evenly to the edges, leaving a 1-inch (2.5 cm) border at the bottom and top of the sheet. Spread 1 tablespoon (5 mL) of the mayonnaise in a single strip from left to right on the rice. Layer one-third of the carrots, avocado, cucumber, lettuce, and ginger over the mayonnaise. Dip your index finger into a bowl of warm water and moisten the top edge of the nori sheet to ensure a good seal when rolled. Using both hands and firm pressure, lift the mat and nori sheet over the filling and snugly tuck the bottom edge of the nori sheet under the filling. Roll the bamboo mat forward with even pressure across the mat in a jelly-roll fashion until the top of the nori sheet is sealed against the top of the roll. Repeat until all three rolls have been assembled.

Place the roll seam-side down on a cutting board. Trim the ends of any food that may have squeezed out during the rolling process. Using a serrated knife, cut each roll in half. Continue cutting each piece in half in order to get eight equal-sized pieces from each roll. Arrange on a serving platter.

For the garnishes, in a small bowl, mix the wasabi powder with a few drops of water, gradually adding more water until a smooth paste is formed. Place wasabi paste on platter along with pickled ginger. Serve with a small bowl of tamari for dipping.

Per roll: calories: 402, protein: 7 g, fat: 9 g, carbohydrate: 73 g (10 g from sugar), dietary fibre: 6 g, calcium: 54 mg, iron: 2 mg, magnesium: 51 mg, phosphorus: 98 mg, potassium: 604 mg, sodium: 455 mg, zinc: 1 mg, thiamin: 0.2 mg, riboflavin: 0.2 mg, niacin: 4 mg, vitamin $B_6$: 0.6 mg, folate: 44 mcg, pantothenic acid: 1 mg, vitamin $B_{12}$: 0 mcg, vitamin A: 504 mcg, vitamin C: 7 mg, vitamin E: 1 mg, omega-6 fatty acids: 1 g, omega-3 fatty acids: 0.1 g

Percentage of calories from protein 7%, fat 20%, carbohydrate 73%

**Note**: Analysis was done without dipping tamari.

**Brown Rice Sushi Rolls**
Brown rice may be used in place of the white rice, though its consistency is less sticky. Use 1 cup (250 mL) brown rice to 2 cups (500 mL) water and cook for 45 minutes.

# Tapenade Pizza

Makes two 12-inch (30 cm) pizzas

Making pizza dough and sauce from scratch, along with all the toppings, might seem daunting, but nothing beats the fresh taste of hot pizza right out of the oven. These tasty combinations make an excellent lunch or supper, or try it as an appetizer at your next dinner party or social event.

1 recipe **Pizza Dough (page 165)**
1 recipe **Walnut, Olive, and Sun-Dried Tomato Tapenade (page 97)**
2 onions, sliced and caramelized (see sidebar, page 173)
1 can (14 ounces/398 mL) artichoke hearts, drained and sliced
1/2 cup (125 mL) roasted garlic, sliced (see sidebar, page 181)
Extra-virgin olive oil, for drizzling (optional)
1/2 teaspoon (2 mL) fresh thyme leaves, for garnish (optional)

Preheat the oven to 375°F (190°C).

Roll out the pizza dough, cut in half, and spread it to fit two 12-inch (30 cm) round baking trays. Spread half of the tapenade evenly over each of the crusts. Distribute the onions, artichokes, and garlic evenly between the two pizzas. If you like, drizzle a thin line of extra-virgin olive oil along the edge of the unbaked pizza. Bake for 10 to 12 minutes or until the edge and bottoms of crusts are golden brown. Garnish with thyme and serve.

Per 1/3 pizza: calories: 374, protein: 11 g, fat: 9 g, carbohydrate: 65 g (6 g from sugar), dietary fibre: 7 g, calcium: 95 mg, iron: 5 mg, magnesium: 70 mg, phosphorus: 195 mg, potassium: 573 mg, sodium: 737 mg, zinc: 1.3 mg, thiamin: 0.6 mg, riboflavin: 0.5 mg, niacin: 7 mg, vitamin $B_6$: 0.4 mg, folate: 170 mcg, pantothenic acid: 1 mg, vitamin $B_{12}$: 0 mcg, vitamin A: 12 mcg, vitamin C: 16 mg, vitamin E: 0.6 mg, omega-6 fatty acids: 2.4 g, omega-3 fatty acids: 0.5 g

**Premade Pizza Shells**
Replace the homemade pizza dough with premade shells and cook according to package directions.

**Pita Bread Pizza**
The ingredients listed for Tapenade Pizza will also make eight 6-inch (15 cm) pita bread pizzas. For each pizza, use 2 1/2 tablespoons (37 mL) tapenade, 2 tablespoons (30 mL) caramelized onion, 3 tablespoons (45 mL) artichoke hearts, and 1 tablespoon (15 mL) roasted garlic. Bake at 375°F (190°C) for 6 minutes.

**Spinach Pizza**
Replace the artichokes with 2 cups (500 mL) washed, stemmed, steamed spinach leaves (squeeze out excess water with your hands), distributed between the two pizzas. If you like, sprinkle 1/2 cup (125 mL) grated non-dairy cheese on top of each pizza.

# Roasting Garlic

Roasting garlic is a simple procedure that transforms the pungency of the fresh cloves into rich, aromatic, and sweet-tasting morsels for which garlic lovers will find many uses in the kitchen. Roasted garlic can be mashed in a bowl and spread over toast or added to mashed potatoes; chopped and put in soups at the start of cooking to deepen the flavour or added to the soup bowl as a garnish, scattered over pizzas as a topping, added to the blender when making salad dressings, sprinkled over top of salads; or left whole and served on a vegetable platter alongside raw or grilled vegetables. Any oil that remains after using the cooking methods below can be used for cooking or salad dressings.

There are many ways to roast garlic. Here are three methods. The first is for oven roasting whole heads of unpeeled garlic; the second is for skillet roasting individually peeled cloves; and the third is for oven roasting individually peeled cloves. The second and third roasting methods yield individual cloves that can be used in many of the ways mentioned above—and you will undoubtedly find many more ways to use it. Roasted garlic will keep, refrigerated in a covered jar, for up to 3 or 4 weeks.

Individually peeled garlic cloves are now sold by the bagful in many grocery stores. This saves a lot of time spent peeling cloves. Peeled garlic does not last as long as unpeeled, but roasting it extends the shelf life by up to 1 month if stored in the refrigerator.

### Method 1: Oven Method with a Whole Garlic Head
Preheat the oven to 300°F (150°C).

Remove most of the papery skin from the head of garlic, leaving the garlic head intact. Slice off 1/4 inch (5 mm) from the top end of the garlic head. Put the head of garlic on a sheet of aluminum foil with the exposed cloves facing upward. Drizzle a small amount of olive oil over top and then tightly wrap the foil around the garlic head. Place the foil package in an ovenproof skillet or on a cookie sheet and roast in the oven for 1 hour. Check the garlic periodically. It is done when it has a light golden colour and the cloves are soft. Remove from the oven and, when cool, remove the cloves from the head, squeezing out the contents into a bowl.

Alternatively, you can put the head of garlic in an ovenproof dish that can be tightly covered, drizzle olive oil over top, cover the dish, and proceed as above.

### Method 2: Skillet Method with Peeled Garlic Cloves
This method yields a good amount of garlic-flavoured oil that has multiple uses. Put the peeled garlic cloves in a skillet and add enough olive oil to cover the cloves. Heat the skillet over medium-high heat. When the oil starts to bubble around the garlic, reduce heat to medium and cook, stirring occasionally, until the cloves are golden brown in colour.

### Method 3: Oven Method with Peeled Garlic Cloves
Preheat the oven to 300°F (150°C).

Place the peeled garlic cloves with a small amount of olive oil in an ovenproof dish and roast, stir occasionally, until the cloves are golden brown.

# Teriyaki Tofu with Japanese Vegetables

Makes 4 cups (1 L)

Native to Japan, teriyaki sauce strikes a balance between sweet and salty. It is a once-in-a-while sauce, as it can be high in sodium. Served over a bed of whole-grain rice or your favourite noodles, this recipe makes for a fully satisfying and attractive meal. The tofu and vegetables are good sources of iron and the vitamin C in the red peppers substantially improves iron absorption.

**1 tablespoon (15 mL) coconut or olive oil**
**1/2 onion, diced**
**1 clove garlic, minced**
**1 tablespoon (15 mL) minced ginger**
**1 cup (250 mL) diced daikon radish**
**1 cup (250 mL) diced sweet potato**
**1 cup (250 mL) diced carrots**
**1 cup (250 mL) diced red or green bell peppers**
**1 cup (250 mL) diced firm tofu**
**3/4 cup (185 mL) Teriyaki Sauce (page 220) or commercial brand**
**2 tablespoons (30 mL) chopped fresh cilantro or parsley**

Heat the oil in a large skillet over medium heat and cook the onion for 3 to 5 minutes until translucent. Add garlic, ginger, radish, sweet potato, carrots, peppers, and tofu and cook for 5 minutes, stirring frequently. Stir in teriyaki sauce; cover, reduce heat, and cook for 3 minutes. Adjust the seasoning, garnish with cilantro, and serve.

Per cup (250 mL): calories: 255, protein: 10 g, fat: 8 g, carbohydrate: 34 g (20 g from sugar), dietary fibre: 4 g, calcium: 349 mg, iron: 6 mg, magnesium: 56 mg, phosphorus: 148 mg, potassium: 557 mg, sodium: 584 mg, zinc: 1 mg, thiamin: 0.2 mg, riboflavin: 0.2 mg, niacin: 4 mg, vitamin $B_6$: 0.3 mg, folate: 41 mcg, pantothenic acid: 0.7 mg, vitamin $B_{12}$: 0 mcg, vitamin A: 595 mcg, vitamin C: 83 mg, vitamin E: 1 mg, omega-6 fatty acids: 2 g, omega-3 fatty acids: 0.3 g

Percentage of calories from protein 15%, fat 25%, carbohydrate 51%, alcohol (from Teriyaki Sauce) 9%

**Note**: Most of the alcohol from the sake in the Teriyaki Sauce is burned off during the cooking process, leaving behind only its taste and fragrance.

## Timesaving Tacos

Makes 10 tacos

For an almost instant meal, one of the fastest yet nutritionally balanced combinations you can serve is the well-loved taco. Just warm the shells and beans, chop the veggies, and set out the colourful fillings in pretty bowls. Let people assemble their own to suit their individual preferences and create their favourite combinations. If you prefer burritos, replace the taco shells with soft tortillas. In some families or at gatherings with mixed dietary needs, a meal of tacos is welcome, as it can allow the inclusion of non-vegan options, such as grated dairy cheese.

1 can (14 ounces/398 mL) vegetarian refried beans
10 taco shells or soft tortillas
2 cups (500 mL) shredded lettuce
1 cup (250 mL) chopped tomato
1 carrot, grated
1 ripe avocado, chopped
1 cup (250 mL) salsa
1 cup (250 mL) grated non-dairy cheese (optional)

Put the refried beans in a small pan and warm through. If the refried beans are too thick, add 1 tablespoon (15 mL) or more of water to thin them. Warm the taco shells in a 250°F (120°C) oven for 1 to 2 minutes. Put out the warm taco shells, warm beans, lettuce, tomato, carrot, avocado, salsa, and cheese in serving bowls, allowing for individual assembly.

Per taco: calories: 145, protein: 4 g, fat: 7 g, carbohydrate: 19 g (1 g from sugar), dietary fibre: 5 g, calcium: 52 mg, iron: 2 mg, magnesium: 42 mg, phosphorus: 91 mg, potassium: 397 mg, sodium: 293 mg, zinc: 1 mg, thiamin: 0.1 mg, riboflavin: 0.1 mg, niacin: 1 mg, vitamin $B_6$: 0.2 mg, folate: 55 mcg, pantothenic acid: 0.4 mg, vitamin $B_{12}$: 0 mcg, vitamin A: 102 mcg, vitamin C: 13 mg, vitamin E: 1 mg, omega-6 fatty acids: 1.5 g, omega-3 fatty acids: 0.1 g

Percentage of calories from protein 11%, fat 39%, carbohydrate 50%

**Tacos with Black Beans or Pinto Beans**
Replace the refried beans with 2 cups (500 mL) mashed cooked black beans or pinto beans.

**Tacos with Mashed Avocado**
Mash the avocado in a small bowl, add 2 teaspoons (10 mL) lemon juice, and mix well.

## Tofu: An Easy Entrée

Makes about 10 slices

Tofu is Asia's number one fast food, and it has become popular in the West as a versatile source of protein for breakfast, lunch, dinner, or dessert. Since tofu is porous, it absorbs the flavours of the other foods it's cooked with. For a good source of dietary calcium, select tofu with calcium listed in the ingredient list on its package. The following sauces, based on favourite flavour combinations from around the world, were developed for 12 ounces (340 g) of tofu. Or use 1/2 cup (125 mL) Teriyaki Sauce (page 220) or a commercial sauce, if you like. Adjust the quantity of seasoning sauce if using larger or smaller amounts of tofu.

### Hawaiian Sauce

Makes 1/2 cup (125 mL) not including the pineapple garnish

1/4 cup (60 mL) orange juice concentrate
1/4 cup (60 mL) pineapple juice
1 tablespoon (15 mL) minced ginger
2 teaspoons (10 mL) tamari or soy sauce
2 cloves garlic, minced
1 cup (250 mL) diced pineapple, for garnish

### Mediterranean Sauce

Makes 1/2 cup (125 mL)

1/2 cup (125 mL) tomato sauce
1/2 teaspoon (2 mL) minced lemon peel
1 teaspoon (5 mL) dried rosemary, crushed
1/2 teaspoon (2 mL) dried marjoram
2 cloves garlic, minced
1/4 teaspoon (1 mL) salt
Pinch of black pepper
1 cup (250 mL) chopped fresh or canned artichoke hearts, for garnish (optional)

## Mexican Sauce

Makes 1/2 cup (125 mL)

1/2 cup (125 mL) salsa
1 to 2 teaspoons (5 to 10 mL) chili powder
1 teaspoon (5 mL) ground toasted cumin seeds (see page 133)
2 cloves garlic, minced
1/2 onion, for garnish (optional)
1/2 jalapeño pepper, minced, for garnish, added after the tofu comes out of the oven

## Thai Sauce

Makes 1/2 cup (125 mL)

1/3 cup (85 mL) coconut milk
2 tablespoons (30 mL) lime juice
1 to 2 teaspoons (5 to 10 mL) Thai curry paste
1 teaspoon (5 mL) dried basil
1/4 teaspoon (1 mL) dried mint
1/2 teaspoon (2 mL) salt
1 cup (250 mL) sliced red bell peppers, for garnish (optional)

Preheat the oven to 350°F (180°C).

After choosing a sauce from the above options, mix those ingredients together in a small bowl and pour a small amount on the bottom of a 9 × 13 inch (23 × 33 cm) baking dish.

Drain and rinse the tofu. Cut the block into 1/3-inch (8 mm) thick slices. Arrange the slices in a single layer side by side in the baking dish. Pour the remaining sauce over the tofu, spread the garnish on top, if using, cover, and bake in the oven for 30 minutes.

Per 1/3 recipe: calories: 166, protein: 11 g, fat: 5 g, carbohydrate: 22 g (8 g from sugar), dietary fibre: 2 g, calcium: 257 mg, iron: 2 mg, magnesium: 64 mg, phosphorus: 170 mg, potassium: 454 mg, sodium: 243 mg, zinc: 1 mg, thiamin: 0.2 mg, riboflavin: 0.1 mg, niacin: 3 mg, vitamin $B_6$: 0.2 mg, folate: 73 mcg, pantothenic acid: 0.4 mg, vitamin $B_{12}$: 0 mcg, vitamin A: 2 mcg, vitamin C: 61 mg, vitamin E: 0.1 mg, omega-6 fatty acids: 2 g, omega-3 fatty acids: 0.2 g

Percentage of calories from protein 25%, fat 25%, carbohydrate 50%

**Note**: Analysis was done using Hawaiian Sauce.

# Vegetable Kebabs

Makes 6 large kebabs

The assorted vegetables in this recipe, assembled on a skewer, make a colourful addition to a barbecue or picnic. The kebabs also can be baked in the oven. The tofu marinade is absorbed all the way through the tofu, giving it a burst of flavour that is bound to make this dish a favourite. As a bonus, the kebabs are excellent sources of protein, calcium, iron, zinc, vitamin C, and many B vitamins.

1 recipe Marinated Tofu (page 160), with tofu cut into 18 cubes of uniform size (each about 1 inch/2.5 cm square)
6 bamboo or metal skewers, 10 inches (25 cm)
24 medium mushrooms
12 pieces red bell pepper, each about 1 1/2 inches (4 cm) square
12 pieces zucchini, each 1 1/2 inches (4 cm) thick
12 cherry tomatoes

Marinate the tofu for 6 to 10 hours in the refrigerator. If using bamboo skewers, soak for 30 minutes before using, to prevent them from burning.

When ready to assemble the skewers, thread the tofu and vegetables onto the skewers, starting and ending each with a mushroom. Thread the food snugly so that the fire from the grill doesn't burn through the bamboo skewer. A good threading sequence is mushroom, red pepper, tofu, mushroom, zucchini, tomato, tofu, tomato, zucchini, mushroom, tofu, red pepper, and mushroom.

Grill skewers on high heat on the barbecue, turning over once, or place on a baking sheet 6 inches (15 cm) under the broiler, for 10 minutes.

Per kebab: calories: 125, protein: 13 g, fat: 6 g, carbohydrate: 9 g (4 g from sugar), dietary fibre: 3 g, calcium: 411 mg, iron: 7 mg, magnesium: 54 mg, phosphorus: 204 mg, potassium: 589 mg, sodium: 206 mg, zinc: 2 mg, thiamin: 0.2 mg, riboflavin: 0.4 mg, niacin: 7 mg, vitamin $B_6$: 0.4 mg, folate: 51 mcg, pantothenic acid: 1 mg, vitamin $B_{12}$: 0 mcg, vitamin A: 89 mcg, vitamin C: 89 mg, vitamin E: 1 mg, omega-6 fatty acids: 3 g, omega-3 fatty acids: 0.4 g

Percentage of calories from protein 36%, fat 39%, carbohydrate 25%

**Note**: Calcium content depends on the brand of tofu used; check the label.

# Veggie Chick'n Paella with Artichokes and Spinach

Make 6 cups (1.5 L)

Paella is a traditional Spanish dish whose signature ingredients are medium-grain rice and saffron. With the addition of Gardein's veggie chicken, here it makes a satisfying entrée. Arborio rice is suggested for this dish, although Spanish varieties such as Calasparra are excellent as well. The cooked rice should be dry and relatively firm, rather than creamy as in risotto.

1 to 2 tablespoons (15 to 30 mL) coconut or olive oil
1/2 onion, cut into 1-inch (2.5 cm) dice
4 cloves garlic, thinly sliced
2 cups (500 mL) chopped tomatoes
1 package (10 ounces/285 g) Gardein Chick'n Scallopini, cut into 1-inch (2.5 cm) pieces
2 cups (500 mL) vegetable stock
1 cup (250 mL) arborio rice
2 cups (500 mL) frozen artichoke hearts, thawed and quartered, or 1 can (14 ounces/398 mL) artichoke hearts, drained and quartered
1 teaspoon (5 mL) dried basil
Pinch of black pepper
Two pinches of saffron
4 cups (1 L) chopped spinach leaves, about 4 ounces (113 g)
1/2 lemon

Heat the oil in a large skillet or wide-bottomed pot over medium-high heat and cook the onion for 5 minutes or until translucent. Add the garlic and tomatoes and cook for 5 minutes, until the tomato starts to break down. Add the Gardein Chick'n Scallopini, stock, rice, artichoke hearts, basil, pepper, and saffron. Reduce heat to medium-low and simmer for 10 minutes, stirring occasionally. Cook for 10 minutes more without disturbing the rice. Turn off the heat, add the spinach, cover, and let sit for 5 minutes. Stir spinach into the paella, squeeze a bit of lemon juice over top, and serve.

Per cup (250 mL): calories: 272, protein: 16 g, fat: 5 g, carbohydrate: 43 g (2 g from sugar), dietary fibre: 6 g, calcium: 107 mg, iron: 2 mg, magnesium: 43 mg, phosphorus: 68 mg, potassium: 490 mg, sodium: 57 mg, zinc: 0.5 mg, thiamin: 0.1 mg, riboflavin: 0.1 mg, niacin: 2 mg, vitamin $B_6$: 0.2 mg, folate: 128 mcg, pantothenic acid: 0.2 mg, vitamin $B_{12}$: 0 mcg, vitamin A: 127 mcg, vitamin C: 20 mg, vitamin E: 1 mg, omega-6 fatty acids: 0.2 g, omega-3 fatty acids: 0.1 g

Percentage of calories from protein 23%, fat 16%, carbohydrate 61%

# Veggie Pepperoni Pizza

Makes two 12-inch (30 cm) pizzas

Pizza is a favourite for kids and adults alike. Children love pizza-building, and this is certainly an easy way to get them to enjoy veggies such as peppers, mushrooms, and tomato. Make this an occasional meal due to the high sodium contents of veggie pepperoni, cheese, tomato sauce, dough, and olives. To keep the pizza from getting too chunky, slice all the vegetable toppings as thinly as possible. Spreading sauce over the pepperoni will prevent it from drying out in the oven. Extra-virgin olive oil, from the first pressing of olives, carries a wealth of flavour and can give a crisp, delicious edge to the baked crust.

1 recipe Pizza Dough (page 165)
3 cups (750 mL) pizza sauce
1 package (8.5 ounces/240 g) Yves Veggie Pizza Pepperoni
1 medium red bell pepper, sliced
2 cups (500 mL) sliced mushrooms
1 cup (250 mL) sliced red onion
1 cup (250 mL) sliced black or green olives
2 to 3 cups (500 to 750 mL) grated non-dairy cheese
Extra-virgin olive oil, for drizzling (optional)

Preheat the oven to 375°F (190°C).

Roll out the pizza dough, cut in half, and transfer to two 12-inch (30 cm) round baking trays. Spread one-quarter of the sauce evenly over each of the crusts. Arrange veggie pepperoni slices on top of sauce, followed by red pepper, mushrooms, onion, and olives. Spread the remaining tomato sauce evenly over the pizzas. Sprinkle the cheese on top. If you like, drizzle a thin line of extra-virgin olive oil on the edge of the unbaked pizzas. Bake for 10 to 12 minutes or until the edge and bottoms of crusts are golden brown.

Per 1/3 pizza: calories: 556, protein: 23 g, fat: 16 g, carbohydrate: 78 g (10 g from sugar), dietary fibre: 11 g, calcium: 77 mg, iron: 6 mg, magnesium: 24 mg, phosphorus: 125 mg, potassium: 385 mg, sodium: 1718 mg, zinc: 1 mg, thiamin: 0.8 mg, riboflavin: 0.5 mg, niacin: 7 mg, vitamin $B_6$: 0.2 mg, folate: 141 mcg, pantothenic acid: 2 mg, vitamin $B_{12}$: 1 mcg, vitamin A: 36 mcg, vitamin C: 42 mg, vitamin E: 1 mg, omega-6 fatty acids: 0.5 g, omega-3 fatty acids: 0 g

Percentage of calories from protein 17%, fat 26%, carbohydrate 57%

**Pineapple, Pepper, and Veggie Ham Pizza**
Use sliced pineapple chunks, green bell pepper, and veggie ham as toppings.

**Individual Pita Pizzas**
To make an individual veggie pepperoni pizza with a pita bread crust, spread 3/4 cup (185 mL) of the sauce across one 6-inch (15 cm) pita bread. Top with 2 ounces (55 g) veggie pepperoni; 1/4 medium red bell pepper, sliced; 1/2 cup (125 mL) sliced mushrooms; 1/4 cup (60 mL) sliced red onion; and 1/4 cup (60 mL) sliced black or green olives. Bake at 375°F (190°C) for 6 minutes or until the bottom starts to brown.

# Side Dishes

## Carrots with Dijon Mustard and Tarragon

Makes 2 cups (500 mL)

The combination of carrots, Dijon mustard, and tarragon is classic. This simple recipe is delicious and provides an easy way to get your powerful protector, vitamin A, along with some calcium, iron, and potassium. Dijon mustard contains plenty of salt, so no additional salt is needed.

**3 cups (750 mL) sliced carrots**
**1 tablespoon (15 mL) freshly squeezed lemon juice**
**2 tablespoons (30 mL) Dijon mustard**
**1 teaspoon (5 mL) dried tarragon, crushed**

Put the carrots in a steamer over medium-high heat and steam for 5 to 7 minutes or until the carrots are tender to the bite. Combine the lemon juice, mustard, and tarragon in a large bowl. Remove the carrots from the heat and toss them in the mustard dressing until well coated. Serve immediately.

Per cup (250 mL): calories: 89, protein: 3 g, fat: 2 g, carbohydrate: 17 g (8 g from sugar), dietary fibre: 5 g, calcium: 81 mg, iron: 1 mg, magnesium: 22 mg, phosphorus: 57 mg, potassium: 528 mg, sodium: 440 mg, zinc: 0.4 mg, thiamin: 0.1 mg, riboflavin: 0.1 mg, niacin: 2 mg, vitamin $B_6$: 0.2 mg, folate: 33 mcg, pantothenic acid: 0.4 mg, vitamin $B_{12}$: 0 mcg, vitamin A: 1298 mcg, vitamin C: 13 mg, vitamin E: 1 mg, omega-6 fatty acids: 0.2 g, omega-3 fatty acids: 0 g

Percentage of calories from protein 11%, fat 16%, carbohydrate 73%

# Aloo Gobi

Makes 4 cups (1 L)

This popular Indian dish is a superb combination of potato *(aloo)* and cauliflower *(gobi)*. The seasonings include golden-hued turmeric and also curry powder, which is a mixture of spices that varies from one household and from one region to another. A tightly lidded pan is needed because the potatoes and cauliflower cook, in part, from steam that they release as they cook.

1 1/2 tablespoons (22 mL) coconut or olive oil
1 large onion, chopped
1 tablespoon (15 mL) minced ginger
2 teaspoons (10 mL) curry powder
1/2 teaspoon (2 mL) turmeric
2 cups (500 mL) chopped potato, cut into 1/2-inch (1 cm) dice
2 cups (500 mL) cauliflower florets
1/2 teaspoon (2 mL) salt
3/4 cup (185 mL) water
2 teaspoons (10 mL) lemon juice

Heat the oil in a saucepan over medium-low heat. Add the onion and cook for 3 to 5 minutes, stirring occasionally, until the onion is translucent. Add the ginger, curry powder, and turmeric and cook for 1 minute, stirring frequently to avoid burning the spices. Add the potato, cauliflower, and salt and stir until the potatoes and cauliflower are all yellow in colour. Add the water. Stir, cover with a tight fitting lid, reduce heat to low and cook for 20 to 25 minutes or until vegetables are soft when pierced with a knife. Stir in lemon juice, adjust seasoning, and serve.

Per cup (250 mL): calories: 142, protein: 3 g, fat: 5 g, carbohydrate: 22 g (4 g from sugar), dietary fibre: 3 g, calcium: 31 mg, iron: 1 mg, magnesium: 32 mg, phosphorus: 75 mg, potassium: 675 mg, sodium: 258 mg, zinc: 1 mg, thiamin: 0.1 mg, riboflavin: 0.1 mg, niacin: 2 mg, vitamin $B_6$: 0.4 mg, folate: 50 mcg, pantothenic acid: 1 mg, vitamin $B_{12}$: 0 mcg, vitamin A: 1 mcg, vitamin C: 44 mg, vitamin E: 1 mg, omega-6 fatty acids: 0.5 g, omega-3 fatty acids: 0.1 g

Percentage of calories from protein 9%, fat 32%, carbohydrate 59%

**Aloo Gobi with Curry Paste**
Replace the curry powder with 2 teaspoons (10 mL) Patak's Mild Curry Paste, or other Indian curry paste, to taste.

# Baked Yams with Lemon and Green Chili

Makes 7 cups (1.75 L)

This recipe is base on about 2 1/2 pounds (1 kg) of yams as purchased. Yams are good sources of antioxidants: vitamins C and E and the orange carotenoids that our bodies convert to vitamin A. This recipe cooks well in a 9 × 13-inch (23 × 33 cm) glass baking dish. If you use a metal cookie sheet, you'll need to turn the yam slices over halfway through the cooking time.

4 medium yams, peeled
1 tablespoon (15 mL) coconut or olive oil
1 teaspoon (5 mL) crushed coriander seeds or 1/2 teaspoon (2 mL) ground coriander
1/4 teaspoon (1 mL) salt
1 teaspoon (5 mL) minced or grated lemon peel
2 tablespoons (30 mL) freshly squeezed lemon juice
2 serrano chilies, halved, seeded, and minced

Preheat the oven to 350°F (180°C).

Slice the yams into 1/4-inch (5 mm) thick coins. Put them into a medium bowl along with the oil, coriander seeds, and salt. Toss the yams to coat, then evenly spread them in a glass baking dish and bake for 25 minutes, checking near the end of the baking time to avoid scorching. The yams are cooked if they are soft when pierced with a knife. Return the yams to bowl, along with the lemon peel, lemon juice, and chilies. Gently toss and serve.

Per cup (250 mL): calories: 186, protein: 2 g, fat: 2 g, carbohydrate: 40 g (1 g from sugar), dietary fibre: 6 g, calcium: 25 mg, iron: 1 mg, magnesium: 30 mg, phosphorus: 78 mg, potassium: 1162 mg, sodium: 80 mg, zinc: 0.4 mg, thiamin: 0.2 mg, riboflavin: 0 mg, niacin: 1 mg, vitamin $B_6$: 0.4 mg, folate: 33 mcg, pantothenic acid: 0.4 mg, vitamin $B_{12}$: 0 mcg, vitamin A: 10 mcg, vitamin C: 30 mg, vitamin E: 1 mg, omega-6 fatty acids: 0.3 g, omega-3 fatty acids: 0.3 g

Percentage of calories from protein 5%, fat 11%, carbohydrate 84%

# Brown Rice, Mushroom, and Walnut Pilaf

Makes about 4 cups (1 L)

Sautéing is a method of cooking food that uses a small amount of oil in a pan over relatively high heat. A pilaf is a dish containing a cereal grain such as rice that is sautéed in vegetable oil and with other, fragrant ingredients, then cooked in a seasoned broth. The oil coats each individual grain and keeps them from sticking together. This dish can be cooked on the stovetop or in the oven (see variation below).

1 tablespoon (15 mL) coconut or olive oil
1/2 onion, diced
2 cups (500 mL) sliced mushrooms
1 cup (250 mL) brown rice
1/2 cup (125 mL) coarsely chopped walnuts
1 teaspoon (5 mL) ground cumin
2 cups (500 mL) water or vegetable stock
1/2 teaspoon (2 mL) salt
**Chopped fresh parsley, for garnish**

Heat the oil in a skillet over medium-high heat. Add the onion and mushrooms and cook for 5 minutes or until the liquid from the mushrooms has evaporated. Add the rice, walnuts, and cumin and stir for 30 seconds to coat the rice with oil. Add the water and salt, bring to a boil, cover, reduce heat to low, and cook for 45 minutes. Serve garnished with parsley.

Per cup (250 mL): calories: 328, protein: 8 g, fat: 15 g, carbohydrate: 43 g (2 g from sugar), dietary fibre: 3 g, calcium: 45 mg, iron: 2 mg, magnesium: 105 mg, phosphorus: 225 mg, potassium: 355 mg, sodium: 244 mg, zinc: 2 mg, thiamin: 0.3 mg, riboflavin: 0.2 mg, niacin: 5 mg, vitamin $B_6$: 0.4 mg, folate: 35 mcg, pantothenic acid: 1.4 mg, vitamin $B_{12}$: 0 mcg, vitamin A: 5 mcg, vitamin C: 3 mg, vitamin E: 0.5 mg, omega-6 fatty acids: 6 g, omega-3 fatty acids: 1.4 g

Percentage of calories from protein 9%, fat 40%, carbohydrate 51%

**Baked Brown Rice, Mushroom, and Walnut Pilaf**
For a baked version, preheat the oven to 350°F (180°C). After cooking the onion and mushrooms in a skillet as directed in the recipe, add the rice, walnuts, cumin, water, and salt. Bring the liquid to a boil, then transfer the mixture to a baking dish. Cover with a lid or foil and bake for 45 to 50 minutes.

# Coconut Saffron Rice with Cardamom and Lime

Makes 3 1/2 cups (875 mL)

Though quick to prepare, the combination of ingredients in this simple dish creates a fabulous blend of flavours. Coconut milk is a good source of iron and potassium. Canned coconut milk separates on standing at room temperature, so you may need to stir or shake it before measuring and using it. Wash the rice, as it may have been buffed or polished with talc powder, which will give a slight cloudiness to the dish. Adding the rice after the liquid has come to a boil will help to keep the grains separate.

**1 cup (250 mL) white basmati rice**
**1 cup (250 mL) coconut milk**
**3/4 cup (185 mL) water**
**2 cardamom pods, crushed, or pinch of ground cardamom**
**1/4 teaspoon (1 mL) salt**
**Pinch of saffron**
**2 tablespoons (30 mL) lime juice**
**Cilantro or parsley, for garnish**

Wash the rice in a large bowl under cold water until the water runs clear. Set the rice in a strainer and drain well. Bring the coconut milk, water, cardamom, salt, and saffron to a boil in a saucepan. Add the rice, reduce heat, cover, and simmer for 20 minutes or until the liquid is absorbed and the rice is cooked. Sprinkle the lime juice evenly over the rice, fluff with a fork, garnish with cilantro, and serve.

Per cup (250 mL): calories: 363, protein: 5 g, fat: 15 g, carbohydrate: 58 g (0 g from sugar), dietary fibre: 2 g, calcium: 18 mg, iron: 4 mg, magnesium: 36 mg, phosphorus: 72 mg, potassium: 179 mg, sodium: 146 mg, zinc: 0.4 mg, thiamin: 0.2 mg, riboflavin: 0 mg, niacin: 2 mg, vitamin $B_6$: 0 mg, folate: 12 mcg, pantothenic acid: 0.1 mg, vitamin $B_{12}$: 0 mcg, vitamin A: 5 mcg, vitamin C: 5 mg, vitamin E: 0 mg, omega-6 fatty acids: 0.3 g, omega-3 fatty acids: 0 g

Percentage of calories from protein 5%, fat 36%, carbohydrate 59%

# Corn, Red Peppers, and Pesto

Makes 3 cups (750 mL)

What a pleasure it is when the season for fresh corn arrives. To remove corn kernels from the ear, slice off the stem and place the ear of corn, stem end down, on a damp cloth, to avoid slipping. Hold a knife at the top of the ear and slice from top to bottom. Slightly rotate the ear and repeat until all the corn is removed. One large ear will produce about 1 cup (250 mL) of corn kernels. Frozen or canned corn niblets also may be used for this recipe.

1 1/2 teaspoons (7 mL) coconut or olive oil
1/2 red onion, chopped
2 cloves garlic, minced
3 cups (750 mL) corn kernels
1/2 cup (125 mL) diced red bell pepper
1/4 cup (60 mL) Pesto-the-Best-Oh (page 92) or other pesto
1 tablespoon (15 mL) lime juice

Heat the oil in a skillet over medium heat. Cook the onion for 3 to 5 minutes or until translucent. Add the garlic, corn, and bell pepper, cover, and cook for 3 minutes or until the corn is warmed through. Mix the pesto and lime juice together in a small bowl. Remove the corn from the heat, stir in the pesto mixture, and serve.

Per cup (250 mL): calories: 262, protein: 8 g, fat: 12 g, carbohydrate: 37 g (8 g from sugar), dietary fibre: 6 g, calcium: 40 mg, iron: 2 mg, magnesium: 88 mg, phosphorus: 197 mg, potassium: 632 mg, sodium: 163 mg, zinc: 1 mg, thiamin: 0.4 mg, riboflavin: 0.2 mg, niacin: 4 mg, vitamin $B_6$: 0.3 mg, folate: 99 mcg, pantothenic acid: 1.4 mg, vitamin $B_{12}$: 0 mcg, vitamin A: 89 mcg, vitamin C: 68 mg, vitamin E: 1 mg, omega-6 fatty acids: 4 g, omega-3 fatty acids: 0.7 g

Percentage of calories from protein 11%, fat 38%, carbohydrate 51%

# Mashed Parsnips and Apple with Toasted Walnuts

Makes 3 cups (750 mL)

Parsnips are similar to potatoes in nutritional value but there are a few differences. Potatoes contain a little more protein, whereas parsnips have more fibre and natural sugar. This recipe is a fabulous autumn and winter side dish and goes very well with Holiday Stuffed Winter Squash (page 154). To toast the walnuts, see the sidebar on page 112.

4 cups (1 L) peeled, chopped parsnips
1 red apple, peeled, cored, and cubed
1/3 cup (85 mL) cooking liquid from the parsnips and apple
2 tablespoons (30 mL) hemp seed or extra-virgin olive oil
1/2 teaspoon (2 mL) nutmeg
1/2 teaspoon (2 mL) grated or minced lemon peel
1/2 teaspoon (2 mL) salt
1/4 teaspoon (1 mL) white pepper
1/2 cup (125 mL) toasted walnuts, chopped
1/4 cup (60 mL) chopped fresh parsley

Put the parsnips and apple in a steamer over water and on medium-high heat and steam for 5 minutes or until the parsnips are tender when pricked with a knife. Reserve some of the cooking liquid. Transfer the parsnips and apple to the bowl of a food processor along with the measured cooking liquid, oil, nutmeg, lemon peel, salt, and pepper. Purée until smooth. Transfer the purée to a warm serving bowl and stir in the walnuts and parsley.

Per cup (250 mL): calories: 367, protein: 6 g, fat: 23 g, carbohydrate: 43 g (14 g from sugar), dietary fibre: 9 g, calcium: 99 mg, iron: 2 mg, magnesium: 92 mg, phosphorus: 213 mg, potassium: 863 mg, sodium: 337 mg, zinc: 2 mg, thiamin: 0.2 mg, riboflavin: 0.1 mg, niacin: 2 mg, vitamin $B_6$: 0.3 mg, folate: 153 mcg, pantothenic acid: 1 mg, vitamin $B_{12}$: 0 mcg, vitamin A: 23 mcg, vitamin C: 41 mg, vitamin E: 0.2 mg, omega-6 fatty acids: 13 g, omega-3 fatty acids: 4 g

Percentage of calories from protein 6%, fat 52%, carbohydrate 42%

## Dijon Scalloped Potatoes

Makes 6 cups (1.5 L)

Scalloped potatoes are generally made with plenty of milk, cream, and butter. This version is dairy-free, and the fat content has been kept to a minimum. It comes to life with the unique combination of miso and Dijon mustard. The sauce begins with a roux, a classical French cooking technique for thickening sauces in which wheat flour and fat (in this case, coconut or olive oil) are cooked together until the raw flour taste is no longer apparent. Using a roux results in a smooth sauce.

### Roux

1/3 cup (85 mL) unbleached all-purpose flour
3 tablespoons (45 mL) coconut or olive oil
2 cups (500 mL) hot low-sodium vegetable broth or stock

### Potatoes

2 pounds (900 g) unpeeled potatoes, cut into 1/4-inch (5 mm) thick slices
1/2 red onion, thinly sliced
3 tablespoons (45 mL) miso
1 1/2 tablespoons (22 mL) Dijon mustard
1/4 teaspoon (1 mL) black pepper

Put the flour and oil in a saucepan over medium heat and stir well to combine. Cook for 3 minutes, stirring frequently to prevent the flour from burning. Remove the roux from the heat and allow to cool for 1 minute before adding liquid. This will prevent clumping when the hot liquid comes in contact with the roux. Add broth gradually, stirring with a whisk or wooden spoon, until it is all incorporated into the roux. Return mixture to heat and bring to a boil. Reduce heat and simmer for 10 minutes, stirring occasionally.

Preheat the oven to 375°F (190°C).

Layer one-half of the potatoes in a lightly oiled 9 × 13-inch (23 × 33 cm) baking dish. Spread the onion slices evenly over top, followed by the remaining potatoes. Combine miso, mustard, and pepper in a small bowl and stir until miso is dissolved. Remove the sauce from heat and stir in the miso mixture. Pour the sauce over the potatoes, cover, put in the oven, and cook for 30 minutes. Remove cover and cook for 20 minutes or until potatoes are cooked.

Per cup (250 mL): calories: 223, protein: 5 g, fat: 8 g, carbohydrate: 34 g (3 g from sugar), dietary fibre: 5 g, calcium: 25 mg, iron: 1.5 mg, magnesium: 38 mg, phosphorus: 118 mg, potassium: 658 mg, sodium: 463 mg, zinc: 1 mg, thiamin: 0.2 mg, riboflavin: 0.1 mg, niacin: 3 mg, vitamin $B_6$: 0.3 mg, folate: 42 mcg, pantothenic acid: 0.5 mg, vitamin $B_{12}$: 0 mcg, vitamin A: 37 mcg, vitamin C: 30 mg, vitamin E: 1 mg, omega-6 fatty acids: 1 g, omega-3 fatty acids: 0.1 g

Percentage of calories from protein 10%, fat 30%, carbohydrate 60%

## Lemon Roasted Potatoes

Makes 6 cups (1.5 L)

The Greeks make spectacular roasted potatoes using lemon juice and olive oil, though the fat content is very high in traditional recipes. This version keeps the lemon and herb flavours but greatly reduces the amount of oil and salt. Yukon Gold or nugget potatoes work best here, although russets work well too. If you prefer, use 1 tablespoon (15 mL) fresh oregano instead of the dried herb or replace it with the same amount of thyme.

6 cups (1.5 L) peeled, cubed potato, about 6 potatoes cut into 1-inch (2.5 cm) cubes
3 tablespoons (45 mL) freshly squeezed lemon juice
3 tablespoons (45 mL) olive oil
1 teaspoon (5 mL) dried oregano
1/2 teaspoon (2 mL) salt
1/4 teaspoon (1 mL) black pepper
2 tablespoons (30 mL) chopped fresh parsley

Preheat the oven to 400°F (200°C).

Put the potatoes, lemon juice, oil, oregano, salt, and pepper in a large bowl and toss to mix well. Transfer the potato mixture to a baking dish and bake, uncovered, for 35 to 40 minutes or until the potatoes are soft, removing once to turn over the potatoes with a steel spatula. Garnish with parsley and serve.

Per cup (250 mL): calories: 209, protein: 3 g, fat: 9 g, carbohydrate: 29 g (3 g from sugar), dietary fibre: 3 g, calcium: 15 mg, iron: 1 mg, magnesium: 35 mg, phosphorus: 75 mg, potassium: 880 mg, sodium: 168 mg, zinc: 1 mg, thiamin: 0.1 mg, riboflavin: 0.1 mg, niacin: 3 mg, vitamin $B_6$: 0.4 mg, folate: 24 mcg, pantothenic acid: 1 mg, vitamin $B_{12}$: 0 mcg, vitamin A: 6 mcg, vitamin C: 37 mg, vitamin E: 1 mg, omega-6 fatty acids: 1 g, omega-3 fatty acids: 0.1 g

Percentage of calories from protein 6%, fat 39%, carbohydrate 55%

# Portobello Mushrooms with Marjoram and Balsamic

Makes 3 cups (750 mL)

A portobello mushroom is a mature cremini mushroom. Once the small brown cremini grows to about 4 or 6 inches (10 or 15 cm) in diameter, it is deemed to be a portobello. These are known in France as *champignons de Paris* and in Italy as *capellone*, meaning "big hat." These large mushrooms can be sautéed, as in this recipe or in Simple Sautéed Portobello Mushrooms (page 206), or stuffed, as in the Portobello Mushroom Burgers with Chickpea Topping (page 166).

3 large portobello mushrooms, about 6 cups (1.5 L) sliced
1 to 2 tablespoons (15 to 30 mL) Earth Balance spread, coconut oil, or olive oil
1 teaspoon (5 mL) dried marjoram
2 cloves garlic, minced
1 tablespoon (15 mL) balsamic vinegar
1 tablespoon (15 mL) tamari or soy sauce

Carefully remove the stems from the mushrooms, cut the stems in half lengthwise, then cut into 1/4-inch (5 mm) thick slices. Cut each mushroom cap into three equal pieces, then cut each piece into 1/4-inch (5 mm) thick slices.

Heat the Earth Balance spread in a large skillet over medium heat, being careful not to burn the spread. Add the mushrooms pieces, including the stems, and the marjoram. Cover and cook for 4 minutes. Add the garlic and cook for 1 minute, stirring occasionally. Remove the skillet from the heat and stir in the vinegar and tamari.

Per cup (250 mL): calories: 66, protein: 3 g, fat: 4 g, carbohydrate: 6 g (2 g from sugar), dietary fibre: 2 g, calcium: 16 mg, iron: 1 mg, magnesium: 13 mg, phosphorus: 122 mg, potassium: 435 mg, sodium: 347 mg, zinc: 1 mg, thiamin: 0.1 mg, riboflavin: 0.4 mg, niacin: 4 mg, vitamin $B_6$: 0.1 mg, folate: 20 mcg, pantothenic acid: 1 mg, vitamin $B_{12}$: 0 mcg, vitamin A: 1 mcg, vitamin C: 1 mg, vitamin E: 0 mg, omega-6 fatty acids: 0.1 g, omega-3 fatty acids: 0 g

Percentage of calories from protein 17%, fat 49%, carbohydrate 34%

# Potato Subji

Makes 7 cups (1.75 L)

India has a tradition of vegetarian cuisine with roots in antiquity. As a consequence, its food combinations have a great deal to offer the West in depth of flavour, colour, richness, and variety. An example is found in this subji (vegetable dish), which is one of the tastiest ways ever created to eat potatoes. Using a heavy-bottomed pan helps to spread the heat evenly and to prevent burning.

1 tablespoon (15 mL) mustard seeds
2 tablespoons (30 mL) coconut or olive oil
1 large onion, cut into 1/4-inch (5 mm) dice
2 teaspoons (10 mL) turmeric
2 1/2 pounds (1 kg) potatoes, cut into 1/2-inch (1 cm) cubes, about 4 potatoes
1/4 cup (60 mL) water, plus more as needed
1 teaspoon (5 mL) salt

Heat the mustard seeds in the oil over medium heat in a pan. Once the seeds begin to pop, cover the pan with the lid and wait until you hear that the seeds have stopped popping, about 1 minute. Add onion and turmeric; cook for about 5 minutes or until the onion is translucent. Stir in potatoes, water, and salt. Cover and simmer for 20 minutes or until potatoes are tender, adding more water if necessary to prevent the potatoes from drying out.

Per cup (250 mL): calories: 177, protein: 4 g, fat: 5 g, carbohydrate: 31 g (4 g from sugar), dietary fibre: 3 g, calcium: 30 mg, iron: 2 mg, magnesium: 40 mg, phosphorus: 93 mg, potassium: 872 mg, sodium: 348 mg, zinc: 1 mg, thiamin: 0.2 mg, riboflavin: 0.1 mg, niacin: 3 mg, vitamin $B_6$: 0.5 mg, folate: 29 mcg, pantothenic acid: 0.6 mg, vitamin $B_{12}$: 0 mcg, vitamin A: 0 mcg, vitamin C: 31 mg, vitamin E: 1 mg, omega-6 fatty acids: 0.4 g, omega-3 fatty acids: 0.1 g

Percentage of calories from protein 8%, fat 23%, carbohydrate 69%

# Red Cabbage with Walnuts

Makes 3 1/2 cups (875 mL)

The brassica family of cabbage and related plant foods provide valuable phytochemicals that help protect us against cancer. The oils in walnuts are rich in essential omega-3 fatty acids. These health-supportive ingredients are enhanced by the sweet, smooth taste of balsamic vinegar, which has been aged in wooden casks for up to 10 years.

**1 tablespoon (15 mL) coconut or olive oil**
**4 cups (1 L) thinly sliced red cabbage, about 1/4 head**
**1/2 cup (125 mL) chopped walnuts**
**2 tablespoons (30 mL) balsamic vinegar**
**1 to 2 teaspoons (5 to 10 mL) extra-virgin olive oil**
**1 to 2 teaspoons (5 to 10 mL) tamari or soy sauce**

Heat the coconut oil in pan over medium heat. Add the cabbage and cook for 5 to 8 minutes or until wilted. Remove from heat and stir in walnuts, vinegar, the olive oil, and tamari. Serve warm—or cooled, as a salad.

Per cup (250 mL): calories: 173, protein: 4 g, fat: 15 g, carbohydrate: 8 g (4 g from sugar), dietary fibre: 3 g, calcium: 51 mg, iron: 1 mg, magnesium: 37 mg, phosphorus: 78 mg, potassium: 265 mg, sodium: 119 mg, zinc: 1 mg, thiamin: 0.1 mg, riboflavin: 0.1 mg, niacin: 1 mg, vitamin $B_6$: 0.2 mg, folate: 30 mcg, pantothenic acid: 0.2 mg, vitamin $B_{12}$: 0 mcg, vitamin A: 45 mcg, vitamin C: 46 mg, vitamin E: 1 mg, omega-6 fatty acids: 6 g, omega-3 fatty acids: 1.5 g

Percentage of calories from protein 8%, fat 75%, carbohydrate 17%

## Maintaining Vibrant Colour in Green and Red Vegetables

Vegetables such as broccoli, bok choy, and green beans contain the pigment chlorophyll, which turns an even brighter and more vivid green when heat is first applied. During the cooking process, green vegetables release acids that surround plant cells. If these acids are not allowed to escape into the atmosphere, particularly when greens are cooked in a pot covered by a lid, such as a steamer, the unstable chlorophyll molecule turns greyish yellow. This can be avoided by leaving the pot lid slightly askew so that the acids are released into the air. Plunging greens into cold water once they have reached a certain degree of doneness arrests the cooking and preserves, or stabilizes, the chlorophyll pigment.

Green pigments also are affected by the addition of acids. In their natural slightly alkaline condition, they are a brighter green, whereas when acids such as lemon juice or vinegar are added, the colour becomes dull. Adding acidic dressings to greens immediately before serving (rather than ahead of time) reduces the likelihood of making your vegetables unappetizing looking.

On the other hand, red vegetables and fruit—for instance, red cabbage, red radishes, and grapes—not only brighten but retain their appealing colour in the presence of acidic foods. These red foods contain a red pigment known as anthocyanin, and a blue pigment called betacyanin, which are stabilized in the presence of acids like vinegar, citrus juice, and wine.

# Roasted Root Vegetables

Makes about 8 cups (2 L)

Our autumn harvest of root vegetables provides a great deal of nourishment and warmth. You may vary the combination below by including other choices, such as sweet potatoes, parsnips, turnips, or squash, using a total of 8 to 9 cups (2 to 2.25 L) chopped root vegetables. The foods with deep yellow and orange hues are particularly rich in vitamin A.

2 carrots
2 yams, peeled
2 potatoes, unpeeled
1 large red, yellow, or white onion
2 tablespoons (30 mL) extra-virgin olive oil
1 tablespoon (15 mL) chopped fresh herbs (such as basil, thyme, oregano, dill)
1/4 teaspoon (1 mL) salt
Pinch of black pepper

Heat the oven to 375°F (190°C).

Cut the carrots, yams, potatoes, and onion into 1-inch (2.5 cm) pieces and place in large bowl. Sprinkle with the oil, herbs, salt, and pepper, tossing the vegetables well to coat. Transfer to a 9 × 13-inch (23 × 33 cm) baking dish or cookie sheet. Bake, uncovered, for 35 to 40 minutes or until the vegetables are tender.

Per cup (250 mL): calories: 162, protein: 2 g, fat: 4 g, carbohydrate: 31 g (1 g from sugar), dietary fibre: 4 g, calcium: 24 mg, iron: 1 mg, magnesium: 29 mg, phosphorus: 71 mg, potassium: 885 mg, sodium: 79 mg, zinc: 0.4 mg, thiamin: 0.1 mg, riboflavin: 0.1 mg, niacin: 2 mg, vitamin $B_6$: 0.4 mg, folate: 28 mcg, pantothenic acid: 0.5 mg, vitamin $B_{12}$: 0 mcg, vitamin A: 129 mcg, vitamin C: 24 mg, vitamin E: 0.2 mg, omega-6 fatty acids: 0.1 g, omega-3 fatty acids: 0 g

Percentage of calories from protein 6%, fat 20%, carbohydrate 74%

# Seasoned Greens

Makes about 3 cups (750 mL)

Greens have an outstanding nutritional profile. Take a look at the protein, calcium, iron, other minerals, and vitamin A values listed in the nutritional analysis for this recipe! Make this robust dish using a single leafy green such as calcium-rich kale, or use any of the following, alone or mixed: collard, dandelion, mustard or beet greens, spinach, Swiss chard. Spinach or Swiss chard will produce a sweeter dish, though the calcium present in these and in beet greens is far less easily absorbed by the body than that in kale. Wash the greens well and remove and discard tough stems and stalks. Tougher greens, such as mature kale, may take a little longer to cook.

1 tablespoon (15 mL) coconut oil or olive oil
1/2 yellow onion, diced
2 cloves garlic, minced
12 cups (3 L) vegetable greens, cut or ripped into bite-size pieces
2 teaspoons (10 mL) ground cumin
1 teaspoon (5 mL) paprika
1/2 teaspoon (2 mL) dried thyme
1/4 teaspoon (1 mL) salt
1 tablespoon (15 mL) freshly squeezed lemon juice

Heat the oil in a large pot over medium heat. Add the onion and cook for 2 to 3 minutes or until translucent. Add the garlic, then the greens, cumin, paprika, thyme, and salt, stirring well to lift the seasonings into the greens. Partially cover and, stirring frequently, cook for 2 to 5 minutes (depending on how tough the greens are) or until the greens are warmed through, wilted, and tender to the bite. Remove from the heat, stir in the lemon juice, and serve warm or at room temperature.

Per cup (250 mL): calories: 192, protein: 9 g, fat: 7 g, carbohydrate: 31 g (1 g from sugar), dietary fibre: 6 g, calcium: 387 mg, iron: 6 mg, magnesium: 99 mg, phosphorus: 166 mg, potassium: 1266 mg, sodium: 276 mg, zinc: 1 mg, thiamin: 0.3 mg, riboflavin: 0.4 mg, niacin: 5 mg, vitamin $B_6$: 1 mg, folate: 83 mcg, pantothenic acid: 0.3 mg, vitamin $B_{12}$: 0 mcg, vitamin A: 2062 mcg, vitamin C: 326 mg, vitamin E: 3 mg, omega-6 fatty acids: 0.8 g, omega-3 fatty acids: 0.5 g

Percentage of calories from protein 17%, fat 28%, carbohydrate 55%

**Note:** Analysis was done using kale.

## Seasoned Potato Wedges

Makes 18 to 24 wedges

You may be surprised to discover that these potato wedges are a good source of protein and minerals as well as of vitamin C and B vitamins. They are a delicious and low-fat alternative to French fries. Easy to prepare, they can be served alone or with Miso Gravy (page 216), Spicy Peanut Sauce (page 218), or other favourite dipping sauces. Experiment with different herb and spice combinations in the yeast mixture. Any leftover yeast can be sprinkled over casseroles, salad, or popcorn.

3 medium unpeeled potatoes
1/4 cup (60 mL) non-dairy milk
1/2 teaspoon (2 mL) salt
1/3 cup (85 mL) nutritional yeast
2 teaspoons (10 mL) onion powder
2 teaspoons (10 mL) chili powder
3/4 teaspoon (4 mL) garlic powder
1/4 teaspoon (1 mL) black pepper

Preheat the oven to 400°F (200°C).

Cut each potato in half lengthwise; cut each half into thirds or quarters, depending on the size of potato. Pour the milk into a flat-bottomed bowl or dish. Add the salt and stir to dissolve. Sprinkle the yeast onto a plate; stir in the onion, chili, and garlic powders and the pepper. Dip the potato wedges into the milk, then into the yeast mixture, coating all surfaces. Arrange the wedges on a nonstick baking sheet and bake for 30 minutes.

Per 6 to 8 wedges (1 potato): calories: 228, protein: 10 g, fat: 1.5 g, carbohydrate: 45 g (3 g from sugar), dietary fibre: 7 g, calcium: 68 mg, iron: 2 mg, magnesium: 70 mg, phosphorus: 286 mg, potassium: 1245 mg, sodium: 357 mg, zinc: 3 mg, thiamin: 7 mg, riboflavin: 7 mg, niacin: 45 mg, vitamin $B_6$: 7 mg, folate: 241 mcg, pantothenic acid: 2 mg, vitamin $B_{12}$: 6 mcg, vitamin A: 35 mcg, vitamin C: 23 mg, vitamin E: 0.1 mg, omega-6 fatty acids: 0.3 g, omega-3 fatty acids: 0 g

Percentage of calories from protein 17%, fat 6%, carbohydrate 77%

**Note**: Analysis was done using fortified soy milk.

**Oiled-Baking-Sheet Method**
For crispy wedges, lightly oil a baking sheet and arrange potatoes cut-side down. Bake in a 400°F (200°C) oven for 15 minutes. Using a fork or metal tongs, turn the wedges and bake for another 15 minutes.

# Shiitake Mushrooms, Kale, and Sesame

Makes 2 1/2 cups (625 mL)

Shiitake mushrooms are native to China and Japan, where they are used extensively in their cuisines. Now popular around the world, they are found in most supermarkets and are known for their possible anti-cancer benefits. They have a strong earthy flavour and meaty texture and taste very good with a few drops of tamari. Always remove the stems, which are tough, before using the mushrooms, saving the stems for making stock for miso soup.

2 teaspoons (10 mL) coconut or olive oil
1 teaspoon (5 mL) toasted sesame oil
2 cups (500 mL) sliced shiitake mushrooms, stems removed
6 cups (1.5 L) sliced kale leaves
1 cup (250 mL) chopped red bell pepper
1 tablespoon (15 mL) tamari or soy sauce
1 tablespoon (15 mL) rice vinegar
1 tablespoon (15 mL) mirin or other Asian cooking wine
1 tablespoon (15 mL) toasted sesame seeds (see page 133)

Heat the coconut and sesame oils in a large skillet over medium heat. Add the mushrooms and cook, covered but stirring frequently, for 3 to 5 minutes, until the moisture has evaporated. Add the kale and bell pepper, cover, and cook for 3 to 5 minutes or until the kale is soft to the bite. Remove from the heat and add the tamari, vinegar, and mirin. Sprinkle the sesame seeds over top and serve.

Per cup (250 mL): calories: 196, protein: 8 g, fat: 9 g, carbohydrate: 26 g (5 g from sugar), dietary fibre: 5 g, calcium: 273 mg, iron: 4 mg, magnesium: 82 mg, phosphorus: 146 mg, potassium: 926 mg, sodium: 483 mg, zinc: 1 mg, thiamin: 0.2 mg, riboflavin: 0.3 mg, niacin: 4 mg, vitamin $B_6$: 1 mg, folate: 66 mcg, pantothenic acid: 0.4 mg, vitamin $B_{12}$: 0 mcg, vitamin A: 1406 mcg, vitamin C: 324 mg, vitamin E: 2 mg, omega-6 fatty acids: 1 g, omega-3 fatty acids: 0.4 g

Percentage of calories from protein 15%, fat 36%, carbohydrate 46%, alcohol (from mirin) 3%

# Simple Sautéed Portobello Mushrooms

Makes 2 mushrooms

Sometimes we return again and again to the simplest meals. Here, the delicate and unique flavour of the mushrooms comes through. These whole sautéed mushrooms can be served as the "meat" on a plate or in a sandwich, used in place of a patty in a whole-wheat hamburger bun, or sliced as a salad topping.

**1 to 2 tablespoons (15 to 30 mL) Earth Balance spread or olive oil**
**2 large whole portobello mushrooms**
**Salt and pepper**

Remove the stems from the mushrooms. Heat the Earth Balance spread in a large skillet over medium-high heat. Place the whole mushrooms in the pan, sprinkle with salt and pepper to taste, and cook for 4 minutes, until the moisture has evaporated. Turn and cook the other side for 2 minutes, until heated through.

Per mushroom: calories: 69, protein: 2 g, fat: 6 g, carbohydrate: 4 g (1 g from sugar), dietary fibre: 2 g, calcium: 6 mg, iron: 0.4 mg, magnesium: 8 mg, phosphorus: 91 mg, potassium: 339 mg, sodium: 4 mg, zinc: 0.4 mg, thiamin: 0.1 mg, riboflavin: 0.3 mg, niacin: 3 mg, vitamin $B_6$: 0.1 mg, folate: 15 mcg, pantothenic acid: 1 mg, vitamin $B_{12}$: 0 mcg, vitamin A: 0 mcg, vitamin C: 0 mg, vitamin E: 0 mg, omega-6 fatty acids: 0 g, omega-3 fatty acids: 0 g

Percentage of calories from protein 10%, fat 70%, carbohydrate 20%

**Note:** Analysis was done without using salt and pepper.

**Sliced Portobello Mushrooms**
Slice 2 large portobello mushrooms into 1/4-inch (5 mm) thick slices, about 3 cups (750 mL), and proceed as directed in the recipe, cooking, stirring occasionally, for 6 minutes or until slightly browned.

# Spanish Rice

Makes 4 cups (1 L)

The origins of this dish are found in Latin American countries, though rice also is a staple in Spain. This rice turns out very moist thanks to the addition of tomatoes, and the bell peppers, herbs, and spices provide a deep, rich flavour. Try it in International Roll-Ups (page 156) or Timesaving Tacos (page 183). Serve it with warmed black beans and a salad for a pleasant colour combination.

1 tablespoon (15 mL) coconut or olive oil
1/2 onion, diced
1 clove garlic, minced
2 cups (500 mL) chopped fresh or drained canned tomatoes
1/2 cup (125 mL) diced green or red bell peppers
1/2 teaspoon (2 mL) dried oregano
1/2 teaspoon (2 mL) ground cumin
1/2 teaspoon (2 mL) chili powder
1/4 teaspoon (1 mL) salt
1/4 teaspoon (1 mL) black pepper
2 cups (500 mL) vegetable stock or water
1 cup (250 mL) brown rice

Heat the oil in a saucepan over medium heat. Add the onion and cook for 3 to 5 minutes or until translucent. Add the garlic, tomatoes, peppers, oregano, cumin, chili powder, salt, and pepper and cook for 5 minutes or until the tomatoes have lost most of their liquid. Add the stock and rice, bring to a boil, reduce heat to low, cover, and simmer for 45 minutes or until the rice is cooked and has absorbed all the liquid.

Per cup (250 mL): calories: 252, protein: 5 g, fat: 5 g, carbohydrate: 48 g (5 g from sugar), dietary fibre: 4 g, calcium: 39 mg, iron: 2 mg, magnesium: 88 mg, phosphorus: 167 mg, potassium: 430 mg, sodium: 421 mg, zinc: 1 mg, thiamin: 0.3 mg, riboflavin: 0.1 mg, niacin: 4 mg, vitamin $B_6$: 0.4 mg, folate: 30 mcg, pantothenic acid: 0.9 mg, vitamin $B_{12}$: 0 mcg, vitamin A: 48 mcg, vitamin C: 29 mg, vitamin E: 1 mg, omega-6 fatty acids: 0.6 g, omega-3 fatty acids: 0 g

Percentage of calories from protein 8%, fat 18%, carbohydrate 74%

**Note:** Analysis was done with soup stock that provided 292 mg sodium per cup (250 mL) Spanish Rice.

# Spinach with Tofu and Garam Masala

Makes 1 1/2 cups (375 mL)

First the bad news. You will have some dishwashing to do after this meal: a steamer, a skillet, and a blender—so be warned. Now the good news. When you serve this exquisitely seasoned vegan version of the Indian dish palak paneer, people's eyes will light up. In Hindi, garam masala means "warm mixture"; the name arose because of the warming effect of this spice mix on the body. It typically consists of cinnamon, cloves, nutmeg, cardamom, nutmeg, mace, and black pepper. Double-boiler steamers or steaming inserts that can be fitted into a saucepan allow you to cook vegetables in a way that allows maximum nutrient retention.

10 cups (2.5 L) spinach leaves and stems, about 10 ounces (284 g)
1 tablespoon (15 mL) coconut or olive oil
1 small onion, diced
1 teaspoon (5 mL) garam masala
1/2 teaspoon (2 mL) ground coriander
1/4 teaspoon (1 mL) garlic powder
1/4 teaspoon (1 mL) salt
1/2 teaspoon (2 mL) lemon juice
1/4 cup (60 mL) cubed firm tofu, in 1/4-inch (5 mm) cubes

Put the spinach in a steamer over medium-high heat and steam for about 3 minutes or until leaves are cooked.

Heat the oil in a skillet over medium heat; add the onion and cook for 3 to 5 minutes or until translucent. Add the garam masala, coriander, garlic powder, and salt and cook for another 2 to 3 minutes. Stir frequently to prevent the spices from sticking to the pan. Transfer the spinach to a blender or food processor, followed by the onion mixture and the lemon juice. Blend until smooth. Return the mixture to the skillet; add the tofu and warm until the tofu is heated through. Transfer to a serving dish and serve.

Per 1/2 cup (125 mL): calories: 90, protein: 5 g, fat: 6 g, carbohydrate: 7 g (2 g from sugar), dietary fibre: 3 g, calcium: 150 mg, iron: 3 mg, magnesium: 91 mg, phosphorus: 84 mg, potassium: 636 mg, sodium: 240 mg, zinc: 1 mg, thiamin: 0.1 mg, riboflavin: 0.2 mg, niacin: 2 mg, vitamin $B_6$: 0.3 mg, folate: 204 mcg, pantothenic acid: 0.2 mg, vitamin $B_{12}$: 0 mcg, vitamin A: 469 mcg, vitamin C: 30 mg, vitamin E: 2 mg, omega-6 fatty acids: 0.5 g, omega-3 fatty acids: 0.2 g

Percentage of calories from protein 20%, fat 53%, carbohydrate 27%

**Note:** Much of the calcium and iron in spinach is bound by oxalates and unavailable for absorption.

### Collard Greens with Tofu and Garam Masala
Replace spinach with de-stemmed, chopped collard greens and add 3 tablespoons (45 mL) of the cooking liquid to the blender or food processor. The calcium in collard greens is more readily absorbed than that in spinach.

### Puréed Spinach with Garam Masala
Make the dish as directed, but without the tofu.

## Stewed Tomatoes with Kale and Garlic

Makes 4 1/2 cups (1.125 L)

This nutritionally well-balanced dish can be a backbone of your calcium-rich recipes, with approximately 200 milligrams of highly available calcium per cup (250 mL). The vitamin C in the tomatoes helps our body to absorb another mineral that is present in the kale in significant amounts: iron. There also is plenty of potassium, folate, and the antioxidant vitamins A, C, and E. Furthermore, the combination tastes very good indeed.

1 tablespoon (15 mL) coconut or olive oil
1 onion, cut in large dice
4 cups (1 L) chopped fresh or canned tomatoes
4 cloves garlic, chopped
1 teaspoon (5 mL) dried basil
1 teaspoon (5 mL) dried thyme
1/2 teaspoon (2 mL) salt
1/4 teaspoon (1 mL) black pepper
8 cups (2 L) sliced kale greens, stems removed

Heat the oil in a large pot over medium heat. Add the onion and cook for 3 minutes or until translucent. Add the tomatoes, garlic, basil, thyme, salt, and pepper. Cover and cook for 3 to 5 minutes or until the tomatoes have a chunky, sauce-like texture. Add the kale greens. Partially cover and, stirring frequently, cook for 3 to 5 minutes or until the kale is tender to the bite.

Per cup (250 mL): calories: 136, protein: 6 g, fat: 4 g, carbohydrate: 23 g (6 g from sugar), dietary fibre: 5 g, calcium: 210 mg, iron: 3 mg, magnesium: 67 mg, phosphorus: 124 mg, potassium: 1024 mg, sodium: 274 mg, zinc: 1 mg, thiamin: 0.2 mg, riboflavin: 0.2 mg, niacin: 3 mg, vitamin $B_6$: 0.6 mg, folate: 68 mcg, pantothenic acid: 0.3 mg, vitamin $B_{12}$: 0 mcg, vitamin A: 1041 mcg, vitamin C: 175 mg, vitamin E: 2 mg, omega-6 fatty acids: 0.6 g, omega-3 fatty acids: 0.3 g

Percentage of calories from protein 16%, fat 25%, carbohydrate 59%

# Sauces and Gravies

## Apple Plum Chutney

Makes 2 1/4 cups (560 mL)

The autumn harvest of apples and plums bring with it a good reason to make this spicy, warm, ruby-red chutney. Take advantage of plum season and double or triple the recipe to freeze in small containers for up to 6 months. Otherwise keep the chutney in a closed container and refrigerated, for up to 2 weeks. Serve it with any of the Indian dishes listed in the Indian Menu on page 64. This chutney also goes well as a topping with the Lem-Un-Cheesecake with Crumb Crust (page 247) and with Vegan Dasz Ice Cream (page 254).

**3 cups (750 mL) unpeeled, diced red apples**
**3 cups (750 mL) quartered prune plums, about 15**
**2 tablespoons (30 mL) maple syrup or other sweetener**
**1 1/2 teaspoons (7 mL) minced lemon peel**
**3 tablespoons (45 mL) freshly squeezed lemon juice**
**2 teaspoons (10 mL) vanilla extract**
**1/2 teaspoon (2 mL) cinnamon**
**Pinch of ground cloves**

Put the apple, plums, maple syrup, lemon peel, lemon juice, vanilla, cinnamon, and cloves in a medium saucepan and bring to a boil over medium heat. Cover, reduce heat to low, and simmer for 20 minutes or until the plums are disintegrated.

Per 1/4 cup (60 mL): calories: 66, protein: 1 g, fat: 0.4 g, carbohydrate: 16 g (13 g from sugar), dietary fibre: 2 g, calcium: 10 mg, iron: 0.2 mg, magnesium: 7 mg, phosphorus: 11 mg, potassium: 158 mg, sodium: 1 mg, zinc: 0.3 mg, thiamin: 0 mg, riboflavin: 0.1 mg, niacin: 0.3 mg, vitamin $B_6$: 0.1 mg, folate: 3 mcg, pantothenic acid: 0.1 mg, vitamin $B_{12}$: 0 mcg, vitamin A: 1 mcg, vitamin C: 10 mg, vitamin E: 0.4 mg, omega-6 fatty acids: 0.1 g, omega-3 fatty acids: 0 g

Percentage of calories from protein 3%, fat 6%, carbohydrate 91%

# Blueberry Orange Sauce

Makes 2 1/2 cups (625 mL)

This easy sauce goes beautifully on Whole-Wheat Pancakes (page 83), Vegan Dasz Ice Cream (page 254), or other desserts. Starch dissolves better in cold liquids than in hot. Use the lesser amount of starch for a thick sauce that can be poured, and the greater amount of starch to make a thick sauce to be spooned on after it cools.

2 cups (500 mL) blueberries, fresh or frozen
1 cup (250 mL) apple juice
1/2 teaspoon (2 mL) cinnamon
3/4 cup (185 mL) orange juice concentrate
2 to 3 tablespoons (30 to 45 mL) arrowroot powder or cornstarch
1/4 cup (60 mL) maple syrup or other sweetener (optional)

Put the blueberries, apple juice, and cinnamon in a saucepan and heat over medium heat for about 5 minutes or until the berries soften and begin to lose their shape. Put the orange juice concentrate and starch in a small bowl and mix well. Add the orange juice mixture to the hot blueberry mixture. Bring sauce to a boil, then lower the heat and simmer 2 to 3 minutes. Sweeten to taste with maple syrup. Serve warm or cold.

Per 1/4 cup (60 mL): calories: 72, protein: 1 g, fat: 0.2 g, carbohydrate: 18 g (6 g from sugar), dietary fibre: 1 g, calcium: 13 mg, iron: 0.3 mg, magnesium: 10 mg, phosphorus: 18 mg, potassium: 206 mg, sodium: 2 mg, zinc: 0.1 mg, thiamin: 0.1 mg, riboflavin: 0 mg, niacin: 0.4 mg, vitamin $B_6$: 0.1 mg, folate: 37 mcg, pantothenic acid: 0.2 mg, vitamin $B_{12}$: 0 mcg, vitamin A: 1 mcg, vitamin C: 37 mg, vitamin E: 0.2 mg, omega-6 fatty acids: 0 g, omega-3 fatty acids: 0 g

Percentage of calories from protein 4%, fat 2%, carbohydrate 94%

# Cranberry Ginger Relish

Makes 3 cups (750 mL)

Cranberries are indigenous to North America and were traditionally used by First Nations people for food and medicine. The bright crimson berries are very tart; how much sweetener you use depends on how tangy you like your food. Cranberry relish evokes wonderful memories of Thanksgiving, Christmas, and other celebration gatherings for many people. Serve it as a side dish with Holiday Stuffed Winter Squash (page 154).

1/4 cup (60 mL) finely diced red onion
12 ounces (340 g) fresh or frozen cranberries
2 medium oranges, peeled, seeded, and chopped
1/4 cup (60 mL) orange juice
1 tablespoon (15 mL) minced ginger
1 teaspoon (5 mL) minced orange peel
1/2 teaspoon (2 mL) cinnamon
1/3 to 1/2 cup (85 to 125 mL) brown sugar or other sweetener

Put the red onion, cranberries, oranges, orange juice, ginger, orange peel, cinnamon, and brown sugar in a medium saucepan. Bring to a boil, reduce heat to low, cover, and simmer for 15 to 20 minutes or until the cranberries have popped open and are disintegrated.

Per 1/4 cup (60 mL): calories: 53, protein: 0.4 g, fat: 0.1 g, carbohydrate: 14 g (10 g from sugar), dietary fibre: 2 g, calcium: 20 mg, iron: 0.3 mg, magnesium: 7 mg, phosphorus: 10 mg, potassium: 105 mg, sodium: 3 mg, zinc: 0.1 mg, thiamin: 0 mg, riboflavin: 0 mg, niacin: 0 mg, vitamin $B_6$: 0 mg, folate: 9 mcg, pantothenic acid: 0.2 mg, vitamin $B_{12}$: 0 mcg, vitamin A: 1 mcg, vitamin C: 19 mg, vitamin E: 0.4 mg, omega-6 fatty acids: 0 g, omega-3 fatty acids: 0 g

Percentage of calories from protein 3%, fat 1%, carbohydrate 96%

# Light Mushroom Gravy

Makes 4 cups (1 L)

This recipe is ideal for Holiday Stuffed Winter Squash (page 154); it also is good with baked or mashed potatoes and with veggie burgers. If you use stock cubes or powder, experiment with different brands, as flavourful stock makes a big difference. Stocks vary in saltiness, so adjust the amount of tamari or salt accordingly. If the gravy is too thick, add more stock or water. If the gravy is too thin, simmer uncovered to let some moisture evaporate, until the gravy is the desired consistency.

1 tablespoon (15 mL) coconut or olive oil
2 cups (500 mL) thinly sliced mushrooms
1/2 cup (125 mL) finely diced onion
2 cloves garlic, minced
4 cups (1 L) cold vegetable stock or water
1/2 cup (125 mL) unbleached all-purpose or whole-wheat flour
2 tablespoons (30 mL) tamari or soy sauce (optional)
1 tablespoon (15 mL) nutritional yeast
1/4 teaspoon (1 mL) dried thyme
1/4 teaspoon (1 mL) dried sage
Salt (optional)
Pinch of black pepper
2 tablespoons (30 mL) chopped fresh parsley

Heat the oil in a saucepan over medium heat. Cook the mushrooms and onion for 5 minutes or until the moisture from the mushrooms has evaporated. Add the garlic and cook for 1 to 2 minutes. Put 1 cup (250 mL) cold vegetable stock or water, flour, tamari, yeast, thyme, and sage in a jar, tightly cover with a lid, and shake until blended. Pour the stock and flour mixture plus the remaining stock into the saucepan, bring to a boil, then reduce heat to low and simmer, covered, for 15 to 20 minutes, stirring frequently. Add salt, pepper, and parsley and serve.

Per 1/4 cup (60 mL): calories: 32, protein: 1 g, fat: 1 g, carbohydrate: 5 g (0.5 g from sugar), dietary fibre: 0.5 g, calcium: 6 mg, iron: 0.4 mg, magnesium: 3 mg, phosphorus: 20 mg, potassium: 62 mg, sodium: 73 mg, zinc: 0.2 mg, thiamin: 0.3 mg, riboflavin: 0.3 mg, niacin: 2 mg, vitamin $B_6$: 0.3 mg, folate: 16 mcg, pantothenic acid: 0.1 mg, vitamin $B_{12}$: 0.2 mcg, vitamin A: 11 mcg, vitamin C: 1 mg, vitamin E: 0 mg, omega-6 fatty acids: 0 g, omega-3 fatty acids: 0 g

Percentage of calories from protein 13%, fat 31%, carbohydrate 56%

# Marinara Tomato Sauce

Makes 3 1/2 cups (875 mL)

Fresh tomatoes at the height of summer are memorable. Growers and consumers get very enthusiastic about them for many good reasons. With over 4,000 varieties to choose from, they are easy to grow, delicious, and they pack a good nutritional punch that delivers vitamin C, iron, and potassium, along with very few calories. This is an easy and versatile sauce to make and can be used in the Tuscan Minestrone Soup (page 141), Cashew Cheese Lasagna (page 148), Tofu: An Easy Entrée (page 184), or as a base for many Italian dishes.

**1/2 to 1 tablespoon (7 to 15 mL) olive oil**
**1/2 onion, diced**
**4 cloves garlic, chopped**
**4 cups (1 L) chopped fresh tomatoes, or 1 can (28 ounces/796 mL) tomatoes, chopped**
**1 tablespoon (15 mL) dried basil**
**1 teaspoon (5 mL) dried oregano**
**1/2 teaspoon (2 mL) chili flakes (optional)**
**Salt and black pepper**

Heat the oil in a medium saucepan over medium heat and cook the onion for 3 to 5 minutes or until translucent. Add the garlic, tomatoes, basil, oregano, chili flakes, and salt and pepper to taste. Cover and cook on medium-low heat for 15 to 20 minutes.

Per cup (250 mL): calories: 80, protein: 3 g, fat: 2 g, carbohydrate: 14 g (7 g from sugar), dietary fibre: 3 g, calcium: 108 mg, iron: 2 mg, magnesium: 37 mg, phosphorus: 60 mg, potassium: 608 mg, sodium: 360 mg, zinc: 0.5 mg, thiamin: 0.1 mg, riboflavin: 0.1 mg, niacin: 2 mg, vitamin $B_6$: 0.3 mg, folate: 27 mcg, pantothenic acid: 0.4 mg, vitamin $B_{12}$: 0 mcg, vitamin A: 84 mcg, vitamin C: 38 mg, vitamin E: 1 mg, omega-6 fatty acids: 0.3 g, omega-3 fatty acids: 0.1 g

Percentage of calories from protein 12%, fat 24%, carbohydrate 64%

# Miso Gravy

Makes 2 3/4 cups (685 mL)

Miso is a thick, sweet, salty paste made from fermented soy beans that adds a tangy taste to soups, dips, and sauces. If it's not in the refrigerated section of your supermarket, look for it in Asian markets or natural food stores. It contains live one-celled organisms that may be beneficial to our digestion or health, and for this reason it is generally added to a soup, sauce, or gravy *after* the cooking process is completed, in order to retain some micro-organism and enzyme activity. This gravy is a great complement to Seasoned Potato Wedges (page 204), or serve as a dipping sauce or over cooked brown rice.

**2 cups (500 mL) vegetable stock**
**1 tablespoon (15 mL) toasted sesame oil**
**1 tablespoon (15 mL) apple cider vinegar**
**1 tablespoon (15 mL) maple syrup or other sweetener**
**1/2 teaspoon (2 mL) chili paste or 1/4 teaspoon (1 mL) cayenne pepper**
**2 cloves garlic, crushed**
**Pinch of turmeric**
**1/4 cup (60 mL) all-purpose flour**
**1/2 cup (125 mL) water**
**1/4 cup (60 mL) miso**

Combine in a medium saucepan over medium-high heat the stock, sesame oil, vinegar, maple syrup, chili paste, garlic, and turmeric. Stir the flour and water together in a small bowl until well blended and pour into the saucepan, using a whisk or fork to mix. Bring the liquid to a boil, reduce heat to low, cover, and simmer for 5 minutes. Remove the gravy from the heat and whisk in the miso until it is well incorporated. Strain and serve.

Per 1/4 cup (60 mL): calories: 42, protein: 1 g, fat: 2 g, carbohydrate: 6 g (2 g from sugar), dietary fibre: 0.5 g, calcium: 8 mg, iron: 0.4 mg, magnesium: 4 mg, phosphorus: 15 mg, potassium: 30 mg, sodium: 290 mg, zinc: 0.3 mg, thiamin: 0 mg, riboflavin: 0 mg, niacin: 0 mg, vitamin $B_6$: 0 mg, folate: 6 mcg, pantothenic acid: 0 mg, vitamin $B_{12}$: 0 mcg, vitamin A: 1 mcg, vitamin C: 0 mg, vitamin E: 0 mg, omega-6 fatty acids: 0.2 g, omega-3 fatty acids: 0 g

Percentage of calories from protein 11%, fat 38%, carbohydrate 51%

# Rosemary Gravy

Makes 3 1/2 cups (875 mL)

Can vegetarian gravy taste outstanding? Yes! You'll find that the familiar Thanksgiving seasonings of rosemary, thyme, and sage make this aromatic gravy a welcome feature at festive meals. This gravy incorporates a roux, a classic mixture of flour and oil, to thicken the vegetable stock. If the gravy is too thick, add more stock. If too thin, simmer uncovered to let moisture evaporate, until it's of the desired consistency.

**1/4 cup (60 mL) coconut or olive oil**
**1/4 cup (60 mL) diced onion**
**1/4 cup (60 mL) diced carrot**
**1/4 cup (60 mL) diced celery**
**2 cloves garlic, chopped**
**1/2 cup (125 mL) unbleached all-purpose or whole-wheat flour**
**3 cups (750 mL) vegetable stock**
**2 to 3 tablespoons (30 to 45 mL) tamari or soy sauce**
**2 tablespoons (30 mL) chopped fresh parsley**
**2 teaspoons (10 mL) dried rosemary**
**1 teaspoon (5 mL) dried thyme**
**1/2 teaspoon (2 mL) dried sage**
**1/4 teaspoon (1 mL) black pepper**
**Salt**

Heat the oil in a medium saucepan over medium heat and cook the onion, carrots, celery, and garlic for 5 minutes or until the onion is translucent. To make the roux, stir the flour into the vegetable mixture to absorb the oil and cook for 3 minutes, stirring frequently to prevent the flour from burning. Add the stock gradually until it is incorporated into the roux, bring the mixture to a boil, then reduce heat to low. Add the tamari, parsley, rosemary, thyme, sage, pepper, and salt to taste and simmer for 10 to 15 minutes, stirring occasionally. Adjust the seasoning, strain, and serve.

Per 1/4 cup (60 mL): calories: 59, protein: 1 g, fat: 4 g, carbohydrate: 5 g (0 g from sugar), dietary fibre: 0 g, calcium: 10 mg, iron: 0.5 mg, magnesium: 4 mg, phosphorus: 12 mg, potassium: 41 mg, sodium: 211 mg, zinc: 0.1 mg, thiamin: 0 mg, riboflavin: 0 mg, niacin: 0.6 mg, vitamin $B_6$: 0 mg, folate: 11 mcg, pantothenic acid: 0 mg, vitamin $B_{12}$: 0 mcg, vitamin A: 22 mcg, vitamin C: 1 mg, vitamin E: 0 mg, omega-6 fatty acids: 0.1 g, omega-3 fatty acids: 0 g

Percentage of calories from protein 6%, fat 61%, carbohydrate 33%

# Spicy Peanut Sauce

Makes 1 3/4 cups (435 mL)

Peanut sauce is widely used in Thai, Indonesian, Malaysian, Vietnamese, and Chinese cuisines. It can be made mild or hot by adjusting the amount of garlic, ginger, or chili paste. This delectable blend can be used as a stir-fry sauce; served over hot rice, noodles, steamed broccoli, cauliflower, or other vegetables; or used as a dip for Vietnamese Salad Roll (page 114). It's also the dressing used in Thai Pasta Salad with Spicy Peanut Dressing (page 113).

1/2 cup (125 mL) unsweetened, unsalted peanut butter
1/2 cup (125 mL) coconut milk
1/4 cup (60 mL) chopped ginger
1/4 cup (60 mL) tamari or soy sauce
3 tablespoons (45 mL) lime juice
3 tablespoons (45 mL) brown sugar
2 teaspoons (10 mL) toasted sesame oil
1 teaspoon (5 mL) chili paste
2 cloves garlic, chopped

Put the peanut butter, coconut milk, ginger, tamari, lime juice, brown sugar, sesame oil, chili paste, and garlic in a food processor or blender and process for 1 minute or until smooth.

This sauce keeps well in the refrigerator, stored in a covered container, for up to 2 weeks. If it thickens after refrigeration, simply thin with a bit of warm water to desired consistency.

Per 2 tablespoons (30 mL): calories: 98, protein: 3 g, fat: 7 g, carbohydrate: 6 g (4 g from sugar), dietary fibre: 1 g, calcium: 11 mg, iron: 1 mg, magnesium: 24 mg, phosphorus: 49 mg, potassium: 127 mg, sodium: 296 mg, zinc: 0.4 mg, thiamin: 0 mg, riboflavin: 0 mg, niacin: 2 mg, vitamin $B_6$: 0.1 mg, folate: 12 mcg, pantothenic acid: 0.2 mg, vitamin $B_{12}$: 0 mcg, vitamin A: 0.2 mcg, vitamin C: 2 mg, vitamin E: 1 mg, omega-6 fatty acids: 2 g, omega-3 fatty acids: 0 g

Percentage of calories from protein 12%, fat 64%, carbohydrate 24%

# Tamarind Date Sauce

Makes 1 1/4 cups (310 mL)

Tamarind is a fruit that is common in Asian and African countries and widely grown in India. This sauce, made from the pulp of the pod, adds unique sweet, lemony sharpness to Potato Subji (page 199), Aloo Gobi (page 190), and Seasoned Potato Wedges (page 204) when served as a condiment; to Indonesian-Style International Roll-Ups (page 156); or to any curried dish. Tamarind date sauce is frequently served with samosas, a small Asian potato-stuffed turnover typically eaten as an appetizer or snack. Tamarind paste can be purchased at Indian groceries. While you're there, enjoy the aromas of exotic ingredients and stock up on papadums, almonds, curry paste, and spices such as curry powder, garam masala, and cumin. This sauce keeps, refrigerated, for several weeks.

3/4 cup (185 mL) boiling water
3/4 cup (185 mL) chopped pitted dates
3 tablespoons (45 mL) tamarind pulp
2 tablespoons (30 mL) apple cider vinegar
1 tablespoon (15 mL) minced ginger
2 teaspoons (10 mL) orange juice concentrate
1/2 teaspoon (2 mL) garam masala
**Pinch of salt**

Pour the water over the dates and tamarind in a bowl and let the mixture sit for 30 minutes. Remove and discard any tamarind seeds. Place the dates, tamarind, soaking water, vinegar, ginger, orange juice concentrate, garam masala, and salt in the bowl of a food processor. Blend until smooth, stopping occasionally to scrape down the sides of the bowl.

Per cup (250 mL): calories: 41, protein: 0.4 g, fat: 0.1 g, carbohydrate: 11 g (9 g from sugar), dietary fibre: 1 g, calcium: 8 mg, iron: 0.2 mg, magnesium: 8 mg, phosphorus: 11 mg, potassium: 102 mg, sodium: 2 mg, zinc: 0 mg, thiamin: 0 mg, riboflavin: 0 mg, niacin: 0.2 mg, vitamin $B_6$: 0 mg, folate: 3 mcg, pantothenic acid: 0.1 mg, vitamin $B_{12}$: 0 mcg, vitamin A: 1 mcg, vitamin C: 2 mg, vitamin E: 0 mg, omega-6 fatty acids: 0 g, omega-3 fatty acids: 0 g

Percentage of calories from protein 4%, fat 2%, carbohydrate 94%

## Teriyaki Sauce

Makes 2 cups (500 mL)

Teriyaki sauce is common in Japanese cuisine. It adds both sweet and salty flavours to the food with which it is blended, and it's fat-free. The first choice for this recipe is sake, a Japanese rice wine that has a clean but distinctive taste and adds a lot of character. If you prefer not to use alcohol in your cooking, the sake can be replaced with stock, preferably a no-salt version. Teriyaki sauce can be added to stir-fries or poured over tofu and baked for 45 minutes at 350°F (180°C).

**1/2 cup (125 mL) light or regular tamari or soy sauce**
**1/2 cup (125 mL) sake or vegetable stock**
**1/2 cup (125 mL) mirin**
**1/2 cup (125 mL) brown sugar**
**1/2 onion, chopped**
**3 tablespoons (45 mL) unpeeled, thinly sliced ginger**
**4 cloves garlic, chopped**
**1 tablespoon (15 mL) arrowroot powder or cornstarch**
**1 tablespoon (15 mL) water**

Bring the tamari, sake, mirin, brown sugar, onion, ginger, and garlic to a boil in a saucepan over high heat. Reduce heat and cook for 10 minutes. Dissolve the arrowroot powder in the water and stir into the saucepan; cook, stirring frequently, for 3 minutes. Strain the sauce and use immediately or store in the refrigerator, where it will keep for several weeks.

Per 2 tablespoons (30 mL): calories: 64, protein: 1 g, fat: 0 g, carbohydrate: 11 g (10 g from sugar), dietary fibre: 0 g, calcium: 11 mg, iron: 0 mg, magnesium: 6 mg, phosphorus: 13 mg, potassium: 52 mg, sodium: 353 mg, zinc: 0 mg, thiamin: 0 mg, riboflavin: 0 mg, niacin: 0.3 mg, vitamin $B_6$: 0 mg, folate: 2 mcg, pantothenic acid: 0 mg, vitamin $B_{12}$: 0 mcg, vitamin A: 0 mcg, vitamin C: 0 mg, vitamin E: 0 mg, omega-6 fatty acids: 0 g, omega-3 fatty acids: 0 g

Percentage of calories from protein 5%, fat 0%, carbohydrate 70%, alcohol (from mirin) 25%

**Note:** Most of the alcohol in the sake is burned off during the cooking process, leaving behind only its taste and fragrance.

# Tofu Marinade

Makes scant 2 cups (500 mL)

Here's a marinade that will make tofu seriously tasty. It also can be used to marinate tempeh, or thickened and used as a sauce for stir-fries or to baste vegetables on the barbecue. It is delicious as a thin, light salad dressing or simply heated and served over brown rice.

1/2 cup (125 mL) chopped fresh or canned tomatoes
1/2 cup (125 mL) water
1/2 cup (125 mL) tamari or soy sauce
1/4 cup (60 mL) rice or apple cider vinegar
2 tablespoons (30 mL) toasted sesame oil
1 tablespoon (15 mL) minced ginger
1 clove garlic
1/2 teaspoon (2 mL) turmeric

Blend the tomatoes, water, tamari, vinegar, sesame oil, ginger, garlic, and turmeric in a blender for 15 seconds or until smooth.

This marinade will keep for up to 2 or 3 weeks in the refrigerator.

Per tablespoon (15 mL): calories: 12, protein: 0.6 g, fat: 1 g, carbohydrate: 0.5 g (0 g from sugar), dietary fibre: 0 g, calcium: 2 mg, iron: 0.1 mg, magnesium: 3 mg, phosphorus: 8 mg, potassium: 20 mg, sodium: 284 mg, zinc: 0 mg, thiamin: 0 mg, riboflavin: 0 mg, niacin: 0.4 mg, vitamin $B_6$: 0 mg, folate: 1 mcg, pantothenic acid: 0 mg, vitamin $B_{12}$: 0 mcg, vitamin A: 3 mcg, vitamin C: 0 mg, vitamin E: 0 mg, omega-6 fatty acids: 0 g, omega-3 fatty acids: 0 g

Percentage of calories from protein 18%, fat 67%, carbohydrate 15%

# Sweet Treats

## Almond, Date, and Coconut Pie Crust

Makes one 8- or 9-inch (20 or 23 cm) pie crust

This raw crust is easy to make and is an excellent source of the antioxidant vitamin E. It is superb as part of the Raw Lime Pie (page 250) and the Raw Mango Strawberry Pie (page 251).

**1 cup (250 mL) almonds**
**1/2 cup (125 mL) pitted Medjool dates**
**1/2 cup (125 mL) shredded, dried unsweetened coconut**

Process the almonds in the food processor until they form a fine meal, but not to the point that the meal becomes oily and start to form a butter. Remove 1 tablespoon (15 mL) of the almond meal and set it aside. Add the dates and coconut and process until the mixture forms a wall on the side of the food processor. Sprinkle the reserved almond meal across the bottom of a 9-inch (23 cm) pie pan; this will help prevent the crust from sticking. Press the dough evenly along the bottom and up the sides of the pie pan. Place the crust in the freezer while you prepare the filling.

Per 1/8 recipe: calories: 174, protein: 5 g, fat: 13 g, carbohydrate: 14 g (9 g from sugar), dietary fibre: 4 g, calcium: 56 mg, iron: 1 mg, magnesium: 63 mg, phosphorus: 107 mg, potassium: 246 mg, sodium: 2 mg, zinc: 1 mg, thiamin: 0.1 mg, riboflavin: 0.2 mg, niacin: 2 mg, vitamin $B_6$: 0.1 mg, folate: 8 mcg, pantothenic acid: 0.2 mg, vitamin $B_{12}$: 0 mcg, vitamin A: 1 mcg, vitamin C: 0 mg, vitamin E: 5 mg, omega-6 fatty acids: 2 g, omega-3 fatty acids: 0 g

Percentage of calories from protein 10%, fat 61%, carbohydrate 29%

# Almond-Butter Balls

Makes 30 balls, each 2 tablespoons (30 mL)

These nut-butter balls are an ideal snack for outdoor adventures such as hiking, riding, or climbing. They are light to carry, take up little space, and yet provide a good amount of quality calories. Four of these balls can fuel a person weighing 150 pounds (68 kg) for 5 miles (8 km) on an uphill hike. Because oils rise to the top of the container in which the nut butter is stored, nut butters can vary in consistency. For this reason, you may need to adjust the amount of added liquid in this recipe to achieve a desirable consistency.

**1 cup (250 mL) rolled oats**
**1 cup (250 mL) almond or peanut butter**
**1/2 cup (125 mL) pumpkin seeds**
**1/2 cup (125 mL) currants**
**1/2 cup (125 mL) dried cranberries, chopped**
**1/2 cup (125 mL) non-dairy chocolate chips**
**1/2 teaspoon (2 mL) grated or minced lemon peel**
**1 tablespoon (15 mL) freshly squeezed lemon juice**
**1 teaspoon (5 mL) cinnamon**
**1/2 teaspoon (2 mL) ground cardamom**
**1/2 teaspoon (2 mL) vanilla extract**
**1 to 2 tablespoons (15 to 30 mL) water**

Process the rolled oats in a food processor for 20 seconds or until finely ground. Transfer the oats to a medium bowl, along with the nut butter, pumpkin seeds, currants, cranberries, chocolate chips, lemon rind, lemon juice, cinnamon, cardamom, and vanilla. Mix with a fork until all ingredients are well combined. Add enough water to hold the mixture together. Roll into small balls, each about 2 tablespoons (30 mL) in size, and store in a covered container in the refrigerator or freezer.

Per ball: calories: 113, protein: 3 g, fat: 8 g, carbohydrate: 11 g (5 g from sugar), dietary fibre: 2 g, calcium: 33 mg, iron: 1 mg, magnesium: 44 mg, phosphorus: 82 mg, potassium: 151 mg, sodium: 41 mg, zinc: 0.5 mg, thiamin: 0 mg, riboflavin: 0.1 mg, niacin: 1 mg, vitamin $B_6$: 0 mg, folate: 8 mcg, pantothenic acid: 0 mg, vitamin $B_{12}$: 0 mcg, vitamin A: 2 mcg, vitamin C: 1 mg, vitamin E: 2 mg, omega-6 fatty acids: 2 g, omega-3 fatty acids: 0 g

Percentage of calories from protein 9%, fat 56%, carbohydrate 35%

# Baked Stuffed Apples

Makes 4 baked apples

This recipe is equally tasty made with McIntosh apples, which are quick to cook, or other varieties such as Golden Delicious or Granny Smith, which may take longer.

4 medium apples
1/4 cup (60 mL) tahini
1/4 cup (60 mL) raisins
2 teaspoons (10 mL) lemon juice
1/2 teaspoon (2 mL) grated lemon peel
2 teaspoons (10 mL) sweetener
1/4 teaspoon (1 mL) cinnamon

Preheat the oven to 300°F (150°C).

Remove the apple stems by piercing the top of each apple, holding a paring knife at a 45-degree angle to the stem. Rotate the knife around the top to produce small cone-shaped tops. Set tops aside. Using a melon baller or teaspoon, remove the core from each apple, being careful not to pierce the bottom of the apples, otherwise the stuffing will leak out as the apple bakes. In a small bowl, stir together tahini, raisins, lemon juice, lemon peel, sweetener, and cinnamon. Fill the apple cavities almost to the top with the raisin mixture. Replace apple tops. Set apples on a baking tray or casserole dish, and bake for 15 minutes or until apples are soft when pierced with toothpick.

Per apple: calories: 151, protein: 3 g, fat: 8 g, carbohydrate: 19 g (3 g from sugar), dietary fibre: 2 g, calcium: 33 mg, iron: 1 mg, magnesium: 20 mg, phosphorus: 135 mg, potassium: 199 mg, sodium: 7 mg, zinc: 1 mg, thiamin: 0.3 mg, riboflavin: 0 mg, niacin: 1 mg, vitamin $B_6$: 0.1 mg, folate: 17 mcg, pantothenic acid: 0 mg, vitamin $B_{12}$: 0 mcg, vitamin A: 31 mcg, vitamin C: 4 mg, vitamin E: 0.4 mg, omega-6 fatty acids: 3 g, omega-3 fatty acids: 0.1 g

Percentage of calories from protein 8%, fat 45%, carbohydrate 47%

**Baked Apple with Figs**
Replace tahini with 3 soaked and chopped dried figs. To prepare the figs, remove their stems and soak in water overnight, then drain and chop.

# Apple Pear Crumble

Makes 9 cups (2.25 L)

Many other fruits can be substituted for apples and pears in this recipe. Try peaches or nectarines with blueberries or raspberries. With any combination, use a total of 7 to 8 cups (1.75 to 2 L) of chopped fruit and berries. With sour fruits, increase the amount of sweetener to taste.

## Topping

- 2 cups (500 mL) rolled oats
- 1/4 cup (60 mL) chopped walnuts
- 1 cup (250 mL) orange juice
- 3 tablespoons (45 mL) maple syrup
- 1 tablespoon (15 mL) minced orange peel
- 1/2 teaspoon (2 mL) cinnamon
- Pinch of nutmeg

## Fruit Layer

- 3 medium apples, unpeeled, cored, and chopped
- 3 pears, unpeeled, cored, and chopped
- 2 tablespoons (30 mL) lemon juice
- 3 tablespoons (45 mL) maple syrup
- 1/4 cup (60 mL) raisins

To make the topping, in a bowl combine the oats, walnuts, orange juice, maple syrup, orange peel, cinnamon, and nutmeg. Let mixture sit for 10 minutes for oats to absorb the liquid.

In the meantime, preheat the oven to 350°F (180°C).

To make the fruit layer, toss apples and pears in the lemon juice and pour into a 9 × 9-inch (23 × 23 cm) baking dish. Drizzle with maple syrup and sprinkle raisins over top.

Spread the topping mixture evenly over the fruit and bake for 30 to 35 minutes or until the topping is golden brown.

Per cup (250 mL): calories: 208, protein: 4 g, fat: 2 g, carbohydrate: 48 g (9 g from sugar), dietary fibre: 5 g, calcium: 40 mg, iron: 1 mg, magnesium: 64 mg, phosphorus: 111 mg, potassium: 377 mg, sodium: 5 mg, zinc: 1 mg, thiamin: 0.2 mg, riboflavin: 0.1 mg, niacin: 0.5 mg, vitamin $B_6$: 0.1 mg, folate: 34 mcg, pantothenic acid: 0.3 mg, vitamin $B_{12}$: 0 mcg, vitamin A: 10 mcg, vitamin C: 29 mg, vitamin E: 0.4 mg, omega-6 fatty acids: 0.5 g, omega-3 fatty acids: 0 g

Percentage of calories from protein 7%, fat 7%, carbohydrate 86%

**Apple Pear Cranberry Crumble**
Replace 1 cup (250 mL) apples or pears with 1 cup (250 mL) cranberries.

## Apple Spice Cake

Makes 20 pieces

Cooking apples are generally more tart than eating apples, and many hold their shape after being cooked. With so many varieties to choose from, if you are not sure what apple to buy for this recipe, ask your grocer. Serve this cake for a family dessert or for a birthday. Serve it plain or with Lemon Glaze (page 245), Vanilla Frosting (page 253), or strawberries and "cream" (see variation on page 229).

3 cups (750 mL) whole-wheat pastry flour
1 tablespoon (15 mL) baking powder
2 teaspoons (10 mL) cinnamon
1 teaspoon (5 mL) baking soda
1 teaspoon (5 mL) ground cloves
1 teaspoon (5 mL) allspice
1 teaspoon (5 mL) nutmeg
1 teaspoon (5 mL) ground ginger
1/2 teaspoon (2 mL) salt
1 cup (250 mL) hemp seed or other non-dairy milk
1 cup (250 mL) maple syrup
2/3 cup (170 mL) sunflower or melted coconut oil
2 tablespoons (30 mL) ground flaxseed
2 cups (500 mL) grated cooking apples
1 cup (250 mL) raisins
1 cup (250 mL) chopped walnuts or pecans

Preheat the oven to 350°F (180°C).

In a medium bowl using a whisk, mix together the flour, baking powder, cinnamon, baking soda, cloves, allspice, nutmeg, ginger, and salt. Combine the hemp milk, maple syrup, oil, and flaxseed in a large bowl. Mix the dry ingredients into the wet mixture and stir until just blended. Fold in the apples, raisins, and nuts. Do not overmix. Pour the batter into an oiled and floured 9 × 13-inch (23 × 33 cm) baking pan. Bake for 30 to 35 minutes or until a toothpick inserted into the centre of the cake comes out clean. Let the cake cool on a wire rack before turning out.

## Sweet Treats

Per piece: calories: 255, protein: 4 g, fat: 12 g, carbohydrate: 35 g (17 g from sugar), dietary fibre: 4 g, calcium: 99 mg, iron: 2 mg, magnesium: 42 mg, phosphorus: 171 mg, potassium: 221 mg, sodium: 170 mg, zinc: 1.5 mg, thiamin: 0.1 mg, riboflavin: 0.1 mg, niacin: 2 mg, vitamin $B_6$: 0.1 mg, folate: 15 mcg, pantothenic acid: 0.2 mg, vitamin $B_{12}$: 0 mcg, vitamin A: 1 mcg, vitamin C: 1 mg, vitamin E: 0.3 mg, omega-6 fatty acids: 3 g, omega-3 fatty acids: 1 g

Percentage of calories from protein 6%, fat 41%, carbohydrate 53%

**Note:** Analysis was done using fortified soy milk.

### Cake, Strawberries, and "Cream"

Make the Apple Spice Cake using either whole-wheat or all-purpose pastry flour and serve it with Cashew Cream Topping (page 234) or Holiday Pie Topping (page 244), plus sliced strawberries.

## Blueberry Cornmeal Muffins

Makes 12 muffins

What better choice for brunch, lunch bags, or afternoon or evening tea than muffins that are delicious and good for you? Use a combination of unbleached or all-purpose flour and whole-wheat pastry flour, as here, or use a single flour. If you use paper liners instead of oiling the muffin cups, keep in mind that the paper peels away most easily after the muffin has cooled. These muffins freeze well.

1 cup (250 mL) cornmeal
1 1/2 cups (375 mL) non-dairy milk
1/3 cup (85 mL) sunflower or vegetable oil
2/3 cup (170 mL) dry sweetener
1 cup (250 mL) unbleached or all-purpose flour
1 cup (250 mL) whole-wheat pastry flour
1 1/2 teaspoons (7 mL) baking powder
1/2 teaspoon (2 mL) baking soda
1/2 teaspoon (2 mL) salt
1 1/2 cups (375 mL) blueberries, fresh or frozen

Preheat the oven to 400°F (200°C).

Place cornmeal, milk, oil, and sweetener in a large bowl; mix well and let sit for 3 minutes. Place flours, baking powder, baking soda, and salt in a smaller bowl and mix well. Stir flour mixture into wet mixture and stir just until blended; do not overmix. Fold in the blueberries. Spoon the dough into muffin tins with paper liners or that are lightly oiled, and bake for 25 to 30 minutes or until golden brown. If using frozen blueberries, you will probably need to bake them for the longer time.

Per muffin: calories: 245, protein: 4 g, fat: 8 g, carbohydrate: 40 g (13 g from sugar), dietary fibre: 3 g, calcium: 104 mg, iron: 2 mg, magnesium: 23 mg, phosphorus: 124 mg, potassium: 104 mg, sodium: 188 mg, zinc: 0.5 mg, thiamin: 0.2 mg, riboflavin: 0.2 mg, niacin: 2 mg, vitamin $B_6$: 0.1 mg, folate: 44 mcg, pantothenic acid: 0.3 mg, vitamin $B_{12}$: 0.4 mcg, vitamin A: 13 mcg, vitamin C: 2 mg, vitamin E: 0.2 mg, omega-6 fatty acids: 3 g, omega-3 fatty acids: 0.1 g

Percentage of calories from protein 7%, fat 28%, carbohydrate 65%

**Note:** Analysis was done using fortified soy milk.

# Blueberry Mince Tart or Pie Filling

Makes 8 cups (2 L) filling, for 30 tarts or two 8-inch (20 cm) pies

Blueberries and cranberries are combined in this mouth-watering, light tart or pie filling. If you use frozen blueberries, the yield will be a little less because the berries will shrink when they thaw. Omit the arrowroot powder if you plan to store the filling in the refrigerator or freezer before using; add the starch just prior to making your tarts or pies. This filling can be stored in the refrigerator for up to 1 week or for up to 6 months in the freezer.

1 1/2 cups (375 mL) sultana raisins
1 1/2 cups (375 mL) golden raisins
1/2 cup (125 mL) dried cranberries
1/2 cup (125 mL) brown sugar or other dry sweetener
1/3 cup (85 mL) mixed candied peel
2 tablespoons (30 mL) fruit juice or brandy
2 tablespoons (30 mL) arrowroot powder or cornstarch
1 tablespoon (15 mL) lemon juice
1 teaspoon (5 mL) grated lemon rind
1 teaspoon (5 mL) cinnamon
1/2 teaspoon (2 mL) ground ginger
1/2 teaspoon (2 mL) nutmeg
1/4 teaspoon (1 mL) ground cloves
4 cups (1 L) fresh or frozen blueberries

Combine sultana and golden raisins, cranberries, sugar, mixed peel, fruit juice, arrowroot powder, lemon juice and rind, cinnamon, ginger, nutmeg, and cloves in a large bowl. Stir in the blueberries.

Per 1/4 cup (60 mL) filling: calories: 80, protein: 1 g, fat: 0.2 g, carbohydrate: 21 g (16 g from sugar), dietary fibre: 1 g, calcium: 11 mg, iron: 0 mg, magnesium: 4 mg, phosphorus: 11 mg, potassium: 136 mg, sodium: 7 mg, zinc: 0 mg, thiamin: 0 mg, riboflavin: 0 mg, niacin: 0 mg, vitamin $B_6$: 0.1 mg, folate: 2 mcg, pantothenic acid: 0 mg, vitamin $B_{12}$: 0 mcg, vitamin A: 1 mcg, vitamin C: 3 mg, vitamin E: 0 mg, omega-6 fatty acids: 0 g, omega-3 fatty acids: 0 g

Percentage of calories from protein 3%, fat 2%, carbohydrate 95%

# Blueberry Mince Tarts or Pies

Makes 30 tarts or two 8 × 1 1/4-inch (20 × 3 cm) open-face pies

There are several ways to roll out the dough for these tarts or pies. You can use two clean plastic produce bags cut along two sides and opened up to create two sheets. Or you can roll it between wax or parchment paper. And, of course, there is the old-fashioned method of using the countertop. All methods require a dusting of flour to prevent the dough from sticking.

**1 recipe Blueberry Mince Tart or Pie Filling (page 231)**
**1 recipe Tart and Pie Pastry (page 252)**

## For Tarts

Roll out one of the two balls of dough to form a circle of pastry 12 inches (30 cm) in diameter. Cut the dough using a 3 1/2-inch (9 cm) diameter cutter or lid from a wide-mouth Mason jar. Lift the circles with a pancake lifter and place each in a lightly oiled or nonstick muffin cup or tart tin. Repeat with the second ball of dough. Gather any loose scraps and reroll until all the dough is used up, making a total of about 30 tart shells. Spoon about 3 tablespoons (45 mL) of the blueberry filling into each tart shell. Bake the tarts at 350°F (180°C) for 20 to 25 minutes or until the crusts are golden brown. Remove the tarts from the tins while they are still warm and allow to cool on a wire rack.

Per tart: calories: 161, protein: 2 g, fat: 4 g, carbohydrate: 31 g (16 g from sugar), dietary fibre: 2 g, calcium: 37 mg, iron: 1 mg, magnesium: 15 mg, phosphorus: 75 mg, potassium: 220 mg, sodium: 39 mg, zinc: 0.3 mg, thiamin: 0.1 mg, riboflavin: 0.1 mg, niacin: 1 mg, vitamin $B_6$: 0.1 mg, folate: 17 mcg, pantothenic acid: 0.1 mg, vitamin $B_{12}$: 0 mcg, vitamin A: 1 mcg, vitamin C: 3 mg, vitamin E: 2 mg, omega-6 fatty acids: 0.2 g, omega-3 fatty acids: 0 g

Percentage of calories from protein 5%, fat 23%, carbohydrate 72%

## For Pies

Roll out one of the two dough pieces to form a circle of pastry 12 inches (30 cm) in diameter. Carefully lift the dough with one or two pancake flippers and position the dough onto a slightly oiled 8-inch (20 cm) pie dish. Arrange the dough in the pie dish using small amounts of dough to fill any gaps and patch any broken areas. Trim any excess overhang with a knife and flute the edges by pressing into the pie dough towards the center of the pie at the edge with the thumb of one hand, and using the forefinger and thumb on your other hand to crimp the crust. Continue this method all around the perimeter of the pie shell to give the pie a decorative look. Put half of the blueberry mince filling into the pie shell. Repeat the whole procedure to make the second pie. Bake at 350°F (180°C) for 45 to 50 minutes.

Per 1/8 pie: calories: 302, protein: 4 g, fat: 8 g, carbohydrate: 57 g (30 g from sugar), dietary fibre: 5 g, calcium: 69 mg, iron: 2 mg, magnesium: 27 mg, phosphorus: 141 mg, potassium: 412 mg, sodium: 73 mg, zinc: 1 mg, thiamin: 0.2 mg, riboflavin: 0.1 mg, niacin: 3 mg, vitamin $B_6$: 0.2 mg, folate: 31 mcg, pantothenic acid: 0.2 mg, vitamin $B_{12}$: 0 mcg, vitamin A: 2 mcg, vitamin C: 6 mg, vitamin E: 3 mg, omega-6 fatty acids: 0.4 g, omega-3 fatty acids: 0 g

Percentage of calories from protein 5%, fat 23%, carbohydrate 72%

## Cashew Cream Topping

Makes 1 1/4 cups (310 mL)

Use this thick, creamy topping on Apple Pear Crumble (page 226), Creamy Rice Pudding (page 240), or Pumpkin Spice Pie (page 249). Two tablespoons (30 mL) provides 4 grams of protein, as well as copper, iron, magnesium, manganese, and zinc.

**1 cup (250 mL) cashews**
**1/4 cup (60 mL) pitted dates or maple syrup**

Soak the cashews in a bowl of hot water for 2 hours, then drain, reserving the soaking water. Place the cashews, dates, and 1/2 cup (125 mL) of the soaking water in a blender and process until smooth. If you wish to have a thinner sauce, add a little more water. Stored in a glass jar with a lid and refrigerated, the cashew cream will keep for up to 1 week.

Per 2 tablespoons (30 mL): calories: 144, protein: 4 g, fat: 10 g, carbohydrate: 11 g (5 g from sugar), dietary fibre: 1 g, calcium: 11 mg, iron: 2 mg, magnesium: 70 mg, phosphorus: 139 mg, potassium: 191 mg, sodium: 3 mg, zinc: 1 mg, thiamin: 0.1 mg, riboflavin: 0 mg, niacin: 1 mg, vitamin $B_6$: 0.1 mg, folate: 7 mcg, pantothenic acid: 0.2 mg, vitamin $B_{12}$: 0 mcg, vitamin A: 0 mcg, vitamin C: 0 mg, vitamin E: 0.2 mg, omega-6 fatty acids: 2 g, omega-3 fatty acids: 0 g

Percentage of calories from protein 11%, fat 59%, carbohydrate 30%

# Chocolate Frosting

Makes 1 1/4 cups (310 mL)

"Frosting" and "icing" are terms that are used interchangeably to mean sweet toppings for cakes, cookies, brownies, and pastries; they keep these desserts from drying out too quickly. Semi-sweet, dark chocolate chips often are dairy-free; check the label. If you prefer, replace the chips with 6 ounces (180 g) semi-sweet baking chocolate. The minerals shown in the nutritional analysis are from ground cocoa beans, which are native to South and Central America and give a wonderful flavour to this frosting. This recipe was developed especially for the Chocolate Orange Cake (page 236) but it's good on other cakes too.

1 cup (250 mL) non-dairy chocolate chips
1/2 cup (125 mL) Earth Balance spread or vegan margarine
1/2 cup (125 mL) icing sugar
1/4 cup (60 mL) cocoa powder
1 teaspoon (5 mL) vanilla extract

Warm the chocolate chips in the top of a double boiler over boiling water or in a small pan over medium-low heat until melted and a thick sauce-like consistency when stirred. Add the Earth Balance spread and icing sugar; stir until evenly mixed. Add the cocoa powder and vanilla and stir until evenly mixed. Spread over your cake.

Per tablespoon (15 mL): calories: 100, protein: 0.6 g, fat: 7 g, carbohydrate: 9 g (8 g from sugar), dietary fibre: 1 g, calcium: 4 mg, iron: 0.4 mg, magnesium: 16 mg, phosphorus: 20 mg, potassium: 49 mg, sodium: 1 mg, zinc: 0.2 mg, thiamin: 0 mg, riboflavin: 0 mg, niacin: 0.2 mg, vitamin $B_6$: 0 mg, folate: 2 mcg, pantothenic acid: 0 mg, vitamin $B_{12}$: 0 mcg, vitamin A: 0 mcg, vitamin C: 0 mg, vitamin E: 0 mg, omega-6 fatty acids: 0.1 g, omega-3 fatty acids: 0 g

Percentage of calories from protein 2%, fat 62%, carbohydrate 36%

# Chocolate Orange Cake

Makes 20 slices

This recipe has a nice texture and it is not too sweet. It is best served with the Chocolate Frosting (page 235) or Blueberry Orange Sauce (page 212). The leavening used in this cake is baking soda, and as with all recipes using powdered leavening agents, it is best to mix together the ingredients as soon as the liquid portion has been added to the dry. This is because when liquid comes in contact with baking soda or powder, gases are instantly released, and this is what gives the batter power to rise. Overmixing the batter knocks down the gas bubbles, resulting in a flatter cake.

1 1/2 cups (375 mL) whole-wheat pastry flour
1 cup (250 mL) unbleached all-purpose white flour
1 1/2 cups (375 mL) brown sugar or other dry sweetener
1/2 cup (125 mL) cocoa powder, sifted
1 teaspoon (5 mL) baking soda, sifted
1/2 teaspoon (2 mL) salt
2 cups (500 mL) orange juice
1/3 cup (85 mL) sunflower oil or melted coconut oil
1 tablespoon (15 mL) minced orange peel
1 tablespoon (15 mL) apple cider vinegar
1 teaspoon (5 mL) vanilla extract

Preheat the oven to 350°F (180°C).

Put the flours, sugar, cocoa powder, baking soda, and salt in a large mixing bowl and mix well. Combine the orange juice, oil, orange peel, vinegar, and vanilla in another bowl. Add the wet ingredients to the dry and mix quickly until the dry ingredients are moist. Immediately pour the batter into a lightly oiled 9 × 13-inch (23 × 33 cm) baking pan. Bake for 30 minutes or until a toothpick inserted into the centre comes out dry. Cool completely on a wire rack before icing.

Per slice: calories: 152, protein: 3 g, fat: 5 g, carbohydrate: 27 g (13 g from sugar), dietary fibre: 2 g, calcium: 20 mg, iron: 1 mg, magnesium: 32 mg, phosphorus: 64 mg, potassium: 173 mg, sodium: 181 mg, zinc: 0.5 mg, thiamin: 0.1 mg, riboflavin: 0.1 mg, niacin: 2 mg, vitamin $B_6$: 0.1 mg, folate: 23 mcg, pantothenic acid: 0.2 mg, vitamin $B_{12}$: 0 mcg, vitamin A: 3 mcg, vitamin C: 14 mg, vitamin E: 0.1 mg, omega-6 fatty acids: 0.2 g, omega-3 fatty acids: 0 g

Percentage of calories from protein 7%, fat 25%, carbohydrate 68%

**Chocolate Chili Cake**
Add 1/2 teaspoon (2 mL) cayenne pepper to the dry ingredients for a cake that has a warming sensation after each bite.

# Coconut Macaroons

Makes 32 cookies

These raw macaroons are delicious and simple to make. If you have a dehydrator, try the variation listed below.

1 1/2 cups (375 mL) pitted dates
1 cup (250 mL) raw cashew pieces, soaked in water for 4 hours, drained, and rinsed
1 teaspoon (5 mL) vanilla extract
1 1/4 cups (310 mL) plus 1/2 cup (125 mL) unsweetened, shredded dried coconut

Place the dates, cashews, and vanilla extract in a food processor. Process for 2 to 3 minutes or until smooth. Add 1 1/4 cups (310 mL) coconut and pulse a few times, just until the coconut is evenly distributed. Take 1 tablespoon (15 mL) of the dough and form it into a ball with your hands. Place the remaining 1/2 cup (125 mL) coconut on a small plate or bowl and roll each cookie so that it is covered in coconut. Stored in an airtight container, these macaroons will keep for up to 1 month in the refrigerator or for up to 4 months in the freezer.

Per cookie: calories: 70, protein: 1 g, fat: 4 g, carbohydrate: 8 g (5 g from sugar), dietary fibre: 1 g, calcium: 5 mg, iron: 0.5 mg, magnesium: 19 mg, phosphorus: 38 mg, potassium: 97 mg, sodium: 2 mg, zinc: 0.4 mg, thiamin: 0 mg, riboflavin: 0 mg, niacin: 0.4 mg, vitamin $B_6$: 0 mg, folate: 3 mcg, pantothenic acid: 0.1 mg, vitamin $B_{12}$: 0 mcg, vitamin A: 0 mcg, vitamin C: 0 mg, vitamin E: 0.1 mg, omega-6 fatty acids: 0.4 g, omega-3 fatty acids: 0 g

Percentage of calories from protein 7%, fat 52%, carbohydrate 41%

**Apricot Macaroons**
Replace half of the dates with unsulphured dried apricots.

**Chocolate Macaroons**
Increase the dates to 2 cups (500 mL). Add 2 tablespoons (30 mL) cocoa powder to the food processor along with the dates, cashews, and vanilla.

**Dehydrator Method**
Place cookies onto one or two dehydrator trays with nonstick sheets. Dehydrate at 115°F (46°C) for about 12 hours.

## Cranberry Pecan Muffins

Makes 12 to 16 muffins

Stock your freezer with cranberries if you are a muffin lover, as you'll want to make these often. The maple syrup offsets the tartness of the cranberries and lends the muffins a deep, sweet flavour.

2 1/2 cups (625 mL) cranberries, fresh, or frozen and thawed
1/2 cup (125 mL) maple syrup
1 teaspoon (5 mL) grated orange or lemon rind
1 package (12.3 ounces/349 g) soft tofu
1/2 cup (125 mL) non-dairy milk
1/3 cup (85 mL) sunflower or melted coconut oil
1 teaspoon (5 mL) vanilla extract
1/2 cup (125 mL) dry sweetener
2 cups (500 mL) whole-wheat pastry flour
2 teaspoons (10 mL) baking powder
2 teaspoons (10 mL) cinnamon
1 teaspoon (5 mL) baking soda
1/2 teaspoon (2 mL) ground cardamom (optional)
1/2 teaspoon (2 mL) allspice
1/2 teaspoon (2 mL) cloves
1/2 teaspoon (2 mL) salt
1 cup (250 mL) chopped pecans

Preheat the oven to 375°F (190°C).

Put 1 1/2 cups (375 mL) of the cranberries plus the maple syrup and orange rind in a saucepan and cook over medium heat for about 10 minutes or until the cranberries have popped and the liquid is thick. Chop the remaining 1 cup (250 mL) of cranberries. Add to the cooked berries and allow the mixture to cool while preparing the muffin batter. Stir together the tofu, non-dairy milk, oil, vanilla, and sweetener in a large bowl. Mix flour, baking powder, cinnamon, baking soda, cardamom, allspice, cloves, and salt in small bowl. Add the cranberries to the wet ingredients and mix well. Stir in the dry ingredients, along with the pecans, until just blended. Spoon the dough into muffin tins that have been lightly oiled or lined with paper liners and bake for 30 to 35 minutes or until a toothpick inserted into the centre of a muffin comes out clean.

Per muffin (1/12 recipe): calories: 302, protein: 5 g, fat: 16 g, carbohydrate: 38 g (16 g from sugar), dietary fibre: 5 g, calcium: 108 mg, iron: 2 mg, magnesium: 27 mg, phosphorus: 75 mg, potassium: 158 mg, sodium: 240 mg, zinc: 1 mg, thiamin: 0.2 mg, riboflavin: 0.1 mg, niacin: 2 mg, vitamin $B_6$: 0.1 mg, folate: 24 mcg, pantothenic acid: 0.5 mg, vitamin $B_{12}$: 0.1 mcg, vitamin A: 2 mcg, vitamin C: 4 mg, vitamin E: 4 mg, omega-6 fatty acids: 7 g, omega-3 fatty acids: 0.2 g

Percentage of calories from protein 7%, fat 45%, carbohydrate 48%

**Note:** Analysis was done using fortified non-dairy milk.

# Creamy Rice Pudding

Makes 4 cups (1 L)

Use short-grain rice for this comforting pudding. Some varieties of short-grain white rice will soften to create a creamy product, whereas with medium, long-grain, or brown rice, the individual rice grains will remain more intact. Italian arborio rice is ideal. If you like, top individual servings with a sprinkle of cinnamon, Cashew Cream Topping (page 234), or Holiday Pie Topping (page 244). Leftovers make a welcome breakfast.

**2 cups (500 mL) water**
**1 cup (250 mL) arborio rice or short-grain brown rice**
**2 cups (500 mL) non-dairy milk**
**1/2 cup (125 mL) raisins or chopped dates**
**1/4 cup (60 mL) maple syrup or other sweetener**
**1 teaspoon (5 mL) vanilla extract**
**1/2 teaspoon (2 mL) cinnamon**
**Pinch of ground cloves or nutmeg**

Preheat the oven to 350°F (180°C).

Place the water and rice in a medium saucepan and bring to a boil. Lower the heat, cover, and simmer for 15 minutes if using white rice, or for 45 minutes if using brown rice, or until all the water has been absorbed.

Transfer the cooked rice to a baking pan. Add the non-dairy milk, raisins, maple syrup, vanilla, cinnamon, and cloves; stir well to combine. Bake for about 30 minutes or until all the liquid has been absorbed.

Per cup (250 mL): calories: 335, protein: 5 g, fat: 2 g, carbohydrate: 77 g (29 g from sugar), dietary fibre: 3 g, calcium: 133 mg, iron: 2 mg, magnesium: 25 mg, phosphorus: 117 mg, potassium: 323 mg, sodium: 88 mg, zinc: 2 mg, thiamin: 0.3 mg, riboflavin: 0.1 mg, niacin: 3 mg, vitamin $B_6$: 0.1 mg, folate: 206 mcg, pantothenic acid: 0.7 mg, vitamin $B_{12}$: 0 mcg, vitamin A: 0 mcg, vitamin C: 1 mg, vitamin E: 5 mg, omega-6 fatty acids: 0.1 g, omega-3 fatty acids: 0 g

Percentage of calories from protein 6%, fat 5%, carbohydrate 89%

**Note:** Analysis was done using fortified almond milk.

**Double-Boiler Rice Pudding**
Instead of baking it in the oven, cook the rice pudding mixture (cooked rice, non-dairy milk, raisins, maple syrup, vanilla, cinnamon, and cloves) in the top of a double boiler over simmering water for about 20 to 30 minutes, until all the liquid has been absorbed.

# Figgy Pudding

Makes 3 cups (750 mL), enough for 4 servings

Figs are among the first foods cultivated by humans. One reason for their recent popularity is the recognition that figs are good sources of calcium. This recipe also provides iron, magnesium, potassium, and protein. The golden Calimyrna fig is suggested here because of its lighter colour. Served in wide-mouthed champagne glasses, it makes an elegant dessert, garnished with slivered almonds or a sprig of mint.

**1 cup (250 mL) dried golden figs, stems removed, about 15 figs**
**1 1/2 cups (375 mL) apple juice**
**1 package (12.3 ounces/349 g) firm silken tofu**
**1 tablespoon (15 mL) lemon juice**
**1 tablespoon (15 mL) sweetener (optional)**
**1/4 teaspoon (1 mL) cinnamon**
**1/4 teaspoon (1 mL) vanilla extract**
**Pinch of ground cloves**

Soak the figs in the apple juice in refrigerator for 12 hours. Place figs, apple juice, tofu, lemon juice, sweetener, cinnamon, vanilla, and cloves in a food processor or blender and purée for 2 to 3 minutes or until very smooth, occasionally scraping down the sides of the bowl. Scoop the pudding into 4 small serving bowls or glasses to serve.

Per 3/4-cup (185 mL) serving: calories: 237, protein: 8 g, fat: 3 g, carbohydrate: 48 g (47 g from sugar), dietary fibre: 7 g, calcium: 113 mg, iron: 2 mg, magnesium: 58 mg, phosphorus: 122 mg, potassium: 668 mg, sodium: 41 mg, zinc: 1 mg, thiamin: 0.2 mg, riboflavin: 0.1 mg, niacin: 2 mg, vitamin $B_6$: 0.2 mg, folate: 5 mcg, pantothenic acid: 0.3 mg, vitamin $B_{12}$: 0 mcg, vitamin A: 7 mcg, vitamin C: 4 mg, vitamin E: 0.2 mg, omega-6 fatty acids: 0.3 g, omega-3 fatty acids: 0 g

Percentage of calories from protein 12%, fat 11%, carbohydrate 77%

## Fresh Fruit as Dessert

Nothing surpasses fresh fruit in the summer when locally grown fruit is at a peak. Fruit also brings welcome vitamins and protective phytochemicals to winter meals. Fruits provide potassium and other minerals that are essential to electrolyte balance, nerve transmission, and body function. Though bananas are famous as sources of potassium, cantaloupe, grapefruits, and strawberries could share in this glory. Oranges and figs are high in calcium. Bananas, raisins, and prunes provide copper. Fresh fruit is ideal for people with food allergies or gluten sensitivities. For a summer celebration extravaganza, try Watermelon Fruit Sculpture (page 255) or the following ways to present fresh fruit.

- Emulate the presentation at those upscale restaurants that serve a single large, ripe heirloom peach, or other fruit, at the peak of its perfection. This is a great opportunity to discuss with family members and guests the idea of a simple life.
- Create a fruit platter using some combination of red strawberries or raspberries; orange papaya, mandarins, or mango; golden apricots or peaches; pink or yellow watermelon, guava, or grapefruit; green honeydew melon or kiwi; white pear, apple, or banana (sprinkled with a little lemon juice to prevent browning); purple plums; and blueberries or blackberries. For an elegant presentation, as often seen on banquet tables, place your fruit platter on a mirror that has a frame or polished or bevelled edges to prevent injury.
- Cut fruit into uniform pieces and thread the pieces on a bamboo skewer to create a colourful presentation for a potluck, picnic, or brunch.
- Slice a pineapple in half and carefully remove the flesh of one half to create a cavity. Use it as a bowl to fill with fruit salad. The same could be done with a melon.
- For children, assemble a dessert plate composed of fruit in the shape of a face, with a curve of melon for a mouth, the pointed end of a banana for a nose, and berries for eyes. Use your imagination to fill in any other features.

Many fruits are nutritional superstars as providers of vitamins and phytochemicals:

**Anthocyanins** are antioxidants that are found in blackberries, black currants, blueberries, cherries, and plums.

**Carotenoids,** a group of protective compounds that are related to vitamin A, act as antioxidants, support communication between cells in the body, and may protect us against several cancers and macular degeneration. They provide the gorgeous hues seen in apricots, guava, mangos, papaya, persimmons (kaki), pink grapefruit, pumpkin, and watermelon.

**Coumaric acid** in an antioxidant and anti-cancer agent in grapes, pineapple, and strawberries.

**Ellagic acid** is an anti-cancer agent in berries, grapes, and pomegranates.

**Flavonols** such as quercetin help to keep the doctor away and are present in apples, berries, and cherries.

**Folate** helps to build amino acids and our genetic material, DNA. Excellent sources are kiwi and oranges.

**Limonoids,** in citrus fruits, support the health of our hearts.

**Vitamin B6** (pyridoxine), essential for protein metabolism, is well distributed among fruits. You can get your day's supply from three bananas.

**Vitamin C** is a powerful antioxidant that helps our bodies to resist disease and infection, absorb iron from our diet, and build essential compounds such as collagen, carnitine, and the neurotransmitter norepinephrine. A few of our best sources of this vitamin are cantaloupe, citrus fruit, mangos, papaya, and strawberries. The vitamin C content of organic foods has been shown to be higher than that in non-organic counterparts.

## Holiday Pie Topping

Makes about 2 cups (500 mL)

This low-fat alternative to whipped cream is a great accompaniment to Pumpkin Spice Pie (page 249), Blueberry Mince Tarts or Pies (page 232), or apple pie.

**1 package (12.3 ounces/349 g) firm silken tofu**
**1/4 cup (60 mL) maple syrup**
**1 tablespoon (15 mL) lemon juice**
**1 teaspoon (5 mL) vanilla extract**

Put the tofu, maple syrup, lemon juice, and vanilla in a blender or food processor and process for about 1 minute or until perfectly smooth. Chill mixture for 1 to 2 hours. Spread over cooled pie or serve on each individual serving.

Per 2 tablespoons (30 mL): calories: 30, protein: 2 g, fat: 1 g, carbohydrate: 4 g (4 g from sugar), dietary fibre: 0 g, calcium: 11 mg, iron: 0.3 mg, magnesium: 7 mg, phosphorus: 58 mg, potassium: 58 mg, sodium: 9 mg, zinc: 0.4 mg, thiamin: 0 mg, riboflavin: 0 mg, niacin: 0.4 mg, vitamin $B_6$: 0 mg, folate: 0.1 mcg, pantothenic acid: 0 mg, vitamin $B_{12}$: 0 mcg, vitamin A: 0 mcg, vitamin C: 0.5 mg, vitamin E: 0.1 mg, omega-6 fatty acids: 0 g, omega-3 fatty acids: 0 g

Percentage of calories from protein 22%, fat 20%, carbohydrate 58%

# Lemon Glaze

Makes 1 2/3 cups (420 mL)

This glaze or thin icing is a lovely blend of sweet and sour. Use it on Apple Spice Cake (page 228).

**1/4 cup (60 mL) Earth Balance spread or other vegan margarine**
**2 cups (500 mL) icing sugar**
**2 tablespoons (30 mL) grated or minced lemon peel**
**1 1/2 tablespoons (22 mL) freshly squeezed lemon juice**

Put the Earth Balance spread in a bowl and cream well using a hand mixer or spoon. Add the icing sugar and mix until most of the sugar is incorporated, pressing out any lumps. Add the lemon peel and lemon juice and mix well.

Per 1/20 recipe (about 4 teaspoons/20 mL): calories: 70, protein: 0 g, fat: 2 g, carbohydrate: 13 g (13 g from sugar), dietary fibre: 0.1 g, calcium: 1 mg, iron: 0 mg, magnesium: 0.2 mg, phosphorus: 0.4 mg, potassium: 3 mg, sodium: 0.2 mg, zinc: 0.1 mg, thiamin: 0 mg, riboflavin: 0 mg, niacin: 0 mg, vitamin $B_6$: 0 mg, folate: 0.2 mcg, pantothenic acid: 0 mg, vitamin $B_{12}$: 0 mcg, vitamin A: 0 mcg, vitamin C: 1 mg, vitamin E: 0 mg, omega-6 fatty acids: 0 g, omega-3 fatty acids: 0 g

Percentage of calories from protein 0%, fat 28%, carbohydrate 72%

# Lemon Sesame Cookies

Makes 36 cookies

These delectable cookies have a moist cake-like texture and lemon-sesame flavour. They are tasty at tea time, make a pleasant dessert accompanied by fresh fruit salad, and are welcome in a lunch bag.

2 cups (500 mL) unbleached or whole-wheat pastry flour
1/2 cup (125 mL) sesame seeds
2 teaspoons (10 mL) baking powder
1/2 teaspoon (2 mL) salt
1 package (12.3 ounces/349 g) soft tofu
1/2 cup (125 mL) sunflower oil
1/2 cup (125 mL) maple syrup
1/4 cup (60 mL) brown sugar or other dry sweetener
2 teaspoons (10 mL) grated lemon peel
1 1/2 teaspoons (7 mL) lemon extract
1 teaspoon (5 mL) vanilla extract

Preheat the oven to 350°F (180°C).

Put the flour, sesame seeds, baking powder, and salt in a bowl and mix well. Put the tofu, oil, maple syrup, sugar, lemon peel, and lemon and vanilla extracts in another bowl; mash together and mix well. Stir flour mixture into wet ingredients, mixing quickly. Drop cookie batter by rounded tablespoonfuls onto 2 oiled baking sheets. Bake for about 20 minutes or until golden brown, rotating the baking sheets after 10 minutes for even baking. Transfer cookies to a rack to cool.

Per cookie: calories: 96, protein: 2 g, fat: 5 g, carbohydrate: 12 g (5 g from sugar), dietary fibre: 0.5 g, calcium: 37 mg, iron: 1 mg, magnesium: 14 mg, phosphorus: 33 mg, potassium: 59 mg, sodium: 43 mg, zinc: 0.5 mg, thiamin: 0.1 mg, riboflavin: 0.1 mg, niacin: 1 mg, vitamin $B_6$: 0 mg, folate: 13 mcg, pantothenic acid: 0 mg, vitamin $B_{12}$: 0 mcg, vitamin A: 0 mcg, vitamin C: 0 mg, vitamin E: 0 mg, omega-6 fatty acids: 2 g, omega-3 fatty acids: 0 g

Percentage of calories from protein 8%, fat 44%, carbohydrate 48%

## Lem-Un-Cheesecake with Crumb Crust

Makes one 8- or 9-inch (20 to 23 cm) pie, enough for 8 servings

This is a delicious way to get protein. Once the cheesecake is chilled, decorate the top with fresh fruit such as blueberries or sliced strawberries, peaches, or kiwis, or serve with Blueberry Orange Sauce (page 212), or Apple Plum Chutney (page 211).

**1 recipe Oats 'N' Flax Crumb Crust (page 248)**
**2 packages (each 12.3 ounces/349 g) firm silken tofu**
**1/3 cup (85 mL) maple or agave syrup**
**4 teaspoons (20 mL) minced lemon peel**
**1/4 cup (60 mL) lemon juice**
**1 1/2 teaspoons (7 mL) vanilla extract**

Prepare the crumb crust and set aside.

Preheat the oven to 350°F (180°C).

Put the tofu, maple syrup, lemon peel, lemon juice, and vanilla in the bowl of a food processor and purée until smooth, occasionally scraping down the sides of the bowl. Pour the mixture into the crumb crust and bake for 1 hour or until a toothpick comes out clean and the crust begins to set. Chill before serving.

Per slice (1/8 pie): calories: 244, protein: 9 g, fat: 12 g, carbohydrate: 25 g (10 g from sugar), dietary fibre: 3 g, calcium: 56 mg, iron: 2 mg, magnesium: 42 mg, phosphorus: 106 mg, potassium: 305 mg, sodium: 55 mg, zinc: 1 mg, thiamin: 0.2 mg, riboflavin: 0.1 mg, niacin: 2 mg, vitamin $B_6$: 0 mg, folate: 5 mcg, pantothenic acid: 0.1 mg, vitamin $B_{12}$: 0 mcg, vitamin A: 0 mcg, vitamin C: 5 mg, vitamin E: 3 mg, omega-6 fatty acids: 0.5 g, omega-3 fatty acids: 1 g

Percentage of calories from protein 15%, fat 44%, carbohydrate 41%

# Oats 'n' Flax Crumb Crust

Makes one 8- or 9-inch (20 or 23 cm) pie crust

The ground flaxseed in this recipe provide a nutty flavour and beneficial omega-3 fatty acids and vitamin E, while also helping to hold the crust together. Place a cup of whole flaxseeds in a blender and process for 30 seconds or until the seeds are cracked open. Store them in a sealed container in the freezer for up to 6 months. Good choices for the cereal flakes are Nature's Path millet rice cereal or corn flakes. This crust was created especially for the Pumpkin Spice Pie (page 249) and the Lem-Un-Cheesecake with Crumb Crust (page 247).

**1 cup (250 mL) rolled oats**
**1 cup (250 mL) ground cold cereal flakes**
**1/4 cup (60 mL) ground flaxseed**
**1/4 cup (60 mL) sunflower oil or melted coconut oil**
**1/4 cup (60 mL) water**
**2 teaspoons (10 mL) vanilla extract**

Put the oats in a food processor and process for 20 seconds or until the oats are a mealy texture. Transfer to a medium bowl. Process the cold cereal flakes in the food processor for 30 seconds or until the cereal is ground. Add them to the oats along with the flaxseed. Whisk together the oil, water, and vanilla in a small bowl. Quickly stir the oil mixture with a fork into the crumb mixture. Work the mixture well with your fingers for a few seconds to form a mealy texture. Lightly coat an 8- or 9-inch (20 or 23 cm) pie plate with oil. Press the crumb mixture firmly and evenly onto the bottom and sides of the pie plate. Bake as directed in your pie recipe.

Per 1/8 crust: calories: 148, protein: 3 g, fat: 10 g, carbohydrate: 13 g (0.5 g from sugar), dietary fibre: 3 g, calcium: 16 mg, iron: 1 mg, magnesium: 16 mg, phosphorus: 27 mg, potassium: 94 mg, sodium: 22 mg, zinc: 0.2 mg, thiamin: 0.1 mg, riboflavin: 0 mg, niacin: 0.4 mg, vitamin $B_6$: 0 mg, folate: 4 mcg, pantothenic acid: 0 mg, vitamin $B_{12}$: 0 mcg, vitamin A: 0 mcg, vitamin C: 0 mg, vitamin E: 3 mg, omega-6 fatty acids: 0.5 g, omega-3 fatty acids: 1 g

Percentage of calories from protein 8%, fat 58%, carbohydrate 34%

# Pumpkin Spice Pie

Makes one 8- or 9-inch (20 or 23 cm) pie, enough for 8 servings

Pumpkin pie has become a symbol of harvest in North America, and it is often eaten at fall and winter celebrations. This recipe, served with Holiday Pie Topping (page 244) or Cashew Cream Topping (page 234), is an excellent substitution for the traditional pie that is made with eggs and milk and served with a dollop of whipped cream.

**1 recipe Oats 'N' Flax Crumb Crust (page 248)**
**1 package (12.3 ounces/349 g) firm silken tofu**
**2 cups (500 mL) mashed, cooked, or canned pumpkin**
**2/3 cup (170 mL) maple syrup or other liquid sweetener**
**1 teaspoon (5 mL) vanilla extract**
**1 1/2 teaspoons (7 mL) cinnamon**
**3/4 teaspoon (4 mL) ground ginger**
**1/4 teaspoon (1 mL) nutmeg**
**Pinch of ground cloves**

Prepare the crumb crust and set aside.

Preheat the oven to 375°F (190°C).

Blend the tofu in a food processor or blender until creamy smooth. Add the pumpkin, maple syrup, vanilla, cinnamon, ginger, nutmeg, and cloves; blend well. Pour mixture into the crumb crust and bake for 50 to 60 minutes or until a toothpick inserted into the centre comes out clean or the pie just begins to crack. Serve chilled.

Per slice (1/8 pie): calories: 266, protein: 6 g, fat: 11 g, carbohydrate: 37 g (19 g from sugar), dietary fibre: 4 g, calcium: 65 mg, iron: 2 mg, magnesium: 39 mg, phosphorus: 87 mg, potassium: 392 mg, sodium: 42 mg, zinc: 2 mg, thiamin: 0.2 mg, riboflavin: 0.1 mg, niacin: 1 mg, vitamin $B_6$: 0.1 mg, folate: 10 mcg, pantothenic acid: 0.2 mg, vitamin $B_{12}$: 0 mcg, vitamin A: 162 mcg, vitamin C: 3 mg, vitamin E: 4 mg, omega-6 fatty acids: 0.5 g, omega-3 fatty acids: 1 g

Percentage of calories from protein 10%, fat 36%, carbohydrate 54%

**Pumpkin Pie with Soft Tofu**
Replace the silken tofu with 1 3/4 cups (435 mL) mashed soft tofu.

# Raw Lime Pie

Makes one 8- or 9-inch (20 or 23 cm) pie, enough for 8 servings

This raw filling has the ideal balance of sweetness and tang. The Almond, Date, and Coconut Pie Crust (page 223) adds a crunchy contrast. Avocado can become brown if you overblend, so blend this filling just until it is smooth. Coconut oil or guar gum will help the slices of pie maintain a firmer edge when cut, though the pie is also excellent without either. It's rich, so you might want to cut the pieces smaller than you might otherwise. (Then again, it's so delicious, you might want to cut the pieces larger!)

1 recipe Almond, Date, and Coconut Pie Crust (page 223)
4 medium to large avocados, peel and pit removed
2/3 cup (170 mL) freshly squeezed lime juice
2/3 cup (170 mL) maple syrup
2 tablespoons (30 mL) melted virgin coconut oil or 2 teaspoons (10 mL) guar gum (optional)
1 tablespoon (15 mL) lime zest
3 kiwi, peeled and sliced, or other sliced fruit, or a little unsweetened, shredded dried coconut, for garnish

Prepare the pie crust and set aside.

Place the avocados, lime juice, maple syrup, and optional coconut oil in a blender and blend just until smooth and fluid. Add lime zest and blend just to mix. Pour the filling into the pie crust and freeze for 1 to 2 hours or place in the refrigerator overnight to set. Garnish with sliced fruit. Serve this pie chilled so that the slices retain their shape.

Per slice (1/8 pie): calories: 434, protein: 7 g, fat: 28 g, carbohydrate: 47 g (29 g from sugar), dietary fibre: 10 g, calcium: 100 mg, iron: 3 mg, magnesium: 113 mg, phosphorus: 161 mg, potassium: 1022 mg, sodium: 16 mg, zinc: 2 mg, thiamin: 0.2 mg, riboflavin: 0.3 mg, niacin: 4 mg, vitamin $B_6$: 0.4 mg, folate: 79 mcg, pantothenic acid: 1 mg, vitamin $B_{12}$: 0 mcg, vitamin A: 66 mcg, vitamin C: 42 mg, vitamin E: 7 mg, omega-6 fatty acids: 4 g, omega-3 fatty acids: 0 g

Percentage of calories from protein 6%, fat 54%, carbohydrate 40%

**Raw Lime Pudding**
Serve the filling in small bowls or cups, as a pudding, without the pie crust.

# Raw Mango Strawberry Pie

Makes one 8- or 9-inch (20 or 23 cm) pie, enough for 8 servings

This raw pie will dazzle your family and friends. Including the optional coconut oil or guar gum will help the slices of pie maintain a firmer edge when cut. However, this filling is also superb with mango alone.

1 recipe Almond, Date, and Coconut Pie Crust (page 223)
1 cup (250 mL) dried mango, soaked in water for 10 minutes
3 cups (750 mL) chopped fresh mango, about 2 mangos
2 tablespoons (30 mL) melted virgin coconut oil or 2 teaspoons (10 mL) guar gum (optional)
1 cup (250 mL) sliced strawberries, for garnish

Prepare the pie crust and set aside.

Drain the soaked dried mango well, then press it in a small sieve or with your hands to remove excess liquid. (Save the liquid for smoothies). Place the dried mango, fresh mango, and coconut oil in a blender or food processor and blend until smooth. Spread the filling on the pie crust. Top with sliced strawberries. Refrigerate for 2 to 3 hours to set. Serve this pie chilled so that the slices retain their shape.

Per slice (1/8 pie): calories: 277, protein: 5 g, fat: 13 g, carbohydrate: 41 g (22 g from sugar), dietary fibre: 6 g, calcium: 71 mg, iron: 1 mg, magnesium: 73 mg, phosphorus: 125 mg, potassium: 402 mg, sodium: 4 mg, zinc: 1 mg, thiamin: 0.1 mg, riboflavin: 0.2 mg, niacin: 3 mg, vitamin $B_6$: 0.2 mg, folate: 22 mcg, pantothenic acid: 0.4 mg, vitamin $B_{12}$: 0 mcg, vitamin A: 53 mcg, vitamin C: 37 mg, vitamin E: 6 mg, omega-6 fatty acids: 2 g, omega-3 fatty acids: 0 g

Percentage of calories from protein 7%, fat 39%, carbohydrate 54%

**Sliced Fruit or Coconut Garnish**
Garnish with sliced fruit other than strawberries, or shredded coconut.

# Tart and Pie Pastry

Makes 30 tarts or two 8-inch (20 cm) pies

Having a pastry recipe without hydrogenated oils or saturated fats is a welcome addition to anyone's repertoire. The amount of water needed for this recipe can vary depending on the type of flour used. Using whole-wheat flour, slightly more water will be needed, as the extra bran will absorb moisture.

1/2 cup (125 mL) ice water (see directions below)
1 1/2 cups (375 mL) whole-wheat pastry or whole-wheat flour
1 1/2 cups (375 mL) unbleached or all-purpose flour
1 tablespoon (15 mL) baking powder
1/2 teaspoon (2 mL) salt
1/2 cup (125 mL) sunflower oil

To make the ice water, put 2 or 3 ice cubes in a glass of water for several minutes, or put cold water in the freezer for 15 minutes if you have no ice. Combine the flours, baking powder, and salt in a medium bowl. Stir in the oil, tossing the mixture with a fork or your fingers to form pea-size balls. Sprinkle the ice water over the mixture, and use your hands to form a ball of dough. Use just enough water to hold the dough together. Divide the dough into 2 equal pieces and use immediately or refrigerate until needed.

Per tart shell: calories: 81, protein: 2 g, fat: 4 g, carbohydrate: 10 g (0 g from sugar), dietary fibre: 1 g, calcium: 25 mg, iron: 0.1 mg, magnesium: 10 mg, phosphorus: 64 mg, potassium: 84 mg, sodium: 32 mg, zinc: 0.2 mg, thiamin: 0.1 mg, riboflavin: 0.1 mg, niacin: 1 mg, vitamin $B_6$: 0 mg, folate: 14 mcg, pantothenic acid: 0.1 mg, vitamin $B_{12}$: 0 mcg, vitamin A: 0 mcg, vitamin C: 0 mg, vitamin E: 2 mg, omega-6 fatty acids: 0.2 g, omega-3 fatty acids: 0 g

Percentage of calories from protein 7%, fat 45%, carbohydrate 48%

# Vanilla Frosting

Makes 1 2/3 cups (420 mL)

Earth Balance is a brand name for a vegan buttery spread made from non-genetically modified, expeller-pressed oils. The frosting is best made when the spread has sat at room temperature for 1 to 2 hours first.

**2/3 cup (170 mL) Earth Balance spread or other vegan margarine**
**2 cups (500 mL) icing sugar**
**1 teaspoon (5 mL) vanilla extract**

Put the Earth Balance spread in a bowl and cream well using a hand mixer or spoon. Add the icing sugar and mix until all of the sugar is incorporated, pressing out any lumps. Add vanilla and mix well.

Per 1/20 recipe (about 4 teaspoons/20 mL): calories: 107, protein: 0 g, fat: 6 g, carbohydrate: 13 g (12 g from sugar), dietary fibre: 0 g, calcium: 0 mg, iron: 0 mg, magnesium: 0 mg, phosphorus: 0 mg, potassium: 1 mg, sodium: 0 mg, zinc: 0 mg, thiamin: 0 mg, riboflavin: 0 mg, niacin: 0 mg, vitamin $B_6$: 0 mg, folate: 0 mcg, pantothenic acid: 0 mg, vitamin $B_{12}$: 0 mcg, vitamin A: 0 mcg, vitamin C: 0 mg, vitamin E: 0 mg, omega-6 fatty acids: 0 g, omega-3 fatty acids: 0 g

Percentage of calories from protein 0%, fat 53%, carbohydrate 47%

# Vegan Dasz Ice Cream

Makes about 2 1/2 cups (625 mL)

If you have a masticating juicer (such as a Champion) or a twin-gear juicer (such as a Green Power or Green Star), you can make the simplest, lowest fat, non-dairy ice cream imaginable. The fat content is low and the potassium high because the only ingredient is bananas! Ice cream will be thicker if the juicer parts and bowl are chilled before processing. To make this ice cream in a food processor, see the variation below.

**4 peeled, frozen ripe bananas**

Feed frozen banana halves or pieces gradually into a juicer that is fitted with a blank (in place of the juicing screen) and process until smooth. Serve immediately.

Per cup (250 mL): calories: 169, protein: 2 g, fat: 1 g, carbohydrate: 43 g (29 g from sugar), dietary fibre: 3 g, calcium: 11 mg, iron: 0.6 mg, magnesium: 53 mg, phosphorus: 37 mg, potassium: 726 mg, sodium: 2 mg, zinc: 0.3 mg, thiamin: 0.1 mg, riboflavin: 0.2 mg, niacin: 1 mg, vitamin $B_6$: 1 mg, folate: 35 mcg, pantothenic acid: 0.5 mg, vitamin $B_{12}$: 0 mcg, vitamin A: 15 mcg, vitamin C: 17 mg, vitamin E: 0.5 mg, omega-6 fatty acids: 0.1 g, omega-3 fatty acids: 0.1 g

Percentage of calories from protein 4%, fat 4%, carbohydrate 92%

**Mixed Fruit Ice Cream**
Create your own treats by using 2 frozen bananas plus 2 cups (500 mL) other frozen fruits, such as mango, strawberries, blueberries, pineapple, or a combination. Serve immediately.

**Chocolate Ice Cream**
Add 2 teaspoons (10 mL) cocoa or carob powder along with each banana so that the cocoa powder is mixed in with the banana as it goes through the juicer. Serve immediately.

**Food Processor Method**
Place 2 cups (500 mL) frozen banana pieces or other frozen fruit in the food processor along with 1 cup (250 mL) non-dairy milk (such as hemp seed, almond, or soy milk) and process until smooth. Serve immediately.

# Watermelon Fruit Sculpture

Makes about 12 servings

This watermelon sculpture is a cool, refreshing treat on a hot summer day. Free of allergens such as eggs, dairy, and wheat, and low in calories, it is colourful, attractive, and thirst-quenching. This is a great dessert creation to do together with children. If you prefer, you may decorate your sculpture with 3 to 4 cups (750 mL to 1 L) of other fruits, such as those suggested on page 256.

**1 large seedless watermelon, about 10 pounds (4.5 kg)**
**1 ripe pineapple**
**1 cup (250 mL) strawberries**
**2 kiwi**
**Toothpicks**

Slice about 1 inch (2.5 cm) off each end of the watermelon. Stand the watermelon on one end and cut it lengthwise down the middle to create two halves. While holding one half on its end, slice off the peel, including the white inner peel.

Cut off both ends of the pineapple. Stand it on one end and cut away the peel. While still standing on its end, slice the pineapple lengthwise into 4 equal pieces. (You will need one-quarter of the pineapple per half of the watermelon.) Cut the core from the pineapple. Slice one of the quarters lengthwise into two long pieces. Slice the pineapple into 1/2-inch (1 cm) thick pieces.

Wash the strawberries, remove their stems, and cut them in half.

Cut the ends off a kiwi, stand it on end, and slice away the peel. Cut the kiwi in half and then each half into 1/4-inch (5 mm) thick cross-sections. Repeat with the second kiwi.

To assemble the sculpture, centre the peeled watermelon on a serving platter flat side down. Skewer each piece of fruit with a toothpick, then stick it into the watermelon, creating a decorative pattern. Arrange any leftover fruit around the base of the sculpture. If you have the space in your refrigerator, chill the sculpture for 1 to 2 hours or longer before serving. To serve, slice the decorated watermelon into pieces.

Per serving: calories: 54, protein: 1 g, fat: 0 g, carbohydrate: 14 g (10 g from sugar), dietary fibre: 1 g, calcium: 17 mg, iron: 0.4 mg, magnesium: 17 mg, phosphorus: 21 mg, potassium: 207 mg, sodium: 2 mg, zinc: 0.2 mg, thiamin: 0.1 mg, riboflavin: 0 mg, niacin: 1 mg, vitamin $B_6$: 0.1 mg, folate: 12 mcg, pantothenic acid: 0.3 mg, vitamin $B_{12}$: 0 mcg, vitamin A: 33 mcg, vitamin C: 35 mg, vitamin E: 0.3 mg, omega-6 fatty acids: 0.1 g, omega-3 fatty acids: 0 g

Percentage of calories from protein 7%, fat 4%, carbohydrate 89%

**Ideas for Fruit Decorations**
Blueberries, several threaded onto a single toothpick
Grapes, whole or cut in half
Starfruit, cut in half, then sliced thinly to form a border along the base of the watermelon
Honeydew or cantaloupe pieces
Raspberries, whole red or black
Pineapple, canned chunks

# Appendix 1
## Foods Grouped According to Six Tastes (Salty, Sweet, Sour, Bitter, Pungent, Astringent)

These lists include fresh and dried fruits and herbs. The taste of a food can be affected by many factors. For example, cucumbers may be bitter if they are grown under particularly hot conditions that stress the plant. Some brands of olive oil or sesame tahini are more bitter than others. Other foods can be particularly sweet or less sweet depending on variety, growing conditions, and maturity. Foods found in more than one list typically have a predominant taste, with another taste coming through as a secondary quality. The lists below are a good start but are not complete—a list of processed foods that are salty would be very long indeed!

| 1. Salty Foods | | | | |
|---|---|---|---|---|
| **Condiments** | | | | |
| Bragg Liquid Aminos | Miso<br>Salt | Shoyu | Soy sauce | Tamari |
| **Snack Foods** | | | | |
| Chips | Crackers | Popcorn | | |
| **Flavourings** | | | | |
| Bottled sauce | Bouillon cube | Marinade | Vegetable stock powder | Yeast extract |
| **Processed Foods** | | | | |
| Canned foods | Olives | Ready-to-eat entrées | Seaweed, dried | |

## 2. Sweet Foods

### Fruits

| | | | | |
|---|---|---|---|---|
| Apple | Cranberry | Honeydew melon | Peach | Prune |
| Apricot | Currant | Kiwi | Pear | Raisin |
| Avocado | Date | Mango | Pineapple | Raspberry |
| Banana | Fig | Orange | Plantain | Strawberry |
| Blackberry | Grape | Papaya | Plum | Sweet cherry |
| Blueberry | Grapefruit | | Pomegranate | Watermelon |

### Vegetables

| | | | | |
|---|---|---|---|---|
| Asparagus | Chestnut | Onion: red, sweet, or caramelized | Roasted vegetables | Sweet potato |
| Beet | Corn | | | Tapioca |
| Bell pepper (red) | Cucumber | | Squash: pumpkin, winter, acorn, butternut, kabocha | Tomato |
| Cabbage, cooked | Garlic | Parsnip | | Yam |
| Carrot | Leek | Peas | | |
| Cauliflower | Okra | Potato | | |

### Grains

| | | | | |
|---|---|---|---|---|
| Amaranth | Buckwheat | Cornmeal | Oatmeal | Spelt |
| Barley | Bulghur | Kamut | Quinoa | Wheat |
| Basmati rice | Corn flour | Millet | Rice | Wild rice |
| Brown rice | | | | |

### Nuts and Seeds

| | | | | |
|---|---|---|---|---|
| Almond | Cashew | Chestnut | Coconut | Pecan |

### Prepared Foods

| | | | | |
|---|---|---|---|---|
| Breads | Cookies | Ice cream | Pancakes | Pies |
| Cakes | Crêpes | Muffins | Pasta | Waffles |

### Sweeteners

| | | | | |
|---|---|---|---|---|
| Agave syrup | Date sugar | Malt | Raw sugar | Sucanat |
| Barley malt | Fructose | Maple syrup | Splenda | Turbinado |
| Brown rice syrup | Icing sugar | Molasses | Stevia | White sugar |
| Brown sugar | | | | |

### Herbs and Spices

| | | | | |
|---|---|---|---|---|
| Allspice | Cardamom | Cinnamon | Fennel seed | Licorice |
| Basil | | | | Nutmeg |

## 3. Sour Foods

### Fruits

| | | | | |
|---|---|---|---|---|
| Apple | Grape | Mango | Pomegranate | Strawberry |
| Blackberry | Grapefruit | Orange | Raspberry | Tamarind |
| Blueberry | Lemon | Pineapple | Sour cherry | Tomato |
| Cranberry | Lime | | | |

### Vegetables

| | |
|---|---|
| Rhubarb | Spinach |

### Herbs and Spices

| | | | | |
|---|---|---|---|---|
| Asafoetida | Dill | Fenugreek | Hibiscus | Sorrel |
| Caraway seed | Fennel | Galangal | Lemon grass | Tarragon |
| Coriander | | | | |

### Condiments

| | | | | |
|---|---|---|---|---|
| Capers | Olives | Pickles | Sauerkraut | Vinegar |

### Miscellaneous

| | | | | |
|---|---|---|---|---|
| Alcohol | Breads: sourdough, rye, and pumpernickel | Miso | Red wine | Tamarind |
| Beer | | Molasses | | |

## 4. Bitter Foods

### Fruits

| | | |
|---|---|---|
| Grapefruit | Lemon | Plum |

### Vegetables

| | | | | |
|---|---|---|---|---|
| Alfalfa sprouts | Bitter melon | Cucumber | Garlic | Radicchio |
| Artichoke hearts | Broccoli | Dandelion leaves | Horseradish | Radish |
| Arugula (rocket) | Brussels sprouts | Eggplant | Kale | Rapini |
| Bean sprouts | Chard | Endive | Lettuce | Rutabaga |
| Beet | Cilantro | Fennel bulb | Mustard greens | Spinach |
| Beet greens | Collard greens | | Parsnip | Turnip |

### Herbs and Spices

| | | | | |
|---|---|---|---|---|
| Basil | Cumin | Nutmeg | Peppermint | Turmeric |
| Coriander | Hops | Parsley | Thyme | |

### Beverages

| | | | |
|---|---|---|---|
| Beer | Black tea | Coffee | Tonic water |

### Miscellaneous

| | | | | |
|---|---|---|---|---|
| Chocolate | Extra-virgin olive oil | Molasses | Seeds | Tahini |
| Cocoa | | | | |

## 5. Pungent Foods

### Fruits

| | | | | |
|---|---|---|---|---|
| Citrus peel: orange, lemon, grapefruit | Green chilies: chipotle, jalapeño, serrano | Red chilies: cayenne, dried flakes, paprika | | |

### Vegetables

| | | | | |
|---|---|---|---|---|
| Arugula | Ginger, fresh | Mizuna | Savoy cabbage | Watercress |
| Garlic, raw | Onions: green, yellow | Mustard leaves | | |

### Herbs

| | | | | |
|---|---|---|---|---|
| Basil | Cilantro | Mint | Safflower | Tarragon |
| Bay leaf | Dill | Parsley | Sage | Thyme |
| Chives | Marjoram | Rosemary | Scallions | |

### Spices

| | | | | |
|---|---|---|---|---|
| Allspice | Caraway | Cloves | Fennel seed | Peppercorn |
| Anise | Cardamom | Coriander seed | Fenugreek | Saffron |
| Asafoetida (hing) | Celery seed | Cumin | Ginger | Star anise |
| | Cinnamon | Curry powder | Mustard | |

### Condiments

| | | | | |
|---|---|---|---|---|
| Chili paste | Curry paste | Extra-virgin olive oil | Garlic paste | Red chili paste |
| Chipotle in adobo sauce | Dijon mustard | | Horseradish | Wasabi |

## 6. Astringent Foods

### Fruits

| | | | | |
|---|---|---|---|---|
| Apple | Blackberry | Lemon | Pomegranate | Strawberry |
| Apricot | Cranberry | Plantain | Raspberry | |

### Vegetables

| | | | | |
|---|---|---|---|---|
| Alfalfa sprouts | Chard | Kale | Okra | Turnip |
| Asparagus | Collard greens | Lettuce | Potato | |

### Legumes

| | | | | |
|---|---|---|---|---|
| Adzuki | Black-eyed peas | Lentils | Pinto beans | Tempeh |
| Bean sprouts | Chickpeas | Lima beans | Soybeans | Tofu |
| Black beans | Kidney beans | Navy beans | | |

### Miscellaneous

| | | | |
|---|---|---|---|
| Black tea | Turmeric | Walnuts | White wine |

# Appendix 2
## Dietary Reference Intakes (DRIs) for Minerals

| Life Stage/Age | Calcium mg | Chromium mcg | Copper mcg | Fluoride mg | Iodine mcg | Iron mg | Magnesium mg | Manganese mg | Molybdenum mcg | Phosphorus mg | Selenium mcg | Zinc mg |
|---|---|---|---|---|---|---|---|---|---|---|---|---|
| **Infants** | | | | | | | | | | | | |
| 0–6 months | 200 | 0.2 | 200 | 0.01 | 110 | 0.27 | 30 | 0.003 | 2 | 100 | 15 | 2 |
| 7–12 months | 260 | 5.5 | 220 | 0.5 | 130 | **11** | 75 | 0.6 | 3 | 275 | 20 | **3** |
| **Children** | | | | | | | | | | | | |
| 1–3 years | **700** | 11 | **340** | 0.7 | **90** | **7** | **80** | 1.2 | **17** | **460** | **20** | **3** |
| 4–8 years | **1000** | 15 | **440** | 1 | **90** | **10** | **130** | 1.5 | **22** | **500** | **30** | **5** |
| **Males** | | | | | | | | | | | | |
| 9–13 years | **1300** | 25 | **700** | 2 | **120** | **8** | **240** | 1.9 | **34** | **1250** | **40** | **8** |
| 14–18 years | **1300** | 35 | **890** | 3 | **150** | **11** | **410** | 2.2 | **43** | **1250** | **55** | **11** |
| 19–30 years | **1000** | 35 | **900** | 4 | **150** | **8** | **400** | 2.3 | **45** | **700** | **55** | **11** |
| 31–50 years | **1000** | 35 | **900** | 4 | **150** | **8** | **420** | 2.3 | **45** | **700** | **55** | **11** |
| 51–70 years | **1200** | 30 | **900** | 4 | **150** | **8** | **420** | 2.3 | **45** | **700** | **55** | **11** |
| > 70 years | **1200** | 30 | **900** | 4 | **150** | **8** | **420** | 2.3 | **45** | **700** | **55** | **11** |
| **Females** | | | | | | | | | | | | |
| 9–13 years | **1300** | 21 | **700** | 2 | **120** | **8** | **240** | 1.6 | **34** | **1250** | **40** | **8** |
| 14–18 years | **1300** | 24 | **890** | 3 | **150** | **15** | **360** | 1.6 | **43** | **1250** | **55** | **9** |
| 19–30 years | **1000** | 25 | **900** | 3 | **150** | **18** | **310** | 1.8 | **45** | **700** | **55** | **8** |
| 31–50 years | **1000** | 25 | **900** | 3 | **150** | **18** | **320** | 1.8 | **45** | **700** | **55** | **8** |
| 51–70 years | **1200** | 20 | **900** | 3 | **150** | **8** | **320** | 1.8 | **45** | **700** | **55** | **8** |
| > 70 years | **1200** | 20 | **900** | 3 | **150** | **8** | **320** | 1.8 | **45** | **700** | **55** | **8** |
| **Pregnancy** | | | | | | | | | | | | |
| < 18 years | **1300** | 29 | **1000** | 3 | **220** | **27** | **400** | 2.0 | **50** | **1250** | **60** | **13** |
| 19–30 years | **1000** | 30 | **1000** | 3 | **220** | **27** | **350** | 2.0 | **50** | **700** | **60** | **11** |
| 31–50 years | **1000** | 30 | **1000** | 3 | **220** | **27** | **360** | 2.0 | **50** | **700** | **60** | **11** |
| **Lactation** | | | | | | | | | | | | |
| < 18 years | **1300** | 44 | **1300** | 3 | **290** | **10** | **360** | 2.6 | **50** | **1,250** | **70** | **14** |
| 19–30 years | **1000** | 45 | **1300** | 3 | **290** | **9** | **310** | 2.6 | **50** | **700** | **70** | **12** |
| 31–50 years | **1000** | 45 | **1300** | 3 | **290** | **9** | **320** | 2.6 | **50** | **700** | **70** | **12** |

*Note:* Recommended Dietary Allowances (RDAs) are in **bold type** and Adequate Intakes (AIs) are in regular type. Both RDA and AI values may be used as goals for individual intake.

*Source:* Food and Nutrition Board, Institute of Medicine of the National Academies. Access Dietary Reference Intake reports at http://www.iom.edu/Reports
(Search for "Dietary Reference Intakes Minerals" for a listing of reports, which can be opened online and read free of charge.)

# Appendix 3
## Dietary Reference Intakes (DRIs) for Vitamins

| Life Stage/Age | Vit A[a] (mcg) | Vit C (mg) | Vit D[b] (IU; International Units) | Vit E (mg) | Vit K (mcg) | Thiamin (mg) | Riboflavin (mg) | Niacin[c] (mg) | Vit B6 (mg) | Folate[d] (mcg) | Vit B12[e] (mcg) | Pantothenic Acid (mg) | Biotin (mcg) | Choline (mg) |
|---|---|---|---|---|---|---|---|---|---|---|---|---|---|---|
| *Infants* | | | | | | | | | | | | | | |
| 0–6 months | 400 | 40 | – | 4 | 2.0 | 0.2 | 0.3 | 2 | 0.1 | 65 | 0.4 | 1.7 | 5 | 125 |
| 7–12 months | 500 | 50 | – | 5 | 2.5 | 0.3 | 0.4 | 4 | 0.3 | 80 | 0.5 | 1.8 | 6 | 150 |
| *Children* | | | | | | | | | | | | | | |
| 1–3 years | 300 | 15 | 600 | 6 | 30 | 0.5 | 0.5 | 6 | 0.5 | 150 | 0.9 | 2 | 8 | 200 |
| 4–8 years | 400 | 25 | 600 | 7 | 55 | 0.6 | 0.6 | 8 | 0.6 | 200 | 1.2 | 3 | 12 | 250 |
| *Males* | | | | | | | | | | | | | | |
| 9–13 years | 600 | 45 | 600 | 11 | 60 | 0.9 | 0.9 | 12 | 1 | 300 | 1.8 | 4 | 20 | 375 |
| 14–18 years | 900 | 75 | 600 | 15 | 75 | 1.2 | 1.3 | 16 | 1.3 | 400 | 2.4 | 5 | 25 | 550 |
| 19–30 years | 900 | 90 | 600 | 15 | 120 | 1.2 | 1.3 | 16 | 1.3 | 400 | 2.4 | 5 | 30 | 550 |
| 31–50 years | 900 | 90 | 600 | 15 | 120 | 1.2 | 1.3 | 16 | 1.3 | 400 | 2.4 | 5 | 30 | 550 |
| 51–70 years | 900 | 90 | 600 | 15 | 120 | 1.2 | 1.3 | 16 | 1.7 | 400 | 2.4 | 5 | 30 | 550 |
| > 70 years | 900 | 90 | 800 | 15 | 120 | 1.2 | 1.3 | 16 | 1.7 | 400 | 2.4 | 5 | 30 | 550 |
| *Females* | | | | | | | | | | | | | | |
| 9–13 years | 600 | 45 | 600 | 11 | 60 | 0.9 | 0.9 | 12 | 1 | 300 | 1.8 | 4 | 20 | 375 |
| 14–18 years | 700 | 65 | 600 | 15 | 75 | 1 | 1 | 14 | 1.2 | 400 | 2.4 | 5 | 25 | 400 |
| 19–30 years | 700 | 75 | 600 | 15 | 90 | 1.1 | 1.1 | 14 | 1.3 | 400 | 2.4 | 5 | 30 | 425 |
| 31–50 years | 700 | 75 | 600 | 15 | 90 | 1.1 | 1.1 | 14 | 1.3 | 400 | 2.4 | 5 | 30 | 425 |
| 51–70 years | 700 | 75 | 600 | 15 | 90 | 1.1 | 1.1 | 14 | 1.5 | 400 | 2.4 | 5 | 30 | 425 |
| > 70 years | 700 | 75 | 800 | 15 | 90 | 1.1 | 1.1 | 14 | 1.5 | 400 | 2.4 | 5 | 30 | 425 |

## Dietary Reference Intakes (DRIs) for Vitamins

| Life Stage/Age | Vit A[a] (mcg) | Vit C (mg) | Vit D[b] (IU; International Units) | Vit E (mg) | Vit K (mcg) | Thiamin (mg) | Riboflavin (mg) | Niacin[c] (mg) | Vit B6 (mg) | Folate[d] (mcg) | Vit B12[e] (mcg) | Pantothenic Acid (mg) | Biotin (mcg) | Choline (mg) |
|---|---|---|---|---|---|---|---|---|---|---|---|---|---|---|
| *Pregnancy* | | | | | | | | | | | | | | |
| < 18 years | **750** | **80** | **600** | **15** | 75 | **1.4** | **1.4** | **18** | **1.9** | **600** | **2.6** | 6 | 30 | 450 |
| 19–30 years | **770** | **85** | **600** | **15** | 90 | **1.4** | **1.4** | **18** | **1.9** | **600** | **2.6** | 6 | 30 | 450 |
| 31–50 years | **770** | **85** | **600** | **15** | 90 | **1.4** | **1.4** | **18** | **1.9** | **600** | **2.6** | 6 | 30 | 450 |
| *Lactation* | | | | | | | | | | | | | | |
| < 18 years | **1200** | **115** | **600** | **19** | 75 | **1.4** | **1.6** | **17** | **2** | **500** | **2.8** | 7 | 35 | 550 |
| 19–30 years | **1300** | **120** | **600** | **19** | 90 | **1.4** | **1.6** | **17** | **2** | **500** | **2.8** | 7 | 35 | 550 |
| 31–50 years | **1300** | **120** | **600** | **19** | 90 | **1.4** | **1.6** | **17** | **2** | **500** | **2.8** | 7 | 35 | 550 |

[a] Vitamin A: as Retinal Activity Equivalents (RAEs). 1 RAE = 1 mcg retinol; 12 mcg beta-carotene; 24 mcg other pro-vitamin A carotenoids in foods.

[b] Vitamin D: 1 mcg cholecalciferol = 40 IU vitamin D.

[c] Niacin: as Niacin Equivalents (NE). 1 mg of niacin = 60 mg tryptophan (0-6 months must receive preformed niacin, not NE).

[d] Folate: as Dietary Folate Equivalents (DFE). 1 DFE = 1 mcg food folate = 0.6 mcg of folic acid from fortified food or supplement consumed with food, or 0.5 mcg of supplement consumed on an empty stomach.

[e] Vitamin B12: 10 to 30 percent of people 50 years and older malabsorb vitamin B12 and thus people 50 years and older are advised to meet the RDA using B12-fortified foods or supplements.

**Note:** Recommended Dietary Allowances (RDAs) are in **bold type** and Adequate Intakes (AIs) are in regular type. Both RDA and AI values may be used as goals for individual intake.

*Source:* Food and Nutrition Board, Institute of Medicine of the National Academies. Access Dietary Reference Intake reports at http://www.iom.edu/Reports
(Search for "Dietary Reference Intakes Vitamins" for a listing of reports, which can be opened online and read free of charge).

# References and Resources

Davis B., Melina V. *Becoming Raw*. The Book Publishing Company, 2010.

Drewnowski A., Gomez-Carneros C. "Bitter taste, phytonutrients, and the consumer: a review." *American Journal of Clinical Nutrition* Vol. 72, No. 6: 1424-35, December 2000. http://www.ajcn.org/content/72/6/1424

Holick M.F., Biancuzzo R.M., Chen T.C., Klein E.K., Young A., Bibuld D., Reitz R., Salameh W., Ameri A., Tannenbaum A.D. "Vitamin D2 is as effective as vitamin D3 in maintaining circulating concentrations of 25-hydroxyvitamin D." *J Clin Endocrinol Metab*. 2008 Mar; 93(3): 677-81.

Institute of Medicine/Food and Nutrition Board. Dietary Reference Intakes for Energy, Carbohydrate, Fiber, Fat, Fatty Acids, Cholesterol, Protein, and Amino Acids (Macronutrients), Food and Nutrition Board, Institute of Medicine, 2005. http://www.nap.edu/catalog.php?record_id=10490

Institute of Medicine/Food and Nutrition Board. *Dietary Reference Intakes*. Reports for vitamins and minerals are online at http://www.iom.edu/Reports.aspx

Joint WHO/FAO Expert Consultation on Diet, Nutrition, and the Prevention of Chronic Diseases. *WHO Technical Report Series 916*. Geneva: World Health Organization, 2003: 916.

Mangels R., Messina V., Messina M. *The Dietitian's Guide to Vegetarian Diets: Issues and Applications*. Jones and Bartlett, 2010.

Melina V., Davis B., *Becoming Vegetarian*. Wiley Canada, 2003.

Melina V., Stepaniak J., Aronson D. *Food Allergy Survival Guide*. The Book Publishing Company, 2004.

Messina V. Food Guide 4 Vegans. http://www.theveganrd.com/food-guide-for-vegans

Messina V., Melina V., Mangels A.R. "A new food guide for North American vegetarians." *J Am Diet Assoc.* 2003 Jun; 103(6): 771-5.

Rodriguez N.R., DiMarco N.M., Langley S. "Position of the American Dietetic Association, Dietitians of Canada, and the American College of Sports Medicine: Nutrition and athletic performance." *J Am Diet Assoc.* 2009 Mar; 109(3): 509-27.

Soria C., Davis B., Melina V. *The Raw Food Revolution Diet.* The Book Publishing Company, 2009.

Stepaniak J., Melina V. *Raising Vegetarian Children.* McGraw-Hill, 2003.

Stepaniak J., Melina V., Aronson D. *Food Allergies: Health and Healing.* The Book Publishing Company, 2010.

United States Department of Agriculture. National Nutrient Database for Standard Reference. http://www.nal.usda.gov/fnic/foodcomp/search/

United States Department of Agriculture, Center for Nutrition Policy and Promotion. http://www.mypyramid.gov/downloads/MiniPoster.pdf

# Endnotes

1. Data drawn from Dietary Reference Intakes for Energy, Carbohydrate, Fiber, Fat, Fatty Acids, Cholesterol, Protein, and Amino Acids (Macronutrients), Food and Nutrition Board, Institute of Medicine, 2005, http://www.nap.edu/catalog.php?record_id=10490, and the Joint WHO/FAO Expert Consultation on Diet, Nutrition and the Prevention of Chronic Diseases, *WHO technical report series 916* (Geneva: WHO, 2003).
2. Data in the Vegetarian Food Guide and Essential Extras section drawn from Messina V., Food Guide 4 Vegans, http://www.theveganrd.com/food-guide-for-vegans; Messina V., Melina V., Mangels A.R., "A new food guide for North American vegetarians," *J Am Diet Assoc,* 2003 Jun; 103(6): 771-5; and United States Department of Agriculture, Center for Nutrition Policy and Promotion, http://www.mypyramid.gov/downloads/MiniPoster.pdf

# Index

African Chickpea Stew, 145
agar, 27
   Gooda Cheeze, 89
almond butter
   Almond-Butter Balls, 224
   Coconut Almond Dressing, 119
   Good Morning Granola, 78
   Orange Ginger Dressing, 124
almonds. *See also* almond butter
   Almond, Date, and Coconut Pie Crust, 223
   Apple Cinnamon Topping, 75
   Design Your Own Muesli (variation), 77
Aloo Gobi, 190
amaranth
   cooking, 31
   Zucchini, Corn, and Amaranth Soup, 142
apple juice
   Blueberry Orange Sauce, 212
   Design Your Own Muesli, 77
   Figgy Pudding, 241
   Good Morning Granola, 78
apples. *See also* apple juice
   Apple Cinnamon Topping, 75
   Apple Pear Crumble, 226
   Apple Plum Chutney, 211
   Apple Spice Cake, 228
   Baked Stuffed Apples, 225
   Green Giant Juice, 79
   Mashed Parsnips and Apple with Toasted Walnuts, 195
   Mulligatawny Soup, 136
arrowroot, 27–28
artichoke hearts
   Italian Style Roll-Ups, 156
   Tapenade Pizza, 180
   Veggie Chick'n Paella with Artichokes and Spinach, 187
Asian Fusion menu, 63
astringent tastes, 9, 260
athletes, 46–47

avocados, 20
   Avocado, Grapefruit, and Chipotle Dressing, 118
   Black Bean, Corn, and Avocado Salsa, 86
   Coconut Mango Black Beans (variation), 147
   Kamut, Tomato, and Avocado Salad, 107
   Limey Avocado Dip, 91
   Maki-Sushi Rolls, 178
   Raw Lime Pie, 250
   Sprouted Lentil Salad Plate, 110
   Timesaving Tacos, 183
   Vietnamese Salad Roll, 114
   Watercress, Avocado, and Grapefruit Salad, 115

"Baked" Beans, Stovetop, 176
Baked Potato and Fixin's Bar, 146
Baked Stuffed Apples, 225
Baked Yams with Lemon and Green Chili, 191
bananas
   frozen, 76
   Banana Blueberry Power Drink, 76
   Design Your Own Muesli, 77
   Green Smoothie, 81
   Vegan Dasz Ice Cream, 254
barley
   cooking, 31
   Design Your Own Muesli (variation), 77
basil (fresh). *See also* herbs
   Carrot, Lemon Grass, and Basil Soup, 130
   Italian Style Roll-Ups, 156
   Pesto-the-Best-Oh!, 92
   Tomato Herb Dressing, 127
   Tuscan Minestrone Soup, 141
   Zucchini, Corn, and Amaranth Soup, 142
beans. *See also* beans, green; legumes
   cooking, 34
   Black Bean, Corn, and Avocado Salsa, 86
   Black Bean Chipotle Dip, 85
   Coconut Mango Black Beans, 147
   Dhal-icious, 151
   Gee Whiz Spread, 88
   Ginger Lemon Adzuki Beans, 144
   Lima Beans, Corn, and Chipotle Pepper, 158

# Index

Moroccan Black Beans with Yams and Carrots, 161
Multi-Coloured Bean and Vegetable Salad, 108
Savoury Black Bean Soup, 138
Sprouted Mung Beans and Lentils, 112
Stovetop "Baked" Beans, 176
Timesaving Tacos, 183
Tuscan Minestrone Soup, 141
White Bean, Olive, and Thyme Spread, 99
beans, green
    Thai Pasta Salad with Spicy Peanut Dressing, 113
    Tuscan Minestrone Soup, 141
beverages, 76, 79, 81
bitter tastes, 8–9, 259
blueberries
    Banana Blueberry Power Drink, 76
    Blueberry Cornmeal Muffins, 230
    Blueberry Mince Tart or Pie Filling, 231
    Blueberry Orange Sauce, 212
    Design Your Own Muesli (variation), 77
bok choy
    Stir-Fry 101, 174
    Sweet-and-Sour Tofu (variation), 177
breakfast dishes, 75–83
broccoli
    Calcium-Rich Greens, 101
    Curried Vegetables with Tofu, 150
    Garden of Plenty Salad, 105
    Stir-Fry 101, 174
brown rice. *See* rice
buckwheat, 31

cabbage
    Calcium-Rich Greens, 101
    Garden of Plenty Salad, 105
    Indonesian Style Roll-Ups, 156
    Red Cabbage with Walnuts, 200
    Scrambled Tofu, 82
calcium, 49–50
    food sources, 55
Calcium-Rich Greens, 101
carbohydrates, 51, 74
carrots
    Carrot, Lemon Grass, and Basil Soup, 130
    Carrots with Dijon Mustard and Tarragon, 189
    Curried Vegetables with Tofu, 150
    Garden of Plenty Salad, 105
    Ginger, Carrot, and Yam Soup, 134
    Gooda Cheeze, 89
    Japanese Style Roll-Ups, 156
    Maki-Sushi Rolls, 178
    Mexican Style Roll-Ups, 157
    Middle Eastern Style Roll-Ups, 157
    Red Lentil Miso Soup, 137
    Roasted Root Vegetables, 202
    Shiitake Mushroom Miso Soup, 139
    Spicy Marinated Tofu Salad, 109
    Split Pea Soup, Classic, 131
    Stir-Fry 101, 174
    Sweet-and-Sour Tofu, 177
    Teriyaki Tofu with Japanese Vegetables, 182
    Tuscan Minestrone Soup, 141
    Vietnamese Salad Roll, 114
cashews
    Cashew Cheese Lasagna, 148
    Cashew Cream Topping, 234
    Coconut Macaroons, 237
    Gooda Cheeze, 89
    Stir-Fry 101 (variation), 174
cauliflower
    Aloo Gobi, 190
    Curried Vegetables with Tofu, 150
    Garden of Plenty Salad, 105
    Sweet-and-Sour Tofu (variation), 177
celery
    Cashew Cheese Lasagna, 148
    Green Giant Juice, 79
    Mulligatawny Soup, 136
    Multi-Coloured Bean and Vegetable Salad, 108
    Quinoa Stuffing for Vegetables, 168
    Spicy Marinated Tofu Salad, 109
    Split Pea Soup, Classic, 131
    Tuscan Minestrone Soup, 141
cheese (non-dairy)
    Mac Un-Cheese, 159
    Mexican Style Roll-Ups, 157
    Tapenade Pizza (variation), 180
    Veggie Pepperoni Pizza, 188
chickpeas
    African Chickpea Stew, 145
    Curried Kabocha Squash and Chickpea Soup, 132
    Heart-Healthy Hummus, 90
    Indian Chickpeas, 152
    Portobello Mushroom Burgers with Chickpea Topping, 166
    Spicy Eggplant Soup with Chickpeas and Olives, 140
    Stir-Fry 101, 174
children, 47
Children's and Family menu, 59
chocolate
    Almond-Butter Balls, 224
    Chocolate Frosting, 235
    Chocolate Orange Cake, 236
    Coconut Macaroons (variation), 237
    Vegan Dasz Ice Cream (variation), 254
cilantro
    Mexican Style Roll-Ups, 157
    Serrano Chili and Cilantro Dressing, 126
cocoa powder. *See* chocolate
coconut, 20. *See also* coconut milk; coconut oil
    Almond, Date, and Coconut Pie Crust, 223
    Coconut Macaroons, 237
    Good Morning Granola (variation), 78

coconut milk, 20
  making your own, 120
  Carrot, Lemon Grass, and Basil Soup, 130
  Coconut Almond Dressing, 119
  Coconut Mango Black Beans, 147
  Coconut Saffron Rice with Cardamom and Lime, 193
  Curried Vegetables with Tofu, 150
  Spicy Peanut Sauce, 218
  Thai Sauce, 185
coconut oil, 23
collard greens. See greens
cooking. See also menus; recipes
  as art, 3
  equipment for, 41–42
  kitchen organization, 12–13
  as science, 3–4
  sensory aspects, 5–11
corn. See also cornmeal; cornstarch
  Black Bean, Corn, and Avocado Salsa, 86
  Corn, Red Peppers, and Pesto, 194
  Fiesta Quinoa Salad with Lime Dressing, 103
  Lima Beans, Corn, and Chipotle Pepper, 158
  Quinoa Stuffing for Vegetables, 168
  Shepherd's Pie, 172
  Zucchini, Corn, and Amaranth Soup, 142
cornmeal
  cooking, 31
  Blueberry Cornmeal Muffins, 230
cornstarch, 28
cranberries
  Almond-Butter Balls, 224
  Apple Pear Crumble (variation), 226
  Blueberry Mince Tart or Pie Filling, 231
  Cranberry Ginger Relish, 213
  Cranberry Pecan Muffins, 238
  Design Your Own Muesli (variation), 77
  Wild Rice, Walnut, and Cranberry Salad, 116
Creamy Rice Pudding, 240
Crispy Tofu Slices, 143
cucumber
  Cucumber Dill Dressing, 121
  Fiesta Quinoa Salad with Lime Dressing, 103
  Green Giant Juice, 79
  Kamut, Tomato, and Avocado Salad, 107
  Maki-Sushi Rolls, 178
  Spicy Marinated Tofu Salad, 109
  Thai Pasta Salad with Spicy Peanut Dressing, 113
currants (dried)
  Almond-Butter Balls, 224
  Curry Basmati Rice Salad with Currants, 102
  Good Morning Granola, 78
  Moroccan Black Beans with Yams and Carrots, 161
Curried Kabocha Squash and Chickpea Soup, 132
Curried Vegetables with Tofu, 150

Curry Basmati Rice Salad with Currants, 102
Curry Sandwich Spread, 87

daikon radish
  Japanese Style Roll-Ups, 156
  Teriyaki Tofu with Japanese Vegetables, 182
dates
  Almond, Date, and Coconut Pie Crust, 223
  Banana Blueberry Power Drink, 76
  Cashew Cream Topping, 234
  Coconut Macaroons, 237
  Creamy Rice Pudding, 240
  Design Your Own Muesli (variation), 77
  Good Morning Granola, 78
  Orange Ginger Dressing, 124
  Tamarind Date Sauce, 219
Design Your Own Muesli, 77
desserts, 223–56
  toppings for, 234, 244–45
Dhal-icious, 151
Dijon Scalloped Potatoes, 196
dips and spreads, 85–92, 96, 99
dressings, 117–27

Earth Balance spreads, 24
Eggplant Soup with Chickpeas and Olives, Spicy, 140
egg replacers, 28
essential fatty acids, 52, 57

fats, 17–18. See also oils
  calories from (in recipes), 74
  hydrogenated, 21–22
  recommended intake, 51–52
  sources, 18–25, 51, 52
fatty acids, 52, 57
fennel
  French Lentils with Fennel and Lemon, 153
  Vegetable Stock, 129
fibre, 51
Fiesta Quinoa Salad with Lime Dressing, 103
figs
  Baked Stuffed Apples (variation), 225
  Figgy Pudding, 241
flavour, 9–10. See also tastes
  combining, 10–11
  of sweeteners, 26
flaxseed oil, 24
  Liquid Gold Dressing, 123
flaxseeds, 18, 28. See also flaxseed oil
  as egg replacer, 28
  Apple Spice Cake, 228
  Liquid Gold Dressing, 123
  Oats 'n' Flax Crumb Crust, 248
flour (as thickener), 29
foods. See also food shopping
  ethically produced, 25–26
  nutritional value, 25, 53–55

# Index

recommended servings, 55
  as sacred, 14–15
  whole, 25
food shopping, 17
  sensory awareness in, 5–6
  shopping list, 39–40
French Lentils with Fennel and Lemon, 153
French menu, 65
French Potato Salad, 104
fruit, 54. *See also specific fruits*
  as dessert, 242
  nutritional benefits, 243
  recommended servings, 56
  Apple Pear Crumble, 226
  Apple Plum Chutney, 211
  Coconut Macaroons (variation), 237
  Design Your Own Muesli, 77
  Vegan Dasz Ice Cream, 254

Gardein products, 35
  Veggie Chick'n Paella with Artichokes and Spinach, 187
Garden of Plenty Salad, 105
garlic
  roasting, 181
  Hawaiian Sauce, 184
  Mediterranean Sauce, 184
  Mexican Sauce, 185
  Pesto-the-Best-Oh!, 92
  Stewed Tomatoes with Kale and Garlic, 210
  Tapenade Pizza, 180
  Teriyaki Sauce, 220
Gee Whiz Spread, 88
ginger
  Coconut Almond Dressing, 119
  Cranberry Ginger Relish, 213
  Ginger, Carrot, and Yam Soup, 134
  Ginger Lemon Adzuki Beans, 144
  Green Giant Juice, 79
  Hawaiian Sauce, 184
  Indonesian Style Roll-Ups, 156
  Japanese Style Roll-Ups, 156
  Lemon Ginger Tempeh, 155
  Maki-Sushi Rolls, 178
  Mulligatawny Soup, 136
  Orange Ginger Dressing, 124
  Oriental Dressing, 125
  Spicy Peanut Sauce, 218
  Stir-Fry 101 (variation), 174
  Tofu Marinade, 221
gluten-free (Japanese) menu, 67
Gooda Cheeze, 89
Good Morning Granola, 78
grains, 29–31, 54. *See also specific grains*
  cooking guidelines, 30–31
  recommended servings, 56
  Design Your Own Muesli, 77

Hearty Whole-Grain Cereal, 80–81
Holiday Stuffed Winter Squash, 154
grapefruit and grapefruit juice
  Avocado, Grapefruit, and Chipotle Dressing, 118
  Watercress, Avocado, and Grapefruit Salad, 115
gravies, 214, 216–17
Green Giant Juice, 79
greens. *See also* cabbage; kale; lettuce; spinach
  African Chickpea Stew, 145
  Seasoned Greens, 203
Green Smoothie, 81

Hawaiian Sauce, 184
hearing, sense of, 6–7
Heart-Healthy Hummus, 90
hemp seed oil, 24
  Pesto-the-Best-Oh!, 92
hemp seeds, 18–19. *See also* hemp seed oil
  Banana Blueberry Power Drink, 76
  Green Smoothie, 81
  Serrano Chili and Cilantro Dressing, 126
herbs (fresh), 38. *See also* basil; cilantro
  Middle Eastern Style Roll-Ups, 157
  Rosemary Gravy, 217
Holiday menu, 70
Holiday Pie Topping, 244
Holiday Stuffed Winter Squash, 154
hummus
  Heart-Healthy Hummus, 90
  Middle Eastern Style Roll-Ups, 157
hydrogenated oils, 21–22

Indian Chickpeas, 152
Indian menu, 64
International Roll-Ups, 156
iodine, 58
iron (dietary), 48
Italian menu, 66

Japanese (gluten-free) menu, 67

kale
  African Chickpea Stew, 145
  African Style Roll-Ups, 156
  Calcium-Rich Greens, 101
  Garden of Plenty Salad, 105
  Green Giant Juice, 79
  Green Smoothie, 81
  Kale and Red Pepper Holly Ring, 106
  Shiitake Mushrooms, Kale, and Sesame, 205
  Stewed Tomatoes with Kale and Garlic, 210
Kamut berries
  cooking, 31
  Kamut, Tomato, and Avocado Salad, 107
kasha, 31

kitchen
  equipment for, 41–42
  organizing, 12–13
kiwi
  Raw Lime Pie, 250
  Watermelon Fruit Sculpture, 255

legumes, 32–34, 53–54. *See also* beans; lentils; peas, dried
  cooking guidelines, 33–34
  gas minimization, 33
  recommended servings, 56
  soaking, 32–33
lemon
  Baked Yams with Lemon and Green Chili, 191
  Green Giant Juice, 79
  Lemon Ginger Tempeh, 155
  Lemon Glaze, 245
  Lemon Roasted Potatoes, 197
  Lemon Sesame Cookies, 246
  Lemon Tahini Dressing, 122
  Lem-Un-Cheesecake with Crumb Crust, 247
  Liquid Gold Dressing, 123
lentils. *See also* legumes
  cooking, 34
  Dhal-icious, 151
  French Lentils with Fennel and Lemon, 153
  Mediterranean Lentil Soup, 135
  Mushroom Lentil Patties, 162
  Red Lentil Miso Soup, 137
  Sprouted Lentil Salad Plate, 110
  Sprouted Mung Beans and Lentils, 112
lettuce
  Garden of Plenty Salad, 105
  Green Giant Juice, 79
  Italian Style Roll-Ups, 156
  Maki-Sushi Rolls, 178
  Mexican Style Roll-Ups, 157
  Middle Eastern Style Roll-Ups, 157
  Timesaving Tacos, 183
Lima Beans, Corn, and Chipotle Pepper, 158
lime
  Avocado, Grapefruit, and Chipotle Dressing, 118
  Black Bean Chipotle Dip, 85
  Coconut Saffron Rice with Cardamom and Lime, 193
  Fiesta Quinoa Salad with Lime Dressing, 103
  Limey Avocado Dip, 91
  Raw Lime Pie, 250
  Thai Sauce, 185
Liquid Gold Dressing, 123

Mac Un-Cheese, 159
magnesium, 48
Maki-Sushi Rolls, 178
mango
  Coconut Mango Black Beans, 147
  Raw Mango Strawberry Pie, 251

maple syrup
  Apple Pear Crumble, 226
  Apple Spice Cake, 228
  Cashew Cream Topping, 234
  Cranberry Pecan Muffins, 238
  Good Morning Granola, 78
  Holiday Pie Topping, 244
  Lemon Sesame Cookies, 246
  Pumpkin Spice Pie, 249
  Raw Lime Pie, 250
  Stovetop "Baked" Beans, 176
Marinara Tomato Sauce, 215
Marinated Tofu, 160
Mashed Parsnips and Apple with Toasted Walnuts, 195
meat analogues/substitutes, 35
  Shepherd's Pie, 172
  Stir-Fry 101 (variation), 174
  Veggie Chick'n Paella with Artichokes and Spinach, 187
  Veggie Pepperoni Pizza, 188
Mediterranean Lentil Soup, 135
Mediterranean Sauce, 184
menus, 58–70
  Asian Fusion, 63
  Children's and Family, 59
  French, 65
  Holiday, 70
  Indian, 64
  Italian, 66
  Japanese (gluten-free), 67
  Mexican, 68
  Middle Eastern, 69
  North American, 60
  Raw Vegan, 62
  Super Simple, 61
Mexican menu, 68
Mexican Sauce, 185
Middle Eastern menu, 69
milk substitutes (non-dairy), 36, 55
  Blueberry Cornmeal Muffins, 230
  Creamy Rice Pudding, 240
  Design Your Own Muesli (variation), 77
  Vegan Dasz Ice Cream (variation), 254
  Whole-Wheat Pancakes, 83
millet, 31
minerals, 48–50, 261
mirepoix, 10
*mise en place,* 12–13
miso
  Miso Gravy, 216
  Orange Ginger Dressing, 124
  Red Lentil Miso Soup, 137
  Shiitake Mushroom Miso Soup, 139
Moroccan Black Beans with Yams and Carrots, 161
Muesli, Design Your Own, 77
Mulligatawny Soup, 136

# Index

mushrooms
  Brown Rice, Mushroom, and Walnut Pilaf, 192
  Cashew Cheese Lasagna, 148
  Light Mushroom Gravy, 214
  Mushroom Lentil Patties, 162
  Portobello Mushroom Burgers with Chickpea Topping, 166
  Portobello Mushrooms with Marjoram and Balsamic, 198
  Scrambled Tofu, 82
  Shiitake Mushroom Miso Soup, 139
  Shiitake Mushrooms, Kale, and Sesame, 205
  Simple Sautéed Portobello Mushrooms, 206
  Vegetable Kebabs, 186
  Veggie Pepperoni Pizza, 188

noodles. *See* pasta
North American menu, 60
nut butters, 29. *See also* almond butter; peanut butter
nut milks, 37
nutrients
  food sources, 53–55, 57–58
  in non-dairy milks, 36
nutrition, 4
nuts, 19–20, 54. *See also* nut butters; nut milks; *specific nuts*
  recommended servings, 56
  roasting, 112
  as thickeners, 29
  Apple Spice Cake, 228
  Cranberry Pecan Muffins, 238
  Holiday Stuffed Winter Squash (variation), 154

oats, rolled
  cooking, 31
  Almond-Butter Balls, 224
  Apple Pear Crumble, 226
  Design Your Own Muesli, 77
  Good Morning Granola, 78
  Oats 'n' Flax Crumb Crust, 248
oils, 20–25. *See also* fats; *specific oils*
  cold-pressed, 22–23
  hydrogenation of, 21–22
  manufacturing processes, 21–23
  smoke point of, 22, 23
olive oil, 23–24
olives, 20
  French Potato Salad, 104
  Spicy Eggplant Soup with Chickpeas and Olives, 140
  Sprouted Lentil Salad Plate, 110
  Veggie Pepperoni Pizza, 188
  Walnut, Olive, and Sun-Dried Tomato Tapenade, 97
  White Bean, Olive, and Thyme Spread, 99
omega-3/-6 fatty acids, 52, 57

onions
  caramelizing, 173
  Roasted Root Vegetables, 202
  Tapenade Pizza, 180
  Teriyaki Sauce, 220
orange
  Apple Pear Crumble, 226
  Blueberry Orange Sauce, 212
  Chocolate Orange Cake, 236
  Cranberry Ginger Relish, 213
  Ginger, Carrot, and Yam Soup, 134
  Green Smoothie, 81
  Hawaiian Sauce, 184
  Orange Ginger Dressing, 124
Oriental Dressing, 125

Pancakes, Whole-Wheat, 83
Parsnips and Apple with Toasted Walnuts, Mashed, 195
pasta
  Cashew Cheese Lasagna, 148
  Mac Un-Cheese, 159
  Thai Pasta Salad with Spicy Peanut Dressing, 113
Pastry, Tart and Pie, 252
peanut butter
  African Chickpea Stew, 145
  Almond-Butter Balls, 224
  Spicy Peanut Sauce, 218
peas, dried. *See also* legumes
  cooking, 34
  Classic Split Pea Soup, 131
peas, snow
  Spicy Marinated Tofu Salad, 109
  Stir-Fry 101, 174
  Sweet-and-Sour Tofu (variation), 177
  Thai Pasta Salad with Spicy Peanut Dressing, 113
peppers, bell
  Corn, Red Peppers, and Pesto, 194
  Curried Vegetables with Tofu, 150
  Curry Basmati Rice Salad with Currants, 102
  French Potato Salad, 104
  Garden of Plenty Salad, 105
  Kale and Red Pepper Holly Ring, 106
  Multi-Coloured Bean and Vegetable Salad, 108
  Spicy Marinated Tofu Salad, 109
  Stir-Fry 101, 174
  Sweet-and-Sour Tofu, 177
  Teriyaki Tofu with Japanese Vegetables, 182
  Vegetable Kebabs, 186
  Veggie Pepperoni Pizza, 188
peppers, chili
  Avocado, Grapefruit, and Chipotle Dressing, 118
  Baked Yams with Lemon and Green Chili, 191
  Black Bean, Corn, and Avocado Salsa, 86
  Black Bean Chipotle Dip, 85
  Lima Beans, Corn, and Chipotle Pepper, 158
  Mexican Sauce, 185

Moroccan Black Beans with Yams and Carrots, 161
Serrano Chili and Cilantro Dressing, 126
Zucchini, Corn, and Amaranth Soup, 142
pesto
   Corn, Red Peppers, and Pesto, 194
   Pesto Pizza, 164
   Pesto-the-Best-Oh!, 92
phosphorus, 49
pineapple
   Hawaiian Sauce, 184
   Sweet-and-Sour Tofu, 177
   Veggie Pepperoni Pizza (variation), 188
   Watermelon Fruit Sculpture, 255
pita breads. *See also* pizzas
   fillings and spreads for, 93
Pizza Dough, 165
pizzas, 164, 180, 188
pomace oil, 24
Portobello Mushroom Burgers with Chickpea Topping, 166
Portobello Mushrooms, Simple Sautéed, 206
Portobello Mushrooms with Marjoram and Balsamic, 198
potassium, 49
potatoes
   Aloo Gobi, 190
   Baked Potato and Fixin's Bar, 146
   Dijon Scalloped Potatoes, 196
   French Potato Salad, 104
   Lemon Roasted Potatoes, 197
   Potato Subji, 199
   Roasted Root Vegetables, 202
   Seasoned Potato Wedges, 204
   Shepherd's Pie, 172
   Tuscan Minestrone Soup, 141
protein, 44–48
   calories from (in recipes), 74
   recommended intake, 45–47
pumpkin seeds, 19
   Almond-Butter Balls, 224
   Design Your Own Muesli (variation), 77
   Roasted Sunflower or Pumpkin Seeds, 94
Pumpkin Spice Pie, 249
pungent tastes, 9, 260

quinoa
   cooking, 31
   Fiesta Quinoa Salad with Lime Dressing, 103
   Holiday Stuffed Winter Squash, 154
   Quinoa Stuffing for Vegetables, 168

raisins
   Apple Pear Crumble, 226
   Apple Spice Cake, 228
   Baked Stuffed Apples, 225
   Blueberry Mince Tart or Pie Filling, 231
   Creamy Rice Pudding, 240

Curried Vegetables with Tofu, 150
Design Your Own Muesli, 77
Good Morning Granola, 78
Raw Lime Pie, 250
Raw Mango Strawberry Pie, 251
Raw Vegan menu, 62
Raw Vegetable Platter, 93
recipes. *See also* menus
   approaching, 73
   composition of, 10–11
   following, 11–12
   nutritional analyses, 73–74
Red Cabbage with Walnuts, 200
Red Lentil Miso Soup, 137
relishes and chutneys, 211, 213
rice. *See also* rice, wild
   cooking, 31
   African Chickpea Stew, 145
   Brown Rice, Mushroom, and Walnut Pilaf, 192
   Coconut Saffron Rice with Cardamom and Lime, 193
   Creamy Rice Pudding, 240
   Curry Basmati Rice Salad with Currants, 102
   International Roll-Ups, 156
   Maki-Sushi Rolls, 178
   Mulligatawny Soup, 136
   Mushroom Lentil Patties, 162
   Shiitake Mushroom Miso Soup, 139
   Spanish Rice, 207
   Veggie Chick'n Paella with Artichokes and Spinach, 187
   Vietnamese Salad Roll, 114
rice, wild
   cooking, 31
   Wild Rice, Walnut, and Cranberry Salad, 116
Roasted Root Vegetables, 202
Roasted Sunflower or Pumpkin Seeds, 94
Rosemary Gravy, 217

Salad Bar, 170–71
salads, 101–16
salsa (as ingredient)
   Mexican Sauce, 185
   Mexican Style Roll-Ups, 157
   Timesaving Tacos, 183
salty tastes, 7–8, 257. *See also* sodium
sandwich fillings, 93, 95
sauces and gravies, 92, 184–85, 212, 214–21
Savoury Black Bean Soup, 138
Scrambled Tofu, 82
Seasoned Greens, 203
Seasoned Potato Wedges, 204
seasonings, 11, 38
seeds, 18–19, 54. *See also specific seeds*
   recommended servings, 56
   roasting, 94, 112, 133
   as thickeners, 29

## Index

senses
  role in cooking, 6–7
  role in food shopping, 5–6
Serrano Chili and Cilantro Dressing, 126
sesame oil, 24
  Oriental Dressing, 125
sesame seeds, 19. *See also* sesame oil; tahini
  roasting, 133
  Lemon Sesame Cookies, 246
  Shiitake Mushrooms, Kale, and Sesame, 205
Shepherd's Pie, 172
Shiitake Mushroom Miso Soup, 139
Shiitake Mushrooms, Kale, and Sesame, 205
sight, sense of, 5, 6
smell, sense of, 5
sodium, 49. *See also* salty tastes
soups, 129–42
sour tastes, 8, 259
soy foods, 35–36
  protein content, 47
soy milk, 37
Spanish Rice, 207
spelt berries
  cooking, 31
  Kamut, Tomato, and Avocado Salad (variation), 107
spices, 38, 133
spiciness, 9
Spicy Eggplant Soup with Chickpeas and Olives, 140
Spicy Marinated Tofu Salad, 109
Spicy Peanut Sauce, 218
spinach
  Italian Style Roll-Ups, 156
  Spinach with Tofu and Garam Masala, 208
  Tapenade Pizza (variation), 180
  Veggie Chick'n Paella with Artichokes and Spinach, 187
Split Pea Soup, Classic, 131
Sprouted Lentil Salad Plate, 110
Sprouted Mung Beans and Lentils, 112
squash. *See also* zucchini
  Curried Kabocha Squash and Chickpea Soup, 132
  Holiday Stuffed Winter Squash, 154
  Pumpkin Spice Pie, 249
Stir-Fry 101, 174
strawberries
  Apple Spice Cake (variation), 228
  Raw Mango Strawberry Pie, 251
  Watermelon Fruit Sculpture, 255
Stuffed Bell Peppers, 169
sugars, 8. *See also* sweeteners
  reducing, 25
sunflower oil, 25
sunflower seeds, 19. *See also* sunflower oil
  Banana Blueberry Power Drink, 76
  Design Your Own Muesli, 77
  Green Smoothie, 81
  Quinoa Stuffing for Vegetables, 168
  Roasted Sunflower or Pumpkin Seeds, 94
  Sunflower Sesame Spread, 96
Super Simple menu, 61
Sweet-and-Sour Tofu, 177
sweeteners, 8, 25–26. *See also* sugars
sweet potatoes. *See also* yams
  African Chickpea Stew, 145
  Teriyaki Tofu with Japanese Vegetables, 182
sweet tastes, 8, 258

Tacos, Timesaving, 183
tahini
  Baked Stuffed Apples, 225
  Black Bean Chipotle Dip, 85
  Gee Whiz Spread, 88
  Gooda Cheeze, 89
  Good Morning Granola, 78
  Heart-Healthy Hummus, 90
  Lemon Tahini Dressing, 122
  Sunflower Sesame Spread, 96
Tamarind Date Sauce, 219
Tapenade Pizza, 180
Tart and Pie Pastry, 252
tastes. *See also* flavour
  in cooking, 7, 10–11
  in food shopping, 5
  six types, 7–9, 257–60
tempeh, 35
  Indonesian Style Roll-Ups, 156
  Lemon Ginger Tempeh, 155
Teriyaki Sauce, 220
Teriyaki Tofu with Japanese Vegetables, 182
Thai Pasta Salad with Spicy Peanut Dressing, 113
Thai Sauce, 185
thickeners, 26–29
Timesaving Tacos, 183
tofu, firm, 36
  Crispy Tofu Slices, 143
  Curried Vegetables with Tofu, 150
  Curry Sandwich Spread, 87
  Marinated Tofu, 160
  Scrambled Tofu, 82
  Spicy Marinated Tofu Salad, 109
  Spinach with Tofu and Garam Masala, 208
  Stir-Fry 101 (variation), 174
  Sweet-and-Sour Tofu, 177
  Teriyaki Tofu with Japanese Vegetables, 182
  Tofu: An Easy Entrée, 184–85
  Vegetable Kebabs, 186
tofu, soft/silken, 36
  Cashew Cheese Lasagna, 148
  Cranberry Pecan Muffins, 238
  Figgy Pudding, 241
  Holiday Pie Topping, 244
  Lemon Sesame Cookies, 246

Lem-Un-Cheesecake with Crumb Crust, 247
Pumpkin Spice Pie, 249
Tofu Marinade, 221
tomatoes. *See also* tomato sauce and juice
   Black Bean, Corn, and Avocado Salsa, 86
   Curried Kabocha Squash and Chickpea Soup, 132
   French Lentils with Fennel and Lemon, 153
   Indian Chickpeas, 152
   Kamut, Tomato, and Avocado Salad, 107
   Mac Un-Cheese, 159
   Marinara Tomato Sauce, 215
   Mediterranean Lentil Soup, 135
   Middle Eastern Style Roll-Ups, 157
   Multi-Coloured Bean and Vegetable Salad, 108
   Pesto Pizza, 164
   Spanish Rice, 207
   Sprouted Lentil Salad Plate, 110
   Stewed Tomatoes with Kale and Garlic, 210
   Thai Pasta Salad with Spicy Peanut Dressing, 113
   Tofu Marinade, 221
   Vegetable Kebabs, 186
   Veggie Chick'n Paella with Artichokes and Spinach, 187
   Walnut, Olive, and Sun-Dried Tomato Tapenade, 97
   Zucchini, Corn, and Amaranth Soup, 142
tomato sauce and juice. *See also* salsa
   Cashew Cheese Lasagna, 148
   Italian Style Roll-Ups, 156
   Mediterranean Sauce, 184
   Tomato Herb Dressing, 127
   Tuscan Minestrone Soup, 141
   Veggie Pepperoni Pizza, 188
tortillas, 95
   International Roll-Ups, 156–57
   Time-Saving Tacos, 183
touch, sense of, 5, 6
trans fats, 22
Tuscan Minestrone Soup, 141

Vanilla Frosting, 253
Vegan Dasz Ice Cream, 254
vegetables, 53. *See also* greens; *specific vegetables*
   bitter, 9
   recommended servings, 56
   retaining colour, 201
   as thickeners, 29
   Gee Whiz Spread, 88
   International Roll-Ups, 156–57
   Multi-Coloured Bean and Vegetable Salad, 108
   Raw Vegetable Platter, 93
   Roasted Root Vegetables, 202
   Rosemary Gravy, 217
   Salad Bar, 170–71
   Stir-Fry 101, 174
   Vegetable Kebabs, 186
   Vegetable Stock, 129
   Veggie Chick'n Paella with Artichokes and Spinach, 187
   Veggie Pepperoni Pizza, 188
Vietnamese Salad Roll, 114
vitamins, 50, 57, 263–64

walnuts
   Apple Pear Crumble, 226
   Apple Spice Cake, 228
   Brown Rice, Mushroom, and Walnut Pilaf, 192
   Design Your Own Muesli (variation), 77
   Mashed Parsnips and Apple with Toasted Walnuts, 195
   Pesto-the-Best-Oh!, 92
   Red Cabbage with Walnuts, 200
   Sprouted Lentil Salad Plate, 110
   Walnut, Olive, and Sun-Dried Tomato Tapenade, 97
   Wild Rice, Walnut, and Cranberry Salad, 116
Watercress, Avocado, and Grapefruit Salad, 115
Watermelon Fruit Sculpture, 255
wheat berries, 31
Whole-Wheat Pancakes, 83
Wild Rice, Walnut, and Cranberry Salad, 116

yams. *See also* sweet potatoes
   African Chickpea Stew, 145
   African Style Roll-Ups, 156
   Baked Yams with Lemon and Green Chili, 191
   Ginger, Carrot, and Yam Soup, 134
   Moroccan Black Beans with Yams and Carrots, 161
   Roasted Root Vegetables, 202
yeast (nutritional)
   Cashew Cheese Lasagna, 148
   Crispy Tofu Slices, 143
   Gee Whiz Spread, 88
   Gooda Cheeze, 89
   Liquid Gold Dressing, 123
   Mushroom Lentil Patties, 162
   Roasted Sunflower or Pumpkin Seeds, 94
   Seasoned Potato Wedges, 204

zinc, 48
zucchini
   Cucumber Dill Dressing, 121
   Portobello Mushroom Burgers with Chickpea Topping, 166
   Tuscan Minestrone Soup, 141
   Vegetable Kebabs, 186
   Zucchini, Corn, and Amaranth Soup, 142